Handbook of
Norse Mythology

TITLES IN ABC-CLIO's
Handbooks of World Mythology

HANDBOOKS OF WORLD MYTHOLOGY

Handbook of Norse Mythology

John Lindow

A B C ☙ C L I O

Santa Barbara, California • Denver, Colorado • Oxford, England

Library of Congress Cataloging-in-Publication Data

Lindow, John.
  Handbook of Norse mythology / John Lindow.
    p. cm. — (Handbooks of world mythology)
Includes index.
  ISBN 1-57607-217-7 (alk. paper) — ISBN 1-57607-573-7 (e-Book)
  1. Mythology, Norse. I. Title. II. Series.
  BL860.L56 2001
  293'.13—dc21

                      2001001351

06 05 04 03 02 01 10 9 8 7 6 5 4 3 2 1

ABC-CLIO, Inc.
130 Cremona Drive, P.O. Box 1911
Santa Barbara, California 93116-1911

This book is printed on acid-free paper ⊚ .
Manufactured in the United States of America

CONTENTS

A NOTE ON ORTHOGRAPHY

Because this book is intended for a general audience, a decision was made to limit the use of the specialized characters usually employed to represent the sounds of the older Germanic languages, including those of Norway and Iceland during the Viking Age and Middle Ages. Specifically, in names and titles the letter þ (thorn) is here represented as *th*, ð (eth) as *d*, and ǫ (o-hook) as *ö*. These letters have, however, been retained in discussions of specific terms, such as *"þylja"* and *"goði."* Other characters, such as *æ*, *œ*, and *ö*, have been retained. In addition, the nominative singular final *r* has been removed from names, and the accent marks have been removed from the names "Odin" and "Thor," since these forms are the most widely used in English.

These compromises naturally create inconsistencies, but I hope they will not divert from the aim of the work, namely, to let the texts speak for themselves and to give the reader an idea of the main issues in the study of Scandinavian mythology.

1

INTRODUCTION

When most of us use the word "myth" in conversation, we refer to something that is not true. When historians of religion use it, they generally refer to a representation of the sacred in words. When anthropologists use it, they often refer to narratives that tell about the formation of some social institution or behavior. None of the definitions, however, will hold directly for the characters and stories this book treats. That is in part because of the enormous time frame: Materials relevant to the study of Scandinavian mythology, broadly defined, span two millennia or more. But even if we limit the discussion to the relatively small body of texts from the Viking Age and later Middle Ages about the gods Odin, Thor, Frey, and the others and their constant battles with forces of evil and chaos, it is difficult to reconcile these texts with any one of the narrow definitions of myth suggested above. Certainly they had some truth value to the people who composed them and those who wrote them down, but these were not always the same people—usually they were not—and it is obvious that what was true, sacred, and an account of how the world got to be the way it is to a Viking Age pagan poet can have been none of the above to a Christian scribe copying the story in a manuscript hundreds of years after the Viking Age. It is therefore easier and more enlightening to talk of formal criteria and content.

In form, then, myth in general, and the texts that comprise Scandinavian mythology in particular, are narrative, although this narrative is couched in both verse and prose. In general, one expects myth to recount important events that took place at the beginning of time and helped shape the world, and Scandinavian mythology indeed has sequences that tell of the origin of the cosmos and of human beings. The story goes on, however, to the destruction and rebirth of the cosmos, and everything in it is presented in light of an enduring struggle between two groups of beings, the gods on the one hand and giants on the other hand. These terms are to some extent misleading: Although the group that creates and orders the cosmos is often referred to by words that can best be translated "gods," the principal word, "æsir," is explicitly presented by the most important medieval interpreter, Snorri Sturluson, as meaning "People of Asia," and indeed the word often has the feel in mythological texts of an extended kin group or tribe rather than of a collective of deities. And the other group, the ones who aim for the destruction of the cosmos and disruption of order, are certainly not "giant" in the sense that they are demonstrably larger than the gods. They are usually called the "jötnar," and again as the term is used in the mythology it feels more like a tribal or kin group than anything else.

The world in which the æsir and jötnar play out their struggle has its own set of place-names but is essentially recognizable as Scandinavia. There are rivers, mountains, forests, oceans, storms, cold weather, fierce winters, eagles, ravens, salmon, and snakes. People get about on ships and on horseback. They eat slaughtered meat and drink beer. As in Scandinavia, north is a difficult direction, and so is east, probably because our mythology comes from west Scandinavia (Norway and Iceland), where travel to the east required going over mountains, and going west on a ship was far easier for this seafaring culture.

It is helpful to think of three time periods in which the mythology takes place. In the mythic past, the æsir created and ordered the world and joined with another group, the vanir, to make up the community of gods. Somehow this golden age was disrupted in the mythic present. As dwarfs, humans, and occasionally elves look on and are sometimes drawn into the struggle, the æsir and the jötnar fight over resources, precious objects, and, especially, women. The flow of such wealth is all in one direction, from the jötnar to the æsir, and in fact one might divide the narratives of the mythic present into those in which the gods acquire something from the giants and those in which an attempt by the giants to acquire something from the gods is foiled. In the mythic future, this world order will come to a fiery end as gods and giants destroy each other and the cosmos, but a new world order is to follow in which the world will be reborn and inhabited by a new generation of æsir.

THE HISTORICAL BACKGROUND

Scandinavia consists of the low-lying Danish islands and the peninsula of Jutland and the great Scandinavian peninsula, which in its northern reaches is divided in two by the huge mountain range known as the keel. On the eastern side lies Sweden with its gentle Baltic Sea coast and a great deal of fertile land, especially in the central parts of Sweden, around the lakes Mälaren, Vännern, and Vättern, and to the south. On the west lies Norway, where tall mountains spring from the coast, which is protected from the Atlantic by a series of small islands. To the south lies Denmark, which until 1658 included not only Jutland and the islands but also southern portions of the Scandinavian peninsula. The names are indicative: Norway, the northern way, the sea route up and down the coast; Denmark, the forest of the Danes, which separated them from the Saxons; Sweden, the kingdom of the Svear, the people around Mälaren who at some point during the Viking Age subdued their southern neighbors in Götaland. The name "Scandinavia" appears to be the Latinized form of an unattested German word, *Scandinaujā. (The asterisk before the word means that it was never recorded but rather was reconstructed by linguists.) This word is a compound, the second part of which, aujā, means "island." What the first part means has been endlessly debated. It appears to contain the same root as the name of the southern part of Sweden, Skåne, and may therefore mean "Skanian island."

As the ice from the last great Ice Age retreated, the low-lying lands of the south were first exposed, and pollen analysis indicates settlement on Sjælland and elsewhere by around 10,000 B.C.E. We know little about these settlements, but by 6500 B.C.E. or so, a hunting and fishing culture may be identified. By 2500 B.C.E. or so, there are indications of agriculture and the raising of animals. At around 2000 B.C.E. the archaeological record begins to show characteristic small ax heads, made of stone but carefully copying the marks of metal pouring that was used for such axes to the south in Europe. A hypothetical culture associated with these axes and an even more hypothetical immigration of persons with them from Europe is known as the Boat-Ax culture. Around 1000 B.C.E. the Scandinavian Bronze Age begins, and from this same period there are numerous spectacular rock carvings, which may have had a religious purpose. The Scandinavian Iron Age begins circa 500–400 B.C.E., and its first stage, up to around the beginning of our era, is known as the Pre-Roman Iron Age, despite incipient trade with the Roman Empire. Around the beginning of our era we begin to get runic inscriptions from Scandinavia and the Continent in a language that is identifiably Germanic, and in Scandinavia the so-called Roman Iron Age begins. On the Continent this is the time when the Germanic peoples confront the Roman Empire, with increasing success. By around 400 C.E. gold appears in Scandinavia, and the Germanic Iron Age begins; the Older Germanic Iron Age, from circa 400 to 550 or 575 C.E., is also know as the Migration Period because of the extensive movements of the Germanic tribes around Europe, as is especially known from accounts of interaction with Germanic peoples written by Roman historians. Scandinavia was probably the homeland for some of these peoples. For example, the Burgundians would appear to have come from the island of Bornholm, the Goths either from Götaland in Sweden or from the island of Gotland off Sweden's east coast, and the Vandals either from the Vendel area of Sweden or what is now Vendsyssel in Denmark. Part of the Anglo-Saxon immigration to England probably came from Angeln in what is now Denmark.

Buckle clasp in silver, gold, and precious stones from Admark, Norway, seventh century C.E. (The Art Archive/Historiska Museet Norway/Dagli Orti)

The period circa 600–800 C.E. is usually called the Younger Germanic Iron Age, although Swedish archaeologists usually called it the Vendel Period because of the wealth of finds from Vendel, an area northeast of Lake Mälaren. During this period, too, there was extensive trade from across the Baltic centered at Helgö, then an island in the southern part of Lake Mälaren. And in Denmark it appears that a Danish state was already beginning to establish itself in Jutland.

Between circa 600 and 800 C.E., a number of linguistic changes occurred in the northern area of the Germanic speech community, and by the end of this period one may speak of Scandinavian languages. By this same time some Scandinavians burst spectacularly on the European scene. Although there appears to have been sporadic raiding before the autumn of 793, in that year Vikings sacked the rich monastery at Lindisfarne off the east coast of northern England, and for nearly three centuries Vikings, and later, the Scandinavian kingdoms, would play a major role in European history. What the word "Viking" originally meant is not known; the European writers, mostly clergymen, who made it famous painted a fairly clear picture of pagan marauders who destroyed and despoiled wherever they went. Certainly there is some truth to such a picture, especially in the early part of the Viking Age, when the Scandinavian sailors do seem to have had military advantages, with their light, swift, maneuverable ships. But it is important to consider that there were individual forays, larger expeditions, armies wintering in England and on the Continent, and, finally, the North Sea empire of Cnut the Great. Besides this military activity there was continuous trade and a pattern of settlement in the lands to which the Scandinavian ships came.

Some of these lands were already settled, such as the French coast and northeast England. In Normandy the Scandinavians left relatively little trace, but in England their influence was great. The creation of the Danelaw—a relatively fixed area in which Scandinavian law obtained—arranged by Alfred the Great and the Danish king Guthrum in the 880s, indicates just how pervasive the Scandinavian presence was. The enormous number of Scandinavian loanwords into English indicates an extended period of contact between the English and the Scandinavians, and as the Scandinavian kingdoms began to emerge during the ninth and tenth centuries, there was not infrequently contact with English courts. For example, one of the sons of Harald Fairhair of Norway, Hákon the Good, had been fostered at the court of King Athalstan of England. According to tradition, Harald had united all Norway into a single kingdom (this had occurred somewhat earlier in Denmark and would probably happen somewhat later in Sweden, for which the sources are rather meager). During the reign of Harald (870–930) serious emigration began over the sea to the islands to the west: the Orkneys, the Shetlands, the Faroes, and Iceland. This push was finally to reach Greenland and North America, and it was paralleled by extensive travel from Sweden to the east, to Finland and Russia, down the great Russian river systems to Constantinople and the Black Sea.

According to the Icelandic sources, powerful chieftains fled western Norway and settled in Iceland in order to avoid the tyranny of Harald Fairhair. There may

Some English jet was exported from Yorkshire to Norway during the Viking Age. This carving of a pair of bear-like gripping beasts brings to mind related examples in amber. (Historisk Museum, Bergen Universitetet)

be some truth in this, and even if Norway was hardly the only source of immigration into Iceland, it remained the country most connected to Iceland and the kingdom into which Iceland was finally folded in 1262–1264. But from the time of the settlement—Iceland was "fully settled" by 897 according to learned authors of the twelfth century—until then, Iceland functioned as a commonwealth in which judicial power was in the hands of a group of chieftains, and there was no king or other central authority. These leaders were called *goðar* (sing., *goði*), and although the sources rarely show much religious activity on their part—and what they do show may not be reliable—the term clearly incorporates the word for "gods." Therefore they must have had some sort of religious function. *Goðar* had "thing-men," who owed them allegiance and whom they in turn helped; every free man had to be some *goði*'s thing-man. The word "thing" (*þing*) means assembly, and one of the duties of a *goði* and his thing-men was to attend the local assemblies and the national assembly *(alþingi)* to participate in litigation and, one assumes, to renew friendships and exchange stories. There were few towns in Scandinavia during the Viking Age and none at all in Iceland, so the assemblies, and especially the annual national assembly, must have played an important social role. There, one-third of the law was recited from memory each year by the only national official in the country, the lawspeaker. The position was one of status and influence but of little direct power. People lived on farms, and the basic social unit was the household. So important was this principle of household membership that people could switch from one household to another only at certain specified times of the year, the "moving days." Farming consisted primarily of raising cattle and the hay that would be needed to support the cattle.

The Viking Age is by definition a period when Scandinavians and Europeans interacted, and without that interaction and the written documents it gave rise to in Europe, archaeologists might have called the period from 800 to circa 1000 the "Scandinavian Iron Age." The beginning of the period, as we have seen, is portrayed by those who wrote the history, the literate members of the Christian church, as a meeting between pagan and Christian, and it was only natural that as time passed attempts would be made to convert the Scandinavians, as Charlemagne had converted the Saxons. Indeed, those Scandinavians who traded or settled in Christian lands had ample contact with Christianity, and many of them either converted or had themselves "prime-signed," that is, they accepted the sign of the cross, the first step toward baptism, so that they could do business with Christians. Furthermore, the gradual emergence of European nation-states in Scandinavia during the Viking Age and their increasing integration with Europe made it inevitable that the issue would arise at the national level as well. There is documented missionary activity in Scandinavia from the early Viking Age onward, most famously by Ansgar, the "apostle of the north," who worked with both Danish and Swedish kings in the first half of the ninth century.

The process was to bear fruit first in Denmark in the later tenth century, when King Harald Bluetooth witnessed the priest Poppo carrying a red-hot piece of iron, with no harm to his hands, as a demonstration that Christ was greater than the pagan gods. At Jelling in Jutland, King Harald Bluetooth erected an elaborate rune stone celebrating his parents and himself, the person who "made the Danes Christian," as the Jelling rune stone says.

In Norway there is evidence of Christian burial from around this time, and Hákon the Good was a Christian king whose reign ended around 960, when Harald converted. But Hákon was buried in a mound and celebrated in pagan poetry. Olaf Tryggvason, who ruled Norway from 995 to 1001, had been baptized in England, and he undertook a program of forcible conversions throughout the country. He was of a family from the Oslo fjord, and the most obdurate pagans were allegedly in the other power center in the country, the area near modern Trondheim. Credit for the final conversion is given to Olaf Haraldsson. When he was killed at the battle of Stiklestad in 1030, a battle having far more to do with national politics than religion—his opponents were supported by Cnut the Great, the Christian king of Denmark and England—people quickly saw signs of his sanctity, and he became the most important saint of northern Europe.

We are less well informed about the conversion in Sweden. Although the kings of Sweden were Christian from the beginning of the eleventh century, the monk Adam of Bremen, in his history (ca. 1070) of the archbishopric of Hamburg-Bremen in northern Germany, which had responsibility for Scandinavia, reported a vast pagan temple at Uppsala, with idols of the pagan gods and gruesome sacri-

Rune stones depicting Thor's hammer like this one in Sweden are fairly easy to find. Compare this to the rune stone on page 10; both are from the late Viking Age. (Statens Historika Museum, Stockholm)

Illustration from Flateyjarbók, *a late-fourteenth-century Icelandic manuscript. The scene may depict St. Olaf killing a monster. (Bob Krist/Corbis)*

fices. But eleventh-century rune stones from that very same part of Sweden are openly Christian: "God rest his soul," many of them ask, in runes surrounding an incised cross. Most historians accept that Sweden was fully Christian by the beginning of the twelfth century at the latest.

The conversion in Iceland followed a fascinating course. Missionaries were active in the latter decades of the tenth century, but so were their pagan opponents. Olaf Tryggvason, whose role in the conversion was championed by twelfth-century and later Icelandic monks, took hostage some wealthy young Icelandic travelers, and there was further resolve among Christians in Iceland to complete the conversion. However, as the two sides approached the althingi in Iceland in the year 1000, it appeared that war would break out. Finally it was agreed that a single arbiter should choose one religion for the entire land, and the lawspeaker Thorgeir, a pagan, was chosen. After spending a night under his cloak, he emerged and decreed that Iceland should be Christian. And so it was. At first some pagan practices were permitted if carried out in secret, but later even this permission was rescinded. However, for reasons that are no longer quite clear, the old stories about the gods were not lost on Iceland. Poems about them lived on in oral tradition, to be recorded more than two centuries after the conversion. Some mythological poems may actually have been composed by

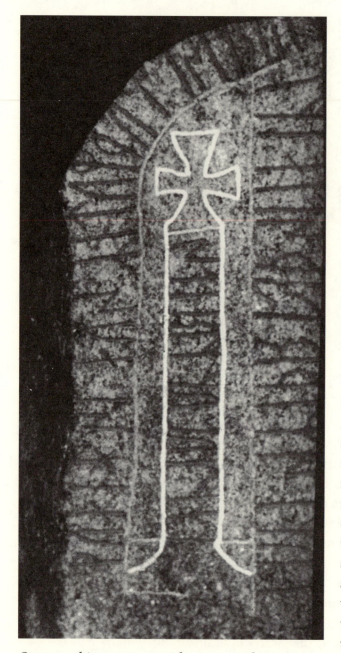

Compare this rune stone with a cross to the one on page 8. (Statens Historika Museum, Stockholm)

Christians in Iceland, and Snorri Sturluson made extensive use of the mythology in his writings.

Thus Scandinavian mythology was, with virtually no exception, written down by Christians, and there is no reason to believe that Christianity in Iceland was any different from Christianity anywhere else in western Europe during the High Middle Ages. Although the earliest bishops were sent out from Norway, quite soon the bishops were native born, and by the end of the eleventh century there were two episcopal sees, the original one at Skálholt and a new one for the north at Hólar. There were several monasteries, adhering both to the Benedictine and Augustinian orders, and there was also one nunnery in Iceland before the demise of the commonwealth in 1262–1264. At least some of the monks were literate, and they composed both Latin and Icelandic texts. Some lay persons of higher status were also apparently literate, at least in Icelandic, but all writing, whether in the international language of the church or in the vernacular, was the result of the conversion to Christianity, which brought with it the technology of manuscript writing.

Before and after the church brought manuscript writing to the north, there was some writing using the native runic writing system. Since in the older runic alphabet there are no horizontal strokes, it is assumed that the system was originally invented for scratching the letters on wooden sticks, whose grain would obscure horizontal strokes. Only special circumstances permit wood to remain

Detail of the rune stone from Rök, Sweden, from the ninth century C.E. *Created by Varin for his dead son, Vemod, with center as ode to Theodoric, king of the Goths. (The Art Archive/ Dagli Orti)*

undecayed in the ground for archaeologists to dig up centuries later, and as a result most (but by no means all) of the extant runic inscriptions are on stones. It is important to stress that carving on wood or stone is a fairly laborious process and that the kinds of things recorded using the runic alphabets tended to be short and of a different nature from texts that can be easily written only in manuscripts. Most runic inscriptions are utilitarian, and despite popular conceptions, they have little to say about mythology or magic.

The oldest runic inscriptions are from around the time of the emergence of the Germanic peoples and are written in an alphabet of 24 characters whose origin is greatly debated. Early in the Viking Age a new runic alphabet developed in Scandinavia, one with 16 characters. Later several variations grew out of this basic Viking Age runic alphabet. Of the approximately 4,000 runic inscriptions, most are from the Viking Age; most of these are from Sweden; and most of these are from the provinces around Lake Mälaren, especially Uppland. Most are memorial: They explain who erected the stone, whose death is memorialized, and what the relationship was between the two. Although the few rune sticks and other kinds of runic inscriptions that have been retained show that runes could be used in a great many ways, Scandinavia through the Viking Age was for all intents and purposes an oral society, one in which nearly all information was encoded in mortal memory—rather than in books that could be stored—and passed from one memory to another through speech acts. Some speech acts were formal in nature, others not. But like speeches that politicians adapt for different audiences, much ancient knowledge must have been prone to change in oral transmission. Without the authority of a written document, there was no way to compare the versions of a text, and we therefore cannot assume that a text recorded in a thirteenth-century source passed unchanged through centuries of oral transmission. This fact makes it extremely difficult to discuss with any authority the time or place of origin of many of the texts of Scandinavian mythology, especially eddic poetry.

"Eddic poetry" is the name we use for a group of about 35 poems, all of them recorded in Iceland during the Middle Ages, nearly all in the thirteenth century. The term "eddic" is a misnomer: Most of these poems are in a single manuscript, and when the learned bishop Brynjólfur Sveinsson first saw this manuscript in the seventeenth century, he perceived a similarity to the book called *Edda* by Snorri Sturluson and imagined that this manuscript, another *"Edda,"* had been composed by Sæmund Sigfússon the Learned, a priest who flourished in the years around 1100 and who according to tradition was the first Icelandic historian, although no works by him have been preserved. This manuscript was therefore called not only *"The Edda of Sæmund"* but also the *"Elder Edda,"* since Sæmund had lived a century before Snorri. It has been more than a century since anyone has taken seriously the idea that Sæmund had anything to do with the composition of this work or that it preceded Snorri, but we still call it *"Edda":* the *Poetic Edda.* Because the manuscript became part of the collection of the Royal Library in Copenhagen, we now call it *"Codex Regius* (royal manuscript) of the *Poetic Edda,"* and we call the kinds of poems in it "eddic poetry."

Codex Regius of the *Poetic Edda,* which is now preserved in Iceland, was written down toward the end of the thirteenth century, probably in the years around 1280. It appears to be a copy of a now lost manuscript, probably written circa 1250, and it seems that some of the poems in it may have been written down as early as the very beginning of the thirteenth century. These are not, however, the mythological poems. *Codex Regius* of the *Poetic Edda* contains 31 poems, sometimes joined or interrupted by prose passages, arranged in a deliberate order by the unknown scribe who wrote it, an order that moves from the mythological to the heroic. It is ordered within the mythological and heroic sections as well.

The manuscript begins with *Völuspá* (Prophecy of the Seeress), which gives a summary of the entire mythology, from the origin of the cosmos to its destruc-

Pages from the famous Codex Regius *of the* Poetic Edda. *(British Library)*

tion to its rebirth. *Völuspá* can also be regarded as an Odin poem, since it is Odin who causes the seeress voicing it to speak. The following three poems are also Odin poems: *Hávamál* (Words of the High One), which contains Odinic wisdom and several stories that describe the acquisition of that wisdom; *Vafthrúdnismál* (Words of Vafthrúdnir), which describes the context of wisdom between Odin and the wise giant Vafthrúdnir; and *Grímnismál* (Words of Grímnir), which describes Odin's ecstatic wisdom performance at the hall of the human king Geirröd. The next poem, *Skírnismál* (Words of Skírnir) or *För Skírnis* (Skírnir's Journey), belongs to Frey, in that it describes the journey of Frey's servant Skírnir to woo the giantess Gerd. The following four poems are probably to be assigned to Thor. The first of these is *Hárbardsljód* (Song of Hárbard), in which Thor and a disguised Odin exchange insults and anecdotes. The next is *Hymiskvida* (Hymir's Poem), an account of Thor's journey to the giant Hymir and fishing up of the Midgard serpent. *Lokasenna* (Loki's Verbal Duel) follows, and in it Loki insults all the gods. It is a Thor poem because it is Thor who finally chases Loki away. The last of the Thor poems is *Thrymskvida* (The Poem of Thrym), a burlesque in which Thor, disguised as Freyja, retrieves his hammer from the giant Thrym. The last two mythological poems are *Völundarkvida* (Völund's Poem) and *Alvíssmál*

(The Words of All-wise). *Völundarkvida* has no gods in it and to us today looks like a heroic poem, but the compiler of *Codex Regius* of the *Poetic Edda* must have thought that Völund's elfish background was good reason to situate the poem here, elves being creatures from the "lower mythology" (neither of the gods nor of the giants). *Alvíssmál* has another such creature in Alvíss, the "all-wise" dwarf who sues for the hand of Thor's daughter and is kept dispensing synonyms by the god until the sun comes up and turns the dwarf to stone.

At this point the heroic poems begin, but the gods are by no means wholly absent, especially from the poems telling the early parts of the story of Sigurd the dragon-slayer. Odin, Hœnir, and Loki appear in the prose header to *Regins-mál* (Reginn's Poem), and Loki appears in the poem itself. There are several allusions to Odin, and these poems contain much fascinating information about such mythological beings as norns, dwarfs, and the like.

There is a second main manuscript containing many of these poems, but, unlike *Codex Regius* of the *Poetic Edda*, it is not apparently ordered. Because it was retained as manuscript number 748 in the Arnamagnæan Collection in Copenhagen, it is called AM 748. It was written down a bit later than *Codex Regius* of the *Poetic Edda*. There are few differences between the texts of the poems in the two manuscripts, but AM 748 contains a mythological poem not included in *Codex Regius* of the *Poetic Edda*, namely, *Baldrs draumar* (Baldr's Dreams), an account of Odin's questioning of a seeress about the fate of Baldr. One additional mythological poem, *Rígsthula* (Ríg's Rhymed List), which tells of the origins of the human social order, is found in a manuscript of Snorri's *Edda*.

Each eddic poem had its own history before it was written down, and there has been much speculation about the dates and origins of the various poems. Most scholars believe strongly in the possibility that some of the mythological poems were composed, after Iceland's conversion to Christianity, by antiquarians secure enough in their Christianity to be able to compose in the old form about the old gods. *Thrymskvida* is the poem most often mentioned in this context, but there are many others. On the other hand, there is no way to tell whether a poem, even one that looks as young as *Thrymskvida*, might have been composed during the Viking Age or even, theoretically, earlier, and changed in oral transmission so as to look like the product of a Christian antiquary. Whatever the original dates and origins of the mythological eddic poems, it seems to me that the similarities outweigh the differences and that the pictures of the gods are fairly consistent.

In form, the eddic poems are short stanzaic poems that rely chiefly on two meters, *fornyrðislag*, "old way of composing," and *ljóðaháttr*, "song meter." *Fornyrðislag* is equivalent to the verse form used in Old English, Old High German, and Old Saxon, the other Germanic languages in which verse has been preserved, although the division into stanzas appears to be a Scandinavian innovation. Like the poems in the second half of *Codex Regius* of the *Poetic Edda*, verse in Old English and Old High German is about heroes, and even the major surviving example of Old Saxon, a verse life of Christ called *Heliand* (Savior), exhibits heroic diction. Heroic eddic poetry, then, especially when it uses *fornyrðislag*, appears to be the heir of common Germanic poetry. We may also surmise that there was verse about gods during the common Germanic period, but only Iceland has preserved any. *Fornyrðislag* tends to be used for third-person narrative, *ljóðaháttr* for dialogue. A version of *ljóðaháttr* is called *galdralag*, "meter of magics," and its use, although sparing, has considerable stylistic power.

Besides these anonymous mythological and heroic poems, there is far more verse that has been transmitted to us with the name of a poet attached to it. The word for "poet" was *skáld*, and these verses are usually called "skaldic." They are far more complex in form than the eddic poems, both with respect to meter and, in the case of the more complex longer poems, with respect to the structure of the poem itself. In addition, they use a far more complex diction. The high degree of formality and complexity make some skaldic verse difficult. Although a great many skalds are known, ranging from Icelandic saga heroes to bishops, some of the most famous skalds served at the courts of kings and other powerful rulers. Sometimes these men gave the skalds valuable gifts, such as a shield, and if the shield was decorated with scenes taken from narrative, the skald might compose a poem describing those scenes as thanks for the gift. Such a shield poem can be of considerable interest in the study of mythology and heroic legend, for the scenes depicted on shields tended to be from those realms. There are other examples of this sort of ekphrasis (Greek: "a plain declaration," in this context a text about an image) in the skaldic corpus, such as Úlf Uggason's *Húsdrápa*, which describes carvings in a newly built hall in late-tenth-century Iceland. In some cases we lack the context of a poem but can surmise the existence of an ekphrasis.

Skaldic poetry is retained as individual verses not (apparently) connected with any poem and as fragmentary or whole poems. The most elaborate poems are called *drápur* (sing., *drápa*), which are broken into sections by means of one or more refrains, which here means lines repeated in the same place within a given stanza. A *drápa* should also have introductory and concluding sections that lack the refrain(s). I will translate *drápa* in this book as "refrain poem." A poem without refrains was called a *flokkr*, "flock."

The earliest known skald is ordinarily taken to be Bragi Boddason the Old, whom most scholars think was Norwegian and active in the second half of the ninth century. According to Snorri, he was associated with the semilegendary Viking Ragnar Lodbrók (Hairy-breeches). Fragments of a poem addressed to Ragnar, *Ragnarsdrápa,* exist. The poem, as we have it reconstructed, describes four scenes on the shield Ragnar gave Bragi, and three of these have to do with the mythology: Thor's fishing up the Midgard serpent, Gefjon's plowing land from Gylfi, and Hild's inciting Högni and Hedin to endless battle.

Another early Norwegian skald was Thjódólf of Hvin, who flourished around the end of the ninth and beginning of the tenth century and was patronized by several Norwegian rulers. Two of the poems attributed to him are important mythological sources. Of these, the first is *Ynglinga tal* (Enumeration of the Ynglingar), which Thjódólf composed for Rögnvald heidumheiri (Honored-highly) Óláfsson, a king from the important Vestfold district in the Oslo fjord. *Ynglinga tal* lists the ways that 22 generations of the Ynglingar, kings centered in Uppsala and predecessors of Rögnvald, met their deaths and where they were buried. The poem clearly originally served a dynastic purpose, but, especially in its discussion of the earliest kings, it has much to tell us about mythology and religion. Thjódólf also composed the shield poem *Haustlöng* (Autumn-long, which may refer to the poem's gestation period). He describes two mythological scenes that adorned the shield: Loki's betrayal of Idun and her apples to the giant Thjazi and her rescue, and Thor's duel with Hrungnir, the strongest of the giants.

From the earliest skaldic tradition come three "eddic praise poems," poems in eddic meters (but in which the meters are ordinarily more strictly adhered to than in eddic poems proper), composed to honor not gods or ancient heroes but recently deceased kings. Two of these describe Valhöll in connection with the arrival there of the king the poet wishes to praise. One, the anonymous *Eiríksmál,* was allegedly commissioned by Gunnhild, the widow of King Eirík Haraldsson Bloodax, who died in 954. The other, attributed to Eyvind Finnsson skáldaspillir (Spoiler-or-debaser-of-poets), praises Hákon the Good, who died in 961.

Úlf Uggason was an Icelandic skald who lived around the tumultuous period of the conversion. Around 985, according to the chronology of *Laxdœla saga,* Úlf composed a *drápa* celebrating the building of an ornate hall by Óláf pái (Peacock), an important chieftain in western Iceland. The hall was decorated within with scenes from the mythology. Three of the scenes are in what we now think we have of the poem, which Úlf recited at the wedding of Óláf's daughter. These are Baldr's funeral, Thor's fishing up of the Midgard serpent, and Loki's fight with Heimdall.

Another skald who lived during this period was Eilíf Godrúnarson, about whom nothing is known—not even his nationality—other than that he was patronized by Hákon Sigurdarson, jarl of Hladir, a notorious pagan. Eilíf composed *Thórsdrápa,* a complex and difficult account of Thor's journey to Geirröd.

Besides these poems treating mythological subjects, there are numerous other relevant texts and fragments. A poem like *Sonatorrek* (Loss of Sons) by Egil

Skallagrímsson, the tenth-century hero of *Egils saga*, may tell us something about his own religious attitudes. "Rán has robbed me greatly," he says, alluding to the drowning death of one of his sons.

In skaldic poetry, Thor is the most frequent mythological subject. The most tantalizing of these are two verses addressing Thor in the second person, both probably from the last years of paganism in Iceland.

Skaldic poetry is valuable not just for the direct exposition of mythological subjects but also for its very diction. The primary stylistic feature is the kenning, a two or more part substitution for a noun. Kennings consist of a base word (e.g., "tree") and a modifier ("of battle"). What is a "tree of battle"? This figure is indeed something like a riddle. Because he stands tall in a battle, a "tree of battle" is a warrior. What is the "din of spears"? Because battles are noisy affairs, the "din of spears" is battle. Kennings are known from eddic poetry and the verse of the other older Germanic languages, but they took on a special importance in skaldic poetry because skalds linked them by using one kenning as the modifier of a base word to create another, for example, "tree of the din of spears" for warrior. The examples I have chosen so far are relatively obvious, but skalds also made kennings based on narrative, that is, on heroic legend and myth. For example, they called gold "the headpiece of Sif," which is only comprehensible if one knows the myth in which Loki cuts off Sif's hair and has the dwarfs make golden hair to replace it. Kennings can be helpful in dating myths, for a kenning that relies on a myth indicates the myth was known to the skald and his audience at a given time. Seeing whether a minor god or goddess is used in the base word of a kenning—for example, "Gná of rings" for woman—can give us some indication as to whether the figure in question was at all known.

Skaldic poetry, then, was a showy, ornate oral poetry, which must have taken much time to master; indeed, it is clear that a certain amount of training would have been needed just to understand it as a member of the audience. It is certainly possible that knowledge of the myths survived the conversion to Christianity because of the value early Christian Iceland placed on the skaldic poems about kings and rulers. In other words, it is possible that the continued transmission of poetry about early kings and battles as historical sources required a continuing knowledge of heroic legend and of myth, not as the object of belief or as something associated with cult but simply as stories that people interested in the history of their own culture had to know. In the same way, students today may study the Bible to be able to understand allusions in older literature. It is even possible to imagine that eddic poems continued to be recited for their narrative value in support of the kenning system, although once belief in the older gods had ended, they could also be recited purely by and for those who enjoyed a good story.

Certainly such a motivation associates the earliest recording of eddic and skaldic poetry and the systematization of the mythology by Snorri Sturluson. Snorri was born during the winter of 1178–1179 into a wealthy family, the Sturlungar, who were to give their name to the turbulent age in which Snorri lived: the Age of the Sturlungs. He grew up at Oddi, the foster son of the most powerful man in Iceland; one of his foster brothers was to become bishop, and Snorri himself was a *goði* and twice held the office of lawspeaker. Through various alliances he soon grew to be one of the most powerful men of his time, and he was deeply involved in the politics of the Age of the Sturlungs. During this time politics became increasingly deadly, and many disputes were settled with weapons. Snorri was assassinated in 1241 by enemies who claimed to be working on behalf of the king of Norway.

Snorri had visited that king, Hákon Hákonarson the Old, in 1218–1219, and he composed a poem in praise of the boy king and his regent, the jarl Skuli. This poem is called *Háttatal* (Enumeration of Meters), and it exemplifies 101 metrical or stylistic variants in its 102 stanzas, equipped with a commentary. From an explication of meter and style, it seems, he moved to a discussion of the system of kennings and rare or poetic words and names called "heiti," which he embodied in a treatise called *Skáldskaparmál* (The Language of Poetry). This text comprises for the most part lists of kennings and heiti arranged by the nouns they can replace, illustrated with a large number of citations from skaldic poetry, quoting in blocks of half a stanza. But besides this, he used a narrative frame to retell some of the more important myths that underlie skaldic kennings. According to this frame, a man named Ægir or Hlér from Hlésey ("Hlér's Island," modern Læssø off the Danish coast), a master of magic, goes to Ásgard, where the æsir receive him well but with visual delusions. The hall is illuminated by swords alone. Twelve male and twelve female æsir are there. Ægir sits next to Bragi, who tells Ægir many stories of events in which the æsir have participated. The first of these is the full story of the alienation and recovery of Idun and her apples, the death of Thjazi, and the compensation granted to Skadi. When Bragi has finished, he and Ægir have a short conversation about a few kennings, and then Ægir asks Bragi the origin of poetry, which elicits the story of the origin and acquisition by Odin of the mead of poetry. At the end of this story Ægir puts questions and Bragi answers them in a way that looks very much like the master-disciple dialogue that so typifies didactic texts in the Middle Ages. Scholars pay special attention to this dialogue, for it sets forth more clearly than in any other place some of the principles of skaldic poetry. After it there follows a paragraph inviting young skalds to pay attention to the narratives that follow if they wish to learn skaldic poetry, but reminding them that Christians are not to believe in pagan gods or the literal truth of the narratives. This can hardly be Bragi's voice; rather, it is that of Snorri or, arguably, one of his copyists, and it intrudes on the framing device of a dialogue between Ægir and Bragi. That device is taken up again when Snorri introduces the story of Thor's duel with Hrungnir and of Thor's journey to Geirröd, but thereafter it is dropped. Additional mythic narratives in *Skáldska-parmál* include the acquisition from one set of dwarfs of Sif's golden hair, the ship Skídbladnir, Odin's spear Gungnir, Odin's ring Draupnir, Frey's boar Gullinborsti, and Thor's hammer Mjöllnir, and the subsequent acquisition from another dwarf of the gold and cursed ring that play a large role in heroic legend. A good deal of heroic legend is also recounted in *Skáldskaparmál.*

It seems that Snorri next was moved to write up the rest of the myths and to do so with a frame story consistently carried out. The result was *Gylfaginning* (Deluding of Gylfi). Here the frame story has a Swedish king, Gylfi, come to visit Ásgard. He does so because he has heard that all goes to the will of the æsir, and he wishes to determine whether it is because of their own nature or because of the gods whom they worship. A wise man with a control of magic, he assumes the form of an old man. But the æsir were wiser in that they possessed the power of prophecy, and, foreseeing his journey, they prepared visual delusions for him. He thinks he arrives at a great hall, and, assuming the name Gangleri, he meets the chieftains there, Hár (High), Jafnhár (Equally-high), and Thridi (Third) and declares his intention to determine whether there is any learned man there. Hár says that Gangleri will not emerge whole if he is not the wiser, and a series of questions and answers ensues, the questions put by Gylfi/Gangleri, the answers given by usually by Hár with occasional amplification by Jafnhár or Thridi. These questions treat the mythology: first the issue of a supreme deity; then the creation of the cosmos, the identity of the gods and goddesses and some of the myths attaching to them, and then myths untreated there or in *Skáldskaparmál;* and finally Ragnarök and its aftermath. Then Gylfi/Gangleri hears a crash, and the hall disappears.

Snorri quotes liberally from eddic poetry in *Gylfaginning*, especially from *Völuspá*, *Vafthrúdnismál*, and *Grímnismál*. The arrangement of the subjects he treats, following the discussion of the "highest and foremost of the gods," which is Gylfi/Gangleri's first question, is essentially that of *Völuspá* in its sweep from beginning to end of mythic time. Snorri also seems to have known eddic poems beyond those he quotes, and he also paraphrases myths that he probably knew from skaldic poetry; but he quotes no skaldic poetry outside the device of the frame, at the beginning of *Gylfaginning*.

If the arrangement of materials to some extent follows *Völuspá*, the frame story itself is reminiscent especially of *Vafthrúdnismál* and other contests of wisdom. We learn Gylfi's motivation for his journey, and he conceals his name. Hár stipulates a wager of heads, but this motif is dropped; indeed, the nearest

King Gylfi of Sweden questions Hár, Jafnhár, and Thridi, from DG 11, a fourteenth-century manuscript containing Snorri Sturluson's Prose Edda. *(Werner Forman/Art Resource)*

analogy to the hall's disappearance at the end of the text is Thor's visit to Útgarda-Loki, not any myth of Odin. Gylfi takes the Odin-role in this contest of wisdom, as the traveler under an assumed name, and indeed this assumed name, Gangleri, is one of Odin's in *Grímnismál*, stanza 46 and elsewhere. This is somewhat ironic, since Hár, Jafnhár, and even Thridi are also names of Odin, the latter two also in *Grímnismál*. But as we shall see, Hár, Jafnhár, and Thridi probably also, in Snorri's view, were no more Odin that Gylfi was.

These three sections, in the opposite order from the one in which I just presented them (i.e., *Gylfaginning, Skáldskaparmál, Háttatal*) and probably in the opposite order from the one in which Snorri wrote them, make up, with a prologue, Snorri's *Edda*, as the work is called in one of its manuscripts. The meaning of this word is not clear, but it seems to have to do with Latin *edo*, in the sense "to compose," and probably therefore meant something like "Poetics." Certainly Snorri's *Edda*, as a whole, is first and foremost a handbook of poetics, even if it is now far more famous as an explication of mythology.

As I have mentioned, *Skáldskaparmál* contains a warning to young skalds about the pagan nature of the material. It seems that Snorri wished to make this statement more forcefully, and he did so in the prologue to his *Edda*. Here, too, he advances his understanding of the historical nature of the gods and gives us the key to understanding *Gylfaginning*. Snorri starts the prologue to his *Edda* by stating, "Almighty God created heaven and earth and all things that accompany them, and finally two people, from whom genealogies are reckoned, Adam and Eve, and their progeny multiplied and went all around the world." Ultimately, however, after the Flood, people lost sight of God, but they observed that there were similarities and yet differences among humans, animals, and the earth, and they began to trace their genealogies from earth. And seeing the importance of the heavenly bodies for time reckoning, they assumed that some being had ordered the course of these bodies and probably existed before they did and might rule all things. This knowledge they possessed was worldly knowledge, for they lacked spiritual knowledge.

This is medieval speculation on the origin of paganism, and it ascribes to pagans a kind of natural religion, one based on unenlightened observation of the environment. It was especially attractive to Icelanders like Snorri, who traced their genealogies from pagans and for whom the conversion of their land to Christianity was a relatively recent event. The first extant work of Icelandic history writing is a little treatise called *Íslendingabók* (Book of Icelanders), by the priest Ari Thorgilsson the Learned, who wrote about a century before Snorri did, and it is plain that for Ari the conversion was the most important event in the history of the Icelanders. In the Sagas of Icelanders, which were composed for the most part in the thirteenth century but which are often set in pagan Iceland, the "noble heathen" is a stock character. All that conversion required, according to this theory of natural religion, was for Icelanders to regain sight of God. Unlike the pagans whom Icelanders learned about when they translated and read the lives of the early saints of the Christian church, Nordic pagans were not doomed souls in league with Satan. They were merely sheep who had lost their way.

Snorri now adds a historical dimension to his prologue. After presenting a standard medieval view of the world as consisting of Africa, Europe, and Asia, he says that near the center of the earth, in Tyrkland, lies the city of Troy. A king there was called Múnón or Mennón, who was married to Tróan, the daughter of King Priam; their son was Trór, "whom we call Thor." He was raised by Duke Loricus, whom he subsequently killed, and he took over the kingdom of Loricus, Trákía (Thrace), "which we call Thrúdheim. Then he traveled widely from country to country, explored the entire continent, and alone defeated all berserks and all giants and the greatest dragon and many animals." He married Síbil, a seeress, "whom we call Sif." He begat an entire family, and eighteen generations later was born Vóden; "we call that one Odin."

Troy was a known place, and Agamemnon and Priam were historical figures known in Iceland from the twelfth century onward. Snorri sets Thor in that environment; that is, he tells us that there was a historical figure whom the Nordic peoples called Thor who lived before Christ was born and who performed historical acts (it is important to remember that berserks and dragons were not as fantastic to medieval historians as they seem to us) that look very much like some of the myths about Thor that later were to be told by the Nordic peoples.

The idea that gods derive from humans whose actions are reinterpreted and deified by later generations is called "euhemerism," after the Greek philosopher Euhemeros (fl. 300 B.C.E.), whose claim to have discovered an inscription showing that Zeus was a mortal king elevated to deity was generalized into a theory that has had considerable currency down into modern times.

Snorri's euhemerism in the prologue to his *Edda* continues with Odin, whose gift of prophecy informs him that his future lies to the north. He sets off from Tyrkland with a large band of followers, young and old, men and women, and they brought many precious things with them. Wherever they went people said great things about them, "so that they seemed more like gods than humans." Odin tarries for a while in Saxony and there sets up his sons as kings. For example, Beldeg, "whom we call Baldr," he makes king of Westphalia. Traveling through Reidgotaland, "which is now called Jutland," he establishes the Skjöldungar as the kings of Denmark. His final destination is Sweden. "That king is there who is named Gylfi. And when he hears of the journey of those Asia-men, who were called æsir, he went to meet them and invited Odin to take as much power in his kingdom as he wished, and those good times went with them, that wherever they stayed in lands, there was peace and prosperity, and everyone believed that they were the cause of that." Odin settles in Sigtúnir (modern Sigtuna, on Lake Mälaren south of Uppsala) and establishes his sons Sæming as king of Norway and Yngvi as king of Sweden after him.

Although the medieval Icelandic word *æsir* (sing., *áss*) etymologically has nothing to do with Asia, the derivation of the æsir from Asia-men completed the euhemeristic process. Snorri tells us who the historical figures were who were deified by his ancestors, and he alleviates somewhat the peripheral northern location of Scandinavia by associating it with the ancient center of the world. It is not difficult to imagine that *Gylfaginning* represents the first encounter between Gylfi and the Asia-men and that Gylfi's delusion was in accepting that the stories told to him by Hár, Jafnhár, and Thridi were about gods. In other words, it is easy to believe that Snorri wishes us to believe that Gylfi's meeting with the æsir contributed to their euhemerization. This theory makes it possible for a learned Christian author to retell and order mythological narratives of his forefathers in a handbook of poetry; the myths in *Gylfaginning* are told by the Asia-men Hár, Jafnhár, and Thridi (none of whom needs to be Odin), just as the myths in *Skáldskaparmál* are told by Bragi, a known skald.

Snorri's *Edda* is thus very much a document of its time, the Christian Middle Ages, and also of its place, an island where the older poetry, for whatever reason, was still transmitted. As it happens, *Skáldskaparmál* quotes much skaldic poetry known from nowhere else, and without it our notion of the genre would be much poorer. And manuscripts of Snorri's *Edda* also contain systematic lists of synonyms called "thulur," doubtless copied there because of the reliance of skaldic poetry on kennings and heiti.

Snorri is also the author of another work, a vast compilation of lives of the kings of Norway known as *Heimskringla* (The Orb of the Earth). Other similar compilations were undertaken in the thirteenth century, but Snorri's is unique in that it starts with prehistory. The first saga in it, *Ynglinga saga*, follows Thjódólf of Hvin's *Ynglinga tal* and expands or paraphrases it in places, but the saga begins before *Ynglinga tal* does, at Troy in Tyrkland. Thor is not in this version, however, as he is in the prologue to Snorri's *Edda*. Additional information not found in the *Edda* prologue is that Vanaland or Vanaheim—the land or world of the vanir—lay along the river Tanais, that is, the Don. To the east lay Ásaland or Ásaheim—the land or world of the æsir—whose capital was Ásgard, a great place of sacrifice. Odin was the chieftain who ruled there, and the opening chapters of *Ynglinga saga* are very much about Odin. Snorri starts the euhemerism in this text by reporting that Odin was constantly victorious, which led his men to believe that if he had "blessed" them before battle they would emerge victorious, and they began to call his name when they were in trouble. From this they got relief, and all their consolation was in him, as Snorri puts it, using vocabulary that is strongly religious. So end the first two chapters.

Chapter 3 of *Ynglinga saga* mentions Odin's long journeys away and the story of his brothers Vili and Vé taking his inheritance and his wife Frigg during one particularly long absence.

Chapter 4 of *Ynglinga saga* offers the fullest account of the war between the æsir and vanir, understood here of course as a historical conflict. The exchange of hostages is present, although with slightly different details. However, the mixing of spittle and creation of the mead of poetry are wholly absent, doubtless in keeping with Snorri's historical project here. Mímir's head is sent back to the æsir and pickled by Odin and used for divination, but we must accept that Snorri found such a concept within historical possibility. He would have been aided in such a supposition by the veneration and use of relics within Christian Europe of the Middle Ages. Also as part of the settlement after the war between the æsir and vanir, Njörd, Frey, and Freyja join the æsir, and Freyja brings the magic art of seid, a form of sorcery and divination, associated in the mythology especially with Odin. Brother-sister incest, which was practiced among the vanir, is dropped when they join the æsir, and Snorri may wish us to believe that the æsir were morally to be preferred to the vanir, even if both groups were pagan.

Chapter 5 describes the emigration from Tyrkland, again motivated by Odin's seeing that his future lay to the north. Again he goes through Saxony, but this time he stops in Ódinsey (modern Odense on the Danish island of Fyn) and sends Gefjon to look for land. The story of her plowing up land from Gylfi and the quotation of the Gefjon stanza by Bragi Boddason the Old are also in *Gylfaginning*, although again the narrative details are slightly different. "Odin and Gylfi contested much in tricks and illusions, and the æsir always were the more powerful," Snorri writes, in an apparent allusion to the euhemeristic frame of *Gylfaginning*. Odin settled at Sigtúnir, and, as in the prologue to Snorri's *Edda*, he established other æsir in their dwelling places.

Chapters 6 and 7 focus on Odin's characteristics and comprise a significant description of him. To his friends he appeared fair of countenance, but to his enemies fierce and grim. He spoke only in verse, and poetry arose from him and his chieftains. In battle he could make his enemies blind or deaf or overcome with fear, but his warriors could go berserk. He was a shape-changer, his body lying apparently inert while he was off and about in some animal form. Here I see the key to this "historical" Odin of Snorri, for this is a classic description of a shamanic trance and journey. If Snorri's historical Odin was a shaman from Tyrkland, he was just a charismatic version of the Sámi shamans who are described in the medieval Scandinavian historical record. To cite but one example among a great many, *Historia Norvegiae* (History of Norway), a work composed presumably in Norway before 1211, describes a shamanic trance and journey to the world of the spirits witnessed by Norwegian traders among the Sámi people in the Norwegian mountains. The author describes the event as though it were fact, as indeed it was for medieval Scandinavians. Odin did not have to be a god to do what Snorri has him do in *Ynglinga saga*. Snorri says explicitly that Odin was a master of seid, which surely refers to the shamanic arts. "His enemies feared him, but his friends relied on him and believed in his strength and in Odin himself." So Snorri expressed his euhemerism at this point. And he extended it by reporting that Odin and his chieftains taught their skills to others, which I take to be an attempt on Snorri's part to account for shamanism among the Sámi. Snorri knew from the saga record (and wrote later about such subjects in *Heimskringla*) that Icelanders, too, had practiced seid during the pagan period, and his historical theory therefore must have been that shamanism originated with Odin and was lost by the Scandinavians upon conversion to Christianity but was retained by the Sámi, who were unconverted in his time.

In chapter 8 Snorri writes that Odin established various pagan customs, primarily cremation funerals, but also various sacrifices. In chapter 9 Odin dies, not in the jaws of a monstrous wolf but of old age. He has himself marked with the point of a spear and gathered for himself all the warriors felled by weapons. He said he wished to go to Godheim or Godheimar, and from this the Swedes concluded, according to Snorri, that Odin had gone to ancient Ásgard and would live there until eternity. "Belief in Odin and calling on him grew up anew." Snorri must have imagined that Godheim was a historical land, misunderstood by the Swedes in connection with their euhemerism, for *goð* is a word for pagan gods. Subsequently in *Ynglinga saga* he has two of the kings of the Ynglingar set out to look for Godheim, to the east in "Greater Sweden."

Njörd ruled the Swedes after Odin. He was followed by Frey, who made Uppsalir (modern Uppsala) the capital. His was a reign of peace and prosperity, the "Peace of Fróði" according to Snorri. Because of this he was worshipped even more than other *goð*. When Snorri uses a word for pagan gods here, he must feel that the euhemerization of the æsir had been completed. Frey is the first of the Ynglingar, and his successor, Fjölnir, is the first king cataloged in Thjódólf's *Ynglinga tal*. From this point, *Ynglinga saga* follows *Ynglinga tal* closely, and the strictly mythological section is at an end. However, the rest of *Ynglinga saga*, and other parts of *Heimskringla* as well, also contains information that is useful for the study of Scandinavian mythology.

Eddic and skaldic poetry, Snorri's *Edda*, and *Ynglinga saga* are the most important direct sources of Scandinavian mythology, and as I have shown, each has its history and is anchored, either by recording or composition, in thirteenth-century Christian Iceland. Iceland recorded its older traditions with extraordinary diligence, and within this large vernacular literature there is much that is of interest for the study of Scandinavian mythology, especially among the sagas.

The word *saga* is related to the verb "to say" and in medieval Icelandic means both "history" and "narrative." There are many kinds of sagas, of which one category, for example, comprises sagas of the Norwegian kings of the sort that are in *Heimskringla*. The other most important saga genres are the mythic-heroic sagas (*fornaldarsögur*, literally "sagas of an ancient age"; sg., *fornaldarsaga*) and the Sagas of Icelanders (*Íslendingasögur*). The mythic-heroic sagas are an amorphous lot joined essentially by being set long ago or far away, that is, before the settlement of Iceland or in the Viking lands to the east. Gods appear as characters in such mythic-heroic sagas as *Völsunga saga*, in part a retelling of some of the heroic materials of the second half of *Codex Regius* of the *Poetic Edda*, or *Gautreks saga*, which tells of an assembly of the gods to set the fate of the hero Starkad. The Sagas of Icelanders recount no myths but rather are seemingly sober accounts of events carried out mostly in Iceland during the pagan period. As a result of this time setting, they sometimes give information about paganism, such as the account of the pagan temple in *Eyrbyggja saga* or of a horse sacred to Frey in *Hrafnkels saga*. Scholars agree that one must proceed with care in using such accounts, since they may include antiquarian reconstructions of the past, but as we have seen, such caution must be used with virtually every text of Scandinavian mythology.

Some other vernacular texts are also of interest. Short independent texts are usually called *þættir* (sing., *þáttr*), which etymologically means "thread" and suggests the interweaving of such texts in larger works, as would be the case when they were recorded in manuscripts. Some of these are quite relevant to the subject. For example, *Sörla þáttr* tells how Freyja acquired the Brísinga men, a torque or necklace, by sleeping with dwarfs in order to outwit a cunning Loki who is Odin's liege man. Whereas *Sörla þáttr* seems like a mythic-heroic saga, *Thidranda þáttr ok Thórhalls* shares the setting of the Sagas of Icelanders and presents some of the evidence regarding the dísir, female spirits.

Not all the important source material is from Iceland or even in the vernacular. An extremely important source is *Gesta Danorum*, a Danish history written by the priest Saxo Grammaticus (that is, "the Grammarian"). Little is known about Saxo, other than that he came from a family of warriors, probably in Jutland, and that he was a member of the household of Absalon, who was archbishop of Lund from 1178–1201. Some of the *Gesta* seems to have been written before the death of Absalon; the rest was probably completed after 1216, or in other words, just a few years before Snorri began his mythological project. Saxo's history consists of 16 books, of which the first 8 treat pagan Denmark and the second 8, Christian Denmark. The first books are therefore, like *Ynglinga saga*, set in prehistory, and gods and heroes play a major role that continues down through the ninth book. Saxo offered a theory of euhemerism similar to that of Snorri, for he says in book 1 that Odin was a man falsely believed to be a god. Höd has become a human king, but Baldr is a demigod, and sometimes Saxo seems to be far more interested in the narratives he is recounting than in any theory of euhemerism. Saxo tells us he got some of his materials from Icelanders, and these materials probably sounded rather like the mythic-heroic sagas. The mythic-heroic sagas are prose with interspersed verse, and Saxo adorns his Latin prose with verse, often rather ornate but still thought to be translated from Scandinavian originals.

Certainly the versions of the myths he presents often vary widely from the versions we have from Iceland. To use the example of Baldr's death: In Saxo's version, Baldr and Höd are not brothers but rivals for the hand of Nanna, a human beauty. Höd is not blind—indeed, he is a most accomplished fellow. Neither Loki nor Frigg appears in the story, and there is no mistletoe. No attempt is made to restore Baldr from the world of the dead, and he enjoys only an attenuated funeral. Saxo's story adds some odd forest maidens and some magic food and sets the death of Baldr in the context of several pitched battles between the forces of Baldr and Höd. Yet Saxo's version does include disquieting dreams, Baldr's invulnerability, and, perhaps most important, the linked story of the siring of an avenger by Odin on Rind (Rinda in Saxo). The extent to which the variation between Saxo's version and the Icelandic sources represents differences between Danish and Icelandic traditions, as opposed to variation within Icelandic tradition reported to Saxo, has never been fully sorted out and probably never will be.

Besides these and a host of other written sources, from inside and outside Scandinavia and in languages ranging from English to Arabic, there are valuable nonwritten sources. Of these the most important is surely the archaeological record. We have, for example, numerous representations from the Viking Age of the encounter between Thor and the Midgard serpent, from Scandinavia and also from England. We have numerous small hammer-shaped amulets, which must be representations in the human world of the protective power conferred by Thor's hammer. We even have dies for casting such hammers and for casting Christian crosses, an eloquent piece of testimony to the mission and conversion. Some small objects with human form have been interpreted as representations of various gods in sculpture. Although these carvings and objects are understood by application of the texts, archaeologists are quite confident in their identifications, and our understanding of Scandinavian mythology would be less rich without them. Some adventurous scholars have even attempted to work from archaeological artifacts back to the mythology, for example, by using the illustrations on

Soapstone mold for making both Thor's hammer and the Christian cross. (National Museum of Denmark)

Migration Period bracteates (small brooches) to reconstruct a set of hypothetical myths about Odin as a healing god.

An example of the importance of the text-object relationship is the large number of small pieces of stamped gold foil that are increasingly being unearthed in apparent cult contexts from Viking Age sites in Scandinavia. Sometimes these portray a man and woman, but there is no direct connection to any text. These fascinating objects belong to the study of the history of religion, but not yet to the study of Scandinavian mythology.

Finally, in discussing the sources of our knowledge of Scandinavian mythology, I must mention etymology (the study of the origin and historical development of words), especially in the study of place-names. Etymology can help us understand the original nature of a god by asking about the meaning of the name of a god in Proto-Germanic, the language of the Germanic peoples around the start of our era, or in Proto-Indo-European, the parent language of Proto-Germanic. Neither of these languages has left any texts, and what we know of them is reconstructed by linguists. For example, according to linguists, the name "Odin," medieval Icelandic Óðinn, derives from a word that would mean something like "leader of the possessed." We cannot be sure what Týr's name meant

Stamped gold foil from Norway depicts embracing figures. (Historisk Museum, Bergen Universitetet)

in Proto-Germanic, but in Proto-Indo-European it was probably a word for "god" or "sky." This may suggest that Týr is an older god than Odin, but such a surmise hardly helps us to understand texts recorded more than a millennium after Proto-Germanic was theoretically spoken and more than two millennia after Proto-Indo-European was spoken. And although it is instructive that Odin's name originally may have meant "leader of the possessed," we cannot assume that Viking Age or later Scandinavians were aware of that fact, and even if we knew they were aware of it, we would still use that fact only as one detail in building up a complete interpretation of Odin.

Most of the place-names of Scandinavia are very old, and over time they have changed enough that only etymology can recover the original meaning. Thus, for example, Copenhagen (Danish København) originally meant "merchants' harbor." Not a few place-names originally contained the names of gods, and the distribution in time and space of these names can tell us much. Nearly all of these theophoric (referring to a deity) names are compounds, in which the name of the god is followed by a noun referring to a natural or cultural feature of the landscape. For example, there are several places in Denmark called "Torshøj," "Thor's hill," and the major city of the Danish island Fyn is Odense, which originally meant "Odin's holy place." Scholars usually distinguish "nature-names" from "cult-names," but the distinction is not as clear as the previous pair of words suggests.

THE INDO-EUROPEAN BACKGROUND

The Germanic languages, of which English, German, Dutch, and the Scandinavian languages are the modern representatives, constitute one branch of the Indo-European family of languages. The name "Indo-European" was coined when the family relationship between Sanskrit, the classic literary language of India, and Greek and Latin, the classic literary languages of Europe, was discovered in the eighteenth century. Most of the languages of modern Europe fall into the Indo-European category, which includes the Germanic, Romance (French, Italian, Spanish, Portuguese, Catalan, Romanian), Slavic (Russian, Polish, Ukrainian, Czech, Slovenian, Croatian, Serbian), Celtic (Irish, Welsh, Manx, and Breton), and Baltic (Lithuanian, Latvian) groups. Finnish and Hungarian are the two national languages of Europe that are not Indo-European; Sámi and Basque represent two other non-Indo-European languages spoken in modern Europe.

Language branches (like Germanic) and families (like Indo-European) are reconstructed on the basis of careful comparison of sounds, words, and grammatical forms. Only such comparison makes possible the etymological research

I discussed above. Going on the assumption that shared language meant shared culture, scholars also tried cultural comparison, and one area in which such comparison was common in the nineteenth century was myth and religion. But although persons who studied comparative mythology were extremely erudite, they did not apply the same rigor to this subject as was used in comparative linguistics. The goal of linguistic comparison was reconstruction of a given language at an earlier state; similarly, comparative mythology hoped to lead to reconstruction of older states of a mythology or, in the Indo-European area, of the myths and conceptions of the hypothetical ancestors of the Indic, Germanic, and other Indo-European peoples from around 2,000 years ago. The project was doomed from the start, however, by notions of what myths were about. Few people thought that a particular sound "meant" something in and of itself. That is, for example, the sound that turned up as ç in Sanskrit, c [= k] in Latin, and h in Germanic was not thought to be anything other than the reflection of a k in Proto-Indo-European, a sound whose meaning was always arbitrary. In myth, however, the situation was quite different. Comparative mythology in the nineteenth century was above all a field driven by interpretations of myths as reflections of natural phenomena, primarily involving the sun, moon, fire, storms, and so forth. This nature mythology was taken as a kind of given, and bits and pieces of myths from all over the world were put to its service. There was no way to test the theory, since even if a bit of mythological lore was taken from a living people, nobody bothered to ask them what they thought it meant, and in fact the comparative method allowed one to ignore living beings, since change could have obscured the original meaning of something.

Although Adalbert Kuhn was an important early adherent of nature mythology, the person most closely associated with it today is Max Müller, a German Indo-Europeanist resident in England who was widely read and very influential for the entire second half of the nineteenth century. Müller's theory of myth was actually based on the notion of a "disease of language," the idea that language itself was inadequate to express everything it had to and therefore was a major contributor to the development of gods and myths, which grew out of linguistic confusion. Müller was an ardent solar mythologist (one who thought that nearly all myths were symbolic stories about the rising and setting sun, light and darkness, and the seasons), and he had followers who were even more ardent than he, if less learned. The indiscriminate aligning of narrative elements to natural phenomena led to the eventual discrediting of comparative mythology, not least when Andrew Lang, a critic of Max Müller, demonstrated that Müller himself was a solar myth.

The discrediting of nature mythology coincided with the growth of anthropology based on field observation in a single culture, and the result was the demise of comparative mythology in the early part of the twentieth century. But Georges Dumézil, the great comparativist, began his academic career at the same time, trained by the Indo-European linguist Antoine Meillet but influenced by the sociologists Marcel Mauss and Émile Durkheim. Dumézil, unlike most of his linguistically trained predecessors, compared structure, not etymology, and he was quite prepared to argue that two deities in different Indo-European traditions were equivalent even when they had no etymological relationship whatever. Nor was he the least bit interested in potential reflection of the phenomena of nature. Rather, he thought that three social "functions" were represented in the mythologies of the various Indo-European peoples. The first function was that of sovereignty, which, according to Dumézil, is ordinarily represented by two deities, each of whom is associated with one or the other side of sovereignty: either with the awe inspired by a leader or with the legal, contractual nature that a sovereign was obligated to uphold. The classic split was found in the Vedic god Varuna and the Persian god Mithra; in Norse mythology, Dumézil argued, Odin represented the awesome side and Týr the legal or contractual side of sovereignty. The second function was might or force, and in Norse mythology Thor fulfilled that function. The third function was fertility, and here the deities are often doubled, as are Frey and Freyja. At one time Dumézil thought these functions represented actual social classes in proto-Indo-European society, but later he backed away from this notion and was content to argue for the structure on a purely mythological plane.

A second aspect of the Dumézilian theory involved the "displacement of myth," that is, the idea that a mythic structure could be "displaced" to the level of divine heroes or in some cases historical fictions. In the Scandinavian area, Dumézil's most forceful argument for such displacement involved the prehistoric king Hadingus, who had many aspects, according to Dumézil, but who also enacted in his life and career all three functions.

Until the late 1950s or early 1960s Dumézil was little known outside France, but thereafter scholars in many fields began to acquaint themselves with his huge output of scholarly writings, and translations of his work began to appear. It was probably inevitable that with such an ambitious project covering so much territory, there would errors at the most specialized level, and in Norse mythology, as in other areas, part of the initial reaction was to point these out. Other critics noted that a tripartite division of the sort Dumézil proposed was relatively common and therefore might have little explanatory power. In medieval Christian Europe, for example, the theory of society involved a division into priest, warriors, and laborers, and that could hardly be an Indo-European inheritance. Even so, the Dumézilian apparatus is by now so widespread that every student of an Indo-European mythology must be aware of it.

Dumézil was not the only person in the twentieth century to seek the Indo-European background of the mythology of one of the daughter traditions, and many contributions have been made outside his theoretical focus. In Norse mythology, study of Thor has especially profited from a look at such figures as the Vedic god Indra and Baltic thunder gods.

CULT, WORSHIP, AND SACRIFICE

This is a book about myths (narratives), not religion (here defined as ritual practice), and as I explained above, few of the narratives were composed during the pagan period and virtually none was recorded then. This makes any study of the cult and ritual that Norse mythology might have accompanied a tricky matter indeed. Nevertheless, we do have some information.

Discussions of the ritual practices associated with Norse mythology usually begin with descriptions by Roman writers of the Germanic peoples, and this is justifiable because the gods we know from our mythological texts also left traces in such forms as the names of the days of the week (see the entry Interpretatio Germanica in chapter 3).

The foremost witness is the *Germania* of Tacitus, from the last years of the first century C.E. Tacitus describes several ritual acts carried out by various Germanic tribes, of which the most famous is surely the worship of the goddess Nerthus described in chapter 40 of his *Germania*. Nerthus, Mother Earth, covered by a cloth, is transported in a cart drawn by cows and accompanied by a priest who recognizes when she is present. This procession takes place in a holy grove on the island on which she lives, and all weapons are laid aside on the days on which it takes place, which are ones of peace and quiet. After the procession, everything is washed in the ocean by slaves who are then drowned.

A number of the aspects of this ceremony agree with what scholars think they know about cult and ritual of the Germanic peoples. Tacitus says elsewhere—and other sources, including place-names, agree—that worship occurs in a sacred grove. The killing of the slaves might also be regarded as a form of sacrifice, a subject to which I will return shortly. Other aspects of the worship of Nerthus find striking agreement with texts recorded much later that are associated specifically with the vanir. Freyja's cart is pulled by cats, and according to *Ögmundar tháttr dytts*, admittedly a late text, (an idol of) Frey is pulled about in a cart accompanied by an attendant, female in this case. Fróði, who shares many characteristics with Frey, was also pulled in a cart, and a time of great peace and prosperity was associated with both Frey and Fróði.

Although there does not seem to have been a separate priestly class, the term *goði*, as suggested above, implies a religious function for the leaders of Icelandic society before the conversion to Christianity. As a Roman, Tacitus used the vocabulary of his own era and therefore called the man who accompanied Nerthus a "priest," but he could easily have been something like a *goði*, a person of status and a secular leader on the days when the goddess was not present. It is the *"goði"* who notices when the goddess is present, and unlike the slaves, he survives to preside over the ceremonies another day. Most or all cults must have been of this nature, led by the chieftain when public ritual was enacted and by the head of household in the case of private ritual. Many historians of religion have argued for a close connection between law, society, and religion, and this connection would be embodied in the men who presided over secular and sacred affairs.

Although Tacitus says the Germanic peoples worshipped in the open, the notion of pagan temples is common in many of the later sources. This probably marks both a change in paganism, perhaps as building techniques changed, and the influence of Christian (and also pagan Roman) worship. In the northern reaches of Scandinavia, the Sámi people seem to have retained an open-air priestless paganism, and they were far from such influences. The eddic poems have references to the building of places of worship (e.g., the "high-timbered" altar and temple of *Völuspá*, stanza 7), and there is one very explicit description of a pagan temple in *Eyrbyggja saga*, which shows, if nothing else, where a thirteenth-century Icelander thought his pagan ancestors had worshipped three centuries earlier. Adam of Bremen's account of the pagan temple at Uppsala, mentioned above, is difficult to discount, but it must be remembered that the end of the eleventh century, when Adam was writing, was a time of enormous Christian influence in Sweden, and it is quite conceivable that the notion of a building reserved for religious purposes could have resulted from such influence. Scandinavian pagans had probably much earlier come in out of the rain for their religious ceremonies: Scholars now agree that large homesteads were the sites of cult activities as well as of other social activities.

The sources mention something called a *hörgr*, which I have translated "altar" in this book. The eddic poems suggest the *hörgr* was something that could be reddened, and they make it appear to be some sort of altar, at least in the sense that sacrifices were made upon it. Etymologically the word seems to have to do with stones or rocks, and it is not difficult to imagine the Germanic *hörgr* as a pile of rocks in a sacred grove; the Old High German cognate is in fact sometimes found with the meaning "sacred rock" and sometimes with the meaning "sacred grove."

Tacitus says the Germanic peoples did not produce images of their gods. Adam of Bremen says the pagan temple at Uppsala had idols of Thor, Wodan (Odin), and Fricco (Frey). Again, the difference lies in the millennium that passed between the times the two authors wrote, and probably also to some extent in the influence of other models. Certainly medieval Scandinavians believed that their pagan forbears had worshipped idols, for they routinely put idols in their historical writings. In the Sagas of Icelanders, the expression "the gods" almost always refers to idols, and when Icelanders translated the lives of the Christian saints, they sometimes attached the names of their own pagan gods to the idols worshipped by the pagans whom the early saints encountered.

The word used for pagan cult activity is *blót*. The etymology is disputed, and that is a pity, for if we could recover the original meaning of the word we would at least know something of the origin and perhaps nature of the activity among the Germanic or pre-Germanic peoples. The two credible suggestions are that *blót* is related to Latin *flamen*, "priest of a specific deity," from a root meaning ultimately something like "sacrificial activity," or to a root meaning "to make strong," ultimately deriving from a root meaning "swollen." The first has the advantage of being associated with religious activity, but it does not tell us much about the actual conception. Far more important are the loans of *blót* into Finnish, namely *luote*, "magic charm," and Sámi *luotte*, "magic song." These show us the importance of verbal activity at a *blót*, specifically verbal activity aimed at producing a result, presumably by means of intervention by the deities.

Another way to influence the deities was of course to make sacrifices to them, and here we have an ample record to draw on. Bogs, wells, lakes, and the earth have yielded such objects as broken weapons, which can only be interpreted as gifts to the gods after battle. Classical sources report that the Germanic peoples killed their defeated enemies rather than take them prisoner, again as a form of sacrifice, and Adam of Bremen says that every ninth year at the pagan temple at Uppsala, sacrifices of all kinds of creatures took place, including humans. But the most important sacrifices at the *blót* were surely animals that were slaughtered and eaten, presumably in some form of honor of a god.

In chapter 8 of his *Ynglinga saga*, Snorri Sturluson says that Odin established the succession of *blót* ceremonies in the north. Toward winter (i.e., in fall) there should be a *blót* for prosperity; at midwinter, one for the growth of the soil; and at summer, a third one, the victory-*blót*. There is an evident connection here, as one would expect, with the rhythm of the year: The fall ceremony would occur after the last harvest was in, and the animals slaughtered would be those who were not to survive the winter. Some of their meat could be eaten fresh at the *blót*, but much would be preserved for winter. The midwinter *blót* would occur after the longest nights had passed and would celebrate the rebirth of the earth; and the summer ceremony, if it was for victory, would coincide with the departure of ships on raiding (and, more mundanely, trading) voyages.

Later in his *Heimskringla*, in *Hákonar saga góða* (The Saga of Hákon the Good), Snorri gives an elaborate description of a *blót* that shows just how pervasive the influence of Christian liturgy was on the view of late Nordic paganism of Snorri and other Icelandic intellectuals. The word *hlaut* is cognate with English "lot," as in "to cast lots." I cannot find a reasonable translation, so I have left it in the original.

> It was the ancient custom, when a *blót* was to be held, that all farmers should come to where the temple was, and to transport there the supplies they would need as long as the banquet lasted. At the banquet everyone was to drink beer. All sorts of cattle and horses were killed there, and all the blood that came from them was called *hlaut,* and the vessels in which it stood *hlaut*-bowls, and the *hlaut*-twigs were made like an aspergillum [a brush used to sprinkle holy water in Catholic liturgy]. With it one was to redden the pedestal together with the walls of the temple inside and out and also to sprinkle it on the people, while the meat of the slaughtered animals was to be cooked for people to enjoy. . . . A tankard was to be carried to the fire, and the one who made the banquet and was the chieftain should bless the tankard and all the sacrificial meat and should first toast Odin—that should be drunk for victory and for the kingdom of his king—and after that a toast to Njörd and Frey for peace and prosperity. Then people were eager to drink the *bragafull* [chieftain's toast] next. People also drank a toast to their kinsmen who had been buried in mounds; that was called *minni* [memorial].

Take away the references to the gods and the blood spattered all about, and one might well have a picture of a wealthy man's feast in medieval Norway or Iceland.

THE IMPORTANCE OF SCANDINAVIAN MYTHOLOGY

Although worship of the Scandinavian gods ended a thousand years ago, and the myths are now exotic and foreign to most people in the English-speaking world, we make implicit reference to the gods and myths almost every day of our lives. That is because the names of the weekdays Tuesday, Wednesday, Thursday, and Friday all contain the names of old Scandinavian gods (Týr, Odin, Thor, and Frigg; the Old English forms were Tiw, Wodæn, Thunor, and Friija), and the choice of the gods for each of these days was based on myths about them. (I treat the subject at greater length in the entry on Interpretatio Germanica in chapter 3.) Furthermore, when we read about or travel in places like Odense, Denmark (probably best known outside Denmark as the birthplace of Hans Christian Andersen), we see a place-name that once bore the name of the god Odin. There are hundreds of these in Scandinavia, but they are seldom obvious, except in Iceland, where there are places with names like Þórsmörk (Thor's forest), a favorite place for hiking and camping. And if you are acquainted with or have heard of anyone called Freyja, Thor, Baldur (a not uncommon name in Iceland), or any Scandinavian name beginning with Tor, you know of the persistence of the names of the gods in personal naming systems.

The era when Norse mythology was most known in more recent times was the Romantic period, when the gods and myths were a popular source of inspiration. Paul Henri Mallet's *Introduction à l'histoire de Dannemarc, ou l'on traite de la religion, des loix, des moeurs, et des usages des anciens danois* (Copenhagen: Berling, 1755) made Norse mythology widely known for the first time in a world language, and the work was translated into English in 1770 as *Northern Antiquities: Or, A Description of The Manners, Customs, Religion, and Laws of The Ancient Danes, and Other Northern Nations; Including Those of Our Own Saxon Ancestors. With a Translation of The Edda, Or System of Runic Mythology, and Other Pieces, from The Ancient Icelandic Tongue* (London: T. Carnan and Co., 1770). The translator was Bishop Percy, who is famous for his *Reliques of Ancient Poetry*, a collection of ballads and other pieces that was one of the most influential works of English Romanticism. The second volume of Mallet contained a translation of the mythological stories of Snorri's *Edda*, in a late arrangement done by Magnús Ólafsson, parson at Laufás in the early seventeenth century and therefore known as the Laufás *Edda*. It was at the end of the eighteenth century, too, that translations of eddic poetry began to appear in the European languages. During the late eighteenth and early nineteenth centuries Norse mythology was the vogue, especially in Germany and Scandinavia, and many of the famous Romantic poets reworked stories from Norse mythology into drama or verse. Romantic painters also found inspiration in the Norse myths.

In a way the ultimate result of this Romantic interest in Norse myth and heroic legend was the opera cycle by the German composer Richard Wagner entitled *Der Ring des Nibelungen* (The Ring of the Nibelung). This mighty work, originally intended to be heard over the course of just three days, consists of a prologue called *Das Rheingold* (The Rhine-gold), followed by three hefty three-act operas, *Die Walküre* (The Valkyrie), *Siegfried*, and *Götterdämmerung* (Twilight of the Gods). Wagner wrote the book as well as the music, using a kind of alliterative, archaic German that has its own strange charm, at least when sung. He based his story loosely on the so-called Burgundian cycle, that is, the heroic poems of the *Poetic Edda* centering on Sigurd, *Völsunga saga*, and the medieval German epic *Das Nibelungenlied* (The Song of the Nibelungs). The major action of the first part of the cycle Wagner took from the story that prefaces *Reginsmál* in the *Poetic Edda*, involving a cursed ring that the gods obtain and must give up. Although many of the gods make only small appearances, Odin, called either Wotan (the German form of his name) or the Wanderer, plays an absolutely pivotal role. He leaves the stage at the end of the second act of *Die Walküre*, but Walhalla, the abode of the gods, is seen crumbling at the end of *Götterdämmerung* as the Rhine overflows its banks and cleanses the world of the cursed ring. It is powerful music and powerful theater.

Wagner was one of Hitler's favorite composers, and Norse mythology had a sad revival in connection with Nazi ideology. Today Norse mythology every once in a while is found in connection with contemptible neo-Nazi activities, but for the most part it is the stuff of either comic books or fantasy literature. There was a revival of "belief in the æsir" some years ago in Iceland, which seemed to have to do at least in part with tax breaks for organized religion, although partying is also important. That revival had its counterpart in Norway, where a group of students announced themselves to be believers in the æsir. In celebration, they drank some beer and sacrificed a sausage.

2

TIME

THE NATURE OF MYTHIC TIME

Religions of the world experience and encode time in various ways: as a linear progression, as a never-ending set of cycles, as a process of degeneration, and so forth. We are most used to a linear system, since it characterizes our Judeo-Christian tradition, which sees a clear progression from the creation of the world through a long present leading to a last time, a day of judgment, an end of history. Similarly, our science gives us increasing detail concerning the origin of the entire universe. We live in the long aftermath of the big boom and the origin of our solar system, and we know that in due course our sun will die. In a cyclical system, however, such a linear progression repeats itself endlessly; each end is followed by a new beginning. Determining the time system of Scandinavian mythology presents special challenges because many of the sources were recorded by Christians, whose notion of time was linear and whose notion of history called for an essentially clear chronology. This is especially so of Snorri Sturluson, whose *Edda* is the clearest and most appealing account of the mythology to modern readers. It must not be forgotten that Snorri was also a historian, the author or compiler of a history of the Norwegian kings *(Heimskringla)* arranged wholly chronologically. The other great overview of the mythology is the eddic poem *Völuspá*. Although nearly all scholars agree that it dates from the pagan period, most would assign it to late paganism, and Christian influence seems apparent. Even so, *Völuspá* seems to show traces of a cyclic arrangement of time as well as a linear arrangement.

Furthermore, the various myths present direct contradictions of relative chronology. Such contradiction is, however, characteristic of myth, which has its own rules. Within Scandinavian mythology, these rules appear to suggest a fairly consistent ordering of events within a given narrative, but no requirement whatever that events within the mythology as a whole can be fit into a precise order. Examples will be cited below, but anyone who confronts the primary sources or even a summary of the mythology will easily identify others.

MYTHIC PAST, PRESENT, AND FUTURE

The mythology as a whole may be divided into events that take place in the past, present, and future, an idea that is expressed in the meanings of the names of the norns Urd, "Became" or "Happened"; Verdandi, "Becoming" or "Happening"; and Skuld, "Is-to-be" or "Will-happen." However, it is convenient to make further distinctions.

The *distant past* would involve the period before the creation of the universe. At that time there was only Ginnunga gap, the vast void of potency and potential, and perhaps also the Élivágar, mysterious waters from which life was to emerge. We must assign Ymir to this distant past, and also his hermaphroditic generation of the races of giants. Similarly, Bur, the first of the gods, existed at this time.

The focus of the *near past* would be the creation of the cosmos, from the body of Ymir according to most sources. The precondition for forming the cosmos was the killing of Ymir by the sons of Bur, so we may say that the movement from the distant past to the near past encompasses a move from a stasis between the two major groups of gods to a state of enmity. During this near past the gods also enabled the reckoning of time by assigning stations to the heavenly bodies (*Völuspá*, stanza 5), and they similarly enabled culture by creating tools (*Völuspá*, stanza 7). They created the races of dwarfs and humans. Finally, I would assign the incorporation of the vanir and of Loki into the æsir as the final events of the near past.

With the completion of these incorporations, the mythological world looks as it does in most of the myths. Snorri's catalog of the gods in *Gylfaginning* includes the vanir and Loki, and also Baldr, whose death is yet to come. I would call this state the *mythological present*, the time when most of the myths take place. Although it hardly matters whether a given myth of the mythological present occurs before or after some other myth, certain events do seem to have to precede or follow others. For example, when in *Skáldskaparmál* of Snorri's *Edda* the gods wish to appease Skadi for the killing of her father Thjazi, they offer her a choice of husband among the gods, letting her select based on an observation of just their lower legs. She chooses what she thinks are Baldr's but ends up with old Njörd. According to the reasoning of this narrative, then, Njörd's marriage to Skadi preceded the death of Baldr. However, Frey's marriage to Gerd appears to have followed Baldr's death. In *Skírnismál*, stanza 21, Skírnir offers the giantess Gerd "the ring which was burned with the young son of Odin," and this can only be Draupnir. If it was burned with the son of Odin, Baldr must already be dead, and Frey and Gerd's marriage has yet even to be arranged, much less consummated after the nine nights that must intervene after the arrangement is made. I think Snorri must have had this sequence of events in mind when he wrote *Gylfaginning*, for in the catalog of gods he says that Njörd is married to Skadi, but he does not say that Frey is married to Gerd. And following this chronology, we might assume that Baldr was, in Snorri's mind, already dead when the gods visited Ægir at the very beginning of *Skáldskaparmál*, for he includes Gerd in the guest list. However, we must take care with such assumptions. In the case of this guest list, for example, Baldr is indeed absent, but Nanna is present. Either she did not after all cast herself on Baldr's funeral pyre, as Snorri says she did in *Gylfaginning*, or the chronology will not hold. Such inconsistencies are, let me stress, not causes for worry. They are in the nature of mythology.

Similarly, we may think of events as occurring relatively early or relatively late in the mythological present. An example of a relatively early event would be the acquisition of the mead of poetry. The mead was in the first place created as a result of the conclusion of hostilities between æsir and vanir and is a token of the incorporation of the two groups. It is one of Odin's most powerful weapons in the ongoing struggle with the jötnar. Similarly, the construction of the wall around the stronghold of the gods, told most fully in Snorri's *Gylfaginning*, is a story of the early mythological present. It explains not only how a wall gets built around Valhöll (which is mentioned in several myths, e.g., Odin's interaction with Hrungnir and Loki's rescue of Idun), but also how Sleipnir, Odin's eight-legged horse, is created. Here again, strict chronological consistency is lacking, for the account of the acquisition of the mead of poetry in *Skáldskaparmál* implies the existence of the wall (the gods put the kettles for it in the enclosure), but the incorporation of the æsir and vanir, which is the precondition for the mead, occurred in the near past. Another story of the early mythological present would be Odin's sending of Hel to the underworld and the Midgard serpent to the outer waters of the ocean, as well as the binding of the wolf Fenrir, when Týr lost his hand. In the mythological present Hel presides over the underworld, Thor fishes up the Midgard serpent in offshore waters, and Týr is without his hand, while Fenrir awaits the end of the world.

Odin's myths tend toward the early part of the mythic present: Already mentioned are the mead of poetry, war and peace with the vanir, oath of blood-brotherhood with Loki, and disposition of Loki's children. In addition there is Odin's self-sacrifice, which gained him much of the rest of the wisdom he uses in the mythological present. Odin myths in the mythological present would include in particular the stories of his visits with the giant Vafthrúdnir and the human king Geirröd, in each of which wisdom plays an important role.

Nearly all of the Thor myths take place in the undifferentiated mythic present. These include, besides his fishing up of the Midgard serpent, his encounters with Hrungnir, Hymir, and Geirröd.

Some events must be fairly late in the mythological present, and the foremost of these is the death of Baldr. As the first death among the gods, it changed all the terms of the game. Even if it did not make Ragnarök inevitable, it made it possible, for now the death of any and therefore of all the gods is a possibility. If we follow the Baldr story in Snorri's *Gylfaginning,* we see that Odin's strategy of swearing blood-brotherhood with Loki has failed, for it was Loki who brought about Baldr's death. The gods now bind Loki, and like his sons the wolf Fenrir and the Midgard serpent, he awaits Ragnarök, the end of the world and the final period in the mythology. Many of the events in the mythic present look forward to Ragnarök: the failed oath of blood-brotherhood, the binding of evil creatures, and the gathering of einherjar, the chosen warriors of Odin, at Valhöll.

The mythic future also has two stages. In the *near future* is Ragnarök, when the power of the gods over the jötnar characteristic of the mythic present will be reversed. Surt will lead the forces of chaos against the gods, who will fall. The creative activities of the near past will be undone: Time reckoning will fail as the sun and moon are swallowed and the heavens destroyed, and the entire cosmos will be consumed by flames and water. Each of the major gods will die in individual combat with a giant adversary, but Odin, at least, will be avenged, by his son Vídar, the silent god, and this vengeance constitutes a bridge to the distant future, the period after Ragnarök when the second-generation gods Vídar and Váli, Magni and Módi, and, perhaps most important, Baldr and Höd, victim and killer, will inhabit the renewed earth. They will possess the cultural property of their ancestors in the form of oral traditions about them as well as in the concrete form of the gaming pieces *Völuspá,* stanza 61, says they will find in the grass. This paradise will be fertile and devoid of jötnar.

As I have thus outlined it, the overall chronology of Scandinavian mythology is neatly symmetrical. The early present looks back to the near past, just as the later present looks forward directly to the near future. The creative work of the near past is undone in the near future, but the vicious relationship between gods and jötnar, which enabled the creation of the cosmos and led to its destruction, is gone in the distant future, just as it was not present in the distant past. But there has still been a progression: In the distant past there was no cosmos, but in the distant future there is a green world with birds and fertile fields. The course of the mythology has indeed led to a better world.

CYCLICAL TIME

Völuspá, stanza 4, states that the creating gods lifted up the earth, and the poem is silent on the killing of Ymir. These facts could imply that when the earth arose from the sea after Ragnarök later in the poem, there was a cyclical notion at work. In other words, the cosmos might be formed and reformed on multiple occasions by rising from the sea. This notion, which accords with the theories of Mircea Eliade as expressed, for example, in his *The Myth of the Eternal Return,* has been expressed most clearly by Jens Peter Schjødt in his 1981 article "Völuspá—cyklisk tidsopfattelse i gammelnordisk religion" (*Danske studier* 76 [1981]: 91–95). Schjødt points especially to the last stanza of *Völuspá,* which refers to the arrival of a dragon and the sinking of the sibyl. In the best treatment of time in Norse mythology, that of Margaret Clunies Ross in volume 1 of her *Prolonged Echoes,* especially chapter 7, Clunies Ross accepts the possibility of underlying traces of cyclic time but offers a linear progression very similar to the one I have outlined here, the differences being that I split the mythic present into periods of early, undifferentiated, and late, and also that I demonstrate the symmetries of the chronology and their implications.

TIME AND SPACE

Clunies Ross also discusses the relationship between time and space that characterized the structural analyses of Eleazar Meletinskij, "Scandinavian Mythology as a System," *The Journal of Structural Anthropology* 1 (1973): 43–58, and 2 (1974): 57–78, and Kirsten Hastrup, *Culture and History in Medieval Iceland: An Anthropological Assessment of Structure and Change* (Oxford: Clarendon, 1985). Both these authors sought to distinguish the vertical from the horizontal axes, the first manifesting itself in the world tree linking heaven and the underworld, and the second, in the disk of the earth on which Ásgard, Midgard, and the worlds of the giants are located. Meletinskij argued that cosmogony and eschatology were distinguished by the axes and that this distinction had a chronological aspect. Hastrup described the difference as one of reversibility: Events on the vertical axis were "irreversible," for they were fated; those on the horizontal axis were "reversible," in that the balance between gods and giants was so close. Both Clunies Ross and Jens Peter Schjødt, "Horizontale und vertikale Achsen in der vorchristlichen skandinavischen Kosmologie," in *Old Norse and Finnish Cultic Religions and Place Names,* ed. Tore Ahlbäck, Scripta Instituti Donneri Aboensis, 13 (Åbo, Finland: Donner Institute for Research in Religious and Cultural History, 1990), 35–57, disagreed. Schjødt takes on the notion of the "eschatological" or "irreversible" nature of the vertical axis and argues that it has cyclical aspects. Clunies Ross argues that events on the horizontal axis (those that for the most part fall into the mythic present) are hardly reversible even in Hastrup's model, for they contribute directly to eschatology (put another way: the mythic present always looks back to the past and forward to the future).

MYTH, NARRATIVE, AND LANGUAGE

The situation is further complicated by two other factors. The first is the "immanence" of the mythology: The entire system is implicit in any of its details, and a myth is equally present in a kenning or an allusive skaldic poem from the pagan period, and neither of these requires any kind of chronology but, instead, implies a kind of simultaneity of myth. The second is a linguistic after-effect and may be presented here by discussing stanza 28 of *Lokasenna*. Frigg has just admonished Loki.

> You know, if here I had in Ægir's hall
> A son like Baldr
> Away you would never get from the sons of the æsir,
> And you would be struck down in anger.

Loki's response is a boast about his role in the slaying of Baldr. The second half of stanza 28 goes literally as follows.

> I arrange it, that you never see
> Baldr afterwards ride up to the hall anymore.

Most translators render the first three words as something like "I am responsible," and indeed the present tense of the verb might be understood that way. Conceivably it might also be read literally as a progressive: "I am arranging," that is, I'm taking care of that right now. But in medieval Icelandic the simple present tense also is used for the future, so Loki may be saying "I will arrange it." And although the word is quite clear in the one manuscript retaining the poem, the difference between present and past tense is just the vowel, and some editors have chosen to print the past tense rather than the present tense. In other words, when Loki was insulting all the gods, he had killed Baldr, was planning it, or would take care of it later.

The same linguistic fact complicates our understanding of other texts. In *Völuspá*, for example, the seeress who speaks the poem says in one manuscript that she *saw* various events connected with Ragnarök (in the other she says she uses the present tense, as one would expect of a vision of the mythic future, as the frame of the poem implies). But around stanza 44 she begins to use the present tense. Is she situated toward the onset of Ragnarök?

MYTH AND HISTORY

For the Christians of the Scandinavian Middle Ages, the gods would have had a place in historical time both through their euhemerization and through their presence in some of the lives of the saints translated from Latin into Icelandic. According to the notion of the euhemerization that prevailed in medieval Iceland, the gods were originally human beings who had emigrated from the Middle East (Tyrkland) to Scandinavia long ago. They would have left their homeland at some point during the Roman Empire, which can be reckoned to around 100 B.C.E. Both Snorri Sturluson and Saxo Grammaticus associate the legendary king Fródi, grandson of Frey according to Snorri, with the peace that occurred when Christ was on earth. And the translated lives of the saints put the Norse gods (in place of Jupiter, Mars, Diana, and other Roman gods) in the time and space of early Christianity—even if they are only for the most part envisioned in these texts as idols animated by demons.

It is furthermore possible—perhaps likely—that Ragnarök was seen by at least some Christians as the demise not only of the pagan gods but of the belief in and worship of them. Their day would have preceded that of Christ, and it had a fiery and perhaps well-deserved end. Certainly the famous stanza 65H of *Völuspá*, found in the late-fourteenth-century redaction of the text, supports such a possibility, for it mentions the coming to power of "the powerful one, from on high, he who rules all." Whoever created this verse appears to have considered the world he and his fellow Christians lived in to be the new world that followed Ragnarök. The conversion to Christianity seems to have been envisioned while it was happening as a struggle between Thor and Christ. Thor and his fellow gods thus exited history at about the time Christ entered it in the north, that is, in the tenth and eleventh centuries.

3

DEITIES, THEMES, AND CONCEPTS

ÆGIR

The sea personified; a famous host to the gods but listed among the jötnar.

The name appears to be identical to a noun for "sea" in skaldic poetry, and that noun, or the name of the figure under discussion here, is the base word in many kennings. For example, "Ægir's horse" is a ship, and "daughters of Ægir" are waves. In *Skáldskaparmál*, Snorri says that Rán is the wife of Ægir and that they have nine daughters, most of whom bear names meaning "wave." Since Rán is listed among the goddesses in the thulur and Ægir has a peaceful relationship with the gods, his inclusion in the thulur as a giant seems questionable.

The eddic poems often show Ægir as host to the gods. *Hymiskvida* is set in motion because the gods expect to visit Ægir and will need a huge cauldron in which to brew the beer that will be consumed. The poem tells how Thor acquires the cauldron from the giant Hymir. The next poem in *Codex Regius* of the *Poetic Edda* is *Lokasenna*, Loki's flyting (that is, verbal duel) with the gods, and it is set at a feast hosted by Ægir. Indeed, paper manuscripts call the poem *Ægisdrekka* (Ægir's Drinking Party). According to the prose header to the poem, "Ægir, who was also called Gymir, had prepared beer for the æsir." After enumerating the guest list (most of the æsir except Thor, who was away to the east bashing trolls), the author reports that bright gold was used there in place of firelight, and the beer served itself. It was a great place of sanctuary, but Loki kills Ægir's servant Fimafeng, and Eldir, Ægir's other servant, is the first with whom Loki exchanges words in the series of flytings that make up the poem. Loki's last words are reserved for Ægir:

> You made the beer, Ægir, and you never more will
> Have a feast again;
> All your possessions, which are here inside,
> May fire play over,
> And may it burn your back.

Ægir's prowess as a host is the final motif Odin reveals to the terrified King Geirröd in *Grímnismál* before beginning the list of names that leads to his epiphany. But Ægir was also a famous guest, according to Snorri. The frame story that he uses in the first sections of *Skáldskaparmál* begins with this introduction of Ægir:

> A man was named Ægir or Hlér; he lived on that island which is now called Hlér's Island [modern Læssø in Denmark]. He had much magic knowledge. He made his way to Ásgard, but the æsir knew of his journey in advance. He was well received, but many things were done with illusions.

The similarities to *Gylfaginning* are remarkable, and they are only extended when Bragi, who is seated next to Ægir, begins to tell Ægir stories: the mythic narratives in *Skáldskaparmál*, beginning with the Thjazi-Idun-Skadi complex. Ægir asks questions after hearing this cycle, and more myths follow. The dialogue between Ægir the questioner and Bragi the narrator continues for many pages in *Skáldskaparmál* and is embedded in many of the myths that are recounted. After a time, speakers are not identified, but the dialogue form is carried on throughout *Skáldskaparmál*, and Ægir reappears as the subject in one of the questions concerning kennings: Why is gold called "fire of the sea" or "fire of Ægir"? The answer is what was found in the prose header to *Lokasenna*: Gold was used to light Ægir's hall when he entertained the æsir.

The beginning of *Orkneyinga saga* (The Saga of the Orkney Islanders) is sometimes called *Fundinn Noregr* (Norway Found), and it is closely related to a section of *Flateyjarbók* called *Hversu Noregr byggdisk* (How Norway Was Settled). It begins with a king called Fornjót, who ruled in northern Norway. "Fornjót had three sons. One was named Hlér, whom we call Ægir, the second Logi, the third Kári." Like *ægir*, *hlér* is a noun meaning "sea." The noun *logi* means "fire," and *kári* is listed among the thulur for "wind." Thus Ægir as a personification of the sea would appear to have been regarded as one of the three elements in a genealogical tradition that presumably was localized in Norway.

See also Ægir's Daughters; Fornjót; Rán

References and further reading: Matthias Tveitane, "Omkring det mytologiske navnet Ægir 'vannmannen,'" *Acta Philologica Scandinavica* 31 (1976): 81–95 (summary in English), argues that the name of the being Ægir, which he understands as "water-man," was originally separate from the noun "mass of water, sea." Francis P. Magoun treated some place-names, including the name of Ægir, in "Fi feldor and the Name of the Eider," *Namn och bygd* 28 (1940): 91–114. Franz Rolf Schröder, "Die Göttin des Urmeeres und ihr männlicher Partner," *Beiträge zur Geschichte der deutschen Sprache und Literatur* (Tübingen) 82 (1960): 221–264, is centered on Nerthus and Njörd but also included discussion of Rán and Ægir/Hlér. Margaret Clunies Ross, "Snorri Sturluson's Use of the Norse Origin Legend of the Sons of Fornjótr in His *Edda*," *Arkiv för nordisk filologi* 98 (1983): 47–66, analyzes Snorri's understanding of natural forces as giants.

ÆGIR'S DAUGHTERS

The waves of the sea; nine sisters, daughters of Ægir and Rán.

Ægir is the sea personified, and his daughters are the waves. The poet known only as Svein, perhaps an Icelander of the eleventh century, describes a wintry storm in which gusts of wind from the mountains riffle and tear apart Ægir's daughters, that is, the waves. *Helgakvida Hundingsbana* I, stanza 29, calls a powerful wave that nearly overturns a ship Ægir's daughter. In *Skáldskaparmál*, Snorri Sturluson says that Rán is Ægir's wife and the mother of Ægir's daughters. Snorri lists their names twice, with a variation in the eighth name only: Himinglæfa (Transparent-on-top), Dúfa (Wave), Blódudhadda (Bloody-hair), Hefring (Lifting), Unn (Wave), Hrönn (Wave), Bylgja (Billow), Kára (Powerful) or Dröfn (Wave), and Kólga (Cool-wave). The only one of these names whose appropriateness is not immediately apparent is "Bloody-hair," which I take to refer to reddish foam atop a wave.

   See also Ægir

ÆSIR

The gods; also the main group of gods, as opposed to the vanir.

The medieval Icelandic word *æsir* is a plural; the singular is *áss*, and a derived feminine form, *ásynja* (pl., *ásynjur*), means "goddess." Etymologically, *áss* appears to be derived from an Indo-European root meaning "breath," and this would suggest an association with life and life-giving forces. A dissenting etymology would understand the term as associated with sovereignty and "binding gods," parallel to the terms *bönd* and *höpt*. The term is found a few times in early runic inscriptions, and the cognate is found in Old English *os*, "god, deity," and in *anses*, "demigods," a Latinized version of a word in Gothic, the language of the well-known Germanic tribe. The word *áss*, or its homonym, also means "beam" or "post," and some scholars seek an association with wooden idols or the equivalent. The rune poems, which are relatively late, give *áss* or its equivalent as the name of the *a*-rune.

In medieval Icelandic the term *æsir* is the one most often found when the gods are being described as a group, in prose and in poetry. In *Thrymskvida*, for example, when it is revealed that Thor's hammer has been stolen by the giant Thrym and that he will exchange it only for Freyja, the poet writes:

Then all the æsir were at an assembly,
And all the *ásynjur* in discussion. (stanza 14)

Often the term *álfar*, "elves," is used as a parallel, probably because of the alliteration that the poetic form required, but also perhaps because of a fundamental association between the two groups. As she describes the world crumbling about them at Ragnarök, for example, the seeress of *Völuspá* asks: "What's with the æsir, / what's with the elves?" (stanza 48), a formula that is repeated in *Thrymskvida*, stanza 7. In the *Ljódatal* section of *Hávamál*, Odin boasts that he can discern the difference between æsir and álfar (stanza 159) and adds that the fifteenth song he has learned was chanted by the dwarf Thjódörir, before the doors of Delling: "He chanted strength for the æsir, / advancement for the álfar, / and mind for Hroptatýr [Odin]" (stanza 160). The formulaic association of æsir and álfar is also found in *Grímnismál*, *Skírnismál*, and *Lokasenna*.

Although the plural refers to all the gods, the singular seems to have a special association with Thor. Thus, when Thor tells Loki about the theft of the hammer early in *Thrymskvida*, he says: "The *áss* has had his hammer stolen" (stanza 2). Thor is called Ása-Thor (Thor of the æsir). No other god is described in this way, and it has been suggested that this extension of the name means that he was regarded as best of the æsir.

The most interesting use of the word *æsir* is that of Snorri Sturluson in the euhemerization project he set forth in the preface to his *Edda* and in the opening chapters of *Ynglinga saga*. *Ásía*, the Old Norse word for Asia, appeared to contain the word *áss*, although of course it does not, and Snorri used the sound similarity to suggest that the original meaning of *æsir* was "men of Asia." Chapter 2 of *Ynglina saga* begins as follows:

> To the east of Tanakvísl [the river Don] in Asia was known as Ásaland [land of the æsir] or Ása-heimr [world of the æsir], and the principle stronghold in the land they called Ásgard.

Because of this usage, one must take care when reading Snorri's *Edda*. When King Gylfi resolves to set off for his encounter with High, Equally-high, and Third, it is because he is curious about the knowledge and power of the Ása-folk, which must refer to "Asians"; the intended euhemerism may even explain Snorri's choice of "Ása-folk," which clearly retains the root of *Ásía*, here instead of "æsir." In the frame to *Skáldskaparmál*, however, he just refers to the inhabitants of Ásgard as æsir, and there the ambiguity may be deliberate.

See also Æsir-Vanir War; Almáttki áss; Ása-Thor; Gods, Words for
References and further reading: Andreas Heusler, *Die gelehrte Urgeschichte im*

altisländischen Schrifttum, Abhandlungen der Königlichen Preussischen Akademie der Wissenschaften, Philosophisch-Historische Klasse; [Jahrg.] 1908, Abh. 3 (Berlin, Verlag der Königlichenen Akademie der Wissenschaften, in Commission bei Georg Reimer, 1908). Waltraud Hunke, "Odins Geburt," in *Edda, Skalden, saga: Festschrift zum 70. Geburtstag von Felix Genzmer,* ed. Hermann Schneider (Heidelberg: C. Winter, 1952), 68–71. Edgar Polomé, "L'étymologie du terme germanique *ansuz 'dieu souverain,'" Études germaniques* 8 (1953): 36–44. Albert Morey Sturtevant, "Regarding the Name Ása-Þórr," *Scandinavian Studies* 15 (1953): 15–16.

ÆSIR-VANIR WAR

War fought at the beginning of time, leading by its truce to the incorporation of the æsir and vanir into a single unified group of gods.

We know the war from *Völuspá* and from Snorri's somewhat varying descriptions in the *Ynglinga saga* of his *Heimskringla* and in the *Skáldskaparmál* of his *Edda.* The sequence in *Völuspá* of stanzas 21–24 refers to the first battle in the world, and in stanza 24 both the æsir and vanir are mentioned. The seeress is speaking of herself in the third person:

21. She remembers the battle of armies, the first one in the world,
When Gullveig with spears they studded
And in the hall of Hár burned her;
Thrice burned, thrice born,
Often, unseldom, though she yet lives.
22. They called her Heid, where she came to [the?] houses,
a seeress very wise, she cast spells;
she performed seid where she could, she performed seid, in a trance,
she was ever the joy of an evil woman.
23. Then all the powers went to the judgment seats
the very holy gods, and discussed this:
whether the æsir should pay a fine,
or all the gods should have tribute.
24. That was yet the battle of armies, the first one in the world.
Odin let fly and shot into the army,
The shield wall of the fortress of the æsir was broken,
The battle-wise vanir knew how to tread the field.

I am uncertain about portions of the above translation, especially the second half of stanza 23. In stanza 21 and stanza 24, the term I have translated as "army" and "armies" is *fólk,* and although the word indeed means "army" in the older poetry, by the Middle Ages it also commonly had the meaning "people." Thus, it is quite possible that the scribes of the *Poetic Edda* and a thirteenth-century audience could have understood the stanza as referring literally to a battle of peoples.

Although these stanzas are anything but clear, they seem to tell of a battle precipitated by the entry of Gullveig or Heid among the æsir. They were unable to kill her with spears or fire, and she was a practitioner of seid, the ancient form of divination and of magic in general. Since Snorri says that Freyja brought seid to the æsir, many scholars have assumed that Gullveig/Heid is actually Freyja, one of the vanir, and that her corruption of the æsir precipitated the war. Gullveig appears to mean "Gold-drink" or possibly "Gold-intoxication"; Heid means perhaps "Shiny." Stanza 23 seems to have to do with an inability to reach a truce during a war, and understood thus it leads nicely into the battle of stanza 24. The move, however, from "æsir" to the inclusive "all the gods" could indicate a move toward a community involving æsir and vanir.

When Snorri tells about the war in *Skáldskaparmál*, it is as part of the much longer story of the origin of the mead of poetry, which Ægir has asked Bragi about. The beginning of this story, Bragi responds, is that the gods had been in conflict with that people *(fólk)* who were called the vanir, and they negotiated a truce settlement in which each side spat into a kettle. From the mingled spittle came Kvasir, and from him in turn came the mead of poetry, but that is another story.

Snorri devotes more attention to the war and its aftermath in *Ynglinga saga*. Here the story is set into the historical or pseudohistorical context of the æsir as Asians and the vanir as a people dwelling by the river Tanakvísl, or, as Snorri says it might be called in violation of every modern linguistic norm but in a perfectly reasonable medieval linguistic jump, Vanakvísl. Snorri, in chapter 4, describes what looks like a real war. The story is as follows:

> Odin went to war against the vanir, but they defended themselves and their land well, and neither side could gain the upper hand. They agreed on a settlement and exchanged hostages [here understood as men exchanged as pledges of good faith]. The vanir sent their most distinguished men, Njörd and Frey, and the æsir in exchange sent Hœnir, whom they declared to be a great leader, and Mímir, who was very wise. In response, the vanir sent Kvasir, who was also very wise. Hœnir proved to be unable of leadership without consulting Mímir, so the vanir, suspecting that they had been cheated, beheaded Mímir and sent the head to Odin. Odin preserved the head and it told him many hidden things. The æsir made Njörd and Frey into leaders of cult. Freyja, Njörd's daughter, first taught seid to the æsir. Brother-sister incest, which had been common among the vanir, was banned among the æsir.

Even if Freyja is not identical to Gullveig/Heid, the various versions seem to share the notion of a disruptive entry of persons into a people (Gullveig/Heid among the æsir, Hœnir and Mímir among the vanir) and the acquisition of tools for the acquisition of wisdom, seid in two accounts and the head of Mímir in one. Both of Snorri's accounts place more emphasis on the settlement than on the war, and from *Skáldskaparmál* we learn that the tangible symbol of the truth, the mixed spittle, ultimately became one of the greatest tools for wisdom, namely the mead of poetry. *Ynglinga saga* also indicates that the most distinguished of the vanir, Njörd and Frey, were fully incorporated into the æsir.

Since the vanir are fertility deities, the war has often been understood as the reflection of the overrunning of local fertility cults somewhere in the Germanic area by a more warlike cult, perhaps that of invading Indo-Europeans. But Georges Dumézil argued forcefully that the story of the war need be no more historical than any other myth: It is set before the emigration from the Middle East, and it is far more focused on the truce than on the details of any battles. The myth of the war between the æsir and vanir (perhaps better termed the "reconciliation of the æsir and vanir"?) explains symbolically how a religious system contains various kinds of deities with varying functions.

See also Hœnir; Mead of Poetry; Mímir; Seid

References and further reading: Dumézil published his ideas on the war in many
   places, but the easiest of access is found in chapter 1 of his *Gods of the
   Ancient Northmen*, ed. Einar Haugen, Publications of the UCLA Center for
   the Study of Comparative Folklore and Mythology, 3 (Berkeley and Los
   Angeles: University of California Press, 1973). A social reading drawing on
   Indo-European parallels is Jarich G. Oosten, *The War of the Gods: The Social
   Code in Indo-European Mythology* (London: Routledge, 1985). Those wishing
   to see how the arguments were constructed for the notion of warring cults
   may consult Karl Weinhold, "Über den Mythus vom Wanenkrieg,"
   *Sitzungsberichte der köninglichen preussischen Akademie der Wissensa-
   haften zu Berlin*, phil.-hist. Kl. 1890: 611–625, or H. W. Stubbs, "Troy, Ásgard,
   and Armageddon," *Folklore* 70 (1959): 440–459. Torbjörg Östvold, "The War
   of the Æsir and the Vanir: A Myth of the Fall in Nordic Religion," *Temenos* 5
   (1969): 169–202, has not found favor.

ÁLFABLÓT

"Elf-sacrifice," pagan ritual known from literary sources.

The Icelandic skald Sighvatr Thórdarson composed verses about his journey to Västergötland, Sweden, circa 1017, gathered under the title *Austrfararvísur*. Often the pagan Swedes refused hospitality, and in one verse this refusal is explicitly linked to the *álfablót* that is going on inside. The verse says that it was an old woman who denied entry, and that she was afraid of the wrath of Odin.

This would appear to associate a cult of the elves explicitly with the gods. *Kormáks saga*, chapter 22, has the prophetess Thórdís give advice to Thorvard, who was wounded in a duel with Kormák and seeks to be healed. He must get a bull slain by Kormák, pour its blood on a hill inhabited by elves, and prepare a feast for them out of the slaughtered meat. Although the word *álfablót* is not used, this too looks like a sacrifice to the elves. Certainly there is a vast difference between a ceremony held indoors, as in the Swedish *álfablót* mentioned by Sighvatr, and sacrificial acts undertaken in nature, as the thirteenth-century *Kormáks saga* suggests for tenth-century Iceland, and this difference appears to be greater than one would expect for regional variation. Since Sighvatr actually uses the term *álfablót*, and is something of an eyewitness, we should probably give his account precedence.

ÁLFHEIM (ELF-LAND)
Property of Frey, presumably a residence.
The information on Álfheim is found in the second half of stanza 5 of *Grímnismál*, which begins the list of residences of the gods:

> Álfheim the gods in ancient times
> Gave to Frey as a tooth-gift.

A tooth-gift was given when a child cut its first tooth, that is, when it was around a year old. The notion of Frey as an infant among the æsir contradicts the myth of the Æsir-Vanir War, in which Frey joined the æsir as a hostage (human pledge) and at the time was a distinguished man.

Perhaps for this reason, in *Gylfaginning* Snorri has a different account of Álfheim: It is, as the name suggests, the abode of the elves—or more precisely, the light-elves; the dark-elves (only Snorri has this distinction) live below the earth. No connection between Frey and the elves is known from other sources.

Álfheimar (plural) was also according to medieval historiography the name of the geographic district between the mouths of the Göta and Glom (Norse Raum) rivers in the coastal border districts between Sweden and Norway. The *Sögubrot af fornkonungum* reports that the people who lived there were fairer than others, which could indicate an association with the elves, but the name of the district probably is derived from a word meaning a gravel layer under a field.

ALFÖDR (ALL-FATHER)

Odin name, found in skaldic and eddic poetry and frequent in the *Gylfaginning* in Snorri's *Edda.*

In *Gylfaginning* the very first question put by Gylfi/Gangleri is "Who is the foremost or eldest of all the gods?" Hár answers, "That one is called Alfödr in our language, but in Old Ásgard he had twelve names." The names listed are Odin names, but Odin is not explicitly identified as Alfödr until later in *Gylfaginning.* Later Snorri writes: "And he may be called Alfödr because he is the father of all the gods and of men and of all that which was done by him and his power. The earth was his daughter and his wife. From her he got his first son, Ása-Thor." Although Snorri seems to use Alfödr and Odin interchangeably (and some manuscripts have Alfödr where others have Odin), it is not until he has formally introduced Odin as the first in his catalog of æsir that the identification of Odin and Alfödr is made explicitly.

> Odin is the foremost and eldest of the æsir; he rules all things, and as powerful as the other gods are, they serve him as children do a father. . . . Odin is called Alfödr.

The form *födr* for "father" appears to be archaic. It is also found in the Odin names Herfödr and Valfödr.

See also Odin

References and further reading: Walter Baetke discussed Snorri's use of the name Alfödr in his *Die Götterlehre der Snorra-Edda,* Berichte über die Verhandlungen der sächsischen Akademie der Wissenschaften zu Leipzig, phil.-hist. Kl., 97:3 (Berlin: Akademie Verlag, 1950). According to Baetke, the obvious Christian analogue to the concept of an all-father has to do with Snorri's attempt to describe the natural religion of his pagan forbears, which Snorri assumes would have tended toward monotheism. Thus Odin, only one of many gods in the mythology itself, was in Baetke's view promoted to a leading position in Snorri's description of it.

ALMÁTTKI ÁSS

"All-powerful deity" of unknown identity.

The expression is found in oaths and is given its fullest expression in *Landnámabók* (in chapter 268 in the *Hauksbók* version). The passage describes the paganism that obtained in Iceland in the early days of the settlement. Every pagan temple should have a ring, and before entering into legal proceedings, each man should swear an oath on that ring:

> I attest that I make an oath on the ring, a legal oath: May Frey and Njörd and the almáttki áss help me in this case as I prosecute or defend or bring witnesses or verdicts or judgments, as I know how to do most rightly or truly or

procedurally correctly, and dispatch all legal pleadings which fall to me, while I am at the assembly.

I cite the full passage to counteract the impression given by some modern writers that the oath served for general purposes; the author of this recension of *Landnámabók* states quite clearly that it is a legal oath.

No certainty as to the identity of the almáttki áss has been reached. An interpretation based purely on the mythology would lead to Odin, the all-father and most powerful of the æsir. A consideration of the role of Thor around the time of the conversion to Christianity and his lengthened name Ása-Thor would lead easily to him. A focus on the ring might lead to Ull, for in *Atlakvida*, stanza 30, Gudún reminds Atli that he has sworn oaths on the ring of Ull. And in his *Lexikon der germanischen Mythologie*, Rudolf Simek even plays with the idea of Týr, which might be possible if one attempted a purely historical reading.

Because Frey and Njörd are vanir, the word *áss* in the formula appears to point specifically away from the vanir. But we must be cautious, as the entire passage in question is the product of a medieval Christian author who was demonstrably far more interested in his ancestors' Christian background than in their pagan background. Perhaps he even meant the "almighty áss" to be a noble pagan anticipation of the new religion that was to come.

References and further reading: Hermann Pálsson, "Áss hinn almáttki," *Skírnir* 130 (1956): 187–192 (in Icelandic; argues for Ull). Jakob Jóh. Smári, "Áss hinn almáttki," *Skírnir* 110 (1936): 161–163 (in Icelandic; argues for a nameless creator). Henry L. Tapp, "Hinn almáttki áss—Thor or Odin?" *Journal of English and Germanic Philology* 55 (1956): 85–89. Gabriel Turville-Petre, "The Cult of Odin in Iceland," in his *Nine Norse Studies*, Viking Society Text Series, 5 (London: Viking Society; University College London, 1972), 1–19.

ALVÍSSMÁL

Eddic poem, "The Words of All-wise."

Found only in *Codex Regius* of the *Poetic Edda*, the poem is situated between *Völundarkvida* and *Helgakvida Hundingsbana* I, the first of the heroic poems in the manuscript. *Alvíssmál* may be the last of the poems in the mythological section because it has a dwarf as a main character; *Völundarkvida* has an elf, and the two together may therefore represent a transitional section from poems of gods to poems of men.

Alvíssmál consists of 35 stanzas of dialogue in the meter usually used for dialogue, *ljóðaháttr*. In the first stanzas one of the speakers announces that he has come for a bride, and when challenged about his identity says, "I am named Alvíss [All-wise], / I live down under the earth, / I have my dwelling under a stone." In stanza 6 the other speaker, the father of the bride, identifies himself as Vingthór, the son of Sídgrani; that is, Thor, the son of Odin. Thor will only give up the girl, whose troth was, he says, given while he was away (stanza 4), if the dwarf will tell him everything he wishes to know. What follows is a series of 13 questions. Each of them begins with the formula "Tell me that, Alvíss, / —all the fates of men / I expect that you know, dwarf." The questions themselves concern vocabulary: What is something called, by which Thor seems to desire a list of synonyms. In his responses Alvíss provides these synonyms according to the races or groups of beings in the mythology. The groups are not always quite the same, but humans, gods, and giants are constants, and vanir (as opposed to the gods in general), elves, dwarfs, and the dead occur frequently. Generally the everyday word is assigned to humans and the other terms are from the poetic vocabulary. Frequently the words assigned to the gods have an elegant feel, while those assigned to the giants feel heavy or clumsy, although admittedly such feelings are to a certain extent subjective.

The categories Thor requests are as follows: earth, heaven, moon, sun, clouds, wind, calm, sea, fire, wood, night, seed, and ale. These categories and the order in which they appear can hardly be arbitrary. The first five are cosmic, and they are presented in the order in which they appear in the creation story. Sea and fire will destroy the cosmos at Ragnarök, wood could represent Yggdrasil, the world tree, and beer, which comes from grain that grows out of seeds, is associated with Odin and wisdom. At the equivalent point in an Odinic wisdom contest there would be an epiphany, as in *Grímnismál* or *Vafthrúdnismál,* leading to the death of the one contending in wisdom with the god, and here something similar happens: Night, the eleventh category, has ended. Thor has the last word, and in his final half-stanza he uses the "magic" meter *galdralag.* "In one breast / I never saw / more ancient wisdom; / with great deceits / I declare you trapped: / you are "dayed out," dwarf, / now the sun shines in the hall." We surmise that the ray of sunlight shatters the dwarf or turns him to stone, as in many dwarf legends; a giantess is turned to stone under precisely the same circumstances in a heroic eddic peom, *Helgakvida Hjörvardssonar.*

Neither Thor nor dwarfs are ordinarily known for skill at verbal dueling, and despite tantalizing hints associating some dwarfs with wisdom, most have none. This and other evidence has been used to propose a late origin for the poem. But Thor is responsible for protecting his females, and thus the result of the action of the poem is appropriate, even if its players strike us as misplaced.

References and further reading: A good study of the language of the poem is Lennart Moberg, "The Language of *Alvíssmál,*" *Saga-Book of the Viking Society* 18 (1973): 299–323. Calvert Watkins, "Language of Gods and Language of Men: Remarks on Some Indo-European Metalinguistic Traditions," in *Myth and Law among the Indo-Europeans: Studies in Indo-European Comparative*

Mythology, ed. Jaan Puhvel (Berkeley and Los Angeles: University of California Press, 1970), 1–17, provides a broader context. The situation of the frame, Thor protecting his daughter from a misalliance, is illuminated in Margaret Clunies Ross, "Þórr's Honour," in *Studien zum Altgermanischen: Festschrift für Heinrich Beck,* ed. Heiko Uecker (Berlin and New York: W. de Gruyter, 1994), 48–76.

ANDHRÍMNIR (SOOTY-IN-FRONT)

Cook at Valhöll.

The key passage is stanza 18 of *Grímnismál.*

> Andhrímnir in Eldhrímnir
> Has Sæhrímnir boiled.

In *Gylfaginning* Snorri understands the passage as a cook (Andhrímnir) cooking pork (the pig Sæhrímnir) in a huge pot (Eldhrímnir), and indeed the rest of this stanza seems to call Sæhrímnir the best of pork and refers to the mysterious nourishment of the einherjar. All three of the names are joined by the element *hrímnir,* which is derived from the word for soot on a cookpot. The element *And-* could refer to (or could have been understood by Snorri as referring to) the front of the cook, who would be facing the cookpot as he worked his culinary magic.

See also Eldhrímnir; Sæhrímnir

ANDLANG

The second of three heavens in the cosmology of Snorri's *Gylfaginning.*

No other text refers to this place or to a second heaven, so it may be Snorri's invention. The name appears to mean "stretched out" but might conceivably derive from a longer form meaning "spiritual heaven."

See also Víðbláinn

ANDVARI (CAREFUL)

Dwarf from whom Loki and the gods extract gold to pay compensation for their killing of Otr, the son Hreidmar.

The story is told in Snorri's *Skáldskaparmál,* in the prose header and opening stanzas of *Reginsmál* in the *Poetic Edda,* and in *Völsunga saga.* The gods involved are Odin, Hœnir, and Loki. Loki kills Otr ("Otter," who had in fact taken the form of an otter), and Hreidmar demands compensation. Using Rán's net, Loki captures Andvari, who has been swimming about in the form of a pike, and extracts from him all his gold, right down to a ring the dwarf wishes to keep. When Loki insists on having it anyway, the dwarf curses it, saying that it will lead to death and discord. So it does.

Andvari is also mentioned in the catalog of dwarfs in *Völuspá* and in the thulur. The thulur also include the word as a noun for "fish."

See also Dwarfs

ANGRBODA (SHE-WHO-OFFERS-SORROW)

Giantess mate of Loki and mother of monsters.

The name is found only once in poetry, in *Hyndluljód*, stanza 40, a part of the "Short *Völuspá*."

> Loki sired the wolf on Angrboda,
> and got Sleipnir on Svadilfari;
> the witch alone seemed most evil
> the one that came from the brother of Byleipt.

Snorri makes Angrboda, "a giantess in Jötunheimar," the mother of three monsters: the Fenrir wolf; Jörmungand, that is, the Midgard serpent; and Hel. This raises the possibility that the witch in lines 3–4 of the stanza quoted above from *Hyndluljód* may be Hel.

See also Fenrir; Hel; Loki; Midgard Serpent

ÁRVAK AND ALSVIN (EARLY-AWAKE AND VERY-SWIFT)

Horses that pull the sun.

Grímnismál, stanza 37, is the main source:

> Árvak and Alsvin, they should up from here,
> The bold ones, pull the sun;
> And under their traces the blithe powers,
> The æsir, hid "iron cold."

The names of the horses are bound by alliteration, and they also occur as a couple on the other occasion when they appear in verse. This is in *Sigrdrífumál*, in a mysterious part of the poem introduced by a stanza saying that Mím's head spoke. The very next stanza, number 15, is where the horses appear:

> On a shield shall be carved, the one which stands before the shining god,
> On the ears of Árvak and on the hoof of Alsvin,

This engraved stone found in Havor, Gotland, might be an unusual depiction of the horses that pull the sun, Árvak and Alsvin. (The Art Archive/Historiska Museet Stockholm/Dagli Orti)

On that wheel, which turns itself under the riding of Rungnir,
On Sleipnir's teeth and on the springs of a sled.

The list goes on, and it becomes no more edifying.

Snorri paraphrases the stanza from *Grímnismál* in his *Gylfaginning*, but, rather uncharacteristically, he has nothing to add about the horses. He does, however, expand the "iron cold" *(ísarn kól)* into wind-driven bellows called "Ísarnkól."

See also Sól

ÁSA-THOR (THOR-OF-THE-ÆSIR)

Name for Thor.

This name is found in *Hárbardsljód*, stanza 52, and frequently in Snorri's *Edda*. Although it is sometimes used in cases where Thor's might is held up to question (e.g., in the Útgarda-Loki story), it may be going a bit far to regard the name as ironic.

References and further reading: Albert Morey Sturtevant, "Regarding the Name Ása-Þórr," *Scandinavian Studies* 15 (1953): 15–16.

ÁS-BRÚ (ÆSIR-BRIDGE)

Alternate name for Bilröst, according to Snorri Sturluson in *Gylfaginning*. He cites *Grímnismál*, stanza 29, which may, however, use the word as a common noun rather than as a name.

See also Bilröst

ÁSGARD (ENCLOSURE-OF-THE-ÆSIR)

The abode of the gods.

The name is found in eddic poetry, in Snorri's *Edda*, and, perhaps most interestingly, in a fragment of a poem about Thor composed by the late-tenth-century skald Thorbjörn dísarskáld, who was one of two skalds to leave us poems addressed to Thor, the only such verse we know of. What Thorbjörn said was "Thor has defended Ásgard and Ygg's [Odin's] people [the gods] with strength." The noun *-gard*, "yard," is used of the domains of the major groups in the mythology: Ásgard for the gods, Midgard (Central-enclosure) for humans, and Útgardar (Outer-enclosures) for the jötnar (the last, however, is found only in connection with Útgarda-Loki). Within Ásgard was Valhöll.

What makes Ásgard an enclosure is the wall around it, which an elaborate story in *Gylfaginning* seems to address. The gods had established Midgard and had built Valhöll when a builder came to them and offered to build a fortress so secure that giants could not get through it. He offered to do the job in a year and a half against a payment of Freyja, the sun, and the moon. The gods thought they had cut a great deal when they got him to agree to do the job within half a year with only the help of his horse Svadilfari. They were mistaken, and when three days were left it appeared all but certain that the wall would be completed. The gods blamed Loki and threatened him. Loki changed himself into a mare and distracted Svadilfari. The wall was never completed, and when Thor returned he killed the giant builder. Loki subsequently gave birth to Sleipnir.

> **References and further reading:** The medieval and folklore analogues to the story of the construction of the wall were long ago pointed out by C. W. von Sydow, "Studier i Finnsägnen och besläktade byggmästarsägner," *Fataburen*, 1907: 65–78, 199–218; and 1908: 19–27; Lotte Motz's discussion, "Snorri's Story of the Cheated Mason and Its Folklore Parallels," *Maal og minne*, 1977: 115–122, adds little. Joseph Harris, "The Masterbuilder Story in Snorri's *Edda* and Two Sagas," *Arkiv för nordisk filologi* 91 (1976): 66–101, argues that Snorri created the story in an attempt to clarify *Völuspá*, stanzas 25–26. His source would have been an oral legend, retained in two of the Sagas of Icelanders, *Eyrbyggja saga* and *Heidarvíga saga*, about two berserks who build a road; this legend was in turn based on the international migratory legend von Sydow had discussed. The argument is quite plausible, but it was disputed by Ursula Dronke, "*Völuspá* and Satiric Tradition," *Annali: Sezione germanica: Studi nederlandesi, studi nordici* 77 (1979): 57–86, who postulated a lost *Lay of Svadilfari* as the source of *Völuspá*, stanzas 25–26.

ASK (ASH-TREE) AND EMBLA

First humans.

The story of the creation of humans is found in *Völuspá*, stanzas 17–18, and in Snorri's *Gylfaginning*. According to *Völuspá*, Ask (the first human man) and Embla (the first human woman) were found on shore, capable of little and fateless. Odin, Hœnir, and Lódur endowed them with the various qualities they needed to live. Odin gave breath or spirit, Hœnir gave mental faculties or voice, and Lódur gave blood, ruddiness, or vital warmth and good coloring. Snorri adds some details and changes others. The creator gods, according to Snorri, are the sons of Bor (elsewhere Bur)—Odin, Vili, and Vé—who find two pieces of wood on the seashore and fashion them into humans. One of Bor's sons gives spirit and life; the second, mind and movement; the third, appearance, speech, hearing, and vision. The sons of Bor also gave these vivified pieces of wood clothing and their names, Ask and Embla, and from them descend the races of mankind.

In *Völuspá*, the stanzas about Ask and Embla follow the catalog of dwarfs, and it is quite possible that stanza 10, which refers to the dwarfs' making of human forms out of the earth, may be involved. In this scenario, the dwarfs would have formed humans, but the gods would have endowed them with life.

Although Ask clearly means "Ash tree," the meaning of Embla is uncertain. "Elm tree" is one possibility, but it encounters serious linguistic obstacles. The other possibility usually offered is "vine," and in connection with this option comes the further suggestion of a relationship between human sexual congress and the turning of a hardwood such as ash into a soft wood to make fire.

See also Hœnir

References and further reading: The possible role of the dwarfs in the creation of Ask and Embla is argued forcefully in Gro Steinsland, "Antrogonimyten i Voluspá: En tekst- og tradisjonskritisk analyse," *Arkiv för nordisk filologi* 98 (1983): 80–107. For Embla as "vine" and the hardwood/softwood hypothesis, see Hans Sperber, "Embla," *Beiträge zur Geschichte der deutschen Sprache und Literatur* 36 (1910): 219–222.

ATLA

One of nine giant mothers, perhaps of Heimdall, listed in *Hyndluljód,* stanza 37 (part of the "Short *Völuspá*").

See also Heimdall; *Hyndluljód*

References and further reading: Lotte Motz, "Giantesses and Their Names," *Früh-mittelalterliche Studien* 15 (1981): 495–511.

AUDHUMLA

The proto-cow, involved in the origin of the races of gods and giants.

Although the name is found among the thulur for "cow," Audhumla's mythological role is found only in Snorri's *Gylfaginning.* Snorri says that Audhumla emerged from the drips of rime just after Ymir was formed, and that four streams of milk ran from her udders and nourished Ymir. She in turn licked salt blocks, and from these there emerged in three days Búri, the first of the æsir.

Although cows are not uncommon in creation stories from around the world, what is most striking about Audhumla is that she unites the two groups of warring groups in the mythology, by nourishing Ymir, ancestor of all the giants, and bringing into the light Búri, progenitor of the æsir. The presumed etymology of her name, "hornless cow rich in milk," is of no help in interpreting her mythological role.

See also Ymir

References and further reading: On the etymology, see Adolf Noreen, "Urkon *Audhumla* och några hennes språkliga släktningar," *Namn och bygd* 6 (1918): 169–172.

AURBODA (GRAVEL-OFFERER)

Giantess, mother of Gerd, Frey's wife.

The relevant source is *Hyndluljód*, stanza 30, lines 5–8:

> Frey possessed Gerd, she was the daughter of Gymir [corrected from Geymir]
> Of the race of giants, and of Aurboda.

In *Gylfaginning* Snorri repeated this information.

Stanza 38 of *Fjölsvinnsmál*, which is stanza 54 in the poem editors create out of *Grógald* and *Fjölsvinnsmál* and which they call *Svipdagsmál*, also mentions an Aurboda. She occurs in a list of nine maidens who sit at the knees of Menglöd. Although Menglöd is a giantess, these are not giantess names—one, indeed, is Eir, an *ásynja* according to Snorri, and the others are adjectives like bright, blithe, and fair. I doubt that we are dealing with the same Aurboda in both cases.

See also Frey, Gerd

AURGELMIR (MUD-YELLER)

Primeval giant.

In *Vafthrúdnismál* Odin asks Vafthrúdnir who was the oldest of the æsir or kin of Ymir. Vafthrúdnir says Bergelmir was born many years before the earth was formed; his father was Thrúdgelmir and his grandfather Aurgelmir. Odin now asks (stanza 30), whence Aurgelmir first came among the sons of the jötnar. The giant responds:

> From the Élivágar spurted poison drops,
> Thus it grew, until a giant emerged.

Odin now asks how that giant got children, since he had no pleasure of giantesses. Vafthrúdnir responds in stanza 33:

> Under an arm of the frost giant, they say, grew
> A maiden and lad together;
> A leg got on a leg of the wise [or fruitful] giant
> A six-headed son.

Snorri quotes these verses but says that Aurgelmir was the name the frost giants used for Ymir. Since that would be unique, we must again assume that Snorri was systematizing, although it is also true that the hermaphroditic birthing process fits better etymologically with Ymir (whose name has to do with doubling) than with Aurgelmir.

See also Bergelmir; Thrúdgelmir; Ymir

AURVANDIL

Giant (?) whose toe was made into a star by Thor; husband of Gróa.

According to Snorri's account of Thor's duel with Hrungnir in *Skáldskaparmál*, Thor was visited by the seeress Gróa, who sang charms over him and thereby loosened the whetstone that was lodged in Thor's head after the duel.

> And when Thor learned that and thought it likely that the whetstone would be removed, then he wanted to repay Gróa for her cure and make her happy. He told her that he had been wading from the north across the Élivágar and had carried Aurvandil on his back in a basket out of Jötunheimar, and a sign of it was that one of Aurvandil's toes had stuck out of the basket and frozen, and Thor broke it off and cast it into the sky and made of it that star which is called Aurvandil's Toe. Thor said that it would not be long before Aurvandil would come home, and Gróa became so happy that she forgot the charms and the whetstone grew no looser.

Although the etymology of the name is unknown, it is cognate with Old English *earendel*, "dawn, ray of light," so there may be a Germanic myth here, despite the absence of Aurvandil from the Norse poetic corpus. Thor also made stars out of Thjazi's eyes, and in my view we should read these acts as his contribution to cosmogony, an area in which he is otherwise absent.

References and further reading: Rudolf Much, "Aurvandils tá," *Altschlesien* 5 (1934): 387–388, speculates on the star that Aurvandil's toe may represent.

BALDR

God, member of the æsir group, killed by his blind half brother Höd, buried in a solemn funeral, and left in the world of the dead when an attempt to retrieve him fails.

The death of Baldr is one of the most important moments in the mythology. Parts of the story are alluded to in various skaldic poems; much of it is told in the *Codex Regius* version of *Völuspá*, and Snorri gives a full version in *Gylfaginning*, using a probably oral version of *Völuspá* and other sources. According to Snorri, Baldr is the second son of Odin, after Thor, and "about him there is good to report; he is the best, and all praise him; he is so fair of face and bright that he seems to shine, and one plant is so white that it is compared to Baldr's brows;

that is the whitest of all plants, and from it you can note his beauty, both of hair and of face; he is the wisest of the æsir and the most eloquent, and the most merciful, but that nature accompanies him, that none of his judgments stands. He lives where it is called Breidablik; that is in heaven; in that place nothing can be nothing impure." A few pages later Snorri reports that Forseti is the son of Baldr and Nanna Nepsdóttir. Later in the *Gylfaginning* he tells about Baldr's death and its aftermath, and these stories take up about 10 percent of the entire *Gylfaginning.*

Baldr's death actually comprises several constituent parts, and Snorri is the first to combine them all in one fluid narrative, even if *Völuspá*, a version of which he clearly had before him, tells most of the story. These parts may conveniently be divided as follows: Baldr's death, his funeral, the attempted revival, and vengeance for him.

The story of Baldr's death and the attempted revival are intertwined, by Snorri at least. It begins, according to him, with Baldr suffering disquieting dreams, presumably that he may be injured or killed. Frigg elicits an oath not to harm him from all things, and thereafter the æsir take sport in attacking him with weapons and stones, and it seems an accomplishment to them that he is unhurt. Loki is displeased that Baldr is unhurt. He takes the form of a woman, goes to Frigg, and asks whether anything can harm Baldr. Frigg responds that she took oaths from everything except mistletoe, which seemed too young. Loki gets some mistletoe, fashions a spear from it, and heads to the assembly. There he sees Baldr's blind half brother, Höd, not participating in the sport. He gives the mistletoe spear to Höd, who casts it at Baldr. It pierces Baldr, and he falls dead to the earth. "The greatest misfortune among gods and men was done," says Snorri.

The gods are stricken, and no vengeance can be taken on the spot because it is a place of sanctuary. Frigg asks for a volunteer to go to Hel to try to retrieve Baldr. Hermód, another son (or a servant) of Odin volunteers. Borrowing Sleipnir, he travels nine nights until he comes to the Gjallar bridge (Gjallarbrú, the bridge between earth and the underworld), where he is challenged by the maiden Módgud. She tells him that the way to Hel is down and north. He rides on, comes to Hel, and sees that Baldr is in the high seat (the seat of honor) in her hall. Hel agrees to release Baldr if all things, living and dead, will weep for him. Bearing tokens from the underworld, Hermód returns to the land of the living. Emissaries are sent to request that everything weep for Baldr, and just when the attempt appears to have succeeded, they come upon an old lady who calls herself Thökk (Thanks). She speaks a verse: "Thökk will weep / dry tears / about Baldr's funeral; / I had no use for Karl's son, / alive or dead; / let Hel keep what she has." People think, Snorri explains, that this old lady who kept Baldr with Hel was Loki.

While Hermód was undertaking his journey, according to Snorri, Baldr's funeral took place. Snorri was probably following the skald Úlf Uggason's *Húsdrápa* here, a poem that describes the rich carved decorations in the newly built hall of Óláf pái (Peacock) from around 1185 or so in western Iceland. Here is what *Húsdrápa* says about the funeral:

> The battle-wise Frey rides on a boar, bristled with gold, first to the pyre of the son of Odin, and leads armies. The exceedingly widely famous Hropta-Týr [Odin] rides to the pyre of his son. There I perceive valkyries and ravens accompany the wise victory-tree [man; here Odin] to the blood of the holy corpse. Thus [the hall] is adorned from within with things remembered. The excellent Heimdall rides a horse to that pyre that the gods had built for the fallen son of the very wise tester of the raven [Odin]. The very powerful Hild of the mountains [giantess] caused the sea-Sleipnir [ship] to trudge forward; but the wielders of the helmet flames of Hropt [Odin] felled her mount.

Snorri has more detail. He adds several gods to the list of those who attended, and he makes sense out of the stanza with the giantess in it by stating that the funeral ship could not be launched and that the gods therefore sent to Jötunheimar for that ogress who was called Hyrrokkin. "She arrived riding a wolf with poisonous snakes for reins, and when she dismounted, Odin called to four berserks to look after the horse, and they could not hold it unless they killed it. Then Hyrrokkin went to the prow of the ship and shot it forward at the first try so that sparks leapt out of the runners and all the lands shook." Thor was enraged and would have killed her had the gods not pleaded for amnesty for her. Thor kicked a little dwarf named Lit into the fire, and Nanna died of grief and was put on the pyre with Baldr. The ring Draupnir and Baldr's horse were also burned with him.

The vengeance sequence comprises two parts. The first, regarding which Snorri is silent in *Gylfaginning,* is told in *Völuspá:* "Baldr's brother was / quickly born; / that son of Odin / killed when he was one night old." In *Skáldskaparmál,* Snorri reports that kennings for Váli include "enemy of Höd and his killer." Vengeance is also taken on Loki, and here Snorri has a very detailed narrative (the prose following *Lokasenna* in the *Poetic Edda* tells much the same story but says that the gods were taking vengeance for Loki's reviling of them). Loki runs off to a mountain and sequesters himself in a house with four doors out of which he peers to watch for the æsir's attack. Frequently changing himself into a salmon, he anticipates the strategy of the æsir and makes a net but burns it and leaps into the river as they approach. Seeing the pattern in the ashes, Kvasir understands the potential it represents, and the æsir pursue Loki with a net. Twice he evades them, but on the third try he attempts a leap over the net and

Thor grabs him by the tail, which is why salmon to this day are thin by the tail. The æsir take Loki to a cave, where they bind him to the rock. They change one of his sons into a wolf and have it tear the other to pieces. They suspend a poisonous snake over him, dripping venom. His wife Sigyn catches the venom in a pot, but when she goes to empty it the venom falls onto his face, and his writhings cause earthquakes.

Saxo Grammaticus has a rather different story of Baldr's death and the aftermath. Høtherus, the foster son of King Gevarus, and Balderus, the son of Othinus and a demigod, have both fallen in love with Nanna. Høtherus acquires a special sword and a magic ring. Nanna refuses Balderus on the grounds that demigods and humans are incompatible. Høtherus and an ally confront Balderus and the gods in a sea battle and gain victory when Høtherus slices the handle off Thor's hammer, the gods' major weapon, with his magic sword.

Høtherus marries Nanna. In a subsequent battle Balderus defeats him. Balderus is plagued by dreams of his desired Nanna. Høtherus is now chosen king of the Danes, but in his absence the Danes vote again, and this time they choose Balderus. In a third battle Høtherus is put to flight. In their final battle he wounds Balderus. Balderus dreams of Proserpina (as Saxo calls her, using the Roman name for the Greek Persephone, who like Hel presided over the underworld), dies, and is buried in a mound.

The story now turns to vengeance. A sorcerer advises Othinus that he must seduce Rinda, the daughter of the king of the Rutenians. After three failed attempts, first disguised as a warrior, then as a smith, and then as a knight, Othinus returns a fourth time, disguised as a woman, and becomes a serving maid to the princess. When Rinda falls sick, Othinus arranges for her to be tied down so that she can be given some medicine. He rapes her, and she bears Bous, who kills Høtherus.

These stories are indeed quite different, but there are important similarities that go beyond Höd killing Baldr and having vengeance taken on him. Dreams are important in both versions, as is a magic weapon. The goddess of the dead plays a role in each. The rape of Rinda is paralleled in medieval Icelandic tradition in a skaldic stanza that states that Odin used the magic seid on Rind, the mother of Váli. The differences in the versions may reflect variants in medieval Icelandic oral tradition, since Saxo learned from Icelanders, but he may also be passing along some genuine Danish traditions.

The story has led to many attempts at interpretation, some of them rather fanciful. The mistletoe remains unexplained, despite Sir James Frazer's attempt to build up a grand theory around it. In fact, the story may have far less to do with the fertility exemplified by various gods who die (in the fall) and are reborn (in the spring) than it does with initiation into a hypothetical cult of Odin. Thus

Höd's name seems to have meant "battle," and his blindness intensifies Odin's sacrifice of a single eye. *Gautreks saga* contains a sham sacrifice to Odin that turns real. When Starkad throws at King Víkar a reed that has been provided to him by another person, the reed turns into a spear and kills the king.

However, analysis of the Baldr story as Odinic ritual runs up against the fact that in *Völuspá* Baldr's death leads directly to Ragnarök (and the victory of Høtherus over all the gods in Saxo may be analogous). For Snorri, too, Baldr's death was a disaster that led to Ragnarök. I understand the story as the mythic reflection of a basic social problem, namely, the fact that a society that used blood feud to resolve disputes—as medieval and presumably saga Iceland did—could not deal with a killing within a family. Simply by requiring a counterattack against the family of the killer, Höd's killing of Baldr puts Odin in an impossible situation. He turns outside the kin group to sire the avenger Váli/Bous, but that is no solution, since it simply displaces the problem of brother killing brother. The Old English epic poem *Beowulf* has a story that looks cognate, in which one brother, Hædcyn (Höd) mistakenly kills another, Herebeald (Baldr?). Hredel, the father, dies of grief.

> *References and further reading:* A comparison of the versions of the story in the Icelandic sources and Saxo, arguing essential similarity, is Margaret Clunies Ross, "Mythic Narrative in Saxo Grammaticus and Snorri Sturluson," in the volume *Saxo Grammaticus: Tra storiografia e letteratura: Bevagna, 27–29 settembre 1990* (Rome: Editrice "Il Calamo," 1992), 47–59. Sir James Frazer's reading of the Baldr myth—still a classic of "armchair anthropology"—may be studied in his "Balder the Beautiful," in *The Golden Bough: A Study in Magic and Religion*, 3rd ed., 2 vols. (New York: St. Martin's Press: 1990 [1890]), part 7; see also John Stanley Martin, "Baldr's Death and *The Golden Bough*," in *Iceland and the Medieval World: Studies in Honour of Ian Maxwell*, ed. Gabriel Turville-Petre and John Stanley Martin (Victoria, Australia: The Organizing Committee for Publishing a Volume in Honour of Professor Maxwell, 1974), 26–32. My reading of the Baldr myth is in my *Murder and Vengeance among the Gods: Baldr in Scandinavian Mythology*, FF Communications, 277 (Helsinki: Societas Scientiarum Fennica, 1997); see also my "Interpreting Baldr, the Dying God," in *Australian Academy of the Humanities Proceedings*, 1993: 155–173 (also in *Old Norse Studies in the New World*, ed. Judy Quinn, Geraldine Barnes, and Margaret Clunies Ross [Sydney: University of Sydney, 1994], 14–25). On blood feud, see William Ian Miller, *Bloodtaking and Peacemaking: Feud, Law, and Society in Saga Iceland* (Chicago and London: University of Chicago Press, 1990), and on its general application to the mythology see my "Blood Feud and Scandinavian Mythology," *Alvíssmál* 4 (1994): 51–68. In her *Prolonged Echoes: Old Norse Myths in Medieval Icelandic Society*, vol. 1: *The Myths* (Odense: Odense University Press, 1994), Margaret Clunies Ross stresses the dynastic implications of the story: Baldr is Odin's legitimate heir, and his death brings about a crisis of succession.

BALDRS DRAUMAR (BALDR'S DREAMS)

Eddic poem.

Found not in *Codex Regius* of the *Poetic Edda* but only in the other main manuscript, AM 748, the poem comprises 14 stanzas in *fornyrðislag*. It begins with the æsir in a state of crisis over Baldr's bad dreams. Odin rides to Hel. He is confronted by a hellhound but rides east of Hel's hall, where he knows the grave of a seeress lies. Aroused, she asks his identity, and he says that he is Vegtam (Accustomed-to-the-road). From stanza 6 onward the poem consists of a series of questions put by Odin and answered by the seeress. The seeress concludes each response except the last by saying she was forced to speak and now will fall silent, but Odin always forces her to continue. First, Odin asks for whom the hall of Hel has been prepared; the seeress answers that it is for Baldr. Second, Odin asks who will kill Baldr, and the answer is Höd. The third question is who will avenge Baldr, and the answer is apparently Váli (the name is omitted in the manuscript but a name beginning with *V* is required to complete the alliteration). The fourth and last question is not clear but has to do with the identity of a group of maidens. Somehow, in a way we no longer understand, the question reveals to the seeress that she is conversing with Odin. To this Odin replies, "You are not a seeress, / nor a wise woman, / but rather of three / giants the mother" (stanza 13). "Go home," she says. The next step is Ragnarök.

The version of the myth of Baldr's death here omits the role of Loki, which is so important in Snorri's version, although some observers have seen a reference to Loki in the mother of three giants of stanza 13, since Loki's children are three of the most famous giants, namely, the Midgard serpent, the wolf Fenrir, and Hel herself. This version would seem to focus on the essentials: Baldr will die, Höd will kill him, Váli will avenge Baldr's death. That is a departure from Snorri's version far greater, in fact, than the omission of Loki's role, for Snorri has nothing to say of vengeance on Höd. Most sources seem to agree that the vengeance is an integral part of the myth.

In form, *Baldrs draumar* shares much with the other eddic contests of wisdom, especially *Vafthrúdnismál*, which also has an unclear reference to a group of females near the end of the poem and a question that reveals Odin's identity, although in *Vafthrúdnimsál* and *Baldrs draumar* these are not the same question.

Although there are striking verbal parallels with *Thrymskvida*, few observers are as confident of a late date for *Baldrs draumar* as they are for that poem.

> ***References and further reading:*** Discussions of the poem in English include John Lindow, *Murder and Vengeance among the Gods: Baldr in Scandinavian Mythology*, FF Communications, 262 (Helsinki: Suomalainen Tiedeakatemia, 1997), 130–134, and Mats Malm, "*Baldrs draumar*: Literally and Literarily," in *Old Norse Myths, Literature, and Society: Proceedings of the Eleventh Inter-*

national Saga Conference, 2–7 July 2000, ed. Margaret Clunies Ross and Geraldine Barnes (Sydney: Centre for Medieval Studies, University of Sydney, 2000), 277–289.

BÁLEYG (FLAME-EYE)

Odin name.

Odin himself includes this in the list of names he gives just before the epiphany in *Grímnismál* (stanza 47). The Icelandic skald Hallfred Óttarson vandrædaskáld used the kenning "Báleyg's wife" to refer to the earth in stanza 6 of his *Hákonardrápa*, composed for Hákon the Hladir jarl toward the end of the tenth century, and in the early twelfth century Gísli Illugason called warriors "trees of Báleyg" in a memorial to the Norwegian king Magnús Bareleg. The name is also found in the thulur. The flame must be metaphorical, a reference to the fierce gaze of Odin's one eye.

In *Grímnismál* Báleyg follows and alliterates with Bileyg (Wavering-eye), and this name pair has been associated with Bolwisus and Bilwisus in Book 6 of the *Gesta Danorum* of Saxo Grammaticus, two old men who counsel King Sigarus in the Hagbard and Signe story. Bilwisus works to reconcile enemies, while Bolwisus sows dissension, even among friends. Many observers have accepted that what Saxo says here reflects two sides of Odin, a distinction that is contrasted in the names Bileyg and Báleyg.

See also Bileyg; Ód

BARRI

The trysting place where Frey will meet Gerd, his giant bride-to-be.

We have the story in *Skírnismál* and in an abbreviated form in Snorri's *Gylfaginning*. In brief, after Frey's emissary Skírnir has cajoled Gerd, the giantess with whom Frey has fallen in love from afar, she agrees to meet him in nine nights' time at Barri (Barrey, according to Snorri).

Magnus Olsen's hoary explanation, that Barri has to do with *barr*, "barley," ties the story to a hypothetical fertility myth, in which Skírnir is understood as the sun's ray and the ensuing marriage as a holy wedding of a god and the earth. Those who are unpersuaded point out that *barr* can just as well mean "pine needle," which would fit with the fact that *Skírnismál* explicitly calls Barri a grove, that Snorri's Barrey (Barley-island or Grain-island) makes no sense in the context of a fertility myth, and that in both texts the marriage is in fact postponed. However, no other explanations of the names themselves have been proposed.

References and further reading: Magnus Olsen's famous article is "Fra gammelnorsk myte og kultus," *Maal og minne,* 1909: 17–36. The most solid philological criticism of Olsen's reading of Barri is that of Jöran Sahlgren, "Lunden Barre i *Skírnismál,*" *Namn och bygd* 50 (1952): 193–203 (summary in English, p. 233).

BAUGI (RING-SHAPED)

Giant, brother of Suttung, the giant from whom Odin obtained the mead of poetry. Baugi is known only from Snorri's *Edda* and from the thulur and is not attested anywhere in poetry. In *Skáldskaparmál* Snorri has Odin setting forth to obtain the mead. He comes upon nine slaves who are cutting hay and sharpens their scythes with a whetstone he has brought along. The scythes are so much sharper that each of the slaves wants the whetstone for himself, and as they are contending over who might purchase it, Odin throws the hone in the air. As they scramble to get it, they cut each other's throats. At this point we learn that these slaves worked for Baugi, and Odin, calling himself Bölverk (Evil-deed), offers to do the work of nine men, for a wage of one drink of the mead. Baugi says that Suttung alone controls the mead but that he will help. After the summer work season is over, Bölverk/Odin asks for his payment, and when Suttung flatly refuses a single drop of the mead, Bölverk/Odin enlists Baugi's help. They drill into the mountain, and when Baugi says the tunnel is finished, Bölverk/Odin blows into the hole. But chips fly back, indicating the other end is still blocked. Bölverk/Odin realizes that Baugi wishes to deceive him. They drill again. Odin then turns himself into a snake and slithers into the hole. Baugi strikes at him but misses, and thereupon he vanishes from the mythology as quickly and puzzlingly as he has entered it.

The major problem with Baugi is his absence outside Snorri, especially from *Hávamál,* which Snorri seems to be paraphrasing in most of the story of the acquisition of the mead of poetry. A. G. van Hamel argued that Snorri found Baugi in another source (indeed, that Odin obtained the mead from Baugi) and that the version we have in *Skáldskaparmál* is thus an artful blending of the two sources. Others have argued that Snorri invented Baugi, and Aage Kabell thought he knew why: because he misunderstood stanza 110 of *Hávamál:*

A ring oath *[baugeiðr]* I think Odin made,
What good are his pledges?
He left Suttung deceived from the feast
And made Gunnlöd weep.

The problem with this hypothesis is that ring oaths were tolerably well known in medieval Iceland, and the stanza is really quite clear. If Margaret Clunies Ross is right in reviving an argument that a ring might stand for the anus in certain contexts and thus be involved in innuendo concerning *ergi* (sexual perversion), Snorri may have been indulging in wordplay; or he may even have imagined a kind of symbolic rape of Suttung through Baugi alongside his rape of Gunnlöd, Suttung's daughter.

> ***See also*** Mead of Poetry; Odin
>
> ***References and further reading:*** Van Hamel's thoughts are expressed in "The Mastering of the Mead," in the volume *Studia Germanica tillägnade Ernst Albin Kock den 6 december 1934* (Lund: C. Blom), 76–85. On Baugi and the ring, see Aage Kabell, "Baugi und der Ringeid," *Arkiv för nordisk filologi* 90 (1975): 30–40. Margaret Clunies Ross wrote on the possible metaphorical value of the ring in "Hild's Ring: A Problem in the Raganarsdrápa, Strophes 8–12," *Mediaeval Scandinavia* 6 (1973): 75–92.

BELI

Giant killed by Frey.

This appears to be one of those lost myths that can be glimpsed only in passing. In kennings Frey is called "killer of Beli," but the only reference to how it might have happened is in Snorri's *Gylfaginning*. Just after sketching the story of the arrangement of Frey's marriage to Gerd, Snorri adds that because Frey gave Skírnir his sword, he was weaponless when he fought with Beli, and therefore he killed the giant with the horn of a hart. Because in *Skírnismál*, stanza 36, Gerd complains of the slaying of her brother by Frey, some observers have wished to believe that Beli was Gerd's brother.

> ***See also*** Frey

BERGBÚA THÁTTR (THE TALE OF THE MOUNTAIN-DWELLER)

Tale incorporating a poem spoken by a thirteenth-century giant, including many mythological references.

The text is retained in manuscripts from the end of the fourteenth century but is usually assigned to the thirteenth century. It tells of how one Thórd and his servant got lost on their way to church in winter and took shelter for the night in a cave. There they heard noises, saw a pair of huge burning eyes, and finally heard the owner of those eyes recite a well-crafted poem of 12 stanzas, repeating it three times over the course of the evening. In the poem the speaker refers to himself as a *bjarg-álfr*, "mountain-elf," which is a kenning for giant and refers to his journeys around mountains and north to the Élivágar in the third netherworld. He has, he says, a house all to himself on the lava field, but few visit him there. In short, he appears to be a supernatural nature being such as have been commonly found in European folklore until very recently—a lone denizen of the areas far from where humans live. But this particular giant has ties to Norse mythology. "Strong Thor makes trouble for people," he says in stanza 10, and "the earth is rent, because I say that Thor thus again came thither," he adds in stanza 11. The word "people" in stanza 10 could, in the language of poetry, refer to the speaker's people, that is, the giants, or it could refer to everyone in the world. The rest of the poem indulges in prophecies: The mountains will tumble, the earth will move, men will be scoured in hot water and burned by fire, and so forth, and this may be a mix of the destruction of the race of giants and of humans, as in Ragnarök (Surt's fire is mentioned in stanza 10). But many of the predictions of disruption on earth could also fit the volcanic activity that is so common in Iceland.

At the end of the poem the speaker tells his listeners to remember it or bear a punishment. Thórd has it word-for-word, but the servant does not. He dies a year after the night in the cave. The cave itself cannot be located, and Thórd moves closer to the church.

See also Ragnarök; Thor

BERGELMIR (BEAR-YELLER, MOUNTAIN-YELLER, OR BARE-YELLER)
Giant, one of those from whom giants traced their genealogy.
Vafthrúdnismál, stanza 29, states the lineage of Bergelmir. Odin has asked Vafthrúdnir who was the oldest of the æsir or of the kin of Ymir. Vafthrúdnir responds,

> A great many years before the earth was formed,
> Bergelmir was born;
> Thrúdgelmir was the father of this one,
> And Aurgelmir the grandfather.

After asking about the monstrous birth of the offspring of Aurgelmir, Odin asks what Vafthrúdnir's oldest memory is. Vafthrúdnir responds in stanza 35:

> A great many years before the earth was formed,
> Bergelmir was born;
> What I first remember is when the wise giant
> Was placed on a *lúðr*.

This verse has occasioned all sorts of speculation. Snorri wrote in *Gylfaginning* that it had to do with a flood story. After the sons of Bor killed Ymir, his blood flooded the earth and "with it all of the frost giants were killed, except one who got away with his family. The giants called that one Bergelmir. He got up on his *lúðr* along with his wife and saved himself there, and from them come the families of the frost giants."

Snorri clearly understood the *lúðr* as something that would float, and the word might in fact have meant "coffin" or "chest" or some wooden part of a mill; the expected meaning, of a cumbersome musical instrument something like an alphorn, makes no sense either in Snorri or his poetic source. If there is any consensus here, it is that what Vafthrúdnir remembered was the funeral of Bergelmir, and what Snorri made of it was an analogue to the Judeo-Christian flood story.

> **See also** Aurgelmir; Thrúdgelmir; *Vafthrúdnismál*; Ymir
> **References and further reading:** The best interpretation of the issues surrounding Bergelmir and his *lúðr* remains that of Anne Holtsmark, "Det norrøne ord *lúðr*," *Maal og minne*, 1946: 49–65.

BERSERKS

Furious warriors, in mythology associated with Odin.

The passage in question is chapter 6 of Snorri's *Ynglinga saga*, which also provides a description of *berserksgangr*, "going berserk." After stating that Odin could make his enemies blind, deaf, or overcome with fear in battle, their weapons useless, Snorri added, "but his men went without armor and were crazed as dogs or wolves, bit their shields, were strong as bears or bulls. They killed men, but neither fire nor iron affected them. That is called going berserk."

Other than this passage, berserks seem to have belonged more to the world of men than of gods, which agrees with the project of euhemerism Snorri had adopted with *Ynglinga saga*. The skaldic poem *Haraldskvædi*, assembled from various fragments and generally attributed to a poet called Thorbjörn hornklofi, assigns berserks to the forces of King Harald Fairhair at the battle of Hafrsfjörd (late ninth century): "The berserks howled, / battle was on their minds, / the wolf-skins growled / and shook their spears" (stanza 8b). In stanza 20 the poet asks about berserks, "who drink blood," and answers himself: "They are called wolf-skins, / who in battle / carry bloody shields; / they redden spears / when they come to battle" (stanza 21a).

According to chapter 9 of *Vatnsdæla saga*, one of the Sagas of Icelanders, probably composed in the years just before 1280, Harald Fairhair had berserks on board his ship who were called *úlfhednar*; they wore wolfskins and defended the prow.

The connection between wolf-skins and berserks supports one of the suggested etymologies for medieval Icelandic *berserkr*, namely, "bear-shirt," and this etymology is ordinarily mentioned in light of such warrior-animal amalgamations as those on the Torslunda helmet plates from Sweden, which suggest warriors wearing animal skins, masks, or both. Adherents of this etymology see

Buckle of gilded bronze from the Anglo-Saxon cemetery at Finglesham, Kent, with bosses and rivets encircled with gold wire. It shows a naked male figure in a horned helmet and belt, holding a spear in each hand. (Courtesy of Ms. Sonia Hawkes)

a connection with a reconstructed Odin cult, which in turn, they argue, may reflect Indo-European ecstatic warrior cults usually known by the German scholarly term *Männerbünde* (sing., *Mänerbund*). The other proposed etymology of *berserkr* is "bare-shirt." Snorri's statement about the lack of armor appears to support this etymology, although there is always the possibility that Snorri wrote these words because of his own understanding of the etymology.

Beside Harald Fairhair and the Odin of *Ynglinga saga,* other kings in older Scandinavian literary tradition are accorded berserks as elite troops, and the medieval Icelandic law code, *Grágás,* has a provision against going berserk. Elsewhere in medieval Icelandic literature, however, berserks are mostly stereotypical figures who threaten but are easily overcome by heroes, sometimes after challenging for the hand of a woman. Although there may be a parallel here with the lusting of the giants for Freyja and the other female æsir, the only direct connection between berserks and the mythology is the passage from Snorri. If, however, there indeed was a cult of warriors in animal disguise, it would almost certainly have centered around Odin.

References and further reading: D. J. Beard, "The Berserkr in Icelandic Literature," in *Approaches to Oral Literature,* ed. Tobin Thelwall (Ulster: New University of Ulster, 1978), 99–114. Benjamin Blaney, "The Berserk Suitor: The Literary Application of a Stereotyped Theme," *Scandinavian Studies* 54 (1982): 279–294.

BESTLA

Odin's mother.

The relationship of Bestla and Odin is set forth in Snorri's *Gylfaginning*. The first man was Búri, whose son was Bor.

> He married that woman who was called Bestla, the daughter of the giant Bölthorn. They had three sons; the first was called Odin, the second Vili, the third Vé.

Hávamál, stanza 140, gives a variant version of the name, Bölthor, and makes him Bestla's grandfather:

> Nine magic songs I got from the famous son
> Of Bölthor, Bestla's father,
> And I got a drink of the precious mead,
> Poured from [by? to?] Ódrerir.

Although there is nothing in this stanza indicating a family relationship with Odin, and although the mead was, according to other sources, stolen, it is not inconceivable that Odin could have obtained magic songs from his maternal uncle (the verb in the first line, literally "got," also means "learned"). And skalds knew of Bestla as Odin's mother and formed kennings based on the relationship. One manuscript of Snorri's *Edda* says that one may make Odin kennings by calling him "father of Bestla or of his other children," but since this contradicts the other sources and is absent from the other manuscripts, we need not pay it too much attention.

It is of course significant that Odin is descended from the giants on his mother's side, since the slaying of Ymir by him and his brothers must therefore be understood as a killing within a family, the slaying or denial of a maternal relation. Another theory, however, advanced by Waltraud Hunke, sees Bestla as the bark of the world tree, on which Odin was perhaps born (or reborn in an initiation?) according to *Hávamál*, stanza 141 ("then I started to grow fruitful"). Hunke would then understand Bestla etymologically as the bark of the maternal tree.

See also Odin

References and further reading: Waltraud Hunke, "Odins Geburt," in *Edda, Skalden, Saga: Festschrift zum 70. Geburtstage von Felix Genzmer*, ed. Hermann Schneider (Heidelberg: C. Winter, 1952), 68–71.

BEYLA

Mythological character.

Beyla is found only in the prose header to *Lokasenna* and stanzas 55–56 of the poem. The prose header says that she and Byggvir were servants of Frey. In stanza 55 she warns Loki that Thor is approaching and will silence the one slandering all the gods. Loki replies in stanza 56: "Shut up, Beyla! / You are Byggvir's wife / and much mixed with evil; / a greater monster / never came among the sons of the gods; / you are entirely filthy, milkmaid." Beyla is one of those figures for whom scholars have had to turn to etymology for interpretation, but the problem is that the etymology is anything but clear. Her name may be related to a word for "cow," "bean," or "bee." Why Loki should accuse her of being entirely filthy remains unclear.

> ***References and further reading:*** Georges Dumézil, "Two Minor Scandinavian Gods: Byggvir and Beyla" (1952), in his *Gods of the Ancient Northmen,* ed. Einar Haugen, Publications of the UCLA Center for the Study of Comparative Folklore and Mythology, 3 (Berkeley and Los Angeles: University of California Press, 1973), 89–117.

BIL AND HJÚKI

Children who accompany the moon, according to Snorri Sturluson.

Snorri includes them in his discussion of the moon in *Gylfaginning;* they were taken up from earth as they left the well called Byrgir, carrying a bucket and a pole. Their father was Vidfinn (Wood-Finn). Now they accompany the moon, as can be seen from the earth.

These names are found only in this passage, with one exception: Later in *Gylfaginning* Snorri says that, along with Sól (Sun), Bil, "whose nature was explained above," is numbered among the æsir. The absence of this whole moon story from other sources has led many observers to the conclusion that they lack mythic significance, or even that Snorri invented them, but Anne Holtsmark advanced a plausible argument to the effect that Snorri had a now lost verse source, probably a learned riddle in which Bil and Hjúki represented the waning and waxing moon. Holtsmark thinks it possible that Bil was one of the dísir (female spirits).

> ***See also*** Máni; Sól; Vidfinn
>
> ***References and further reading:*** Anne Holtsmark, "Bil og Hjuke," *Maal og minne,* 1945: 139–154. Alfred Wolf, "Die germanische Sippe *bil:* Entsprechung zu *Mana:* Mit einem Anhang über den Bilwis," *Språkvetenskapliga sällskapets i Uppsala förhandlingar,* 1928–1930: 17–156, thought that the root *bil* meant "supernatural power" and referred to a concept like mana, a supernatural power in gods and objects.

BILEYG (WAVERING-EYE)

Odin name.

Odin himself includes this in the list of names he gives just before the epiphany in *Grímnismál* (stanza 47). It is not, however, known from other sources, although it is listed among the thulur.

This name is found in the same line, and alliterates with Báleyg (Flame-eye), and some observers think two sides of Odin are represented in the pair.

See also Báleyg; Odin

BILLING'S GIRL

Subject of a section of the poem *Hávamál,* one of the so-called Odin's examples.

Told in the first person by Odin, the section begins by announcing that Odin awaited his beloved (presumably Billing's girl) in the reeds. She was dear to him but he had never possessed her. He found Billing's girl asleep on the bed and desired her. She made an assignation with him. He returned for this assignation, but the way was blocked by flame and an efficient warrior band. In the morning he returned and found a bitch bound on the bed in place of the woman. Stanza 102 appears to be a reflection on the episode and has numerous verbal parallels with stanza 96. Stanzas 96 and 102 therefore bracket the incident.

Sigurður Nordal understood the episode as a display of the magic of Billing's girl, who thwarted Odin's advances by deflecting his magic powers onto a dog on her bed. In this light, the binding of the dog would be a magic binding imposed by Odin in anticipation of a rape. Most other observers content themselves with contrasting the failed seduction with the successful seduction of Gunnlöd in the following episode in the poem.

Billing is listed as a dwarf name in the *Hauksbók* version of *Völuspá* and is found in a kenning for poetry: "cup of the son of Billing." Since both the dwarfs and giants possessed the mead of poetry before Odin retrieved it, this kenning works whether Billing is a dwarf or a giant. The problem with understanding Billing as a dwarf is not one of sexual congress between gods and dwarfs, for Freyja slept with three dwarfs to obtain the Brísinga men, and the dwarf Alvíss coveted Thor's daughter and even claimed to have affianced himself to her (*Alvíssmál*). However, if Billing is a dwarf, his "girl" (presumably daughter) would be one of the very few female dwarfs in the mythology. Certainly Billing's girl is a member of an out-group, and Odin seduces and rapes many of these.

The most telling analogue is stanza 18 of *Hárbardsljód*, in which Odin boasts of having his way with giant girls on the island Algrœn (All-green) in precisely the same language he uses in *Hávamál*, stanza 99, for his desire for Billing's daughter: To possess a woman is to have "all her mind and pleasure." If the common language indicates a common story, the reeds in stanza 96 would be near the island Algrœn, but that is surmise.

Odin ought not to come up short in any of his encounters, and for that reason it is useful to speculate on how Odin's failure to seduce Billing's girl may in fact be a success. I have suggested that failing to sleep with the bitch keeps him from committing an act of bestiality, which properly belongs in the realm of the giants. A parallel in Icelandic folklore in which the motif of a bitch bound in place of a girl is used to prevent father-daughter incest may also be relevant.

> **References and further reading:** Two articles are devoted to this incident: Sigurður Nordal, "Billings mær," in the volume *Bidrag till nordisk filologi tillägnade Emil Olson den 9 Juni 1936* (Lund: C. W. K. Gleerup; Copenhagen: Levin & Munksgaard, 1936), 288–295, and John Lindow, "Billings mær," in *Gudar på jorden: Festskrift till Lars Lönnroth*, ed. Stina Hansson and Mats Malm (Stockholm: Brutus Östlings Bokförlag Symposion, 2000), 57–66.

BILRÖST

The bridge between the world of humans and the world of the gods or between earth and heaven.

Grímnismál, stanza 44, is a list of the foremost or best of things: Yggdrasil of trees, Odin of æsir, and so forth. There Bilröst is called best of bridges. In *Fáfnismál*, stanza 15, Fáfnir responds to a question asking what the island is called where Surt and the æsir will fight, presumably at Ragnarök.

> Óskópnir it is called, and there shall all
> The gods make play with spears;
> Bilröst will break, when they go away,
> And horses will swim in the current.

Bilröst is compounded of *bil*, "stopping place, time, instant, weak spot," and *röst*, ordinarily "league" or "current" but here apparently with the meaning "road." Snorri uses instead the form "Bifröst," whose first component has to do with wavering or shaking. Snorri mentions "Bifröst" several times. Asked about the path to heaven from earth, Hár tells Gylfi/Gangleri that it is Bilröst, that the gods made it, and that it may be called the rainbow. It is of three colors, very strong, and made with great skill and knowledge, but it will break when the sons of Muspell ride over it. Nothing can survive the harrying of the sons of Muspell, and much later in the text, describing Ragnarök, Snorri says that Bilröst will break, "as was previously stated." Jafnhár also tells Gylfi/Gangleri that the gods ride this bridge, which may also be called the Ás-Brú (Æsir-bridge), up to the Urdarbrunn (Well-of-Urd), where they go to make judgments. And a bit after that, Gylfi/Gangleri asks whether fire burns over Bilröst. Hár responds that the red "in the bow" is indeed fire, and he implies that it is there to keep the giants away. From *Gylfaginning* we also learn that at the upper end of the bridge there stands Himinbjörg, where Heimdall lives.

Fire on the bridge is also found in *Grímnismál*, stanza 29, which reports that Thor crosses the rivers Körmt and Örmt and two named Kerlaug each day when he goes to judge at the ash of Yggdrasil,

> Because the Ás-Brú burns all with fire,
> The holy waters boil.

The notion of the bridge between earth and heaven, or earth and the world of the gods, has a parallel in the Gjallarbrú, a bridge between earth and the underworld, or earth and the world of the dead.

> ***See also*** Gjallarbrú
> ***References and further reading:*** Åke Ohlmarks, "Stellt die mythische Bilröst den Regenbogen oder die Milchstrasse dar? Eine textkritische-religionshistorische Untersuchung zur mythographischen Arbeitsmethode Snorri Sturlusons," *Meddelanden från Lunds astronomiska observatorium*, ser. 2, 110 (1940): 1–40, asks whether Bilröst represents the rainbow or the Milky Way and concludes that Bilröst originally was the Milky Way but that Snorri reinterpreted the bridge as the rainbow when confronted with the variations in the terminology. Bilröst as the Milky Way is hardly a new concept; see, for example, Franz Rolf Schröder, *Germanentum und Hellenismus: Untersuchungen zur germanischen Religionsgeschichte*, Germanische Bibliothek, Abteilung 2, vol. 17 (Heidelberg: C. Winter, 1924). William MacArthur thought he saw Bilröst among "Norse Myths Illustrated on Ancient Manx Crosses," *Notes and Queries*, ser. 11, 5 (1912): 506, but no one else has done so.

BILSKÍRNIR
Thor's hall.
Grímnismál, stanza 24, has Odin reveal the following vision as he catalogs the dwellings of the gods:

> Five hundred rooms and forty
> There are, I think, under the arches of Bilskírnir
> Of those halls which I know to be roofed,
> My son's is the biggest.

In *Gylfaginning*, when he introduces Thor, Snorri has Hár say that Thor has a kingdom at Thrúdvangar and a hall called Bilskírnir with 540 rooms, which is the greatest of buildings. He then cites this verse. In *Skáldskaparmál* Snorri says that "owner of Bilskírnir" is a valid Thor kenning, and in fact "prince of Bilskírnir" is attested in the skaldic corpus.

The meaning of the name is unclear, but it seems to be either "suddenly illuminated [by lightning]" or "everlasting."

See also Thrúdvangar

BLÁIN

In *Völuspá,* stanza 9, apparently an alternate name for Ymir:

> Then all the powers went to their judgment seats
> The very holy gods, and discussed,
> Who should form the lord of dwarfs,
> Out of the blood of Brimir and the limbs of Bláin.

Containing as it does the adjective "blue," the name might refer to the blue sky. It is, however, also found in the thulur as a dwarf name.

See also Brimir

BÖLTHOR(N)

Father or grandfather of Bestla, Odin's giant mother.

The form "Bölthor" is found in *Hávamál,* stanza 140, where he is referred to as the father of Bestla and of a famous but unnamed son, from whom Odin got or learned nine magic songs. The form "Bölthorn" is found in Snorri, who says that Odin married that woman who was called Bestla, the daughter of Bölthorn. The difference in name forms does not appear to be significant, but Bölthorn obviously means "Evil-thorn," whereas the form "Bölthor" would not have had an obvious meaning to a Viking or medieval Scandinavian.

A special relationship with the maternal uncle is mentioned by Tacitus and is found in Norse texts and a proverb from medieval Iceland: "Men turn out most like their maternal uncles." Certainly Odin, of all the gods, turned out most like a giant.

See also Bestla, Odin

BOUND MONSTER

Enemy of the gods bound or restrained in some way during the mythological present but destined to break free at Ragnarök.

The monster who best fits the pattern is the wolf Fenrir, whose sole function in the mythology is to be bound by the gods and then to break free at Ragnarök and wreak havoc: to swallow the sun according to *Vafthrúdnismál* and to kill Odin according to *Völuspá*. Fenrir was bound with a magic fetter and bit off Týr's hand, which was placed in his mouth as a pledge that the binding was in sport. Fenrir may be identical with Garm, who according to a refrain in *Völuspá* howls before the cave Gnipahellir: "The bond will burst, / and the wolf run free."

Fenrir was the son of Loki and the giantess Angrboda, one of a brood of three. In light of the binding of Fenrir, we may be justified in regarding the exile of his siblings—the Midgard serpent to the outer waters of the sea and Hel to the world of the dead—as a kind of binding. No fetters are used, but the serpent does lied coiled about the earth, biting its own tail, and this linking of mouth to tail might be taken as a kind of binding. Like Fenrir, the Midgard serpent will be "unbound" from the ocean at Ragnarök and will kill Thor. There is no parallel "unbinding" for Hel, however.

Loki is the most important and studied of the bound monsters in Scandinavian mythology. His binding occurs, according to Snorri, as vengeance for the killing of Baldr. According to the prose colophon to *Lokasenna*, however, Loki was bound as vengeance for his reviling of the gods at the feast of Ægir. Loki's binding is more uncomfortable than that of his monster children, however, for a snake hangs over his head dripping venom. His wife Sigyn collects the venom in a bowl, but when she goes to empty the bowl Loki writhes in anguish and shakes the earth, "and that is now called earthquakes," as the passage following *Lokasenna* puts it. Loki of course gets free at Ragnarök and according to *Völuspá* will steer a ship full of the forces of evil against the gods. Snorri also grants him a mutually fatal single combat with Heimdall.

Since the early twentieth century, and especially through the influential study of Ragnarök by Axel Olrik, Loki as bound monster has been associated with similar figures from traditions of people living in the Caucasus. However, at least Fenrir and Garm are also clearly bound monsters, and the notion of bound forces of evil who will break free at Ragnarök could be extended to nearly all the forces who will assail the gods at that time. If we are to take seriously the notion of a loan from the Caucasus, it would affect nearly the entire mythology. And of course there was the analog within Christian legend of the bound Antichrist awaiting the Last Judgment.

See also Fenrir; Garm; Hel; Loki; Midgard Serpent; Ragnarök

References and further reading: The early studies of the bound monster and the Caucasian analogs included M. Anholm, "Den bundne jætte i Kavkasus," *Danske studier* 1 (1904): 141–151; Bernhard Kahle, "Der gefesselte Riese," *Archiv für Religionswissenschaft* 8 (1905): 314–316; and Friedrich von der

Leyen, "Der gefesselte Unhold: Eine mythologische Studie," in *Untersuchungen und Quellen zur germanischen und romanischen Philologie: Johan von Kelle dargebracht von seinen Kollegen und Schülern*, Prager deutsche Studien, 8 (Prague: C. Bellman, 1908), vol. 1: 7–35. Axel Olrik's study appeared originally in Danish in 1914 but found its canonical form in the 1922 translation by Wilhelm Ranisch, *Ragnarök: Die Sagen vom Weltuntergang* (Berlin and Leipzig: W. de Gruyter); a book-length chapter (pp. 133–290) treats the bound giant in the Caucasus and is followed by a consideration of the bound wolf (pp. 291–326). A more recent study was that of Alexander Haggerty Krappe, "The Snake Tower," *Scandinavian Studies* 16 (1940): 22–33, which associated Loki with the hero Gunnar in the snake pit and saw England as the conduit.

BOUS

Avenger of Baldr in the version of the story in Saxo's *Gesta Danorum*.

Bous was the result of Othinus's rape of the Rutenian princess Rinda. He grows up skilled with weapons, and when he is ten, Odin summons him and argues that vengeance is more noble than killing random adversaries. When Bous and Høtherus (in Saxo's version, Balderus's competitor for the affections of Nanna) meet in battle, Bous kills Høtherus but himself receives a mortal wound; he dies the next day. Thus Bous differs from Váli, the avenger of Baldr in the vernacular west Scandinavian traditions, not just in his name, for Váli survives not only the encounter with Höd but also, and far more significantly, the cataclysmic demise of gods, giants, and the cosmos that is Ragnarök. Váli is truly an enduring figure, but Bous is a very minor player in Saxo's history.

The name Bous is ordinarily understood to represent a Danish version of the medieval Icelandic name Búi, and since the name is ultimately related to the verb meaning "to dwell, settle," earlier scholars associated it with their theories of fertility myth and ritual associated with Baldr's death. But "Búi" was an ordinary man's name, and indeed was not infrequently used in heroic legend: One of the most famous of the Jómsvíkingar, for example, was Búi the Stout, and a Búi also turns up among the sons of Karl in *Rígsthula*.

See also Baldr; Rind; Váli, Son of Odin

BRACTEATES

Small round golden disks, stamped with images on one side and occasionally also with runic inscriptions.

Bracteates date from the late Migration Period (5th–6th centuries C.E.) and have been found in graves and hoards and as isolated finds. They were probably intended

Gold bracteate found in Denmark showing a figure in a horned helmet, horse, bird, and swastika. (Universitets Oldsaksamling, Oslo)

to be worn as pendants hanging around the neck. More than 900 bracteates exist, mostly from Scandinavia but also from England and the Continent.

Bracteates are significant for the study of Norse mythology not for the runic inscriptions but for the human and animal images on them. These were based on Roman iconography, but they soon developed characteristic Germanic forms that some scholars have thought involved especially the god Odin. In a huge body of work, Karl Hauck argued that the bracteates present a "wind-god" who is involved with healing, and specifically that certain bracteates containing this figure and that of an animal show Odin healing Baldr's horse, as he does in the Second Merseburg Charm. He interprets another characteristic image, that of three figures together (the so-called three-god bracteates) as presenting Odin, Baldr, and Loki, or perhaps Odin, Baldr, and Hel, either of which would correspond to the Baldr myth as we have it in the Scandinavian sources. In addition, the divine twins have been identified in images with two figures. Although Hauck's work is enormously learned and thorough, the mythological interpretations remain speculative and would seem to invite fresh investigations.

> ***See also*** Baldr; Hel; Loki; Merseburg Charms; Odin
>
> ***References and further reading:*** Karl Hauck provided a relatively short summary of his analyses in the encyclopedia article "Brakteatenikonlogie," *Reallexikon der germanischen Altertumskunde,* ed. Heinrich Beck, Herbert Jankuhn, Kurt Ranke, and Reinhard Wenskus, 2nd ed. (Berlin and New York: W. de Gruyter, 1973–), vol. 3 (1978): 361–401. The details are in his *Goldbrakteaten aus Sievern: Spätantike Amulett-Bilder der "Dania Saxonica" und die Sachsen-"Origo" bei Widukind von Corvey,* Münstersche Mittelalter-Schriften, 1 (Munich: W. Fink, 1970), and in a long series of articles from 1971 onward, published in a variety of sources, called "Zur Ikonologie der Goldbrakteaten." The bracteates themselves may be found in Hauck, *Die Goldbrakteaten der Völkerwanderungszeit,* 3 vols. (Munich: W. Fink, 1985–1989). A recent work reassessing Hauck's thinking is Kathryn Starkey, "Imagining an Early Odin: Gold Bracteates as Visual Evidence?" *Scandinavian Studies* 71 (1999): 373–392.

BRAGI

God of poetry according to Snorri Sturluson; perhaps identical with Bragi Boddason the Old, traditionally reckoned the first skald.

Bragi is listed fourth in Snorri's catalog of the æsir in *Gylfaginning:*

> One is called Bragi. He is excellent with respect to wisdom and foremost in linguistic genius and speech. He knows most about poetry, and because of him *bragr* is called poetry, and from his name that one is called a *bragr* of men or a *bragr* of women who possesses verbal talent beyond others, a man or a woman. His wife is Idun.

Snorri has no more to say of Bragi in *Gylfaginning,* but he used Bragi extensively in *Skáldskaparmál.* This usage occurs in the frame. Ægir has come to visit the æsir, and at the splendid banquet that ensues he is seated next to Bragi, who tells him "many tidings about the æsir." These are the mythic narratives of *Skáldskaparmál,* and many are told in the context of a dialogue between Ægir and Bragi that precisely parallels the one between Gylfi/Gangleri and Hár, Jafnhár, and Thridi in *Gylfaginning.*

Grímnismál, stanza 44, calls Bragi "best of poets" in a list of other "bests"—Odin of the æsir, Sleipnir of horses, and so forth. In *Lokasenna*, Bragi has an early exchange with Loki. Loki has just joined the æsir after calling on his blood brother relationship with Odin, and Vídar has poured him a drink.

11. [Loki:] Hail æsir, hail *ásynjur*
and all the very holy gods,
except that one *áss*, who sits further in,
Bragi, on the bench.
12. [Bragi:] Steed and sword will I give you of my riches,
and Bragi will thus fix it for you with a ring;
lest you repay jealousy to the gods;
do not provoke the gods to anger at you.
13. [Loki:] Horse and arm rings will you ever
lack both, Bragi;
of æsir and elves who are in here
you are the most wary of battle
and most shy of a shot.
14. [Bragi:] I know that if I were outside, as I am inside
come into Ægir's hall,
your head I would carry in my hands
I see that for your lying.
15. [Loki:] You are brave in your seat, you will never do thus,
Bragi, you adornment of the bench.
Go your way, if you are angry
You seem not brave at all.

Bragi's cowardice is not elsewhere mentioned, and in fact this accusation is common in *Lokasenna*.

Bragi is found at Valhöll in both *Hákonarmál* (stanza 14) and *Eiríksmál* (stanza 3). Each of these late-tenth-century poems shows the arrival of a human king at Valhöll, and it is not inconceivable that the poets imagined Bragi Boddason the poet there as an earlier arrival from the world of humans. If this was indeed the source of Bragi the god, it had to have preceded the stanzas from *Grímnismál* and *Lokasenna*, and this level of relative chronology eludes us.

References and further reading: Two of the giants of the nineteenth century debated the question of Bragi the poet and Bragi the god. Eugen Mogk, "Bragi als Gott und Dichter," *Beiträge zur Geschichte der deutschen Sprache und Literatur* 12 (1887): 383–392, derived the god from the poet and thought that Bragi's promotion to Valhöll had occurred as early as the late ninth century. Opposition came from Sophus Bugge, "Der Gott Bragi in den norrönen Gedichten," *Beiträge zur Geschichte der deutschen Sprache und Literatur* 13

(1888): 187–201, who thought that time frame for the process was too short. Mogk had the last word: "Bragi," *Beiträge zur Geschichte der deutschen Sprache und Literatur* 14 (1889): 81–90.

BREIDABLIK

Baldr's dwelling, according to *Grímnismál,* stanza 12, and Snorri in *Gylfaginning.* Interpreting the verse, which says that fewest evils are at Breidablik, Snorri says that nothing impure is there, and he surely had in mind Baldr's "goodness" when he said this. The name means either "wide-gleam" or "wide-view."

See also Baldr

BRIMIR

In *Völuspá,* stanza 9, apparently an alternate name for Ymir:

> Then all the powers went to their judgment seats
> The very holy gods, and discussed,
> Who should form the lord of dwarfs,
> Out of the blood of Brimir and the limbs of Bláin.

Containing as it does the word *brim,* "surf, seaway," the name might allude to the making of the sea from Ymir's blood. It is also found in *Völuspá,* stanza 37, where it appears to refer to a beer hall of the giants, although it is not wholly impossible that it refers to the owner of the beer hall. This hall stands at (or is named, if Brimir owns it) Ókólnir (Uncold).

See also Bláin

BRÍSINGA MEN

Torque or necklace belonging to Freyja.

In eddic poetry, the Brísinga men is found in *Thrymskvida.* It jerks when Freyja is angered at the suggestion that she should go to Giantland (stanza 13), and at Heimdall's suggestion (stanza 15), it is put onto Thor as he assumed Freyja's disguise (stanza 19). Otherwise the Brísinga men is found only in Snorri's *Edda.* In both *Gylfaginning* and *Skáldskaparmál,* Snorri says simply that Freyja owned it, but in *Skáldskaparmál* he also gives two very interesting pieces of information: Loki and Heimdall fought over it, and Loki is known as the "thief of the giants, of the goat, of the Brísinga men, and of the apples of Idun." A battle between Heimdall and Loki is known from one stanza of the late-tenth-century Icelandic skaldic poem *Húsdrápa* by Úlf Uggason. It is difficult to interpret, but some scholars think they may indeed have been fighting over the Brísinga men. In stanza 9 of the *Haustlöng* of Thjódólf of Hvin, one of the very earliest skaldic poems, Loki is called "hoop-thief of Brísing's people," an apparent reference to his theft of the necklace. The same myth also appears to be recounted in the late *Sörla tháttr*, in which Loki, taking on the form of a fly, steals from Freyja a golden necklace made for her by dwarfs, but the necklace is not explicitly called the Brísinga men.

Lines 1197–1201 of the Old English epic *Beowulf* allude to a legendary narrative in which the hero Hama takes away the necklace of the Brosings (Brosinga mene), fleeing the terror of Ermaneric. This necklace is clearly an analog of the Brísinga men, and many scholars have tried to relate the story attached to it to Loki's battle with Heimdall or theft of the necklace, an enterprise that is not easy. What the *Beowulf* analog does seem to show is that Brísinga men should be understood as "torque of the Brísings," not, as some scholars have thought, "gleaming torque" or "sunny torque." But who the Brísings might be remains an unanswered question. The Brísing of *Haustlöng* is not found elsewhere, although the thulur refer to a Norwegian island of that name. The simplest explanation might be to regard the Brísings as dwarfs, the ones who, according to *Sörla tháttr*, made Freyja's precious necklace.

> *References and further reading:* Perhaps the most famous treatment of the Brísinga men is an essay by Karl Müllenhoff, "Frija und der Halsbandmythus," *Zeitschrift für deutsches Altertumn* 30 (1886): 217–260, which argues for a kind of solar myth that, as F. Klaeber put it, "compels admiration rather than acceptance" (*Beowulf and the Fight at Finnsburg: Edited with Introduction, Bibliography, Notes, Glossary, and Appendices*, 3rd ed., with first and second supplements [Boston: D. C. Heath, 1950], 178). The archaeological background is explored by Birgit Arrhenius, "Det flammande smycket," *Fornvännen* 57 (1962): 79–101, and "Zum symbolischen Sinn des Almadin im früheren Mittelalter," *Frühmittelalterliche Studien* 3 (1969): 47–59. The parallel between Brosinge mene and Brísinga men is treated by Ursula Dronke, "Beowulf and Ragnarǫk," *Saga-Book of the Viking Society* 17 (1968): 302–325, and Helen Damico, "*Sörlaþáttr* and the Hama Episode in *Beowulf*," *Scandinavian Studies* 55 (1983): 222–235.

BROKK

Dwarf; helped create some of the precious objects of the gods.

Snorri tells the story in *Skáldskaparmál*. Loki had cut the hair off Sif, Thor's wife, and he avoided a beating only by promising to have the dwarfs make for Sif a headpiece that would grow into golden hair. After having the sons of Ívaldi make the headpiece and also the ship Skídbladnir and Odin's spear, Gungnir, he bets the dwarf Brokk that Brokk's brother Eitri cannot make three equally good objects. Brokk is to work the bellows for Eitri, and Loki changes himself into a fly and pesters Brokk. Eitri makes first a boar with gold bristles, then the ring Draupnir, finally Mjöllnir, Thor's hammer. The hammer's handle is short because Brokk's bellows work was nearly interrupted when the fly bit him between the eyes so that blood flowed.

Brokk is known from no other source.

See also Dwarfs

BUR, BOR (SON)

Son of Búri, father of Odin, Vili, and Vé.

Bur is found in eddic poetry and in Snorri's *Edda*, where the name is spelled Bor. The word *bur* is a poetic noun meaning "son." With the giantess Bestla, Bur had the three sons Odin, Vili, and Vé.

See also Bestla; Búri; Odin

BÚRI

First of the æsir, father of Bur and therefore grandfather of Odin.

Búri is found in Snorri's *Gylfaginning* but not in eddic poetry. He is part of the creation story, for he was licked from salt blocks by the primeval cow Audhumla. Snorri describes him as "fair in appearance, large, and powerful. He begat that son called Bor." Although the text does not make it explicit, we may, I think, assume that he did so through an ordinary human sexual act, in contrast to the monstrous hermaphroditic procreation of Ymir.

See also Audhumla; Bur, Bor; Ymir

BYGGVIR

Mythological character.

Byggvir is found only in the prose header to *Lokasenna* and stanzas 55–56 of the poem. The prose header says that he and Beyla were servants of Frey. Byggvir's intervention with Loki in the poem proper follows that of Frey. In stanza 43 Byggvir apparently says (the stanza is difficult) that if he could measure up to Frey, he would give Loki a beating, the evil crow! Loki's response is dismissive: "What is that little thing, / I see strutting about, / a hungry parasite? / At the ears of Frey / you will always be / and will cluck under the millstone" (stanza 45). Byggvir responds by proclaiming his name and stating that all men and gods call him rapid: "I am proud here / that the sons of Hropt [i.e., of Odin] / all drink beer together." Loki responds: "Shut up, Byggvir! / You were never able / to divide food among people. / And in the straw of the floor / you were never seen / when people fought."

Like his wife Beyla (according to *Lokasenna* stanza 56), Byggvir is mostly understood through the etymology of his name, although the problem is complicated by the competing form in the poem, "Beyggvir." *Bygg* is the word for barley, and much of what the poem says of Byggvir can be imagined to fit barley, which is tiny, ground in a mill, and used in beer. Barley would be associated with Frey insofar as Frey is a fertility god.

If Byggvir is indeed a personification of barley, he is virtually unique in Scandinavian mythology, which otherwise has little to say of such figures.

> *See also* Beyla
> *References and further reading:* Georges Dumézil, "Two Minor Scandinavian Gods: Byggvir and Beyla" (1952), in his *Gods of the Ancient Northmen*, ed. Einar Haugen, Publications of the UCLA Center for the Study of Comparative Folklore and Mythology, 3 (Berkeley and Los Angeles: University of California Press, 1973), 89–117, surveys the evidence.

BYLEIST (BYLEIPT, BYLEIFT)

Loki's brother.

Although he acts in no extant myth, Byleist is found in a number of passages in poetry in the kenning "Byleist's brother" for Loki. Snorri states directly in both *Gylfaginning* and *Skáldskaparmál* that Byleist is one of Loki's two brothers; the other is Helblindi.

Unlike Helblindi, whose meaning is transparent (Hel-blind), Byleist's name is obscure. Most attempts at etymology have come up with some sort of meteorological phenomenon, which is hardly helpful.

> *See also* Loki

DAG (DAY)

Personification of the day.

Dag is found in *Vafthrúdnismál*, stanza 25, Vafthrúdnir's response to Odin's question in stanza 24, "Whence comes the day / that goes over people / or the night with tides?"

> Delling he is called, he is Dag's father,
> And Nótt [Night] was born to Nör.
> New moon and tides the useful powers created
> For people to tell time.

An alternate translation of the second half of the first line would be "he is father of the day."

In *Gylfaginning* Snorri has an interesting expansion of the idea in this stanza:

> Nörfi or Narfi was a giant who lived in Jötunheimar. He had a daughter named Nótt [Night]; she was swarthy and dark, as she had the lineage for. [She had two marriages, to Naglfari, then to Ánar.] Last she married Delling, and he was of the lineage of the æsir. Their son was Dag, according to his paternal heritage.

This is a typical example of Snorri's view of the mythological difference between jötnar and æsir. But it also shows the importance in the mythology of patriliny, which in medieval Iceland operated within a bilateral kinship system; that is, people could reckon their kin through father *and* mother (and we might expect that they thought they inherited characteristics of both, not just of the father). As in the genealogy of the æsir as a whole, so it is with the heavenly bodies. Dag and Odin each has a giant mother (Nótt, Bestla) and ultimately a giant progenitor on the mother's side (Ymir, Nörfi), but each is regarded exclusively as a member of the æsir.

Snorri goes on in *Gylfaginning* to say that Alfödr gave Dag and Nótt each a horse and carriage and put them up in the sky, where they go around the earth once a day. "The horse that Dag has is called Skínfaxi, and all the sky and earth glow from its mane."

See also Delling; Nótt; Nari and/or Narfi

DÁIN (DEAD)

According to *Grímnismál,* stanza 33 (and therefore Snorri in *Gylfaginning*), one of the four harts that gnaws on Yggdrasil; elsewhere an appropriate and much-used dwarf name, except in *Hávamál,* stanza 143, where he appears to be an elf.

This last stanza lists various people who carve runes, and since Odin carves for the æsir, the others presumably are of the race for which they carve, and Dáin carves for the elves. Perhaps the name "Dead" was just very useful mythologically.

See also Dvalin; Yggdrasil

DELLING

Father of Dag, who is day personified.

Delling is found in *Vafthrúdnismál,* stanza 25, Vafthrúdnir's response to Odin's question in stanza 24, "Whence comes the day / that goes over people / or the night with tides?"

Delling he is called, he is Dag's father,
And Nótt [Night] was born to Nör.
New moon and tides the useful powers created
For people to tell time.

An alternate translation of the second half of the first line would be "he is father of the day."

In *Gylfaginning*, Snorri has an interesting expansion of the idea in this stanza:

Nörfi or Narfi was a giant who lived in Jötunheimar. He had a daughter named Nótt; she was swarthy and dark, as she had the lineage for. [She had two marriages.] Last she married Delling and he was of the lineage of the æsir. Their son was Dag, according to his paternal heritage.

This is a typical example of Snorri's view of the mythological difference between jötnar and æsir. As I point out above, in the entry on Dag, it shows the typical mythological emphasis on patriliny. Dag is of the æsir because his father was of the æsir, even though his mother was not.

Delling probably means something like "shining," which would be an appropriate name for the father of the day. But the situation is complicated by *Hávamál*, stanza 160, in which Odin is enumerating charms he has learned:

I know a fifteenth, which Thjódrörir howled,
The dwarf, before Delling's door.

Unless Delling's door is a metaphor for sunrise, there may have been two figures called Delling, the second a dwarf, and Delling is indeed listed in the thulur as a dwarf name.

See also Dag

References and further reading: Rudolf Much, "Der germanische Himmelsgott," in the volume *Abhandlungen zur germanischen Philologie: Festgabe für R. Heinzel* (Halle an der Saale: M. Niemeyer, 1898), 189–278, argued, based on the etymological connection between *Dell-* and *-dall*, that Delling was a representation of Heimdall.

DÍSABLÓT

Sacrifice to the dísir.

From the point of view of the mythology the most interesting reference to the dísablót is found in a version of *Hervarar saga ok Heidreks konungs* (The Saga of Hervör and King Heidrek), which scholars ordinarily date to around the end of the thirteenth century, although the dating is difficult. This version of the saga opens with an account of the Learned Prehistory and tells about Starkad Áludreng. Starkad abducts Álfhild, the daughter of King Álf of Álfheimar, after she has reddened the altar *(hörgr)* with blood at a great dísablót one autumn. The prefix *Álf-* means "elf," and although there is no other evidence connecting the elves with the dísablót, on its face the text offers a mythological model for human behavior. The ceremony takes place at the home of a king, is presided over by a woman (one indeed of royal lineage), and involves the spilling of blood, presumably from an animal that was sacrificed. Angered at the abduction of his daughter, King Álf calls on Thor, who subsequently kills Starkad and restores Álfhild to her father. It is at least conceivable that the author of the saga thought that Thor was inclined to intervene because the dísablót had been successfully carried out, in other words, that in the eyes of this author at least, a dísablót could have been aimed at the æsir.

This ceremony is also mentioned in thirteenth-century Icelandic sources of a more historical nature. Two set the ceremony in Viking Age Norway and the other, Snorri's *Ynglinga saga,* chapter 29, in Uppsala. Snorri says that at the dísablót, King Adils was riding around the *dísarsal,* "hall of the dís," when his horse stumbled and threw him. The king's head struck a rock in such a way that his skull was split and his brain spilled onto the rock, and that was his death. Snorri then quotes Thjódólf of Hvin's *Ynglinga tal,* which does not mention the dísablót but says that a "creature of magic" or witch was to deprive Adils of his life; the brave descendent of Frey was to fall from his horse and his brain to be mixed with wet sand. Presumably Snorri understood the creature of magic as a witch, and he may also have thought that the dísablót involved riding a horse around a building sacred to or temporarily set aside for one of the dísir. Here the connection of the dísir with death would be echoed. The story is told with less detail in *Historia Norvegiae.*

The other two accounts come from the Sagas of Icelanders. Both set the dísablót at a banquet or feast in the midtenth century in Norway. *Egils saga,* which is from the early part of the thirteenth century—perhaps, according to some, from the pen of Snorri Sturluson—says that a feast was prepared at a farm owned by King Eirík Bloodax and Queen Gunnhild and that on an evening when the king and queen had just arrived, "there was to be a dísablót there." The actual account of the proceedings has to do pretty much exclusively with drinking huge mugs of beer, but it includes a skaldic stanza by Egil alluding to the dísablót. *Víga-Glúms saga,* which was composed a bit later than *Egils saga* and perhaps with that saga in mind, says that Víga-Glúm comes to Voss, in western Norway, and that a feast was prepared at the "winter-nights" (the onset of winter in late October), and the dísablót was done.

Thus the dísablót appears to have had a connection with autumn and to have been a relatively public event, insofar as it involved the participation of royalty. Beyond that we know little. A *dísathing* (assembly of or for the dísir) was held in Uppsala in early February, and there are many place-names attesting to the worship of the dísir.

DÍSIR
Collective female spirits.

In the mythological sources proper the dísir are hardly to be found. Their only secure appearance is in the eddic poem *Grímnismál*, stanza 53. Odin is about to reveal his identity to the doomed Geirröd:

> Slaughtered carrion
> will Ygg [Odin] have now,
> I know that your life has run its course;
> angry are the dísir—
> now you may see Odin,
> approach me, if you can!

The association with impending death seems to be a commonplace of the usage of the term "dísir" in eddic poetry. In *Reginsmál*, stanza 24, Hnikar tells Sigurd that there is great danger if he should trip going into battle: "Malicious dísir / stand on both sides of you / and wish to see you wounded." In *Hamdismál*, stanza 28, Hamdir, bemoaning the killing of their half-brother at their own hands, tell Sörli that the dísir had incited them. Sometimes the dísir look like valkyries, as in *Atlamál*, stanza 28, where Glaumvör tells her husband Gunnar a disquieting dream:

> I thought dead women
> came hither into the hall,
> not poorly decked out.
> They wished to choose you,
> would have invited you quickly
> to their benches;
> I declare of no value
> these dísir to you.

These dísir who would choose a doomed warrior and invite him to their benches look rather like valkyries, the choosers of the dead and the maidens who serve them in Valhöll. And indeed, the expression "Herjann's [Odin's] dísir,"

Figures found all over Scandinavia are believed to represent valkyries or dísir. (The Art Archive/Historiska Museet Stockholm/Dagli Orti)

which is found in *Gudrúnarkvida* I, stanza 19, looks like a kenning for the valkyries, Odin's maidens, but since the noun *dís* can also mean just "lady," that stanza may tell us nothing at all about the dísir.

Snorri uses the singular form, *dís*, in connection with two figures in *Gylfaginning*. After recounting the story of the failed marriage between Njörd and Skadi, Snorri says that Skadi moved to the mountains and lived at Thrymhrim, "and she goes about much on skis and with a bow and shoots animals; she is called 'snow-shoe god' or 'snow-shoe dís.'" Snorri says later in *Gylfaginning* that Freyja "is also called Vanadís," that is, dís of the vanir.

The text in which dísir play the greatest role is *Thidranda tháttr ok Thórhalls*, which is found in late-fourteenth-century manuscripts of the *Great Saga of Olaf Tryggvason* but is believed by some observers to have been included in the late-twelfth-century Latin life of Olaf Tryggvason, now lost, by the Icelandic monk Gunnlaug Leifsson. It is set before the conversion of Iceland to Christianity at the farmstead of Sídu-Hall, a leading chieftain who later was to be among those who advanced the cause of the conversion. The prophet Thorhall has foreseen that a prophet is to die at the sacrifice of the winter nights, but Sídu-Hall has a bull named Prophet slaughtered. Thorhall then decrees that none should leave the house at night, but when there are three mighty knocks on the door, Sídu-Hall's son Thidrandi opens it and goes outside. He is attacked by nine women in black riding from the north, while nine women in white ride from the south. Thorhall later guesses that there will be a change of religion for the better. The women were fylgjur (fetches) of Sídu-Hall's family. The nine women in black were dísir who wanted their share before being forever parted from the family, while the nine in white were dísir who arrived too late to help.

Many interpretations of these strange women and the events in which they figure have been advanced. Some scholars argue that Sídu-Hall angered the dísir by failing to hold the dísablót (sacrifice to the dísir), but there is no evidence for that in the text. What the text does tell us unequivocally is that some time between the late twelfth and late fourteenth centuries a learned author saw little difference between fylgjur and dísir and saw no difficulty depicting them in terms of color symbolism to represent the opposition between the old faith and the new. The destructive and benign nature of the two groups reminds us further of the good and bad fates doled out by valkyries. Once again the distinction among these groups of collective female spirits breaks down.

Another connection with the conversion is the nickname of the poet Thorbjörn dísarskáld (Skald of the dís), who is one of two poets who left fragments of poetry directly addressed to Thor.

Place-names suggest a cult of the dísir, and written sources tell of a sacrifice to the dísir, the dísablót.

See also Dísablót

References and further reading: General treatments of the dísir include Erik Brate, "Disen," *Zeitschrift für deutsche Wortforschung* 13 (1911–1912): 143–152; Folke Ström, "Diser, norner, valkyrjor: Frukbarhetskult och sakralt kungadöme i Norden," *Kungliga vitterhets, historie och antikvitetsadademiens handlingar*, Filologisk-filosofiska serien 1 (Stockholm: Almqvist & Wiksell, 1954); and the second part of Dag Strömbäck's "Tidrande och disarna: Ett filologiskt-folkloristiskt utkast," in his *Folklore och filologi: Valda uppsatser utgivna av Kungl. Gustav Adolfs akademien 13.8.1970*, Skrifter utgivna av Kungliga Gustav Adolfs akademien, 48 (Uppsala: Kungliga Gustav Adolfs akademien, 1970), 181–191. For a discussion of *Thidranda tháttr*, see also Merrill Kaplan, "Prefiguration and the Writing of History in Þáttr Þiðranda ok Þórhalls," *Journal of English and Germanic Philology* 99 (2000): 379–394.

DRAUPNIR (DRIPPER)

Odin's golden arm ring.

Many skalds use "Draupnir" in kennings for gold, so it must have been well known, although the only Draupnir to be found in eddic poetry by name is a dwarf in the catalog of dwarfs in *Völuspá*. However, in *Skírnismál*, stanza 21,

Skírnir offers Gerd a ring that had been burned with Odin's young son, from which drip every ninth night eight rings of equal weight. This can only be Draupnir, for in *Gylfaginning* Snorri says that Odin put the ring Draupnir on Baldr's funeral pyre and adds the information about its magically replicating itself, information that he also includes in *Skáldskaparmál* when he tells of the origin of Draupnir. Like Sif's golden hair, Frey's ship Skídbladnir, Odin's spear Gungnir, Frey's golden boar, and Thor's hammer, it was made by the dwarfs. Along with the boar and the hammer, Draupnir is one of three treasures forged by Eitri while Loki in the form of a fly pestered Brokk, who was working the bellows.

Draupnir has truly been to Hel and back, for Snorri says, in his account of Baldr's death, that when Hermód leaves the realm of the dead after having acquired Hel's consent to release Baldr if all creation will weep, he takes with him Draupnir, sent by Baldr to Odin as a memorial. Indeed, *Skáldskaparmál* lists among Baldr kennings "owner of Draupnir," and the passage of Draupnir through funeral fire and the world of the dead must truly have enhanced its value.

    See also Brokk; Eitri; Odin

DRÓMI
See **FENRIR**

DUNEYR
According to *Grímnismál,* stanza 33 (and therefore Snorri in *Gylfaginning*), one of the four harts that gnaws on Yggdrasil.
The name appears to mean "dark-ear."

    See also Dáin; Durathrór; Yggdrasil

DURATHRÓR
According to *Grímnismál,* stanza 33 (and therefore Snorri in *Gylfaginning*), one of the four harts that gnaws on Yggdrasil.
The meaning of the name is unclear.

    See also Dáin; Duneyr; Yggdrasil

DVALIN (DELAYED)
Dwarf name; also according to *Grímnismál,* stanza 33 (and therefore Snorri in *Gylfaginning*), one of the four harts that gnaws on Yggdrasil.
Dvalin is mentioned in stanza 11 of *Völuspá* in the catalog of dwarfs, then again in stanza 17, as the catalog of dwarfs is drawing to a close, when the "dwarfs in

Dvalin's group" are mentioned. In stanza 145 of *Hávamál*, Dvalin stands as a representative of the dwarfs, along with Odin for the æsir, Dáin for the elves, and Alsvinn for the giants. According to stanza 16 of *Alvíssmál*, the dwarfs call the sun "Dvalin's deluder" (or so the expression is understood, as a reference to the sun turning dwarfs to stone). When, then, *Fáfnismál*, stanza 13, says that some of the norns are of the family of the æsir, some are of the elves, and some are the daughters of Dvalin, it seems apparent that the dwarfs are what is meant. The skalds often used "Dvalin's drink" or something similar as a kenning for poetry, clearly because the mead of poetry had at one time been in the possession of dwarfs. Finally, Dvalin is the name of one of the dwarfs to whom Freyja gave herself in *Sörla tháttr* in exchange for a golden necklace, presumably the Brísinga men. Dvalin is, then, one of the most common of the dwarf names. Why he should be "delayed" is not clear.

As for the hart, the thulur list "Dvalar" as a hart name, but not "Dvalin," and some observers think that the hart who gnaws at Yggdrasil should be Dvalar.

   See also Dwarfs

DWARFS
Mythological beings.

Völuspá turns its attention to the dwarfs just after the æsir have created the cosmos, arranged for time reckoning, and acquired gold. The æsir were blissful "until three came, / giant maidens, / very powerful, / out of Jötunheimar" (stanza 8). For the first of several times in the poem, when crisis threatens, the gods repair to their "judgment seats." On this occasion they consider "which dwarfs are to create a lord" *(Codex Regius)* or "who is to create troops of dwarfs" *(Hauksbók)* "out of bloody surf and out of dark limbs" *(Codex Regius)*. The passage is difficult, and the editions ordinarily render it as something like "who should create a lord of dwarfs out of the blood of Brimir and out of the limbs of Bláin." The following stanza, however, is clear:

> There Mótsognir had
> become the foremost
> of all dwarfs,
> and Durinn the second;
> human likenesses they
> made many, those dwarfs, out of earth,
> as Durinn told.

There follows a catalog of dwarfs that takes up several stanzas. Thus *Völuspá* actually has more information on dwarfs than on the gods. The names in this and other catalogs of dwarfs suggest something about their characteristics: They are associated with the dead, with battle, with wisdom, with craftsmanship, with the supernatural, and even to some extent with the elves.

It is not clear why the arrival of giant maidens in *Völuspá* should provoke a crisis involving the dwarfs. However, the response appears to have something to do with the creation of order in the already existing community of dwarfs, or the creation of troops of dwarfs themselves. What these dwarfs do is to create "human likenesses," and it is not implausible that these are the human beings whom the æsir will endow with the characteristics of life. Perhaps the arrival of giant maidens made it clear that humans would be needed, since dead human warriors make up the ranks of the einherjar who will fight alongside Odin against the forces of chaos.

Certainly the fashioning of "human likenesses" is consistent with the general picture in the mythology of dwarfs as craftsmen. According to Snorri in *Skáldskaparmál*, the dwarfs Fjalar and Galar made the mead of poetry out of the blood of Kvasir. Mostly, however, the dwarfs make objects. Snorri also tells in *Skáldskaparmál* of the creation of some of the most important and precious possessions of the gods. Loki had cut the hair off Sif, Thor's wife, and Loki avoided a beating only by promising to have the dwarfs make for Sif a headpiece that would grow into golden hair. He has the sons of Ívaldi make the headpiece, and also the ship Skídbladnir and Odin's spear, Gungnir. Then he bets the dwarf Brokk that Brokk's brother Eitri cannot make three equally good objects. Brokk is to work the bellows for Eitri, and Loki changes himself into a fly and pesters Brokk. Eitri makes first a boar with gold bristles, then the ring Draupnir, and finally Mjöllnir, Thor's hammer. The hammer's handle is short because Brokk's bellows work was nearly interrupted when the fly bit him between the eyes so that blood flowed.

Thus, if we assign Sif's hair to the realm of Thor, each of the three major gods gets two objects. Odin gets his spear, which he can use to throw an enemy army into panic, and the ring that duplicates itself in multiple copies. Thor gets the hammer with which he kills giants, and Frey gets the ship that can be folded up and put in a pocket and the gold-bristled boar, Gullinborsti. It may be worth noting that each god gets one object of gold and one of iron or wood. Furthermore, Odin commissioned the dwarfs to make the fetter Gleipnir, which he used to bind Fenrir. And when Odin, Hœnir, and Loki needed gold to compensate Hreidmar for the death of his son Otr in *Skáldskaparmál*, it was to the dwarfs that Odin sent Loki. Like the male gods, Freyja also had precious objects fashioned by the dwarfs: She had her own gold-bristled boar (*Hyndluljód*, stanza 7) and obtained a necklace (*Sörla tháttr*, which is probably a rather late text), perhaps the Brísinga men. Besides making precious objects for the gods, the dwarfs may also have supported them with magic. According to *Hávamál*, stanza 160,

Odin learned a charm first sung by the dwarf Thjódrörir: "[H]e sang wealth for the æsir, / and prosperity for the elves, / mind for Hroptatýr." Hroptatýr is Odin, and to have endowed him with mind would be a great gift.

However, in the overall scheme of Scandinavian mythology, the dwarfs appear to occupy a position closer to that of the giants than to some kind of allies of the gods. The flow of goods is always from the dwarfs to the gods, never the reverse, and sometimes hostilities are involved, as when Loki gets gold from Andvari to compensate Hreidmar for the death of Otr. Alvíss wishes to marry Thor's daughter and winds up dead for this presumption *(Alvíssmál)*, just as did the giants Thrym and Thjazi, who coveted Freyja and Idun (Freyja did, however, apparently sleep with some dwarfs to get her necklace in *Sörla tháttr*). The poet Thjódólf of Hvin said in his *Ynglinga tal* (stanza 5) that a dwarf tricked the Swedish king Sveigdir, when the king jumped into the rock after the dwarf, and "the bright hall of Sökmímir and his people, inhabited by giants [jötnar], gaped open." Paraphrasing the poem in *Ynglinga saga*, Snorri tells us that the king Sveigdir one evening after sundown at a farm called Steinn (Stone) saw a dwarf sitting by the stone and was summoned into the stone by the dwarf, never to return.

The conception of dwarfs as dwelling in the earth or in rocks or mountains is deeply rooted. Alvíss tells Thor that he lives down under the earth, under a stone. When Odin sent for the fetter Gleipnir, the direction was down. Here, however, and in *Skáldskaparmál* as well, in the story of the acquisition of gold from Andvari, Snorri calls the destination Svartálfaheim (world of the black-elves), which suggests that for him the category of elves and dwarfs was somewhat blurred.

Snorri tells us in *Gylfaginning* that the dwarfs originated as maggots in the flesh of the proto-giant Ymir, whose body the gods used to fashion the cosmos. Snorri also gives dwarfs a cosmological function and equates them with the cardinal directions when he writes that the dwarfs Nordri (North), Sudri (South), Austri (East), and Vestri (West) hold up the sky.

In later medieval Icelandic literature dwarfs appear as stereotypical figures similar to those in medieval literature elsewhere in Europe.

> **See also** *Alvíssmál; Völuspá*
>
> **References and further reading:** On the names of the dwarfs and their implications, see Chester N. Gould, "Dwarf-Names in Old Icelandic," *Publications of the Modern Language Association* 44 (1929): 949–967, and Lotte Motz, "New Thoughts on Dwarf-Names in Old Icelandic." *Frühmittelalterliche Studien* 7 (1973): 100–117 (with an epilogue by Dietrich Hoffmann). Motz also contributed several other studies of dwarfs: "Of Elves and Dwarfs," *Arv* 29–30 (1973–1974): 93–127; "The Craftsman in the Mound," *Folklore* 88 (1977): 46–60; and *The Wise One of the Mountain: A Study in Folklore*, Göppinger Arbeiten zur Germanistik, 379 (Göttingen: Kümmerle, 1983).

EGGTHÉR

In *Völuspá,* stanza 42, the herdsman of a giantess:

> He sat there on a mound and played a harp,
> The herdsman of a giantess, happy Eggthér.

The giantess in question might be the one from stanza 40, who raised the brood of Fenrir in Járnvid (Iron-woods), possibly therefore Angrboda. Why anyone working for her would be happy is unexplained; perhaps Eggthér was especially fond of the harp. In any case, his name is identical to that of Ecgtheow, who in the Old English epic *Beowulf* is the father of Beowulf. Andy Orchard, in his *Dictionary of Norse Myth and Legend,* says that this parallel "is almost certainly a red herring," a statement with which I agree.

> *References and further reading:* Peter H. Salus and Paul Beekman Tayler, "Eikinskjaldi, Fjalar, and Eggthér," *Neophilologus* 53 (1969): 76–81. Andy Orchard, *Dictionary of Norse Myth and Legend* (London: Cassell, 1997), 35.

EGIL

According to *Hymiskvida,* stanza 7, the one who looked after Thor's goats while Thor was visiting Hymir; possibly the father of Thor's human servants Thjálfi and Röskva.

The surmise concerning Thjálfi and Röskva is based on *Hymiskvida,* stanza 37, the third from last stanza in the poem and the one that follows Thor's acquisition of the kettle and killing of the pursuing giants. Parts of it are difficult, especially in the third line, but it means something like this:

> They went for a long time, before lay down
> Hlorridi's [Thor's] goat, half dead, in front;
> The team-mate of the trace was limping on its leg;
> And the crafty Loki caused it.

According to *Gylfaginning,* when Thor and Loki set off on the visit to Jötunheimar that would take them to Útgarda-Loki, they stopped for the night at a farmer's house. Thor killed and cooked his goats and then revived them next morning. One was lame, because Thjálfi had broken it to get at the marrow. Those who are able to put aside the different destinations of the two trips and the differing roles of Loki (he did not accompany Thor in *Hymiskvida,* and he was not responsible for the laming in *Gylfaginning*) and who like to sew things up neatly will find attractive the possibility of linking Egil to Thjálfi and Röskva.

Egil was a common given name in medieval Scandinavia. One Egil turns up as the brother of Völund, and another is the subject of one of the grandest of the sagas of Icelanders.

See also Thjálfi; Útgarda-Loki

EIKINSKJALDI (WITH-AN-OAKEN-SHIELD)

Dwarf name, found in *Völuspá*, stanzas 13 and 16.

See also Dwarfs

References and further reading: Peter H. Salus and Paul Beekman Tayler, "Eikin-skjaldi, Fjalar, and Eggthér," *Neophilologus* 53 (1969): 76–81.

EIKTHYRNIR (OAK-ENCIRCLER)

Hart that nibbles on the leaves of Yggdrasil, the world tree.
The major source is *Grímnismál*, stanza 26:

> Eikthyrnir is the name of a hart, who stands at the hall of Herjafödr [Odin]
> And bites from the limbs of Lærad.
> Yet from his horns it drips into Hvergelmir,
> Thence all waters have their ways.

In *Gylfaginning*, Snorri paraphrases this stanza nearly verbatim, at least for the first half, but he clarifies the last line to mean a bunch of rivers, which he names.

See also Lærad; Yggdrasil

References and further reading: The high water mark for Eikthyrnir studies (and also the only year in which anything significant has ever appeared) was 1917: Axel Olrik, "Yggdrasil," *Danske studier* 14 (1917): 49–62, used the confluence of oak tree and large stag to assign the provenance of Yggdrasil to Denmark or western Norway. Uno Holmberg (Harva), "Valhall och världsträdet," *Finsk tidskrift för vitterhet, vetenskap, konst och politik* 48 (1917): 349–377, thought that Eikthyrnir was an Icelandic invention based on the constellation Ursa Major.

EIN(D)RIDI (LONE-RIDER)

Thor name.
The name is found in stanza 19 of the *Haustlöng* of Thjódólf of Hvin, one of the very earliest skalds, in the scene in Thor's duel with Hrungnir in which the whetstone is lodged in the god's head. Elsewhere in this stanza Einridi is called both earth's son and Odin's son. It is also found in the *Vellekla* of Einar Helga-

son skálaglamm, a poem in praise of Hákon the Hladir jarl, probably from around 975–985 C.E. In this stanza he refers to the temple lands of Einridi and all the gods *(bönd)*.

The form with *d* in the second syllable is younger. My translation of the name (either form) is what I think a Norseman would have thought it meant; some scholars have thought that etymologically it may originally have meant "lone ruler." It is worth noting that this name is attested on rune stones for human beings, who may therefore have been named after the god.

See also Hlórridi; Thor

EINHERJAR (LONE-FIGHTERS)

The chosen warriors of Odin, who sport at Valhöll awaiting the last battle at Ragnarök.

Vafthrúdnismál, stanza 41, describes life at Valhöll:

> All the einherjar in Odin's fields
> Hack each other each day.
> They choose slaughter and ride from the field
> Later sit reconciled together.

Grímnismál, stanza 18, says that the einherjar are nourished on Sæhrímnir, cooked in Eldhrímnir by Andhrímnir. Stanza 23 says that 800 einherjar go out of each of the doors of Valhöll. Stanza 36 lists the valkyries who bring beer to them. At the end of the poem, when Odin reveals his identity to Geirröd, Odin tells him that he has lost the grace of all the einherjar and of Odin.

The anonymous *Eiríksmál*, from the second half of the tenth century, describes Valhöll and puts the einherjar there. Indeed, stanza 1 has Odin dream that he awakened the einherjar and bade them prepare for an honored guest. The similar poem *Hákonarmál*, attributed to Eyvind Finnsson skáldaspillir, also mentions the einherjar: Odin tells the retinue of Hákon the Good, as they are arriving in Valhöll, that they shall have a truce with the einherjar and invites them to drink beer.

In *Gylfaginning* Snorri uses and expands on these sources, adding, among other things, that the einherjar are "all those men who have fallen in battle since the beginning of the world." He also sends the einherjar out against the forces of chaos at the last battle but gives no details of their fights and fates.

The emphasis in the sources is twofold: the eternal fighting and revival of the einherjar, and their special relationship with Odin, which is manifested in part by their feasting endlessly with him and in part by their sharing in his grace.

Many scholars think there may be a basis for the myth in an ancient Odin cult, which would have centered on young warriors who entered into an ecstatic relationship with Odin. Sometimes this notion is juxtaposed to the description in the *Germania* of Tacitus, chapter 43, of an army of the dead. The people are called the Harii, a name that some say is etymologically related to *-herjar* in einherjar. In *Lokasenna*, stanza 60, Loki addresses Thor as *einheri*, the singular of *einherjar* and the only time the singular is attested. Thor certainly has a special relationship with Odin, as his son with Jörd.

See also Andhrímnir; Eldhrímnir; Odin; Sæhrímnir; Valhöll

References and further reading: The notion of an ecstatic Odin cult was best articulated by Otto Höfler, *Kultische Geheimbünde der Germanen* (Frankfurt: M. Diesterweg, 1934) and numerous later works. A more recent take is that of Bruce Lincoln, articulated in his *Priests, Warriors, and Cattle: A Study in the Ecology of Religions* (Berkeley and Los Angeles: University of California Press, 1981), 122–133. A credible alternative etymology of einherjar, proposing that the word meant "peerless warriors," is in Lennart Elmevik, "Fisl. einherjar 'krigare i Valhall' och några andra fornnord. sammansättningar med -ein," *Saga och sed*, 1982: 75–84.

EIR

Minor goddess.

Snorri lists Eir third in his catalog in *Gylfaginning* of goddesses among the æsir and calls her "best of physicians." Her name is identical with the noun *eir*, "peace, clemency." Eir plays no role in the mythology, but in *Fjölsvinnsmál*, stanza 38, Eir is found in a list of the maidens who serve Menglöd; none of the others is a deity, and many are just feminine adjectives ("bright," "happy," "fair"). Eir is listed among the names of valkyries in the thulur, but not among those of the goddesses. The name is common as a base word in skaldic kennings, but whether we should trust Snorri and imagine the existence of a goddess Eir is problematic.

EIRÍKSMÁL

Anonymous poem composed after the death of King Eirík Bloodax at the battle of Stainmoor, Westmoreland, England in 954, recounting his glorious arrival in Valhöll. The poem as we have it is only nine stanzas, and two different meters are used. Nevertheless, it appears to offer a picture of Valhöll that actually was rooted in late paganism. The poem begins with Odin recounting a dream: He thought he awoke early and bade the einherjar and valkyries prepare Valhöll for the arrival of a great ruler. He asks Bragi what great noise resounds, as though Baldr himself were returning to the hall. But it is Eirík Bloodax, and Odin bids the heroes

Sigmund and Sinfjötli arise and invite the guest into the hall, if it is Eirík. Bragi asks why Odin thinks it is Eirík, and Odin responds that the guest has reddened his sword in many a land. Why deprive such a great king of victory, asks Bragi. Because, Odin answers, one can never know—the gray wolf gazes upon the abodes of the gods. Eirík now arrives and is welcomed into the hall and asked who accompanies him. Five kings, he says. Here the poem ends.

The mythological details are familiar: Einherjar and valkyries inhabit Valhöll, and Baldr is missing. Bragi here is presumably to be regarded as the human poet, for the poem specifically mentions also the human heroes Sigmund and Sinfjötli, and, of course, Eirík; the five kings who accompany him have not been identified with any certainty. The poet explains why it is that a warrior favored by Odin might be defeated in battle, and he implies that Ragnarök may be near, or at least that in tenth-century Denmark Odin was consciously gathering troops for the final battle.

> **See also** *Hákonarmál*
>
> **References and further reading:** The literary relationship between *Eiríksmál* and *Hákonarmál* is discussed by Klaus von See, "Zwei eddische Preislieder," in *Festgabe Ulrich Pretzel zum 65. Geburtstag dargebracht von seinen Freunden und Schülern*, ed. Walter Simon, Wolfgang Bachofer, and Wolfgang Dittmann (Berlin: Schmidt, 1963), 107–117. Edith Marold, "Das Walhallbild in den *Eiríksmál* und *Hákonarmál*," *Mediaeval Scandinavia* 5 (1972): 19–33, acknowledges that the portrait of Valhöll in *Hákonarmál* is darker and conceivably more archaic than that of *Eiríksmál* and analyzes especially the duality of the conceptions in *Hákonarmál*. Axel Seeberg treats the identity of those who accompany Eirík to Valhöll in "Five Kings," *Saga-Book of the Viking Society*, 20 (1979–1980): 106–113.

EISTLA

One of nine giant mothers, perhaps of Heimdall, listed in *Hyndluljód,* stanza 37 (part of the "Short *Völuspá*").

> **See also** Heimdall; *Hyndluljód*
>
> **References and further reading:** Lotte Motz, "Giantesses and Their Names," *Frühmittelalterliche Studien* 15 (1981): 495–511.

EITRI

Dwarf; helped create some of the precious objects of the gods.

Snorri tells the story in *Skáldskaparmál*. Loki had cut the hair off Sif, Thor's wife, and he avoided a beating only by promising to have the dwarfs make for Sif a headpiece that would grow into golden hair. After having the sons of Ívaldi make the headpiece, and also the ship Skídbladnir and Odin's spear, Gungnir, he bets the dwarf Brokk that Brokk's brother Eitri cannot make three equally good objects. Brokk is to work the bellows for Eitri, and Loki changes himself into a fly and pesters Brokk. Eitri makes first a boar with gold bristles, then the ring Draupnir, finally Mjöllnir, Thor's hammer. The hammer's handle is short because Brokk's bellows work was interrupted when the fly bit him between the eyes so that blood flowed.

Eitri is known from no other source.

See also Dwarfs

ELDHRÍMNIR (FIRE-SOOTY)

Cookpot at Valhöll.

The key passage is stanza 18 of *Grímnismál*.

> Andhrímnir in Eldhrímnir
> Has Sæhrímnir boiled.

In *Gylfaginning*, Snorri understands the passage as a cook (Andhrímnir) cooking pork (the pig Sæhrímnir) in a huge pot (Eldhrímnir), and indeed the rest of this stanza seems to call Sæhrímnir the best of pork and refers to the mysterious nourishment of the einherjar. All three of the names are joined by the element *hrímnir*, which is derived from the word for soot on a cookpot. "Fire-sooty" as the cookpot is the most appropriate of the three.

See also Andhrímnir; Sæhrímnir

ELDIR

Servant of Ægir; Loki's first verbal opponent in *Lokasenna*.

The prose header to *Lokasenna* says that people greatly praised Ægir's two servants (who cannot have had much to do, as the beer carried itself into the hall), and out of jealousy Loki killed one of them, Fimafeng. After the gods chased him off to the forest, Loki returned and confronted Eldir. Their exchange makes up the first five stanzas of the poem. Loki asks what the æsir are discussing in the hall (stanza 1) and Eldir replies that they are judging their weapons and prowess. No one, he says, is a friend of Loki's in words (has good things to say to or about Loki) (stanza 2). Loki declares his intention to enter the hall and blend mead with harmful or sinister power (stanza 3). Stanzas 4–5 appear to be Eldir's challenge to Loki, rebuffed:

4. [Eldir:] You know, if you enter Ægir's hall,
   To gaze on that feast,

If slander and calumny you pour into the hall of the æsir,
On you they will dry it.
5. [Loki:]You know, Eldir, if we two alone should
Contend with harmful words,
Rich will I be in answers
If you speak much about it.

This silences Eldir, and Loki enters the hall.

Eldir fits the character type of the outer guardian, often a herdsman as in *Skírnismál*, stanzas 11–16, with whom someone contends before entering a place for the main confrontation.

See also *Lokasenna*

ÉLIVÁGAR (HAILSTORM-WAVES)

Mythic rivers, associated with the proto-giant Aurgelmir/Ymir or with the ends of the world.

The association with the proto-giant is explicit in *Vafthrúdnismál*, stanza 31. Odin has asked Vafthrúdnir whence came Aurgelmir, the oldest being according to stanza 29, among the giants. Vafthrúdnir replies:

> From the Élivágar spurted poison drops,
> Thus it grew, until a giant emerged.

Snorri says that Aurgelmir is the name Ymir bore among the giants and expands considerably on the above stanza, which must have been at least part of his source. Hár is the speaker of this section, and he is responding to this question from Gylfi/Gangleri: "How was it arranged, before clans came into being or mankind was increased?"

> Those rivers which are called the Élivágar, when they had come so far from their source that the fermentation that accompanied them there, hardened like the slag that runs out of fires, as it was freezing, and when the ice stopped and froze solid, and that drizzling rain that arose from the poison, froze into frost, and the frost grew over all Ginnunga gap.

The discussion now turns to Ginnunga gap and Ymir's eventual emergence from it.

Most editors read "fermentation" as "poisonous yeast" to make the passage accord better with *Vafthrúdnismál*, stanza 29. But there is still a substantial difference between the two accounts, a vast gap between the two lines of *Vafthrúd-*

nismál that is filled by the detail leading to Ginnunga gap. In Snorri's account, then, the Élivágar preceded even Ginnunga gap and were the first fixed point in the cosmos, although he never mentions them again.

Hymiskvida gives us good reason to think that the Élivágar were located on the periphery of the mythological world. Toward the beginning of the poem, as the gods ponder how they are to obtain the kettle to brew beer for Ægir's party, Týr gives Thor a "great loving counsel," in stanza 5:

> There dwells east of the Élivágar
> Exceedingly wise Hymir, at the edge of heaven.
> My father, the powerful one, owns a kettle,
> A huge pot, a league deep.

Finally there is the curious set of stanzas found in *Bergbúa tháttr*, a thirteenth-century account of one Thórd and his servant who get lost on his way to church in winter and take shelter for the night in a cave. There they hear the supernatural inhabitant of the cave recite a poem predicting various cataclysmic events. In the seventh (of twelve) stanzas, the poet says that he travels north down into the third netherworld, and there someone fears his arrival at the Élivágar. The poem is sometimes difficult to understand, but here at least the peripheral location of the Élivágar is assured.

There is little useful direct discussion of the Élivágar, but it is clear that they are meant to be far removed in time, space, or both.

See also Aurgelmir; *Bergbúa tháttr*; *Hymiskvida*; Ymir

ELLI (OLD-AGE)
Old woman with whom Thor wrestles when he visits Útgarda-Loki.

Thor is unable to throw Elli, and in the end he loses the match when one of his knees touches down. Only later does Útgarda-Loki explain that Thor's performance was extraordinary, for Old Age could only make him kneel. Elli is found only in Snorri's *Gylfaginning*.

See also Útgarda-Loki

ELVES
Medieval Icelandic *álfar*, sg. *álfr*, mythological beings.

The formula "æsir and elves" is a commonplace in eddic poetry, and as Ragnarök approaches in *Völuspá*, the seeress asks "What's with the æsir? / What's with the elves?" This same line is echoed in *Thrymskvida*. Despite this usage, however, and despite the appearance of the elves in other lists of mythological beings, such as those in *Alvíssmál*, where vocabulary items of the mythological races are cataloged, little concrete is known about them. The only important figure explicitly assigned to the elves is Völund: The eddic poem *Völundarkvida* calls him prince of the álfar (stanzas 13 and 32), and "countryman of the álfar" (stanza 10). But he has no interaction with elves in or outside of the poem, and although he does marry a swan maiden and fly off on wings at the end of the poem, his skill as a smith would suggest association with the dwarfs, as his cognate Wayland the Smith confirms. Nor does Völund have any contact with the gods or giants of the mythology; his story as we have it belongs to heroic poetry, even though the person who arranged the *Poetic Edda* as we have it put it before *Alvíssmál*. There Thor indeed plays a role, but so does a dwarf. In fact, the word *álfr* appears by itself as a dwarf name in lists of such names and is compounded with other nouns to make other dwarf names in medieval Icelandic tradition. Besides Völund, the only other explicitly named elf is Dáin (*Hávamál*, stanza 143), and that too is more frequently found as a dwarf name.

Snorri introduces in *Gylfaginning* a distinction between light-elves and dark-elves. "There is yet that place, which is called Álfheim (Elf-world); there lives that people, which is called the light-elves, but the dark-elves dwell down in the earth, and they are unlike in appearance and much more unlike in experience. The light-elves are fairer than the sun in appearance, but the dark-elves are blacker than pitch." A few lines later, Snorri has Hár tell Gylfi/Ganglerí that there are three heavens, the highest of which the light-elves alone inhabit. Insofar as they live in the earth, the dark-elves would appear to be similar, or more likely identical to, the dwarfs. Twice Snorri says the dwarfs live in Svartálfaheim (World-of-the-black-elves), and whether he intended a distinction between the dark-elves and black-elves is unknown, as in fact is any distinction among the elves outside of Snorri.

The relative lack of information about the elves in the mythology is made more tantalizing by the references retained in medieval Icelandic tradition to the *álfablót*. In recent Scandinavian folklore elves are important as supernatural nature beings in Danish and Icelandic tradition.

See also Æsir; *Álfablót*; Álfheim; Völund

References and further reading: Two readable treatments in English are those of Jón Hnefill Aðalsteinsson, "Folk Narrative and Norse Mythology," *Arv* 46 (1989): 115–122 (reprinted as "Giants and Elves in Mythology and Folktales," in Jón Hnefill Aðalsteinsson, *A Piece of Horse Liver: Myth, Ritual, and Folklore in Old Icelandic Sources*, 129–139 (Reykjavík: Háskólaútgáfan, 1998), and Lotte Motz, "Of Elves and Dwarfs," *Arv* 29–30 (1973–1974): 93–127.

EYRGJAFA

One of nine giant mothers, perhaps of Heimdall, listed in *Hyndluljód,* stanza 37 (part of the "Short *Völuspá*").

> ***See also*** Heimdall; *Hyndluljód*
> ***References and further reading:*** Lotte Motz, "Giantesses and Their Names," *Früh-mittelalterliche Studien* 15 (1981): 495–511.

FALHÓFNIR (PALE-HOOFED)

Horse name found in *Grímnismál,* stanza 30, which lists the horses the æsir ride each day when they go to make judgments at Yggdrasil.

Snorri Sturluson includes Falhófnir in his list of the horses of the æsir in *Gylfaginning* but does not assign the horse to any specific god. Falhófnir is also listed in the thulur for horses.

FÁRBAUTI (ANGER-STRIKER)

Loki's father.

Two tenth-century skalds call Loki son of Fárbauti (using, however, the poetic word *mögr* for "son" rather than the usual *sonr*), so the genealogy is assured. When introducing Loki in *Gylfaginning,* Snorri tells us that Loki is the son of Fárbauti the giant, and there is no reason to doubt the assignment of Fárbauti to the giants, especially given the meaning of his name. Doubtless Loki's ill will toward the æsir had to do with his father's affiliation.

> ***See also*** Laufey; Loki

FENRIR

Wolf; enemy of the gods.

Fenrir is also called Fenrisúlf, that is, the wolf of Fenrir, and this usage has never been satisfactorily explained. He has two roles in the mythology: one as the maimer of Týr early in the mythic present, the other as the killer of Odin at Rag-narök. In between, he lies bound.

Hyndluljód, stanza 40, a part of the "Short *Völuspá*," states that Loki sired the (or a) wolf on Angrboda, and Snorri agrees that Fenrir is the offspring of Loki and this giantess and that their brood also included Jörmungand (the Midgard serpent) and Hel. The wolf's great act in the mythological present is to deprive Týr of his right hand, an event alluded to directly in *Lokasenna,* stanza 38. Loki is upbraiding Týr:

> Shut up, Týr. You never knew how
> To mediate something good between two people

Your right hand, that one will I mention
Which Fenrir tore from you.

"To mediate something good between two people" is the standard translation, but an attractive alternative, given what happens next, would be "to carry
something well with two [hands]."

Snorri tells the myth twice in *Gylfaginning*. On the first occasion, he is
describing Týr and cites the episode as a token of Týr's bravery:

> When the æsir enticed the wolf of Fenrir to permit the fetter to be put on him,
> then he did not believe that they would release him, until they placed the hand
> of Týr as a pledge in his mouth. And when the æsir were unwilling to release
> him, then he bit the hand off, where it is now called the "wolf's joint" [wrist],
> and Týr is one-handed and not called a peacemaker.

A few pages later Snorri tells the full story. When the gods learned that
Loki's evil offspring with Angrboda were being raised in Jötunheimar, they discovered through prophecy that this brood would be trouble for them, and Odin
had them brought to him. He cast the Midgard serpent into the sea and Hel into
the world of the dead. For reasons that are unclear (because Odin had a connection with wolves? Because Loki was Odin's blood brother?), the gods raised the
wolf with them, and only Týr was brave enough to feed it. But when they saw
how quickly it was growing and reconsidered the prophecies, they decided to
bind the wolf. First they brought a great fetter called Lœding, but Fenrir allowed
them to bind him with it and burst it with his first movements. Next the gods
got a stronger fetter, Drómi, and following a thought process that in English is
reflected in the proverb "Nothing ventured, nothing gained," the wolf allowed
them to bind him with that fetter and burst it into bits. For this reason, Snorri
tells us, there are proverbs "to loose oneself from Lœding" and "to break out of
Drómi;" neither, however, has left any other trace. The gods now turned to
magic. Alfödr (Odin) sent Skírnir to the dwarfs to obtain a fetter, Gleipnir (perhaps "Entangler"), made from cat noise and woman beard and mountain roots
and bear sinews and fish breath and bird spittle. On the island Lyngvi (Heathery)
in the lake Ámsvartnir (Red-black), they invited the wolf to let himself be bound
again. Needless to say, the wolf was suspicious. What renown could there be in
bursting this fetter, which looked like a silken band? Fenrir stipulated that
someone had to place a hand in his mouth.

> And each of the æsir looked at another and thought that now their troubles had
> doubled, but none would put forth his hand, until Týr stretched forth his right
> hand and put it into the mouth of the wolf. And when the wolf moved, then the

fetter hardened, and the more he struggled, the sharper it became. Then all the gods laughed except Týr; he lost his hand.

Lokasenna, stanzas 37–40, comprise an exchange between Týr and Loki. Loki boasts that Fenrir tore off Týr's arm; Týr responds that although he may be missing his hand, Loki is missing Hródrsvitnir, that is, the famous wolf, Fenrir. *Málsháttakvædi*, a poem of the twelfth or thirteenth century and usually thought to have been composed in the Orkneys, is the only poem to refer to the binding of Fenrir. It has been argued that Týr and Fenrir appear on the eighth-century Alskog Tjängvide picture stone from Gotland.

Vafthrúdnismál gives information about the wolf's further career. Toward the end of the poem Odin is asking about the aftermath of Ragnarök, and he poses this question to Vafthrúdnir:

Whence will come the sun into the smooth heaven,
After Fenrir has destroyed it?

In describing the sun and moon, Snorri says in *Gylfaginning* that the sun is ultimately to be swallowed by a wolf called Sköll. When he comes to Ragnarök, Snorri says simply that a wolf swallows the sun, and another the moon, and it is apparent that he regards neither of these as identical to Fenrir, for only after describing the swallowing of the sun and moon and a devastating earthquake does he report that Fenrir has gotten loose. But Fenrir's subsequent action echoes the swallowing of the heavenly bodies, for he "goes about with a gaping mouth, and the lower jaw is on the earth and the upper against the sky—he would gape wider if there were room—fires burn from his eyes and nostrils."

In the series of duels that make up the gods' last stand against the forces of chaos, Odin fights with and is killed by Fenrir. *Völuspá*, stanza 53, reads:

Then the second sorrow of Hlín [Frigg] occurs,
When Odin goes to fight with the wolf.

Völuspá gives no details on Odin's death, only on the subsequent vengeance:

Then comes the great son of Sigfather [Odin];
Vídar, to fight with the beast of battle;
For the son of Hvedrung, he makes stand with his hand
A sword in the heart; thus the father is avenged.

Hvedrung is surely Loki, since *Ynglinga tal*, stanza 32, refers to Hel as Hvedrung's daughter. It is also to be found among the thulur as a word for giant, and, confusingly, as an Odin name.

Vafthrúdnismál, stanza 53, also tells of Odin's death in the jaws of the wolf of Vídar's vengeance. Odin has just asked Vafthrúdnir about Odin's fate.

> The wolf will swallow Aldafödr [Odin]
> Vídar will avenge this;
> The malevolent jaws he will cleave
> At the death of the wolf.

Snorri agrees that Fenrir swallows Odin and goes on to describe the vengeance thus:

> Immediately thereafter Vídar will come forth and put one foot on the lower jaw of the wolf. . . . With one hand he will take hold of the upper jaw of the wolf and tear apart his gullet, and that will be the death of the wolf.

Like his father Loki and his brother the Midgard serpent, then, Fenrir is a creature who spends time among the gods, is bound or cast out by them, and returns at the end of the current mythic order to destroy them, only to be destroyed himself as a younger generation of gods, one of them his slayer, survives into the new world order.

See also Hel; Midgard Serpent; Vídar

References and further reading: The alternative translation of *Lokasenna*, stanza 38, is discussed by Alfred Jakobsen, *"Bera tilt með tveim:* Til tolkning av Lokasenna 38," *Maal og minne*, 1979: 34–39, reprinted in his *Studier i norrøn filologi* ([Trondheim:] Tapir, 1979), 43–48. On the Alskog Tjängvide picture stone from Gotland, see Karl Helm, "Zu den gotländischen Bildsteinen," *Beiträge zur deutschen Geschichte und Literatur* 62 (1938): 357–361.

FENSALIR (BOG-HALLS)

The abode of Frigg.

The assignment of Fensalir to Frigg is based on a poignant stanza in *Völuspá*, stanza 33 (not found in the late *Hauksbók* version of the poem). The poet is telling us that vengeance will be taken for Baldr's killing, "and yet Frigg weeps over Valhöll's woe at Fensalir." Cruelly, Snorri says in *Gylfaginning* that it was at Fensalir that Loki wheedled the information from Frigg about Baldr's vulnerability to mistletoe; earlier he had said that Frigg lives at Fensalir, "and it is most esteemed." In *Skáldskaparmál* he says that Frigg may be called "Ruler of Fensalir." I have no idea why Frigg should live in a boggy place, despite the old argument that there is an association with a cult situated at a spring.

See also Frigg

References and further reading: The notion of a spring cult was advanced by A. Edzardi, "Fensalir und Vegtamskviq 12, 5ff," *Germania* 27 (1882): 330–339.

FIMAFENG

Servant of Ægir, killed by Loki according to the prose header to *Lokasenna* and Snorri in *Skáldskaparmál.*

According to the prose header to *Lokasenna,* Loki could not bear to hear people praise Fimafeng and Ægir's other servant, Eldir, and so he killed Fimafeng. For this outrage he was driven off into the forest. Immediate vengeance was impossible, since the site of the feast was a "great place of sanctuary." Fimafeng might mean something like "hurrying service."

See also Eldir; *Lokasenna*

FIMBUL-

Adjective meaning "mighty," found only in mythological contexts.

Völuspá, stanza 60, refers to the ancient runes of Fimbultýr (Mighty-god), who must be Odin. Stanzas 80 and 142 of *Hávamál* refer to a *fimbulthulr,* "mighty sage or poet," who again is Odin. *Grímnismál,* stanza 27, has a list of mythological rivers, including Fimbulthul (Mighty-roar?). The most important of the *fimbul-* words is Fimbulvetr (Mighty-winter), which is to occur at the onset of Ragnarök.

Finally there is Fimbulfambi, mentioned at the end of *Hávamál,* stanza 103:

He is called Fimbulfambi, who can say little,
That is the nature of an unwise man.

I call this a mythological context, despite the sententious nature of the lines, because they stand between the Billing's girl and Gunnlöd episodes in the poem. In the first Odin fails to get a woman; in the second he succeeds. Odin is a master of seduction and of words, and everyone else is a fimbul-fool.

See also Billing's Girl; Gunnlöd; *Hávamál*

FJALAR (DECEIVER)

One of the most-used names in the mythology, presumably because of all the deception that goes on.

Völuspá appears to have two beings called Fjalar, the first occurring in the catalog of dwarfs, the second, in stanza 42, a beautiful red rooster that crowed near the happy harping herdsman Eggthér at the onset of Ragnarök. In *Hávamál*, stanza 14, Fjalar the Learned is a host whose beer the speaker (Odin?) got drunk on. In *Hárbardsljód*, stanza 26, Odin is chiding Thor about the latter's misadventures with the giant Skrýmir on the journey to Útgarda-Loki and says that Thor did not dare sneeze or fart, lest Fjalar—presumably Skrýmir—were to hear it. The most important Fjalar is one of the two dwarfs who killed Kvasir and made the mead of poetry from his blood, according to Snorri in *Skáldskaparmál*.

If we take *Hávamál*, stanza 14, as a reference to Odin's consumption of the mead of poetry, we are left with Fjalar the dwarf, Fjalar the rooster, and Fjalar as Skrýmir. In the last case it is tempting to think of the name simply as a noun, "deceiver," to refer to the shape-changing Skrýmir.

See also Mead of Poetry; Ragnarök; Útgarda-Loki

References and further reading: Peter H. Salus and Paul Beekman Tayler, "Eikinskjaldi, Fjalar, and Eggthér," *Neophilologus* 53 (1969): 76–81.

FJÖLNIR

Odin name; son of Frey in the Learned Prehistory (a medieval historical theory holding that Scandinavians had emigrated from Troy).

In *Grímnismál* Odin announces a long series of his names (stanzas 46–50) that constitute the beginning of his epiphany before Geirröd. Fjölnir appears among them in stanza 47. In *Reginsmál* a man standing on a mountain, clearly Odin, uses the name to refer to himself; the stanza is quoted in *Völsunga saga*. In Snorri's *Gylfaginning* Fjölnir is among the 12 names given for Alfödr and is listed again when Snorri quotes from *Grímnismál*. It is also common in skaldic poetry.

The other Fjölnir, or tradition about Fjölnir, is captured most fully in Snorri's *Ynglinga saga*. There Fjölnir is the son of Frey, king and deity of the Swedes in Uppsala. During Fjölnir's reign the Peace of Fródi, which had started during Frey's reign, continues, "at Lejre," that is, in Denmark, according to Snorri. Fjölnir visits Fródi, and a huge vat of beer is brewed up in the basement with the floors open above it. That night, sleepy and dead drunk, Fjölnir wanders out from his bedchamber to relieve himself and falls into the vat, where he perishes. The first stanza from Thjódólf's *Ynglinga tal* was probably Snorri's source, and he cites it here, but it just says that Fjölnir died visiting Fródi.

The etymology of the name is disputed. When Odin bears it, something like "all-knowing" seems appropriate, but many other possibilities have been advanced for the prehistoric Swedish king.

See also Frey

FJÖLVAR

Being, perhaps a giant, with whom Odin spent some time, according the *Hárbards-ljód*, stanza 17:

> I was with Fjölvar all of five winters,
> In that island, which is called Algrœn [All-green];
> We could fight and fell carrion,
> To test much, to try our luck with a maiden.

Since a female Fjölvör is listed among the thulur for giantesses, it seems likely that Fjölvar would be her male counterpart, and therefore also a giant. In *Hárbardsljód*, stanza 18, Odin says that he alone slept with seven sisters on Algrœn. The incident is otherwise unknown, but it would appear to fit the pattern of Odinic seductions in Giantland, known, for example, from the story of his seduction of Gunnlöd. Algrœn is also found only in this passage.

See also Gunnlöd; *Hárbardsljód*; Odin

FJÖRGYN

An alternative name for Jörd (Earth) when feminine; the father of Frigg when masculine (a distinction lost in the system used in this book for medieval Icelandic names). Fjörgyn as Jörd is found in *Völuspá*, stanza 56, in the kenning "Fjörgyn's son" for Thor, and even more clearly in *Hárbardsljód*, stanza 56. Odin as Hárbard has finally refused to ferry Thor over the sound. The stanza ends this way:

> So keep to the left on the road, until you find Verland;
> There Fjörgyn will find Thor, her son,
> And she will teach him the ways of kinsmen to Odin's lands.

A few skalds used Fjörgyn (or a noun *fjörgyn*) for "earth" or "land" in their verse.

Fjörgyn (masc.) as the father of Frigg is known from Snorri's *Edda*, where it is found in both *Gylfaginning* and *Skáldskaparmál*. *Lokasenna*, stanza 26, appears to give the same information. Loki is responding to Frigg:

> Shut up, Frigg! You are Fjörgyn's daughter
> and have ever been most eager for men,
> when Vé and Vili you allowed, wife of Vidrir,
> To embrace you.

There is a small measure of ambiguity here, since the word I have rendered "daughter" is used in the kenning "Ód's maiden" for Freyja, who is the wife of

Óð. But if we accept Snorri, who says in both *Gylfaginning* and *Skáldskaparmál* that Frigg is Fjörgyn's daughter, we must assume that the information about Fjörgyn is purely genealogical and has nothing to do with the charge of sexual insatiability that follows.

> *See also* Jörð
>
> *References and further reading:* Those who can read Dutch may wish to read Jan de Vries, "Studien over germaansche mythologie, I: Fjorgyn en Fjorgynn," *Tijdschrift voor nederlandsche taal- en letterkunde* 50 (1931): 1–25, which finds that the masculine form of the name is late and that the name originally meant something like "life" or "vital power."

FÓLKVANG (PEOPLE-FIELD OR ARMY-FIELD)

Freyja's abode.

Odin's vision of the dwelling places of the gods in *Grímnismál* includes Fólkvang, in stanza 14:

> Fólkvang is the ninth, and there Freyja rules
> The choice of seats in the hall.
> Half the dead she chooses each day,
> And Odin has half.

According to Snorri's *Gylfaginning*, the hall itself at Fólkvang is called Sessrúmnir (Seat-roomy), but this information is not found elsewhere.

If we understand *Fólk-* as "army," Fólkvang begins to look like some kind of alternative to Valhöll, where the einherjar dwell until Ragnarök. Freyja too has an association with warriors who, like the einherjar, fight each day and feast each night, in that she presides over the Hjaðningavíg (an eternal combat of warriors). In that case, however, the end comes not with Ragnarök but with the intervention of a Christian.

> *See also* Freyja; Hjaðningavíg

FORNJÓT

Progenitor of the elements, according to Norwegian tradition.

This tradition is located in *Fundinn Noregr* (Norway Found), as the beginning of *Orkneyinga saga* (The Saga of the Orkney Islanders) is sometimes called, and in a section of *Flateyjarbók* called *Hversu Noregr byggðisk* (How Norway Was Settled). According to them Fornjót was a king who ruled Gotland or Jutland, "which is called Finnland [i.e., the land of the Sámi or Lapps] and Kvenland [the Finnish-settled part of northern Norway]." Some editors alter "Gotland" or "Jutland" to "that land." Fornjót had three sons: Hlér ("whom we call Ægir," according to

Fundinn Noregr), Logi, and Kári. *Ægir* and *hlér* are nouns meaning "sea." The noun *logi* means "fire," and *kári* is listed among the thulur for "wind." Kári, according to *Fundinn Noregr,* was the father of Frosti (Frost), the father of Snær (Snow) the Old. From there the genealogy goes into some of the month names of the old Scandinavian system. *Hversu Noregr byggdisk* has a somewhat more elaborate genealogy: Kári's son is Jökull (Glacier); his son, Snær (Snow); his children, Thorri (the name of the fourth month of winter), Fönn (Heap-of-snow), Drífa (Snowdrift), and Mjöll (Fresh-powdery-snow). The last three nouns are feminine, and we are presumably to understand these children as daughters, but Thorri is a masculine noun, and Thorri is a king. He had three children, sons Nór and Gór and a daughter Gói. She vanished, and when Thorri held the sacrifice a month later than usual, they named the month after her (Gói followed Thorri in the old Scandinavian calendar).

Fornjót is found only twice in older poetry. In *Ynglinga tal,* stanza 29, Thjódólf of Hvin seems to use the kenning "son of Fornjót" to mean fire, and a poet known only as Svein apparently uses the kenning "ugly sons of Fornjót" for wind (Snorri quotes the line in *Skáldskaparmál* as an example of this kenning). Fornjót is included among the thulur for giants.

The meaning of the name is unclear. It can be analyzed as Forn-jótr (Ancient-Jutlander, or possibly Giant), or For-njótr (Early-user or Early-destroyer), Forn-njótr (One-who-enjoys-sacrifices), or even perhaps Forn-þjótr (Ancient-screamer).

See also Ægir

References and further reading: Margaret Clunies Ross, "Snorri Sturluson's Use of the Norse Origin Legend of the Sons of Fornjót in his *Edda,*" *Arkiv för nordisk filologi* 98 (1983): 47–66, analyzes Snorri's understanding of natural forces as giants.

FORSETI (CHAIRMAN)

Baldr and Nanna's son.

In poetry Forseti is found only in *Grímnismál,* stanza 15, in Odin's vision enumerating the abodes of the gods.

> Glitnir is the tenth. It is studded with gold
> And thatched with silver as well.
> And there Forseti dwells most of the day
> And settles all lawsuits.

Snorri includes Forseti in the catalog of æsir in *Gylfaginning:*

> Forseti is the son of Baldr and Nanna Nepsdóttir. He has that hall in heaven, which is called Glitnir, and all who come to him in legal difficulties go away reconciled. That is the best place of judgment of gods and men.

Except for his presence at Ægir's banquet in the beginning of *Skáldskap-armál* and in the list of Baldr kennings (in "Forseti's father"), Forseti is otherwise unknown in the mythology. Since the nineteenth century some scholars have wished to associate him with Fosite, a god after whom a Frisian island is supposed to be named, according to Alcuin's *Life of St. Willebrord* from the end of the ninth century. The original Germanic form would be closer to the Frisian and would have been converted by the Scandinavians into the common noun *forseti* (which is still in use today as the title of the president of Iceland).

See also Baldr; Glitnir

References and further reading: The implications of the hypothetical connection between Fosite and Forseti (doubted by Theodor Siebs, "Der Gott Fos[e]te und sein Land," *Beiträge zur Geschichte der deutschen Sprache und Literatur* 35 [1909]: 535–553) are investigated by Stephen Schwartz, *Poetry and Law in Germanic Myth,* University of California Publications, Folklore Studies, 27 (Berkeley and Los Angeles: University of California Press, 1973).

FREKI (RAVENOUS-ONE)
One of Odin's wolves.

Grímnismál, stanza 19, part of Odin's vision of the abodes of the gods, mentions Freki:

Geri and Freki the one accustomed to battle feeds,
Glorious Herjafödr [Odin];
And on wine alone the weapon-noble
Odin ever lives.

Snorri quotes this stanza in *Gylfaginning* and puts the two halves together, saying that Odin gives his own food to the wolves, as he lives on wine alone.

The name is simply the definite form of an adjective, and it is more than a little ironic that the same adjective is used in *Völuspá* in a repeated stanza (44, 49, 58) about Ragnarök:

Garm howls much before Gnipahellir.
Fetters will burst, and the ravenous one *[freki]* run free.

Thus Odin feeds one ravenous one at his side in Valhöll and another—with his body—at Ragnarök.

See also Geri; Odin

FREY

Important god, member of the vanir.

Frey is the son of Njörd, either by his sister when he lived among the vanir or by Skadi. When Snorri says in *Gylfaginning* that Njörd had two children, apparently by Skadi, he first introduces Frey and Freyja, saying that they were both good-looking and powerful:

> Frey is the most noble of the æsir. He rules over rain and sunshine and with that the growth of the earth, and it is good to call on him for prosperity and peace. He also rules over the wealth of men.

This is practically a textbook description of a fertility god. In the warlike culture of the æsir, there is little for him to do, and the mythology only grants him three moments: his entry into the æsir, his marriage, and his death.

Frey joined the æsir as a result of the Æsir-Vanir War, according to Snorri in *Ynglinga saga*. When a settlement was reached, the two groups "exchanged hostages [here understood as

Small figure from Rällinge, Sweden, possibly Frey, and if so probably used as an amulet. (Statens Historika Museum, Stockholm)

men exchanged as pledges of good faith]. The vanir sent their most distinguished men, Njörd and Frey, and the æsir in exchange sent Hœnir, whom they declared to be a great leader, and Mímir, who was very wise." Although Hœnir could make no decision without Mímir, whom the vanir finally decapitated, Njörd and Frey were a success, and the æsir made them into leaders of cult.

Frey's courtship of Gerd is the one full narrative about him in the mythology, although in fact he acts rather passively in it. The story is the subject of the eddic poem *Skírnismál* and is paraphrased in much shorter form by Snorri in *Gylfaginning*. To follow the story in *Skírnismál*: Frey had seated himself in Hlidskjálf, Odin's high seat, with its view into all the worlds. Looking into Jötunheimar, he saw a beautiful maiden and immediately fell lovesick. Skírnir, Frey's servant, is asked to look into the matter. Frey explains that the gleaming arms of a maiden at Gymir's farmstead have captivated him:

7. The maiden is more dear to me than to any young
Man, in days of yore;
No one wishes, of the æsir and elves,
That the two of us come together.

Given Frey's horse and sword, Skírnir sets out to woo the girl on his master's behalf. At Gymir's homestead he is challenged first by a shepherd, then by the girl herself, Gerd. Invited in (though she fears, Gerd says, that he may be the slayer of her brother), Skírnir begins his blandishments. Gerd refuses first golden apples and then the ring Draupnir, saying she has no need of gold. Skírnir now turns to threats: He will kill her and her father; he will tame her through magic. He turns to curses: She will be a laughingstock, forced to live among the giants, with a three-headed giant or with no man at all. The æsir are angry at her. She is forbidden joy of men, will live with a giant beneath the Corpse-gate (Nágrind, one of the gates to Hel's realm), be offered goat urine. Finally Skírnir goes into some kind of runic threat, and Gerd capitulates. The wedding will be in nine nights, at a place called Barri. Skírnir returns home and tells the news to Frey, who does not rejoice; he laments:

42. A night is long, longer are two,
How will I endure three?
Oft to me a month seemed shorter
Than this half honeymoon.

For most of the twentieth century Magnus Olsen's nature mythological interpretation of this myth held sway: Skírnir is the sun's ray, sent down from heaven to retrieve Gerd ("earth") from the underworld; the tryst will be at Barri ("in the seed"). Most serious scholars of Norse mythology today would point out that the etymologies required to support this reading are questionable and would not have been at all apparent to a medieval audience. The myth can instead be read as part of the ongoing struggle between the æsir and jötnar, in which the æsir nearly always succeed in obtaining valuables, often women, from the world of the giants. The flow of such wealth is nearly always in one direction only. Furthermore, as Margaret Clunies Ross showed, this and the Njörd-Skadi myth serve to place the vanir hierarchically below the rest of the æsir: The æsir can take wives from among the *ásynjur*, but the vanir must turn to the giants, where the other gods find concubines but not wives.

At Ragnarök Frey will fight Surt (*Völuspá*, stanza 53). In *Gylfaginning* Snorri carries Frey's giving of his sword to Skírnir over to this scene, where, he says, Frey will be swordless and will therefore perish. This is not, according to Snorri, the first time Frey has fought without a sword; at the end of his presentation of

Large grave mounds at Gamla Uppsala, Sweden. According to Snorri's Ynglinga saga, *the historical Frey was buried in such a mound. (Courtesy of Roger Buton)*

the Gerd myth, Snorri says that Frey fought the giant Beli without his sword and killed him with the antler of a hart.

According to *Grímnismál*, stanza 5, the gods gave Álfheim to Frey as a gift in days of yore when he cut his first tooth, and this was therefore presumably Frey's dwelling place. Snorri, on the other hand, assigns Álfheim to the so-called light-elves. Frey has two precious objects, the ship Skídbladnir (although Snorri in *Ynglinga saga* assigns this ship to Odin) and the boar Gullinborsti (Gold-bristle) or Slídrugtanni. Both these objects were made by the dwarfs Ívaldi and Brokk, according to Snorri's *Skáldskaparmál* (*Grímnismál*, stanza 43, mentions only the ship). In his account of Baldr's funeral, Úlf Uggason says that Frey arrived riding a boar with golden bristles, and Snorri understood this to be Gullinborsti and added that it was pulling the cart in which Frey rode.

Lokasenna assigns two servants to Frey, Byggvir and Beyla, whom scholars interpret through etymology as associated with barley and either cows, beans, or bees; all of these can be made to fit with the notion of a fertility god. Loki's insult to Frey in the poem is a reminder of the sword given up for Gerd and the problem that its loss will pose at Ragnarök.

In Snorri's version of the Learned Prehistory in chapter 10 of *Ynglinga saga*, Frey is one of the important early kings of Sweden. He succeeds his father Njörd, who succeeded Odin. He was popular and prosperous like his father. Frey erected a large temple at Uppsala and established his principal residence there, gave it all that was owed him, lands, and money. Then began the wealth of Uppsala, and it has lasted ever since.

> In his days the Peace of Fródi began. At that time there was also prosperity throughout all lands. The Swedes attributed that to Frey. The more wealthy the people became through peace and prosperity, the more he was worshipped than the other gods.

The passage goes on to say that Frey married Gerd the daughter of Gymir, that their son was Fjölnir (in the *Eddas* this is an Odin name), that Frey's other name was Yngvi, and that for this reason his descendants are called the Ynglingar.

Snorri next tells a curious story about Frey's death. After Frey dies, his men place the corpse in a mound but do not reveal his death. Freyja takes over the sacrifices, and Frey's men maintain the body for three years. When the Swedes finally learn of Frey's death, they believe that their peace and prosperity is dependent on his body being present in Sweden and do not wish to have him cremated. They declare him to be the *veraldar* god ("world god") and forever after sacrifice to him for peace and prosperity.

This story bears a close similarity to that of the concealed death of King Frotho (Fródi) III in Book 5 of Saxo's *Gesta Danorum*, which also lasts for three years. And Fródi is also famously associated with peace and prosperity. Clearly the two figures played out the same mythic pattern, and many scholars think they may once have been the same figure.

According to Book 1 of Saxo's *Gesta Danorum*, the prehistoric Danish king Hadingus carried out a sacrifice to Frey and established an annual sacrifice to Frø (Frey), which the Swedes call Frøblot.

The tale *Ögmundar tháttr dytts* gives information on what a high medieval Icelandic audience thought about the worship of Frey in Uppsala. Ögmund, an Icelander, has fled the court of Olaf Tryggvason in Norway because he is falsely suspected of the murder of one of the king's men. Coming to Sweden, he meets and befriends a priestess of Frey. The god is a statue, inhabited by a demon and pulled about on a cart. Ögmund wrestles away the demon through the divine intervention of King Olaf and thereafter impersonates Frey. The Swedes are delighted that their god deigns to eat and drink with them and are impressed when his priestess becomes pregnant. Unlike before, Frey is now willing to be propitiated with gold and fine clothing. Times are good until King Olaf arrives to bring Ögmund back to Norway. Ögmund marries Frey's priestess and both are baptized.

Place-names showing worship of Frey are especially popular in eastern Sweden. Writing around the year 1070, Adam of Bremen, in his history of the archbishopric of Hamburg-Bremen, described the pagan temple at Uppsala. In it were statues of three gods, one of them, Fricco, who clearly reflects Frey, equipped with an enormous phallus. A small figurine found in Rällinge, Sweden, has a similar feature and has been interpreted as Frey and associated with a statement in *Vatnsdœla saga* to the effect that a worshiper of Frey carried a figurine of the god. Other Sagas of Icelanders mention people who were priests *(goðar)* of Frey. The most famous of them, Hrafnkel, the title character of *Hrafnkels saga*, owned a horse he kept sacred to Frey. The extent to which these materials represent worship of Frey is not clear, but Frey was certainly known as an important deity.

> **See also** Æsir-Vanir War; Álfheim; Aurboda; Beyla; Byggvir; Fjölnir; Freyja; Fródi; Hadingus; Ingunar-Frey; *Ögmundar tháttr dytts*; Slídrugtanni; Yngvi
>
> **References and further reading:** Magnus Olsen's reading of the myth behind *Skírnismál* is in "Fra gammelnorsk myte og kultus," *Maal og minne*, 1909: 17–36. Margaret Clunies Ross's reading of the mythology, including the hierarchical role of vanir-giant marriages, is in *Prolonged Echoes: Old Norse Myths in Medieval Icelandic Society*, vol. 1: *The Myths* (Odense: Odense University Press, 1994). The first serious objection to Olsen's seasonal hypothesis was by Jöran Sahlgren, *Eddica et Scaldica: Fornvästnordiska studier 1–2*, Nordisk filologi, undersökningar och handlingar, 1 (Lund: C. W. K. Gleerup, 1927–1928), who on pages 209–303 argued that there are parallels with folk tale and saga. More recently, Lars Lönnroth interpreted the myth sociologically in "Skírnismál och den fornisländska äktenskapsnormen," in *Opuscula Septentrionalia: Festskrift til Ole Widding, 10.10.1977*, ed. Bent Chr. Jacobsen et al. (Copenhagen: C. A. Reitzel, 1977), 154–178; Lotte Motz attempted a reading more in the heroic realm, in "Gerðr: A New Interpretation of the Lay of Skírnir," *Maal og minne*, 1981: 121–136; and Stephen A. Mitchell tried a structural analysis in "For Scírnis as Mythological Model: Frið at kaupa," *Arkiv för nordisk filologi* 98 (1983): 109–122. The implications of a presumed sacral marriage, however, animate the literary analysis of Ursula Dronke, "Art

and Tradition in *Skírnismál*," in *English and Medieval Studies, Presented to J. R. R. Tolkien on the Occasion of His Seventieth Birthday*, ed. Norman Davis and C. L. Wrenn (London: Allen and Unwen, 1962), 250–268, and the comparative analysis of Annelise Talbot, "The Withdrawal of the Fertility God," *Folklore* 93 (1982): 31–46. The detailed analysis of Gro Steinsland, *Det hellige bryllup og norrøn kongeideologi: En analyse av hierogami-myten i Skírnismál, Ynglingatal, Háleygjatal, og Hyndluljód* (N.p.: Solum, 1991), the most recent serious study of the myth as a whole, again departs from the notion of a sacred marriage, but Steinsland associates it both with fertility and with kingship. On Skírnir's curse, see Joseph Harris, "Cursing with the Thistle: *Skírnismál* 31, 6–8, and OE Metrical Charm 9, 16–17," *Neuphilologische Mitteilungen* 76 (1975): 26–33. On Frey and animals, see Helge Rosén, "Freykult och djurkult," *Fornvännen* 8 (1913): 213–244.

FREYJA (LADY)

Important goddess; only named female of the vanir; object of giants' lust.

Freyja is the daughter of Njörd, either by his sister when he lived among the vanir or by Skadi. When Snorri says in *Gylfaginning* that Njörd had two children, apparently by Skadi, he first introduces Frey and Freyja, saying that they were both good-looking and powerful.

> And Freyja is the most excellent of the goddesses. She has that homestead in heaven which is called Fólkvang, and wherever she rides to battle she has half the dead, and Odin half. . . . Her hall is Sessrúmnir; it is great and handsome. And when she travels, she drives her cats and sits in a carriage. She is the most accessible for people to call on, and from her name it is a sign of respect that women of substance are called *frúvur* [ladies]. She enjoys erotic poetry. It is good to call on her for love.

In the first half of this passage, Snorri was paraphrasing *Grímnismál*, stanza 14, which he had just quoted. Then, a few pages later, seemingly contradicting his statement that Freyja was the most excellent of the *ásynjur*, Snorri listed her only sixth in the catalog of *ásynjur*, although he did say that she is equal in nobility to Frigg.

> She is married to Ód, and their daughter is Hnoss. . . . Ód went away on long journeys, and Freyja weeps for him, and her tears are red gold. Freyja has many names, and the reason for that is that she called herself by various names when she went about among unknown peoples looking for Ód. She is called Mardöll and Hörn, Gefn, Sýr. Freyja owned the Brísinga men.

Ód's journeys are not mentioned in the older poetry, although "Ód's bedfriend" is a Freyja kenning in skaldic poetry, and Freyja's journeys in search of him are completely undocumented. Her ownership of the Brísinga men is alluded to in *Thrymskvida* and perhaps explained in *Sörla tháttr*. *Thrymskvida* also mentions a feather coat that Freyja lends to Loki, giving him the gift of flight. Loki borrows the same item from Freyja in the story of his retrieval of Idun from Thjazi in *Skáldskaparmál*.

In the extant mythology Freyja exists primarily as an object of lust for male giants. Thrym will only return Thor's stolen hammer if he gets Freyja in return; the giant who is to build the wall around Ásgard demands Freyja, the sun, and the moon as his wages; and Hrungnir boasts drunkenly in Ásgard that he will kill all the æsir except Freyja and Sif, whom he will carry off. Freyja's reputation, meanwhile, is somewhat questionable. When asked to go off as Thrym's bride so that Thor can get his hammer back, she protests that everyone will know her to be most eager for men if she does so. In *Lokasenna* Loki tells her that she has been lover of all the assembled æsir and elves; she even was caught in flagrante delicto with her brother, and then, Loki says, "you had to fart"—an insult or joke whose exact tenor escapes us today. Of course, Loki accuses all the goddesses of sexual indiscretion, but *Sörla tháttr* says flat out that Freyja plies the oldest profession, for she gives herself to four dwarfs in order to obtain a beautiful necklace, perhaps the Brísinga men. In *Hyndluljód* Hyndla accuses Freyja of being the lover of Óttar, the human whose genealogy the poem explores.

This sexual history, and her fondness for erotic poetry, make plausible Snorri's assertion that it is to Freyja whom one must turn in affairs of the heart. Presumably this attachment to human love accords with the notion of the vanir as fertility deities. We might reasonably expect a fertility deity to be associated with the dead, but in this mythology, at least, the evidence all goes in the other direction. Odin, the god of wisdom and magic, has the closest association with the dead, and the other vanir, Njörd and Frey, have no such connection. Indeed, the word Snorri used for the dead whom Freyja shares equally with Odin refers to those who die in battle. This association with the battle-dead may also underlie Freyja's connection with the eternal battle of the Hjadningavíg, which has obvious parallels to the endless battles of the einherjar.

Freyja is also connected with magic, especially the kind of shamanic magic called seid. In *Ynglinga saga* Snorri says that Freyja first taught seid among the æsir, and many scholars surmise that Freyja is identical with the figure Gullveig in *Völuspá*, whom the æsir cannot kill and who apparently under the name Heid performs seid. Seid, like the dead, is something that Freyja and Odin share. It may thus be pertinent to recall here Odin's sexual promiscuity and his many names. Finally, the names Ód (Óðr) and Odin (Óðinn) look like a doublet, parallel to Ull and Ullin, and Saxo has a story in Book 1 of *Gesta Danorum* about a long absence of Odin from his realm, which some scholars think is parallel to Ód's absences.

We know that Freyja was a potent force in the last years of paganism, in Iceland at least, because of a famous incident recounted in connection with the conversion. Hjalti Skeggjason, one of the supporters of the conversion, was outlawed for blasphemy at the althingi because of a little ditty he recited calling Freyja a bitch (i.e., a female dog; it has been suggested that he wished to suggest that she was a whore). She also appeared frequently as a base word in woman kennings of the early skalds, and many place-names indicate a worship of her.

> **See also** Æsir-Vanir War; Frey; Gullveig; Njörd; Odin; Seid; Vanir
>
> **References and further reading:** Treatments of Hjalti Skeggjason's blasphemous verse include Felix Genzmer, "Der Spottvers des Hjalti Skeggjason," *Arkiv för nordisk filologi* 44 (1928): 311–314, and Klaus von See, "Der Spottvers des Hjalti Skeggjason," *Zeitschrift für deutsches Altertum* 97 (1968): 155–158 (reprinted in von See, *Edda, saga, Skaldendichtung* [Heidelberg: C. Winter, 1981], 380–383). Jan de Vries, "Studien over germaansche mythologie, VII: De skaldenkenningen met de namen der godinnen Freyja en Frigg," *Tijdschrift voor nederlandsche taal- en letterkunde* 53 (1934): 210–217, is a comprehensive study of the kennings for Freyja and Frigg.

FRIGG

Goddess, wife of Odin and mother of Baldr.

In *Gylfaginning* Snorri cites Frigg as foremost among the goddesses, as would be appropriate for the consort of Odin. Indeed, in the mythology as we have it she mostly functions as wife and mother. She warns Odin not to contest in wisdom with Vafthrúdnir, the wisest giant, but wishes him well when he perseveres (*Vafthrúdnismál*, stanzas 1–4), and sorrows upon his death at Ragnarök (*Völuspá*, stanza 53). In the prose header to *Grímnismál* she quarrels with Odin over the fate of their protégés. In Snorri's version of the Baldr story she first extracts an oath from all things not to harm Baldr, and when that fails, as the result of her own interaction with the disguised Loki, she dispatches Hermód to Hel to try to retrieve him. According to *Völuspá*, stanza 33, she weeps at Fensalir after Baldr's death, and Snorri says that Fensalir is her dwelling. And in the Second Merseburg Charm, from the tenth century or earlier, Frija, the Old High German equivalent to Frigg, participates in the curing of Baldere's (Baldr's) horse; Odin is also present.

However, there is tantalizing information of a far different nature. According to Snorri in *Ynglinga saga*, once when Odin had been away on a journey for a particularly long time, Odin's brothers, Vili and Vé, divided his inheritance and both possessed Frigg, but Odin later returned and took her back. Saxo Grammaticus tells a somewhat similar story in Book 1 of the *Gesta Danorum*. In order to adorn herself with gold, Frigga despoils a statue of Othinus and then gives herself to a servant in order to enlist his aid in taking down the statue. In shame, Othinus goes into self-imposed exile, and during his exile a sorcerer called Mithothyn takes his place and institutes a change in cult procedures. Upon Othinus's return Mithothyn flees to Fyn and is killed by the inhabitants there.

Loki knew a version of this story and was not above reminding Frigg about it. In *Lokasenna*, stanza 26, when Frigg tries to silence Loki, he rebukes her.

> Shut up, Frigg! You are Fjörgyn's daughter
> and have ever been most eager for men,
> when Vé and Vili you allowed, wife of Vidrir [Odin],
> to embrace you.

Frigg does not dispute the charge, but in response she says that if she had a son like Baldr on the scene, Loki would not get out alive. This gives Loki a chance to claim responsibility for the death of Baldr (stanzas 27–28). At this point Freyja intervenes, warning Loki that Frigg knows the fates of all people, although she chooses not to disclose them (stanza 29, also quoted by Snorri in *Gylfaginning*).

It is not easy to make sense of this material. To be called "Fjörgyn's daughter" (Snorri has the same information, but the name is otherwise unattested) is hardly an insult. Fjörgyn, in the feminine form of the name (a distinction lost in the system used in this book for medieval Icelandic names), is Thor's mother. The taking of Odin's inheritance by Vili and Vé in Odin's absence in *Ynglinga saga* might indicate the absence of a legitimate heir, so this incident might have occurred early in Odin's career. Frigga's infidelity with the slave is hardly of the same order. The discord suggested by the prose header to *Grímnismál* finds a parallel in an incident in Paul the Deacon's *History of the Langobards*, written in the second half of the eighth century. Here Godan (Odin) and Frea (Frigg) dispute over an upcoming battle between the Vandals, whom Godan favors, and the people who will become the Langobards, whom Frea favors.

The name Frigg is derived from an Indo-European root meaning "love," and in the Interpretatio Germanica, it was Frigg who was given the day of Venus, that is, Friday. This may accord with the Scandinavian stories of Frigg's infidelity. Her silent gift of prophecy, however, remains unexplained. It would belong more properly to Freyja, with her association with seid. The name Frigg is frequently found in Scandinavian place-names indicating cult activity. Based on the Swedish place-name evidence, Hugo Jungner argued that Frigg and Freyja were once identical. Although that cannot be proved, there certainly are similarities, not least in Freyja's marriage to Ód, who also is frequently away on journeys. *Oddrúnargrátr*, stanza 9, has a formula: "May the gracious beings help you, / Frigg and Freyja / and more gods."

See also Interpretatio Germanica; Merseburg Charms; Seid

References and further reading: Hugo Jungner's study is *Gudinnan Frigg och Als härad: En studie i Västergötlands religions-, språk- och bebyggelsehistoria* (Uppsala: Wretman, 1922). Jan de Vries, "Studien over germaansche mythologie, VII: De skaldenkenningen met de namen der godinnen Freyja en Frigg," *Tijdschrift voor nederlandsche taal- en letterkunde* 53 (1934): 210–217, is a comprehensive study of the kennings for Freyja and Frigg.

FRÓDI

Ancient Danish king and figure of heroic legend.

In his account of the story told to explain the kenning "Fródi's flour" for gold in *Skáldskaparmál*, Snorri says that Skjöld was a son of Odin and the founder of the Skjöldung dynasty in Denmark. His son was Fridleif, and Fridleif's son was Fródi. Fródi ascended to the throne at the time Emperor Augustus had imposed peace on the entire world when Christ was born.

But because Fródi was the most powerful of all kings in the northern lands, the peace was ascribed to him wherever Scandinavian was spoken, and the people of the north call it the Peace of Fródi. No man harmed another, even if he encountered the killer of his father or brother, free or bound. At that time there was no thief or robber, so that a certain gold ring lay for a long time on Jelling heath.

Snorri probably got the precise details of the Peace of Fródi from stanza 6 of the poem *Grottasöng* (which he cited right after telling about Fródi's demise through the actions of two slave girls he had purchased to turn an enormous mill).

> Here no one should harm another,
> Live for evil or work for death,
> Nor strike with a sharp sword,
> Even if the killer of his brother he find bound.

In the poem this peace appears to relate to Fródi's seat at Hleiðra (modern Lejre in Denmark), whereas in Snorri's version the peace is temporal and euhemerized with the birth of Christ. Scholars believe that Snorri took both of these notions from *Skjöldunga saga,* an account of the early Danish kings that is now known only through a seventeenth-century Latin paraphrase. But Snorri knew (or told of) another version of the Peace of Fródi, which he recounted in chapter 10 of his *Ynglinga saga.* According to this account, the Peace of Fródi was associated with Frey, here euhemerized as a king of Sweden who had succeeded Njörd, who had succeeded Odin himself. But Snorri slips out of his euhemerization somewhat:

In his days the Peace of Fródi began. At that time there was also prosperity in all lands. The Swedes attributed that to Frey. The more wealthy the people became through peace and prosperity, the more he was worshipped than the other gods.

Interestingly, Snorri introduces Fródi in the next chapter, calling him "Peace-Fródi" and putting him in Lejre at the same time that Frey's son Fjölnir is in Uppsala. Perhaps Snorri moved the Peace from Fródi to Frey, or perhaps, as some scholars have come to believe, Frey and Fródi were in effect two versions of the same figure, a local fertility god. That assumption finds strength in the references to Frey in stanzas 1 and 2 of *Skírnismál* as "the fródi," that is, "the wise one" or "the fruitful one."

In *Vellekla*, a poem from the end of the tenth century praising Hákon the Hladir jarl, the poet Einar Helgason skálaglamm said that no ruler had brought about such peace and prosperity except Fródi.

Saxo names several kings called Frotho, the Latin equivalent of the Norse Fródi. Of these the most relevant is Frotho III, who is the subject of the pivotal fifth book of *Gesta Danorum*. This Fródi, the son of Fridleif, is a successful Danish king renowned for lawgiving. Having defeated his enemies, he institutes an era of peace in his land, ridding it of theft, and to test this peace he hangs a heavy golden arm ring at a crossroads. Fearful of his authority, no thief dares take it, and he derives great fame from this act. Saxo tells us that this period coincides with Christ's stay on earth, and it is ended when a wicked woman urges her son to steal the arm ring, and then, trying to hide from Fródi's wrath in the form of a sea cow, she gores and kills him. To forestall the possibility of rebellion or invasion, the Danes conceal Fródi's death, embalm the body, and carry it about in a cart for three years before finally burying it. This story bears close similarity to Snorri's account of the death of Frey in *Ynglinga saga*, since Frey's death also is concealed for three years, during which time peace and prosperity continue. *Ögmundar tháttr dytts* tells of the worship of an idol of Frey transported in a cart near Uppsala, and, more distantly, Tacitus reports this of the goddess Nerthus.

Fródi would therefore appear to be a historicized remnant of one or more aspects of the myth and cult of the vanir, associated with peace and prosperity.

See also Frey; Njörd; *Ögmundar tháttr dytts*

References and further reading: The cults of Frey, Fródi, and Nerthus are scrutinized and associated with Baldr by Gustav Neckel in the fourth chapter of his influential book on Baldr, *Die Überlieferungen vom Gotte Balder* (Dortmund: F. W. Ruhfus, 1920). The *Festschrift für Otto Höfler zum 65. Geburtstage*, ed. Helmut Birkhan and Otto Gschwantler (Vienna: Notring, 1968), contains two articles on Fródi: Albert Ebenbauer, "Fróði und seine Fried," treats the Peace of Fródi, and Kurt Schier, "Freys und Fróðis Bestattung," (389–409), shows the essential unity of Fródi's and Frey's funerals. In "Appolon emintheús and the Teutonic Mysing," *Archiv für Religionswissenschaft* 33 (1936): 40–56, Alexander Haggerty Krappe argued an implausible connection between Fródi's killer Mýsing in the Norse tradition and the Greek *emintheús* (mouse-god), perhaps the plague.

FULLA

Minor goddess.

Snorri lists Fulla fifth in his catalog in *Gylfaginning* of goddesses among the æsir and says, "She is still a virgin and goes about with her hair down and a gold band about her head; she carries Frigg's trunk and looks after her shoes and shares secret counsels with her." The prose preceding *Grímnismál* in the *Poetic Edda* says that Frigg sent her "trunk-maiden" Fulla to Geirröd to trick him into mistreating the disguised Odin, and in *Skáldskaparmál* Snorri says that "ruler of Fulla" is a kenning for Frigg. Nanna sent a finger ring back to Fulla from the world of the dead in Snorri's recounting of the Baldr story, and Fulla is numbered with other important goddesses among the guests at Ægir's party, according to the beginning of *Skáldskaparmál*.

Fulla is presumably identical to the Volla of the Second Merseburg Charm. The etymology of the name appears to have to do with fullness, perhaps therefore fertility.

See also Merseburg Charms

GALAR (YELLER)
See **Mead of Poetry**

GALDRAR

Magic charms.

What we think we know about galdrar we get from the sagas. In the mythology, these are especially associated with Odin. In *Baldrs draumar*, stanza 3, Odin is called the father of galdrar, and *Hávamál*, from about stanza 135 onward, describes his mastery of magic songs. Although these are called songs rather than charms, they clearly are galdrar. Euhemerizing in chapter 7 of his *Ynglinga saga*, Snorri wrote of Odin's magic arts,

> All these skills he taught with runes and those songs that are called galdrar. Because of this the æsir were called smiths of galdrar. Odin knew that art called seid, and he carried it out himself.

The noun appears to be a simple past participle of the verb *gala*, "crow, yell." Although some commentators distinguish galdrar from *ljóð* as spoken rather than sung, it is difficult to find any primary source material than enforces the distinction.

Interestingly, one of the meters of eddic poetry is called galdrar meter. It is an extended form of *ljóðaháttr*, "song or chant meter."

See also Seid

GAME OF THE GODS
Motif associated with the golden age of the gods and with the survival of the race of gods after Ragnarök.

The key passages are in *Völuspá*, which gives a synopsis of the entire mythology. In stanza 8 the gods have just completed their creation and ordering of the cosmos and their building of cult sites and tools:

8. They played a game in the home field, were merry
For them there was no lack of gold.

At this point their "golden age" is disrupted by the arrival of three powerful giant maidens from Jötunheimar. The rest of the poem details the struggles and conflicts of the world of the gods, until finally they and the cosmos are destroyed at Ragnarök. But after Ragnarök the earth comes up a second time, and æsir will meet and inhabit it. They have memories of the old mythology (stanza 60), but they also have concrete objects from the earlier times.

61. There they will find wondrous
Golden gaming pieces in the grass,
Those which in ancient times they had had before.

Unsown fields will grow, and Baldr will return—surely this is some kind of new golden age, or perhaps a return to that time when the world was not solely defined as a place of conflict.

The gaming pieces, then, are clearly symbolic, and what kind of game might have been played with them is anybody's guess. There was an elaborate "hunting game" (so-called because one player, with a greater number of pieces, attacks the other, who starts with a smaller number of pieces) called *hnefatafl*, but we cannot be certain this is what the *Völuspá* poet had in mind. Certainly gaming pieces were items of high status, as the Lewis chess set and other finds indicate. It may also be noteworthy that the very late *Sturlaugs saga starfsama* places a golden gaming set in a supposed temple of Thor.

A. G. van Hamel advanced an elaborate and not very convincing hypothesis to the effect that the game ruled the world independently of the will of the gods and that its end caused Ragnarök. Perhaps more intriguing is the answer to one of the riddles in the riddle sequence in *Hervarar saga.* The riddles are put by Gestumblindi, who is actually Odin in disguise, and are solved by King Heidrek up to the very last one, which repeats the question at the epiphany in *Vafthrúdnismál:* What did Odin say into the ear of Baldr before he was put on the funeral pyre? Three of the riddles involve *hnefatafl,* and the first of them is as follows:

> Who are those thanes who ride to the assembly
> All reconciled together; their peoples
> They send over lands to build settlements.
> King Heidrek, ponder the riddle.

The answer varies according to the manuscripts: either Ítrek's board game or Ítrek and Andad, sitting at their board game. If, as some have suggested, Ítrek is an Odin name, the first reading might suggest the game of the gods. But since Andud, a possible variant of Andad, is a giant name, according to the thulur, the second reading would situate the game in the ongoing struggle between gods and giants.

> ***References and further reading:*** A. G. van Hamel's "The Game of the Gods"
> appeared in *Arkiv för nordisk filologi* 50 (1934): 218–242. On *hnefatafl,* see
> Appendix D of *The Saga of King Heidrek the Wise,* translated and with introduction, notes, and appendices by Christopher Tolkien (London: T. Nelson, 1960).

GARM

Dog, "best of hounds" according to *Grímnismál,* stanza 44.

The stanza is recited by Odin as he hangs in the fire at the home of King Geirröd toward the end of the poem and just before he begins the recitation of his names that culminates in an epiphany. Stanza 44 has a list of things that are best in the mythological world: Yggdrasil of trees, Skídbladnir of ships, Odin of æsir, Sleipnir of horses, Bilröst of bridges, Bragi of skalds, Hábrók of hawks, and, finally, Garm of hounds. In this company we would expect Garm to be a positive figure, but in his only other appearance in poetry, repeated three times more or less verbatim in *Völuspá* (stanzas 44, 49, and 58), he is anything but:

> Garm howls loudly before Gnipahellir
> The bond will burst, and the wolf run free.

Here Garm appears to be identical with Fenrir, the bound wolf who will get free at Ragnarök. Writing about Ragnarök in *Gylfaginning*, Snorri, who knew and had already quoted in another context the stanza from *Grímnismál*, calls Garm "the greatest monster" and says that after getting from the place before Gnipahellir where he is bound, he will fight with Týr and they will kill each other.

The name (or noun?) is used as a base word in kennings, always with the connotation of one who destroys (e.g., fire is the "Garm of wood"). Thus, Snorri's beast Mánagarm (Moon-dog) must be the destroyer of the moon, and that is precisely what Snorri says he is in *Gylfaginning*.

See also Bound Monster; Mánagarm

GEFJON

Minor goddess and/or female figure of legendary prehistory.

Snorri lists Gefjon fourth in his catalog in *Gylfaginning* of goddesses among the æsir and says she is a virgin, served by those women who died unmarried. Snorri also numbers her among the goddesses at Ægir's party at the beginning of *Skáldskaparmál* and again when he is discussing gold kennings. She also makes an appearance in *Lokasenna*, where she follows Idun in trying to discourage the verbal dueling. Loki says to her: "Shut up, Gefjon! / That one will I now mention, / who seduced you: / the white lad, / who gave you a piece of jewelry, / and you lay your thigh over him."

The most intriguing Gefjon story is recorded as part of the *Ragnarsdrápa* of Bragi Boddason the Old, taken to be the earliest known skald. Bragi is describing scenes decorating a shield, and one difficult stanza says that Gefjon, using four oxen, plowed land that she then took from Gylfi and added to Denmark. This verse is found in some manuscripts of Snorri's *Edda* and in his *Heimskringla*. In the manuscripts of Snorri's *Edda* that have the verse, it accompanies the following story, which opens *Gylfaginning*: Gylfi, the prehistoric Swedish king whose "delusions" at the hands of the æsir will make up the subject of this section of the *Edda*, had once given "to a traveling woman as payment for his pleasure" (that is, as payment to a prostitute) the land she could plow up in a day and a night using four oxen. That woman was Gefjon, of the family of the æsir. "She took four oxen from the north out of Jötunheimar, and those were the sons of a giant and her," and with their supernatural power they plowed up an entire piece of land and took it west to a sound, where they put it down. Gefjon named it Selund (modern Sjælland, the main island of Denmark, on which the city of Copenhagen is now located). And a body of water was left behind in Sweden, Gylfi's realm, called Lögrinn (the lake, i.e., Lake Mälaren, west of Stockholm), and the bays in Lögrinn match the headlands on Seland.

When Snorri told this story and quoted the verse in *Ynglinga saga*, he says that Odin had just settled at Óðinsey (Odin's island, modern Odense in Denmark; the name is more likely to derive from "Odin's holy place," but that would not have suited Snorri's purpose in *Ynglinga saga*). From there, Odin sent Gefjon north to look for land, and she came to Gylfi, who gave her plow land; no motivation for the gift is provided. She went to Jötunheimar, got four sons by a certain giant, changed them into oxen, and plowed up and transported the land that was to be Seland, thereby creating Lögrinn, whose fjords match the headlands of Seland. She settled in Seland, and Odin married her to his son Skjöld.

These varying conceptions and stories are not easy to reconcile. We are faced with a prostitute who is said to be a virgin goddess, and a goddess—virgin or not—who is said to have had children with a giant, which should disqualify her as a goddess because the sexual traffic is all in the opposite direction. In other words, we have both physical and mythological impossibilities. Some of the inconsistencies recede if we understand Gefjon as a figure of prehistory, a member of the æsir not in their roles as gods but in their role as "Asia-men," as the Icelandic Learned Prehistory understood them, and as Snorri presented them in the Prologue to his *Edda*, the frame to *Gylfaginning*, and *Ynglinga saga*. This Gefjon had a clear association with Denmark, especially Sjælland, even if no other texts support a marriage with Skjöld, the founder of the Danish royal family known as the Skjöldungar in medieval Scandinavian tradition and the Scyldingas in Old English. Her interaction with the giants would have been on the order of other such human-supernatural interactions. However, many scholars have found themselves persuaded that Gefjon originally was a goddess. They believe that her name has to do etymologically with gifts or giving and that she was therefore a fertility deity, perhaps localized to Denmark. It is also possible that her name was the source of a Finnish word meaning "bride's outfit, trousseau." Finally, in some translations of the lives of the saints into medieval Icelandic, the translator substituted the name of Gefjon for a pagan Roman god or used it in a list of pagan Scandinavian gods where there was a list of pagan Roman gods in the original text. Sometimes Diana is the Roman goddess in question, and that has led to the idea that Gefjon's split between virgin and whore may have originated in an analogy with Diana.

The lack of the Gefjon/Gylfi story in one branch of the manuscripts of Snorri's *Edda*, and the fact that Gylfi is reintroduced directly after it in the other manuscripts, suggests that it was not part of Snorri's original text but may have been added by a later scribe. If this passage is not from Snorri's pen, it is possible that whoever wrote it either knew about the Gefjon-Diana equivalence or took the view of the pagan gods as demons and therefore made a whore out of Gefjon. However, *Lokasenna* suggests that the notion of Gefjon's sexual activity was more widespread. Since having children with a giant is ordinarily inconceivable for a goddess, as I have noted, perhaps in the end we must simply accept that there were shifting, sometimes contradictory conceptions of Gefjon.

> ***References and further reading:*** Two recent articles in English treat Gefjon: John Lindow, "The Two Skaldic Stanzas in *Gylfaginning:* Notes on Sources and Text History," *Arkiv för nordisk filologi* 92 (1977): 106–124, and Margaret Clunies Ross, "The Myth of Gefjon and Gylfi," *Arkiv för nordisk filologi* 93 (1978): 149–165.

GEFN

Name for Freyja.

Snorri says in *Gylfaginning* that Freyja has many names because she took on different names among the various peoples she encountered when she went to search for her missing husband, Ód. Gefn is listed as a Freyja name in *Skáldskaparmál* and the thulur and turns up in kennings in skaldic poetry, but there is no extant narrative in which Freyja bears the name. The meaning of the name has to do with the verb "to give" and would therefore accord with the notion of Freyja as a fertility deity.

> ***See also*** Freyja

GEIRRÖD

Giant visited by Thor, who killed the giant's daughters.

The myth is known from the poem *Thórsdrápa*, by the skald Eilíf Godrúnarson, about whom we only know that he was associated with the court of Hákon Sigurdarson, jarl of Hladir toward the end of the tenth century and portrayed in the sources as an enthusiastic pagan. *Thórsdrápa* is an extremely difficult poem, but we have an account of the myth in Snorri Sturluson's *Skáldskaparmál*, preceding the citation of the poem itself. It begins with Loki flying to Geirrödargardar, the abode of the giant, in Frigg's falcon coat. Captured by Geirröd and starved in a locked chest for three months, Loki agrees to bring Thor there without his hammer or belt of strength. Accompanied by Loki (Thjálfi in *Thórsdrápa*), Thor comes first to the home of the giantess Gríd, the mother of Vídar the silent. She warns him about Geirröd and equips him with a belt of strength, an iron glove, and a staff called Grídarvöl (Gríd's-staff). Thor sets out and arrives at Vimur, greatest of all rivers. Wearing the belt of strength and bracing himself against the current with the staff, Thor fights through deep waters. Then he sees that Gjálp, the daughter of Geirröd, is standing astride the river and causing it to swell with urine or menstrual fluids. Saying, "A river must be dammed at its source," he throws a rock and hits the target. At that moment he comes ashore and grabs a rowan, which is why, Snorri says, the rowan is called "Thor's protection." At Geirrödargardar he sits on a seat and finds that Geirröd's daughters Gjálp and Greip are pushing up from beneath, obviously trying to crush him against the ceiling. He presses Grídarvöl against the ceiling and forces the chair down on the girls, breaking their backs. Then Geirröd challenges him to a game in the hall. Geirröd throws a piece of red-hot iron at Thor, who catches it in the iron glove. Geirröd jumps behind a pillar, but Thor throws the piece of iron through the pillar, Geirröd, and the wall behind and into the earth.

Saxo Grammaticus tells in Book 8 of his *Gesta Danorum* of the visit of Thorkillus to the vile hall of the dead Geruthus, where he and his companions see the pierced body of an old man and three dead women with their backs broken. Thorkillus tells them that Thor had driven a hot ingot through Geruthus and killed his daughters with thunderbolts.

The myth shows several characteristics of Thor stories—the dangerous journey to the otherworld, the special enmity of female giantesses, and the killing of a male giant—and it also introduces notions of smithing that sometimes seem to lurk behind Thor.

An entirely unrelated figure also bears the name Geirröd, in the eddic poem *Grímnismál.*

> **References and further reading:** Eugen Mogk, "Die Überlieferungen von Thors Kampf mit dem Riesen Geirröð" in *Festskrift tillägnad Hugo Pipping på hans sextoårsdag den 5 november 1924*, Skrifter utgivna av Svenska litteratursällskapet i Finland, 175 (Helsinki: Mercator, 1924), 379–388, discusses the sources: *Thorsdrápa, Snorra Edda*, Saxo, and a transposed version in the late-Icelandic *Thorsteins saga bæjarmagns*. In "An Interpretation of the Myth of Þórr's Encounter with Geirröðr and His Daughters," in *Speculum Norroenum: Norse Studies in Memory of Gabriel Turville-Petre*, ed. Ursula Dronke, Guðrún P. Helgadóttir, Gerd Wolfgang Weber, and Hans-Bekker Nielsen ([Odense:] Odense University Press, 1981), 370–391, Margaret Clunies Ross offered an essentially psychological reading, in which Thor had to free himself from "the female objects of his primary bonding and the destructive rivalry with his father" (p. 390).

GERD

Giantess wife of Frey.

Gerd is the daughter of the giants Gymir (Geyser according to one source) and Aurboda. Frey caught sight of her from Odin's seat, Hlidskjálf, fell in love with her, and dispatched his servant Skírnir to woo her. Gerd yielded not to Skírnir's blandishments but to his threatened curses, and a wedding was arranged for nine nights later. Frey complained that this wait would be too long. However, Frey and Gerd do appear to be married in the mythological present. Frey gave up his sword to obtain Gerd, and without it he will be weaponless when he faces Surt at Ragnarök.

Gerd's name has been associated etymologically with the earth and with enclosures, and the wedding is often taken to be the divine coupling of sky and earth, or at least of fertility god and representative of the soil. It can also be read as a simple case of the gods getting what they want from the giants.

See also Frey; Hrímgrímnir

GERI (RAVENOUS-ONE)
One of Odin's wolves.
Grímnismál, stanza 19, part of Odin's vision of the abodes of the gods, mentions Geri:

> Geri and Freki the one accus-
> tomed to battle feeds,
> Glorious Herjafödr [Odin];
> And on wine alone the weapon-
> noble
> Odin ever lives.

Stamped gold foil from Helgö, Sweden, showing a couple embracing. (Statens Historiska Museet, Stockholm)

Snorri quotes this stanza in *Gylfaginning* and puts the two halves together, saying that Odin gives his own food to the wolves, as he lives on wine alone.

The name is simply the definite form of an adjective.

See also Freki, Odin

GESTUMBLINDI (ONE-BLIND-TO-GUESTS?)
A name taken by Odin when he participates in a riddling contest in *Hervarar saga ok Heidreks konungs*.
A man called Gestumblindi has been summoned by his enemy, King Heidrek. Seeking help, he sacrifices to Odin. That night a stranger arrives at the door, says

his name is Gestumblindi, and changes places with the original Gestumblindi. This second Gestumblindi, clearly Odin in disguise, goes to Heidrek and elects to propound riddles rather than to be judged by Heidrek's wise men. "That is right and proper," says the king. Gestumblindi puts 30 riddles, and Heidrek easily guesses the answer to the first 29. The answers refer mostly to household situations and natural phenomena, but one is "the women of Ægir," and the twenty-ninth is "Odin riding Sleipnir." The thirtieth is the unanswerable question that doomed Vafthrúdnir: What did Odin say into the ear of Baldr before he was put on the funeral pyre? Heidrek now recognizes Odin and slashes at him with a sword, but Odin flies off in the form of a hawk. He curses Heidrek, prophesying that the worst slaves will kill the king, and this quickly comes to pass.

Despite the mostly mundane content of the riddles themselves, the story fits the type of the contest of wisdom, several of which involve Odin in the mythology. *Vafthrúdnismál* is the closest analogue, not just for the final question but also because the giant has wagered his head on the contest. In *Grímnismál* Geirröd, the human king who fastened Odin in the fire and has been listening to his ecstatic wisdom performance, falls onto his sword at the end of the story and is thus killed. Both human kings suffer ignominious deaths.

> **References and further reading:** Jan de Vries, "Om Eddaens visdomsdigtning," *Arkiv för nordisk filologi* 50 (1934): 1–19, treats the Gestumblindi story in association with eddic wisdom poetry. An analysis of the story itself is that of Elias Wessén, "Gestumblinde," in *Festskrift tillägnad Hugo Pipping på hans sextoårsdag den 5 november 1924,* Skrifter utgivna av Svenska litteratursällskapet i Finland, 175 (Helsinki: Mercator, 1924), 537–548.

GIMLÉ
Hall where people live after Ragnarök.
The main source is *Völuspá,* stanza 65, where the seeress, describing the situation after Ragnarök, has this to say:

> She sees a hall standing, fairer than the sun,
> Thatched with gold, at Gimlé;
> There shall trustworthy people dwell
> And throughout all ages enjoy bliss.

Snorri Sturluson quotes the stanza in the *Gylfaginning* of his *Edda,* where he mentions Gimlé three times. It appears that he thought of it, or perhaps more accurately, wished the æsir to present it to Gylfi/Ganglier, as a kind of pagan heaven.

GINNUNGA GAP

The primeval void that existed before the creation of the cosmos.
The major source is *Völuspá*, stanza 3:

> It was early of ages, when Ymir dwelled,
> There was not sand nor sea nor cool waves;
> Earth did not exist nor heaven above,
> Ginnunga gap existed, but no grass at all.

In *Gylfaginning* Snorri does not explain what Ginnunga gap was, but he uses
it in his creation story:

> Those rivers which are called the Élivágar, when they had come so far from their
> source that the fermentation that accompanied them there, hardened like the
> slag that runs out of fires, as it was freezing, and when the ice stopped and froze
> solid, then it was covered over with frost, and that drizzling rain which arose
> from the poison, froze into frost, and the frost grew over all Ginnunga gap. . . .
> That part of Ginnunga gap, which faced the north, was filled with a load and
> heaviness of ice, and in from there drizzle and a gust of wind; and the southern
> part of Ginnunga gap turned toward those sparks and embers, which flew out of
> Muspellsheim. . . . Just as cold and all bad things came from Niflheim, all that
> which came from Muspell was hot and bright, but Ginnunga gap was as calm as
> a windless sky, and when the warm breeze met the frost, it melted and dripped.
> And from those drops of poison life emerged, with the power that the heat sent,
> and it grew into a human form, and that one is called Ymir, but the frost giants
> call him Aurgelmir, and all the families of frost giants descend from him.

Later Snorri makes it clear that he understood Ginnunga gap as the center
of the universe, for it is there that the sons of Bor place the body parts of Ymir
to make the cosmos, and one of the roots of Yggdrasil runs where Ginnunga gap
used to be.

Formally, Ginnunga gap must be parsed as "Gap of ginnungs." What ginnungs are is not wholly clear, but the first syllable *ginn-* in mythological contexts was used to intensify what followed, as in *ginn*-holy, "extremely holy,"
gods, or *ginnregin*, "great powers," that is, the gods. At the same time, as a noun
(in poetry) *ginn* meant "falsehood, deception," and there was a common verb
ginna, "deceive." A gap of ginnungs, then, was probably a proto-space filled with
magic powers.

> ***References and further reading:*** The meaning I propose in the last sentence is
> taken from Jan de Vries, "Ginnungagap," *Arkiv för nordisk filologi* 5 (1930):
> 41–66, reprinted in his *Kleine Schriften*, ed. Klaas Heeroma and Andries Kyl-
> stra (Berlin: W. de Gruyter, 1965), 113–132.

GÍSL

Horse name found in *Grímnismál,* stanza 30, which lists the horses the æsir ride each day when they go to make judgments at Yggdrasil.

Snorri Sturluson includes Gísl in his list of the horses of the æsir in *Gylfaginning* but does not assign the horse to any specific god. Gísl is also listed in the thulur for horses. The name looks like the common noun for hostage, but etymologically it can be connected with the word for "beam" or "ray," which would make more sense for a horse, especially one with a particularly shiny coat.

GJALLARBRÚ

Bridge that must be crossed on the way to Hel.

Our knowledge of the Gjallarbrú is derived almost exclusively from Snorri Sturluson's *Gylfaginning,* in the section of the Baldr myth describing the journey of Hermód to Hel in an attempt to retrieve Baldr. After riding nine dark nights, Hermód comes to the bridge, and there he has a conversation with Módgud, the maiden who guards the bridge. That this bridge leads to the world of the dead is made clear by their dialogue. She asks Hermód his name and family and informs him that although five troops of dead men rode over the bridge yesterday, it resounds no less under Hermód alone. When she asks Hermód his mission, he tells her and asks whether Baldr has come that way. He has, she replies, and she tells him that the way to Hel lies down and north. Snorri adds the puzzling detail that the bridge is all "roofed with bright gold."

Gjallarbrú means "bridge of [i.e., over] Gjöll," but we have little information about this river. Earlier in *Gylfaginning,* when he cataloged the rivers flowing from Hvergelmir, Snorri said that Gjöll is "closest to the gate of Hel," but this he may have got from his conception of Baldr's journey. The wolf Fenrir is bound by means of a flat rock called Gjöll, but there is no compelling reason to associate the stone and the river.

The Gjallarbrú is found only once outside of Snorri in medieval Iceland, namely in a verse by his nephew, Sturla Thórdarson, who once used the expression "travel the Gjallarbrú" for "die." But it also turns up several times in *Draumkvæde,* a Norwegian ballad telling of the otherworld journey of one Olav Åsteson, who fell asleep Christmas Eve and awoke on Epiphany having had a vision of the fate of dead souls, including, among other things, a passage over the forbidding bridge Gjallarbrú. *Draumkvæde* is known from numerous oral recordings made in Telemark in the 1840s, but the vision it describes probably derives from the high Middle Ages. Thus, the Gjallarbrú appears to be one of the few pagan motifs to flourish in a Christian environment, obviously because a cruel bridge to the other world figures frequently in medieval vision literature. However, Snorri's medieval audience could hardly have conceived of the Gjallarbrú outside of the well-known visionary tradition. Perhaps Snorri covered the bridge with gold to differentiate it somewhat from the bridges of medieval Christian vision literature.

> ***See also*** Baldr; Gjallarhorn
>
> ***References and further reading:*** For an English translation of *Draumkvæde*, with discussion, see Knut Liestøl, *Draumkvæde: A Norwegian Visionary Poem from the Middle Ages*, Studia Norvegia, 3 (Oslo: Aschehoug, 1946). More recent discussion is in Dag Strömbäck, "Resan till den andra världen: Kring medeltidsvisionerna och Draumkvæde," *Saga och sed*, 1976: 15–29, and Peter Dinzelberger, "Zur Entstehung von Draumkvæde," *Skandinavistik* 10 (1980): 89–96.

GJALLARHORN (SCREAMING-HORN)

Heimdall's horn, sounded at the onset of Ragnarök.

The relevant source is *Völuspá*, stanza 46:

> Mím's sons sport, and the world tree trembles
> At the old Gjallarhorn.
> Loudly blows Heimdall, the horn is aloft,
> Odin is speaking to Mím's head.

In *Gylfaginning* Snorri paraphrases this verse and adds the information that Heimdall blows the Gjallarhorn in order to awaken all the gods for a meeting to deal with the oncoming forces of chaos.

Snorri had mentioned the Gjallarhorn twice previously in *Gylfaginning*. In describing Heimdall, he has duly ascribed the horn to him, using the word for a long brass instrument that would answer today to an unvalved trumpet. Heimdall's blast on it can be heard throughout the entire world. How odd it is, then, that in the very first reference to the Gjallarhorn, Snorri refers to it as a drinking horn and associates it with Mímir, who acquires wisdom by drinking from it out of the well that is associated with him, the Mímisbrunn. The association, if there is one, may be retrievable from stanzas 27 of *Völuspá*:

> She knows that Heimdall's hearing is hidden
> Under the holy tree, accustomed to brightness;
> She sees a river washed with a muddy waterfall
> From the pledge of Valfödr—would you know yet more?

We know from various sources (including the next stanza of *Völuspá*), that Odin pledged his eye in the well. If Heimdall's hearing (ear?) is also pledged there, as the stanza seems to suggest, he ought to have supernatural hearing, just as Odin has supernatural vision. But what of the horn? Perhaps Snorri was influenced by *Grímnismál*, stanza 13, which says that Heimdall (not Mím) drinks good mead at his hall, Himinbjörg. Or perhaps he simply turned the notion of hearing inside out and imagined it as noise. Or perhaps this Gjallarhorn, like the Gjallarbrú, is associated with the river Gjöll, which flowed from Hvergelmir, like Mím's well, a spring located near the center of the cosmos.

> ***See also*** Gjallarbrú; Heimdall; Mímir
>
> ***References and further reading:*** Åke Ohlmarks, *Heimdalls Horn und Odins Auge: Studein zur nordischen und vergleichenden Relgionsgeschichte,* vol. 1: *Heimdall und das Horn* (Lund: C. W. K. Gleerup, 1937), has a chapter devoted to the horn, but it follows an outmoded methodology and is highly speculative.

GJÁLP

Giantess, daughter of Geirröd, killed by Thor.

According to Snorri Sturluson writing in *Skáldskaparmál*, Gjálp was the giantess straddling the river Vimur and causing it to swell with urine or menstrual fluids when Thor was trying to cross it on his way to Geirröd. Thor threw a rock at her, saying, "A river must be dammed at its source," and he hit the target. Later he killed Gjálp and her sister Greip by breaking their backs beneath his seat as they tried to push it up against the ceiling to crush him.

Gjálp is also found in stanza 37 of *Hyndluljód*, in the "Short *Völuspá*," where she is listed as one of the nine giant mothers of an unnamed character, presumably Heimdall. Gjálp also turns up in the thulur and in kennings in skaldic poetry. The meaning of the name may be something like "screamer."

> ***See also*** Geirröd; Greip; Heimdall
>
> ***References and further reading:*** Lotte Motz, "Giantesses and Their Names," *Frühmittelalterliche Studien* 15 (1981): 495–511.

GLAD (GLAD)

Horse name found in *Grímnismál,* stanza 30, a stanza listing the horses the æsir ride each day when they go to make judgments at Yggdrasil.

Snorri Sturluson includes Glad in his list of the horses of the æsir in *Gylfaginning* but does not assign the horse to any specific god. Glad is also listed in the thulur for horses.

GLADSHEIM

One of the abodes of the æsir, described in *Grímnismál,* stanza 8, in the list of such abodes.

> Gladsheim is the fifth, where the gold bright
> Valhöll lies widely situated;
> And there Hropt [Odin] chooses each day
> Weapon-dead men.

This would appear to be a larger place in which Valhöll is situated; that is, it seems that Valhöll is a hall, perhaps one of many, at Gladsheim. Snorri knew *Grímnismál*, so it is interesting to note that he says Gladsheim was a temple erected at Idavöll by Alfödr, with 12 high seats: "That is the best and greatest building made on earth; outside and inside it is like a single piece of gold." Although Gladsheim looks as though it should mean "Happy home," Snorri may therefore have understood it to mean "Gleaming home."

See also Idavöll; Valhöll

GLÆR (GLASSY)

Horse name found in *Grímnismál,* stanza 30, a stanza listing the horses the æsir ride each day when they go to make judgments at Yggdrasil.

Snorri Sturluson includes Glær in his list of the horses of the æsir in *Gylfaginning* but does not assign the horse to any specific god. Glær is also listed in the thulur for horses.

GLEIPNIR

The fetter with which the wolf Fenrir was finally bound.

According to Snorri Sturluson in *Gylfaginning,* after Fenrir broke out of two previous fetters, Lœding and Drómi, the æsir feared they would never be able to bind the wolf.

> Then Alfödr [Odin] sent Skírnir, Frey's servant, down into the world of the dark-elves to some dwarfs and had that fetter made, which is called Gleipnir. It was made of six things: cat noise, woman beard, mountain roots, bear sinews, fish breath, and bird spittle. . . . The fetter was smooth and soft as a silk ribbon.

The wolf thought little renown could be won from breaking out of such a bond, and he feared a trick, but he allowed himself to be bound with Gleipnir when Týr put his hand in the wolf's mouth. Thus he was bound, and thus Týr lost his hand.

See also Fenrir; Týr

GLEN

Husband of Sól (Sun), according to Snorri Sturluson.

Writing in *Gylfaginning*, Snorri alludes to *Vafthrúdnismál*, stanza 23, which personifies the sun and moon. But Snorri has a somewhat different and more elaborate story: Mundilfœri is a man who had two children who were so beautiful that he named them Máni and Sól (i.e., Moon and Sun), and he married Sól to a man called Glen. Thereafter the gods punished this act of pride by placing the children in heaven to serve the actual heavenly bodies, which the gods had created. Sól drives the horses that pull the sun, and Máni controls the motion of the moon and its waxings and wanings.

I have paraphrased the text fairly closely. The implication that the act of pride was marrying his daughter to Glen, and not naming one's children Sun and Moon, is right there in Snorri, but like most people I prefer to ignore it and think that the gods punished Mundilfœri for the names and not the marriage. There is certainly no evidence that Sól's marriage to Glen annoyed the gods, for indeed there is no other evidence whatever about this marriage. Glen is discussed in passing in various reference works, and most writers make an effort to find an appropriate etymology for his name, in one root or another having to do with shining or gleaming.

See also Máni; Mundilfœri; Sól

GLITNIR

The hall of Forseti, Baldr's son.

Glitnir is enumerated among the abodes of the æsir in *Grímnismál*, stanza 15:

> Glitnir is the tenth. It is studded with gold
> And thatched with silver as well.
> And there Forseti dwells most of the day
> And settles all lawsuits.

In *Gylfaginning* in his *Edda* Snorri Sturluson repeats this information.

See also Forseti

GNÁ

Minor goddess.

Snorri lists her fourteenth and last in his catalog in *Gylfaginning* of goddesses among the æsir and says that Frigg sends her into various worlds on errands. She has a horse called Hófvarpnir (Hoof-thrower) that runs over air and sea. Snorri now cites a strange verse exchange. Seeing her riding in the sky, vanir (why it should be vanir is unclear) ask in verse what is flying there. She answers, "I am not flying, / although I travel / and move through the sky / on Hófvarpnir / whom Hamskerpir sired with Gardrofa." The name Hamskerpir is not transparent, and Gardrofa looks as though it should mean "Fence-breaker," but these horses and any myth connected with them are not known from any other source. Snorri ends his discussion of Gná by saying that from her name what goes high up is said to *gnæfa* ("to project").

GNIPAHELLIR (GNIPA-CAVE)

Cave where the hound Garm is bound, in *Völuspá,* stanzas 44, 49, and 53, and in the *Gylfaginning* of Snorri Sturluson's *Edda.*

The meaning of the entire name is sometimes taken to be "overhanging cave."

GODS, WORDS FOR

Terms used to designate the gods collectively in medieval Icelandic, especially in the written texts of the mythology. This entry treats the individual terms other than *æsir,* which has its own entry, and attempts to draw a few conclusions based on general trends.

Probably the most commonly found term after *æsir* is *goð* or *guð* (both forms are attested), which is obviously cognate with English "god." Etymologically, the word is usually understood as deriving from something like "one called on." This is the term that is used in translations of saints' lives to render Latin *deus* with the sense of pagan idol, and the sense of an idol is often found in the native Icelandic literature as well. But in the mythological texts, the word appears to be essentially interchangeable with *æsir;* that is, it is a plural and refers to the gods as a group, usually including both æsir and vanir. It was used in the singular only of the sun (the "shining god," *Grímnismál,* stanzas 38–39, *Sigrdrífumál,* stanza 15). There are Odin kennings such as *hanga-goð* (god of the hanged) and *hjaldr-goð* (noise [i.e., of battle]-god), but such kennings could also be used of giants: *stál-goð* (steel-god, apparently Hrungnir), *öndur-goð* (snowshoe-god, i.e., Skadi), used of her before her marriage to Njörd and entry into the community of the gods. According to the principles of kenning formation, there is considerable freedom in the use of such base words. What is far more striking is that *goð* was also used in the singular to refer to the Christian god, but with masculine grammatical gender, not the original neuter grammatical gender of all other uses of the word.

Another term is *regin,* like *goð* grammatically a neuter plural noun. It is perhaps most familiar in the genitive plural form *ragna,* in Ragnarök (literally, "fates of the gods"), the term for the end of the reign of the gods and the demise of the cosmos. Etymologically, *regin* appears to be derived from a root meaning "to give counsel." A runic inscription from around 600 C.E. has the word in a compound that scholars read as "descended from the divine powers." If this interpretation is correct, then this word has quite a prehistory. Compounds like *reginkunnr*, "descended from the gods," are relatively clear in eddic poetry, but in other cases the usage of the word as a prefix meaning "great" or "tremendous," which is common in modern Icelandic (e.g., *reginvitleysa*, "great stupidity"), may be at work. Thus, does *regindómr* in *Völuspá*, stanza 65, mean "tribunal of the gods, divine rule," or something similar, or does it mean "great judgment"? The *regin-þing* in *Helgakvida Hundingsbana* I appears simply to be a great assembly, as there is no sign of the gods at this point in the poem.

An interesting aside to the above discussion, in which a "god" word is used as an intensifier, is that "giant" words often fulfill this function, as in English (e.g., "giant mistake") or Swedish (*jättekul*, "way cool").

The language of eddic poetry suggests that these terms are very nearly synonymous:

> Then all the *regin* went to the judgment seats,
> The very holy *goð*, and considered that . . . (*Völuspá*, stanzas 6, 9, 23, and 25)

> Hail æsir,
> hail *ásynjur* [goddesses],
> hail all the very holy *goð*. (*Lokasenna*, stanza 11)

Finally, there are two words that are transparently plurals meaning bonds (*bönd*) or fetters (*höpt*), both again neuter. Both are limited to poetry, especially skaldic poetry. Indo-European comparative mythology suggests that binding gods were common. For the Germanic area, Tacitus states in *Germania*, chapter 39, that the Semnones, the "oldest and noblest of the Suebi," conduct sacrifices in a grove that no one enters unless bound by a chain. Anyone who falls must somehow wiggle out of the grove without help. Some scholars think that the mysterious Fjöturlund, "Fetter-grove," of *Helgakvida Hundingsbana* II may be related. The practice of the bravest warriors of another tribe, the Chatti, described by Tacitus in chapter 31 of *Germania*, may also be relevant: Novice warriors were not permitted to shave or groom themselves until they had first slain an enemy; the bravest wore an iron ring in token of chains, to be removed by the slaughter of an enemy.

In general, the presence of these various words for the collective of the gods may serve to remind us that the vivid pictures of individual deities with various personalities given by the mythological texts may not tell the whole story. The collective of gods must also at some time have been a potent force.

> *See also* Æsir; Regnator Omnium Deus
> *References and further reading:* Walter Gehl, *Der germanische Schicksalsglaube* (Berlin: Junker & Dünnhaupt, 1939), associates *regin, bönd,* and *höpt* with conceptions of fate. On *regin,* see Albert Morey Sturtevant, "A Study of the Old Norse Word *regin,*" *Journal of English and Germanic Philology* 15 (1916): 251–266.

GREIP (GRIP)

Giantess, daughter of Geirröd, killed by Thor.

According to Snorri Sturluson writing in *Skáldskaparmál,* Greip was one of the two daughters of Geirröd whom Thor killed by breaking their backs beneath his seat as they tried to push it up against the ceiling to crush him.

Greip is also found in stanza 37 of *Hyndluljód,* in the "Short *Völuspá,*" where she is listed as one of the nine giant mothers of an unnamed character, presumably Heimdall. Greip is not found in the thulur, but she is used once in a kenning in skaldic poetry.

> *See also* Geirröd; Gjálp; Heimdall
> *References and further reading:* Lotte Motz, "Giantesses and Their Names," *Früh-mittelalterliche Studien* 15 (1981): 495–511.

GRÍD

Giantess who equips Thor on his journey to Geirröd, according to the *Skáldskap-armál* of Snorri Sturluson's *Edda.*

Thor came to stay with that giantess who is called Gríd. She is the mother of Vídar the silent. She told Thor about Geirröd, said he was an exceedingly wise giant and difficult to deal with. She lent him her belt of strength, her iron glove, and her staff, which is called Grídarvöl (Gríd's-staff).

As the mother of Vídar the silent, Gríd is a consort of Odin, and this may explain her willingness to help Thor. In the arrangement of this narrative, she plays a role very like that of an old woman in a fairy tale who equips a hero with information and things he needs. Folklorists call such a figure a donor and note that it is a commonplace of folk narrative.

> *See also* Geirröd; Vídar

GRÍMNISMÁL

Eddic poem.

Grímnismál (Words of Grímnir) is found in both of the main manuscripts of eddic poetry and is quoted extensively by Snorri Sturluson in *Gylfaginning*. In *Codex Regius* of the *Poetic Edda* it is located between *Vafthrúdnismál* and *Skírnismál* and was therefore probably regarded by the compiler as the last of the Odin poems, perhaps because here Odin contends with a human king. It consists of 54 stanzas, mostly in *ljóðaháttr*; other stanzas are in *galdralag*, and some editors set some stanzas as *fornyrðislag*. The poem is preceded by a prose header under the rubric "About the Sons of King Hraudung" and is followed by a prose colophon.

The prose frame tells of two sons of King Hraudung, a name that turns up as the father of Hjördís in *Sigrdrífumál*, stanza 26, and in the thulur as a sea king. Agnar and Geirröd set out fishing but are blown out to a distant island where a couple takes them in. The old woman fosters Agnar and the old man Geirröd. In spring they return home, but Geirröd, following the old man's whispered advice, pushes his older brother back out to sea. We learn that the old couple were Frigg and Odin, and when Odin boasts that his foster son is a king while Frigg's is getting children on a giantess in a cave, Frigg counters that Geirröd is stingy with food—a false accusation—and the couple make a bet. Frigg sends Fulla to Geirröd to warn him of the impending visit of a man with magic powers, and when Odin arrives, calling himself Grímnir (Masked-one), Geirröd puts Grímnir in the fire. Geirröd's son Agnar offers him a drink, and as the flames lick higher the Masked One speaks. The first three stanzas relate to the frame story: He has been eight nights in the fire and is grateful for the sustenance from Agnar, who will become a king. With stanza 4 he begins a series of visions of the dwellings of the gods, Thor at Thrúdheim, Ull at Ýdalir, Frey at Álfheim, and so forth. Stanzas 9 and 10 describe Valhöll, with its spear shafts, shields, and byrnies within and a wolf and eagle outside. Eleven residences are described, but in place of a twelfth, stanza 17 says that Vídar's land grows with brush and high grass. Stanzas 18–26 tell about life in Valhöll, including the food of the einherjar, the many doors, and Heidrún and Eikthyrnir. Stanzas 27–30 catalog rivers and other bodies of water, and 31–35 describe Yggdrasil. Stanza 36 lists valkyries. Stanzas 37–39 are about the heavenly bodies. Stanzas 40–41 tell of the creation of the cosmos from the body of Ymir. Stanza 42 calls down the protection of Ull and may therefore be related to the frame. Stanzas 43–44 list the best of things.

In stanza 45 Grímnir says, in *galdralag*, that he has revealed his face to æsir and elves. In stanza 46 he begins to list his names, and these lead to an epiphany.

Sword-weakened carrion
Ygg [Odin] will have now;
I know that your life has run its course;
the dísir are angry—
now you can see Odin,
approach me if you can. (stanza 53)

"Odin I am named now," he says to begin the last stanza, the final catalog of his names.

According to the prose colophon, Geirröd arises to free Odin from the fire but trips and falls on his sword. Odin disappears at that point, and Agnar enjoys a long reign in his father's place.

Outside of the frame, the core of the verses represent a catalog of mythological knowledge. This knowledge is largely cosmological and is the sort of thing that is used in such eddic contests of wisdom as *Vafthrúdnismál* and *Alvíssmál*. And although Geirröd does not exchange verses with Odin, he does die at the end of the episode, thus sharing the fate of Vafthrúdnir and Alvíss. In short, there is an implicit contest of wisdom here despite Geirröd's silence. Thus, just as Odin has triumphed over the giant Vafthrúdnir, so he triumphs over a human king.

There are, however, additional aspects that are of interest. Odin's performance is set off not only by his consumption of a drink, as is normal in contests of wisdom, but also by his being hung in the fire. Here one thinks first of his self-sacrifice, as told in *Hávamál*. Pain and deprivation lead to the performance or acquisition of wisdom. Without necessarily imagining *Grímnismál* to represent a shamanic event, we may readily imagine that Odin's verses, especially the cosmological ones, report a vision.

Much of the recent discussion of the poem has centered around the relationship of the prose to the verse and the frame to the catalog of mythological knowledge. Whether the prose is late, or whether the frame and cosmological catalogs were once separate entities, is not easy to discern. The poem is impossible to date, but it is not difficult to imagine something like it being performed during the pagan period.

References and further reading: Bo Ralph, "The Composition of the *Grímnismál*,"
Arkiv för nordisk filologi 87 (1972): 97–118.

GROTTASÖNG

Eddic poem, spoken by two giant women who turn a magic mill and foretell the demise of King Fródi of Denmark.

The poem is found only in manuscripts of Snorri Sturluson's *Edda*, in the section called *Skáldskaparmál*. Snorri cites it after explaining the kenning "Fródi's flour" for gold. Skjöld, he says, was a son of Odin and the founder of the Skjöldung dynasty in Denmark. His son was Fridleif, and Fridleif's son was Fródi. Fródi ascended to the throne at the time Emperor Augustus had imposed peace on the entire world when Christ was born, and this was called the Peace of Fródi in Scandinavia. Fródi visited the Swedish king Fjölnir and purchased from him two slave girls, Fenja and Menja, who were large and strong. At that time there was a magic mill in Denmark, named Grotti, which no one had been strong enough to operate. Fródi set the slaves to turning it and bade them grind out gold, which they did, and also peace and prosperity for Fródi. But he did not allow them rest, and finally they ground out an army against Fródi, led by the sea king Mýsing. Mýsing killed Fródi and took much booty, and so ended the peace of Fródi. Mýsing took the mill and the slaves and bade them grind salt. He too allowed them no rest. A little later the ship sank, presumably through the grinding of the slave girls, and that is why the sea is salty.

Although Fródi is descended from Odin, the story belongs to heroic legend. The poem itself, which Snorri goes on to cite, is also a part of heroic legend, but it approaches the mythology more closely because of the explicit association of the slaves with the race of giants. In the very first stanza, the slaves are called "prescient." They grind away, contentedly at first, and they indeed grind gold, prosperity, and even the Peace of Fródi (stanza 6). But Fródi will not let them rest, and their good will evaporates. Stanzas 8 and 9 reveal that Fródi's problem has a mythological side.

> 8. You did not, Fródi, wisely guard your interests,
> Eloquent friend of men, when you purchased slaves;
> You chose on the basis of strength and appearance
> But about family you did not enquire.
> 9. Hard was Hrungnir and his father,
> Yet was Thjazi more powerful than they;
> Idi and Aurnir, our kinsmen,
> Brothers of mountain giants, to them we were born.

As girls they played beneath the earth, casting boulders about (stanza 11), causing the earth to shake (12). Then they fought battles, deposed princes, helped a hero, reddened blades (13–15). Now they are slaves of Fródi and are not pleased with their lot. Grinding ever more fiercely, they see fire approach the stronghold (19) and warn Fródi that he will not keep the throne of Hleiðra (20). They grind on, seeing the fates of men (21). The son of Yrsa and Hálfdan will avenge Fródi (22). Their fearsome grinding grows, and in a giant rage, they destroy the mill. The last stanza gives one of them the last word:

Still the mountain giant's bride spoke words:
We have ground, Fródi, as we dared;
The women have completed the grinding.

The poem gives us the sense that the giants threaten humans as well as gods, but that whereas the gods can mostly keep the giants in check, humans cannot. The giants have great powers, but attempting to harness those powers can be dangerous and destructive. Odin and the gods may be able to acquire precious objects from the giants, but humans had better be very careful about such matters.

> *See also* Fródi
>
> *References and further reading:* Folklore descendants and analogues are presented in Alfred W. Johnson, "*Grotta Söngr* and the Orkney and Shetland Quern," *Saga-Book of the Viking Society* 6 (1908–1909): 296–304, and Alexander Haggerty Krappe, "The Song of Grotte," *Modern Language Review* 19 (1924). An intelligent recent reading is that of Joseph Harris, "Reflections on Genre and Intertextuality in Eddic Poetry (with Special Reference to Grottasöngr)," in *Proceedings of the Seventh International Saga Conference*, ed. Theresa Pàroli (Spoleto: Centro Italiano di Studi sull' Alto Medioevo, 1990), 231–243.

GULLINBORSTI (GOLD-BRISTLE)

Frey's boar; the boar Slídrugtanni.

In his account of Baldr's funeral in *Húsdrápa*, composed circa 985 in western Iceland, Úlf Uggason said that Frey arrived at the funeral riding a boar with golden bristles, and this was presumably Gullinborsti (indeed, it is possible that the name derived from this verse). When Snorri Sturluson gave his famous account of the same funeral, he said that Gullinborsti pulled the cart in which Frey was riding. In *Hyndluljód*, stanza 7, Freyja apparently refers to her friend (lover? protégé?) Óttar as a boar, and the word *gullinbusti* follows, which most editors read as the adjective "gold-bristled" rather than the name of Frey's boar, since in the following line, this boar is named Hildisvíni (Battle-pig). It is therefore possible that both Frey and Freyja had a boar with golden bristles.

According to Snorri's *Skáldskaparmál*, Gullinborsti was made by the dwarfs Brokk and Eitri, in a wager with Loki, at the same time that other precious objects for the gods were made. Snorri mentions in both *Gylfaginning* and *Skáldskaparmál* that Gullinborsti had another name, Slídrugtanni.

Scholars understand the boar as associated with the fertility of the vanir but also with the early Swedish kings.

> *See also* Dwarfs; Frey; Freyja; Slídrugtanni

GULLINTANNI (GILDED-TOOTH)

Name for Heimdall.

The name is given by Snorri when he describes Heimdall in the catalog of the æsir in *Gylfaginning,* where he adds that Heimdall's teeth were of gold. It is not attested elsewhere, but in stanza 13 of his *Gráfeldardrápa,* a poem memorializing Harald Greycloak, who died circa 974, the poet Glúm Geirason called gold the "teeth of Hallinskídi," using another of Heimdall's names.

See also Gulltopp; Heimdall

GULLTOPP (GOLD-TOP)

Heimdall's horse.

Gulltopp is listed as one of the horses of the æsir in *Grímnismál,* stanza 30, and as a horse name in the thulur. Only Snorri assigns the horse to Heimdall. He does so in his description of Heimdall in the catalog of æsir in *Gylfaginning.* Snorri says that Gulltopp is one of the horses ridden by the æsir to daily judgments near Yggdrasil, but he does not associate the horse with Heimdall. In his description of Baldr's funeral, however, Snorri fills out his source, Úlf Uggason's *Húsdrápa* (which just says that Heimdall came riding), by stating that Heimdall rode Gulltopp.

The name Gold-top could refer to a horse with a reddish-yellow mane, but given that Heimdall himself is called Gullintanni (Gilded-tooth), we may perhaps be permitted to think of the precious metal.

See also Gullintanni; Heimdall

GULLVEIG

Mysterious female in *Völuspá,* stanzas 21–22, apparently associated with the war between the æsir and vanir.

> 21. She remembers the war of peoples first in the world,
> When Gullveig with spears they studded
> And in Hár's hall burned her;
> Thrice burned, thrice born,
> Often, unseldom, though she yet lives.
> 22. Heid they called her, wherever she came to houses,
> A seeress skilled in prophecy, she observed magic staffs;
> She performed seid, wherever she could, she performed seid in a trance,
> She was ever the joy of an evil woman.

These stanzas are obscure, but it is hardly going too far to say that Gullveig came to the hall of Odin (Hár), was attacked but could not be killed, and under the name Heid went about performing seid. Since *Ynglinga saga* says that Freyja first brought seid to the æsir, it is not impossible that Gullveig is Freyja, and that she brought seid to the æsir in the first instance either as a strategy in the war, or that her bringing of seid started the war. Beyond this, many fanciful attempts have been made to interpret Gullveig, some based on a literal understanding of her name as "gold-drink."

> *See also* Æsir-Vanir War; Freyja; Seid
>
> *References and further reading:* Heino Gehrts, "Die Gullveig-Mythe der *Völuspá*," *Zeitschrift für deutsche Philologie* 88 (1969): 312–378, seeks a background in cult, which seems very speculative. An analysis based on myth is that of Ursula Dronke, "The War of the Æsir and Vanir in *Völuspá*," in *Idee Gestalt Geschichte: Festschrift Klaus von See*, ed. Gerd Wolfgang Weber (Odense: Odense University Press, 1988), 223–238; Gullveig might, she thinks, have been some kind of idol burned by the æsir because Freyja, a woman, led the vanir in battle. In her *Prolonged Echoes: Old Norse Myths in Medieval Icelandic Society*, vol. 1: *The Myths* (Odense: Odense University Press, 1994), Margaret Clunies Ross suggests that Gullveig/Freyja was sent by the vanir, perhaps as a possible sexual partner, and rejected by the æsir because they did not take wives from lower social groups, and that their vehement reaction, the attempt to kill her, may have precipitated the war.

GUNGNIR

Odin's spear.

Like Sif's golden hair, Frey's ship Skídbladnir, Odin's ring Draupnir, Frey's golden boar, and Thor's hammer, Gungnir was made by the dwarfs. Although it is not specifically named as Gungnir, Odin throws a spear over an opposing army, was "wounded with a spear and given to Odin, myself to myself," when he hung on the tree in his self-sacrifice according to *Hávamál*, stanza 138, and had himself marked with a spear when he died, as did Njörd, according to the historicized account of the æsir in the early chapters of *Ynglinga saga*. Skalds call Odin the lord and god of the spear.

> *See also* Odin
>
> *References and further reading:* Julius Schwietering, "Wodans Speer," *Zeitschrift für deutsches Altertum* 60 (1923): 290–292, reprint in Schwietering, *Philologische Schriften*, ed. Friedrich Ohly and Max Wehrli (Munich: W. Fink, 1969), 234–236, advances the clever but almost certainly wrong idea that advances in military technology promoted Odin, god of the spear, ahead of Týr, god of the sword.

GUNNLÖD

The giantess seduced by Odin when he obtained the mead of poetry.

The story is told allusively in *Hávamál*, stanzas 108–110, and at length by Snorri Sturluson in the *Skáldskaparmál* of his *Edda*. *Hávamál* 108 says,

> I doubt that I would yet have come
> Out of the giants lands,
> If I had not had use of Gunnlöd, the good woman,
> Around whom I put my arm.

Snorri has Odin, in the form of a snake, gain access to Gunnlöd in her father Suttung's mountain abode Hnitbjörg, where Suttung has set her to guard the mead. Odin sleeps with her for three nights, and she permits him three drinks of the mead. With that she leaves the story.

Gunnlöd looks as though it ought to mean "Battle-invitation," which would be a better valkyrie name than giant name.

See also Mead of Poetry; Suttung

GYLLIR

Horse name found in *Grímnismál,* stanza 30, a stanza listing the horses the æsir ride each day when they go to make judgments at Yggdrasil.

Snorri Sturluson includes Gyllir in his list of the horses of the æsir in *Gylfaginning* but does not assign the horse to any specific god. Gyllir is also found listed in the thulur for giants, perhaps because the name could mean "Yeller" as well as the appropriate horse name, "Golden."

GYMIR

Father of Gerd, the giantess who married Frey; possibly also identical with Ægir.

Gymir is indeed identified as the father of Gerd, and Aurboda as his wife and her mother, in *Skírnismál*. In the *Gylfaginning* in his *Edda*, Snorri Sturluson repeats this information, adding that Aurboda was of the lineage of mountain giants. In *Skáldskaparmál*, however, in a discussion of kennings for the sea, Snorri quotes a verse by the skald Ref Gestsson and then says that Ægir and Gymir are one and the same. Ref was an eleventh-century skald quite given to mythological kennings, and the verse in question seems to say that the cold seeress of Gymir often transports the bear of twisted lines into the jaw of Ægir; that is, that the wave (Ægir's daughters are the nine waves) often drives a ship deep into the water. The prose header to *Lokasenna* also says that Ægir was also known as Gymir, and if he was, the in-law relationship with Frey might explain his well-known banqueting with the gods.

See also Gerd

HÁBRÓK (HIGH-PANTS)

Best of hawks, according to *Grímnismál,* stanza 44.

This stanza comprises a list of the best of various things: Odin of the æsir, Sleipnir of horses, and so forth. Although Snorri Sturluson quotes this stanza in *Gylfaginning,* he has nothing more to say of Hábrók, and the other sources are silent as well, except for the thulur, which list the name under "hawk" and "rooster."

"High-pants" could refer to long legs.

HADDINGJAR

Royal family in heroic literature; when doubled, possible reflex of the divine twins.

The prose colophon to *Helgakvida Hundingsbana* II says the ancients believed in rebirth, and that Helgi Hundingsbani was thought to have been reborn as Helgi Haddingja skati, that is, prince of the Haddingjar. The so-called *Kálfsvísa,* a fragmentary list of horses and riders, says that Haddingja skati rode Skævad, a horse name known from other sources.

Haddingjar is the plural of Haddingi (related perhaps to Hadingus in Saxo), and the name is attested most interestingly as a doublet. *Hyndluljód,* stanza 23, mentions "two Haddingjar," as does a verse spoken by Hjálmar in *Örvar-Odds saga* before the battle of Samsey. Another of the *fornaldarsögur, Hervarar saga ok Heidreks konungs,* also names "two Haddingjar," brothers of the hero Angantýr. There thus appears to have been a tradition of a doubled Haddingi, and some observers have associated them with the divine twins, especially since according to tradition each was powerless on his own but together they made up a strong warrior.

> ***See also*** Hadingus
>
> ***References and further reading:*** Georges Dumézil, *From Myth to Fiction: The Saga of Hadingus,* trans. Derek Coltman (Chicago: University of Chicago Press, 1973).

HADINGUS

Danish king in Book 1 of Saxo's *Gesta Danorum;* shows remarkable similarities to both Odin and Njörd.

Hadingus (sometimes referred to in the secondary literature as Haddingus or Hadding because the Scandinavian form would have had *-dd-*) is the son of Gram and descendant of the first Danish kings but raised by giants. He becomes the lover of his nursemaid, the giantess Harthgrepa, who travels with him disguised as a man and performs necromancy with him. After she is torn apart by other giants, an old man with only one eye puts Hadingus in touch with the pirate

Liserus, and when Hadingus is wounded he makes an otherworld journey on a horse (Sleipnir?). Later he makes a second otherworld journey when an old woman transports him to the world of the dead. Before an important battle, Hadingus puts his ship ashore to confer with an old man waving his cloak and learns from him the secret of the wedge formation. And when he learns that Hundingus, whom he had put on the throne at Uppsala, had drowned in a vat of beer, Hadingus hanged himself before the eyes of his populace.

The partnership with a giantess, otherworld journeys, necromancy, wedge formation, and voluntary hanging make it clear that Hadingus had obvious Odinic associations, and indeed the story of Odin and Mithothyn is inserted into the life of Hadingus with no discernible association. And yet there are very strong associations with Njörd as well. Hadingus's wife Regnhild chooses him after an examination of the lower legs of the men assembled at a banquet. Hadingus had saved her from marriage to a giant, and though ignorant of his identity, while nursing him back to health she had put a ring in a leg wound. Recognizing this token, she chooses him. Even if this motif seems only distantly related to Skadi's choosing of Njörd by his lower legs, the other parallel is spot on: Hadingus complains, in verse, of life away from the sea, and Regnhild complains of life at the shore. And their complaints echo those of the verses cited in Snorri's *Gylfaginning:* Hadingus is disturbed by the howls of wolves, and Regnhild by the crying of seagulls.

One other motif captures perfectly the way Hadingus combines aspects of Odin and Njörd. One of his acts was to sacrifice to Frey. Indeed, he is said to have established an annual sacrifice to Frø (Frey), "The Swedes call it Frøblot," Saxo says, using the Norse word *blót*. In the Learned Prehistory, it was Odin who established sacrifices and was especially associated with the *blót*, but Frey carried on the tradition and was of course a member of the vanir and Njörd's son.

See also Haddingjar; Harthgrepa; Njörd; Skadi

References and further reading: For the Odinic side, see Otto Höfler, *Germanisches Sakralkönigtum*, vol. 1: *Der Runenstein von Rök und die germanische Individualweihe* (Tübingen: M. Niemeyer, 1952). For the Njörd side, see Georges Dumézil, *From Myth to Fiction: The Saga of Hadingus*, trans. Derek Coltman (Chicago: University of Chicago Press, 1973). Dumézil argues that Hadingus passes through all three functions and ends as an Odin hero, just as Njörd himself passed from the vanir to the æsir.

HÁKONARMÁL

Skaldic praise poem attributed to Eyvind Finnsson skáldaspillir (Spoiler- or Debaser-of-poets; often understood to mean plagiarist), following the death of the Norwegian king Hákon the Good at the battle of Stord, Norway, in 961.

The poem's 21 stanzas are found in manuscripts of Snorri's *Heimskringla*, and some are also cited in Snorri's *Edda* and in the kings' saga synoptic manuscript *Fagrskinna*. According to that manuscript, Eyvind composed the poem in direct imitation of *Eiríksmál*, the anonymous poem describing the entry of Hákon's brother Eirík Bloodax into Valhöll.

Hákonarmál consists of two scenes followed by four stanzas of praise for the fallen king. The first scene describes the battle, which we know from the very first stanza is being observed by valkyries. Exhorting his men, Hákon tears off his armor before the battle. His sword cuts through armor as if through water, and swords glow in wounds. But now the valkyrie Göndul speaks: It is time to depart for Valhöll. The forces of the gods have grown, now that Hákon and his army are to join them. Hákon asks why the battle turned out as it did, and the valkyrie Skögul responds that the valkyries gave Hákon victory and will now transport him to the green world of the gods. Now the scene shifts to Valhöll. Odin bids Hermód and Bragi greet the king. Hákon, covered with gore, expresses concern about Odin's ill will but is assured that he has the sanctuary of all the einherjar. "Thus it was known, how well that king had spared the holy places, when all the gods bade Hákon welcome" (stanza 18). The final two stanzas are quite lovely:

20. Unbound through the homes of men
The wolf will run,
Before on the abandoned path
An equally good king will come.
21. Cattle die, kinsmen die,
Country and land are laid waste
Since Hákon went among the pagan gods,
The people are much oppressed.

As the final line indicates, the poem must have had a direct political purpose, presumably to comment unfavorably on the rule of Harald gráfeld (Greycloak), who succeeded Hákon. Such comment would especially have suited the interests of the Hladir jarls (the rulers of the area around Trondheim), with whom the poet Eyvind was associated. The beginning of the final stanza echoes very famous lines from the gnomic section of *Hávamál*, and although the relationship between the two poems remains unknown, the effect is certainly powerful here.

Like the *Eiríksmál*, *Hákonarmál* is a document that can be specifically assigned to late paganism. Although Odin is the central deity in both poems, the attitudes toward him are strikingly different. In *Eiríksmál* he chooses that the king should die to build up the army of the gods, but in *Hákonarmál* the valkyries appear to make the choice (in stanza 13, Skögul says that they should ride off to inform Odin of what has transpired), and Hákon is suspicious of Odin. Except for Odin, only former human heroes appear in *Eiríksmál*'s Valhöll, but Hermód, presumably a god rather than a human hero, appears there in *Hákonarmál*. Finally, *Hákonarmál* uses a number of the collective words for gods (e.g., *bönd, regin*). As Eirík had Danish connections and died in England, whereas *Hákonarmál* appears to have been intended for consumption in the circles of the Hladir jarls, what we are seeing may be variation in regional belief, but it may be no more than variation that is to be expected from the work of two different poets working in different political circumstances.

> **See also** *Eiríksmál*; Gods, Words for; *Hávamál*
>
> **References and further reading:** On Eyvind and the politics of the situation, see Folke Ström, "Poetry as an Instrument of Propaganda: Jarl Hákon and his Poets," in *Speculum Norroenum: Norse Studies in Memory of Gabriel Turville-Petre*, ed. Ursula Dronke, Guðrún P. Helgadóttir, Gerd Wolfgang Weber, and Hans Bekker-Nielsen ([Odense:] Odense University Press, 1981), 310-327. The literary relationship between *Eiríksmál* and *Hákonarmál* is discussed by Klaus von See, "Zwei eddische Preislieder," in *Festgabe Ulrich Pretzel m 65. Geburtstag dargebracht von seinen Freunden und Schülern*, ed. Walter Simon, Wolfgang Bachofer, and Wolfgang Dittmann (Berlin: Schmidt, 1963), 107–117. Edith Marold, "Das Walhallbild in den Eiríksmál und Hákonarmál," *Mediaeval Scandinavia* 5 (1972): 19–33, acknowledges that the portrait of Valhöll in *Hákonarmál* is darker and conceivably more archaic than that of *Eiríksmál* and analyzes especially the duality of the conceptions in *Hákonarmál*.

HÁLEYGJATAL

Fragmentary genealogical poem, attributed to Eyvind Finnsson skáldaspillir (Spoiler or Debaser of poets; often understood to mean plagiarist).

The poem one finds in modern editions consists of 16 stanzas and half-stanzas assembled by editors from manuscripts of Snorri's *Edda, Heimskringla*, and two other manuscripts of kings' sagas. It is in *kviðuháttr*, the meter used by Thjódólf of Hvin for his *Ynglinga tal*, and although the text is difficult in places, it appears, like that poem, to enumerate the deaths of a line of kings, in this case of Hálologaland, the area of Norway north of Trondheim. It is usually assumed that the poem was intended to provide for the Hladir jarls, that is, the rulers of the Trondheim area, the genealogical link to the pagan gods that *Ynglinga tal* provided for the kings of the Oslo fjord region. Eyvind had been a court poet of one of those kings, Hákon the Good, but by the end of the tenth century he was working for the Hladir jarls, and he composed *Háleygjatal* for Hákon jarl after the jarl's victory over the Jómsvikings in 985.

The extant stanzas appear to make Odin and Skadi, while they were living in Manheim, the progenitors of the rulers, although one stanza uses the kenning for earth, "bride of slaughter-Týr" (Odin is the slaughter-Týr, or slaughter-god, and his "bride" was Jörd, or earth). According to *Ynglinga tal* Njörd and Skadi lived at Manheim, and one would to be tempted to assume that the poet is referring to Njörd and not Odin here in *Háleygjatal* were it not for the explicit statement that Skadi had many children with Odin.

> ***References and further reading:*** Folke Ström, "Poetry as an Instrument of Propaganda: Jarl Hákon and His Poets," in *Speculum Norroenum: Norse Studies in Memory of Gabriel Turville-Petre*, ed. Ursula Dronke, Guðrún P. Helgadóttir, Gerd Wolfgang Weber, and Hans Bekker-Nielsen ([Odense:] Odense University Press, 1981), 310–327.

HALLINSKÍDI

Name of Heimdall associating him with the ram.

Snorri gives Hallinskídi as a name for Heimdall, and the thulur list it as a name for ram. In a late-tenth-century skaldic stanza, gold is called the "teeth of Hallinskídi," which accords with the general association between Heimdall and gold words. Varying attempts have been made to explain the name Hallinskídi, associating it with horns bent backwards, a stony peak or cranium, crooked teeth, and even skates and skis, but all smack of desperation.

> ***See also*** Gullintanni; Heimdall

HÁRBARDSLJÓD

Eddic poem.

Hárbardsljód (Song of Hárbard) is retained in *Codex Regius* of the *Poetic Edda* and, from near the end of stanza 19, in AM 748. In *Codex Regius* it is found between *Skírnismál* and *Hymiskvida*, which probably means that the organizer of *Codex Regius* regarded it as a Thor poem, although the title, which is found in a rubric, refers to the Odin name Hárbard (Greybeard), and in the course of the poem, Odin gets the upper hand. As edited, the poem consists of 60 stanzas; the dominant meter is *ljóðaháttr*, but numerous stanzas appear to be in *fornyrðislag* or even alliterative metrical prose. The poem is a dialogue, an exchange of boasts and insults, between Thor and a disguised Odin.

The frame centers on Thor's attempt to be ferried across a sound while returning from one of his trips to the east. Thor insultingly calls to the ferryman for transport over the water, but the ferryman upbraids the traveler and even tells him that his mother is dead (stanza 4); taken literally, this is an allusion to Ragnarök, for Thor's mother is Jörd (Earth). Thor is nonplused, but soon asks who owns the ferry (stanza 7). "Hildólf" (Battle-wolf) replies the ferryman (stanza 8). The name is found among the thulur as a son of Odin, but Thor does not react to it. When asked his own name (stanza 8), Thor announces three generations of his lineage: son of Odin, father of Meili. "Here you can see Thor." The expression "Here you can see" is precisely what Odin says to Geirröd in the epiphany at the end of *Grímnismál* when Odin terrifyingly reveals his identity to the human King Geirröd, but on the ferryman it has no effect. Thor lamely asks the ferryman what his name is. Odin's response is deeply ironic. "I am called Hárbard, / seldom I conceal my name" (stanza 10).

Having named themselves, the two return to the original question: Will Thor get a ride across the sound? When Odin makes it clear that Thor will get no such ride, the two settle into a series of questions and answers. These are to be regarded as a *mannjafnaðr,* "comparison of men," a form of verbal dueling in which one boasts about oneself and, often, tries to top the opponent's previous boast. Thor boasts of his battles with giants and mentions such well-known myths as his killing of Hrungnir (stanza 15) and Thjazi (stanza 19), as well as some incidents about which we are not well informed, such as, for example, a battle with the "sons of Svárangr" (stanza 29). Odin's boasts are more varied, but they very frequently refer to his seductions. Thor seems nonplused by Odin's boasts about such a subject, and he often replies rather lamely. Twice he accuses Hárbard of *ergi* (sexual perversion), but in a vexed rather than forceful way. Odin declines Thor's direct order in stanza 53 to row to shore and transport Thor, and he has the last word when he ends the poem by saying to Thor, "Go now where all evil things may have you."

In *Hárbardsljód,* then, the two major gods have a verbal duel. Each plays to his strengths in the actual boasts, but Odin is a master of verbal dueling, and he emerges the clear winner, despite the apparent disadvantage that boasts about sexual conquests ought to have in comparison with boasts about warlike deeds of cosmic importance. The poem serves to order the two main gods on the basis of verbal skills. In other eddic poems, Odin establishes his superiority over the wisest of giants *(Vafthrúdnismál)* and a human king *(Grímnismál).* Here he does the same with the strongest of gods.

References and further reading: Marcel Bax and Tineke Padmos, "Two Types of Verbal Dueling in Old Icelandic: The Interactional Structure of the *senna* and the *mannjafnaðr* in *Hárbardsljód," Scandinavian Studies* 55 (1983): 149–174. Carol J. Clover, "*Hárbarðsljóð* as Generic Farce," *Scandinavian Studies* 51 (1979): 124–145.

HARTHGREPA (HARD-GRIP)

Giantess nursemaid, lover, and companion of Hadingus in Book 1 of Saxo's *Gesta Danorum.*

Harthgrepa is one of the two giants who raised Hadingus, a Danish king with numerous Odinic traits (and not a few that associate him with Njörd). Certainly tarrying with a giantess is an Odinic act, but Hadingus was only able to bring himself to do so after Harthgrepa explained that as a giantess she could change her shape at will. Thereafter they travel together, she disguised as a man, and when they come upon a corpse she has Hadingus place a stick carved with spells (in runes?) under its tongue, thereby initiating him into another of Odin's realms, necromancy. Her name is explained when, as she and Hadingus are sheltering in a cave, a huge hand tries to enter. Swelling herself back up to great size, she grasped the hand for Hadingus to chop off. She paid for this offense against her own race subsequently when she was torn apart by them.

The Norse equivalent of Harthgrepa, Hardgreip, is listed in the thulur for giantesses but is otherwise unknown.

See also Hadingus

HATI HRÓDVITNISSON

Wolf; precedes the sun in the sky and will swallow it or the moon.

Grimnismál, stanza 39, tells of the wolves who threaten the sun:

> Sköll is the name of a wolf who accompanies the shining god
> As a defense of the forest;
> And the other Hati, he is the son of Hródvitnir,
> That one shall be before the bright bride of heaven.

These lines are enigmatic. Snorri paraphrased them as follows in *Gylfaginning:*

> Gangleri said: "The sun moves fast, and almost as if she were frightened; she would not hasten her journey more, if she feared her death." Then Hár answers: "It is not surprising that she goes quickly. The one who seeks her is right nearby, and she has no other way out than to run away." Then Gangleri said: "Who is it who makes this trouble?" Hár says: "It is two wolves, and the one who chases her is Sköll; she is afraid of him, and he will take her, and the one who runs in front of her is called Hati Hródvitnisson, and he will take the moon.

I rendered the last word of this passage "moon," although it can mean either sun or moon. Clearly Snorri has adapted these wolves to his notion of Ragnarök, when Garm will bay and Fenrir will get loose to slay Odin.

Many scholars accept that Hati's father Hródvitnir is the Hródrsvitnir mentioned in *Lokasenna*, stanza 39. Either name (or both forms of the name) would mean something like "famous wolf." In *Lokasenna* that famous wolf is clearly the wolf Fenrir. We have, however, no other indication that Fenrir had offspring, and since he was bound from an early age until Ragnarök, we may wonder.

The name Hati also appears in *Helgakvida Hjörvardssonar*. In a prose section between stanzas 11 and 12, we learn that Helgi killed "Hati the giant," and in stanza 17 Hati's son identifies himself:

> I am called Hrímgerd, Hati was the name of my father,
> I know him to have been the most powerful giant;
> Many women he had abducted from farms
> Until Helgi killed him.

Probably the two creatures who bore the name Hati were not identical, but each was hateful. This is wholly appropriate: Hati probably meant something like "hater."

See also Fenrir; Hródvitnir; Sköll

HÁVAMÁL

Eddic poem (Words of the High One).

Hávamál is the second poem in *Codex Regius* of the *Poetic Edda*, located between *Völuspá* and *Vafthrúdnismál*. The "High One" of the poem's title is Odin. The poem breaks clearly into several parts. The first 80 or so stanzas consist of a set of maxims. These range from the very mundane (Be careful when you travel; Don't drink too much) to beautiful stanzas that have often been taken to present some kind of heroic ideal:

> 76. Cattle die,
> kinsmen die,
> one dies oneself in the same way,
> but a reputation
> never dies
> for the one who acquires a good one.
> 77. Cattle die,
> kinsmen die,
> one dies oneself in the same way.
> I know one thing
> that never dies
> the judgment of each dead person.

Stanzas 96–110 are sometimes called "Odin's examples." Two "examples" are offered: the story of Billing's girl and the story of Odin's seduction of Gunnlöd in connection with his acquisition of the mead of poetry. Stanzas 111–137 comprise the *Loddfáfnismál*. Stanzas 138–145 tell of Odin's self-sacrifice; this section is sometimes called *Rúnatal* (Enumeration of Runes) because Odin acquires runes in it. Stanzas 146 to the end of the poem are sometimes called the *Ljódatal* (Enumeration of Chants).

Although the poem obviously has material that relates directly to paganism as well as to the mythology, and older scholarship often sought to reconstruct forms that could have existed during the Viking Age or even earlier, today there is a tolerable consensus that *Hávamál* as we have it is a medieval artifact and that its organization, current form, and even language in some cases is the work of a late-twelfth- or thirteenth-century redactor. For that reason I have chosen to treat the pieces separately in this book. There are separate entries for Billing's Girl, *Loddfáfnismál*, and the *Ljódatal*. The second of the "Odin's examples," his seduction or rape of Gunnlöd, is treated in the entry Mead of Poetry, and the self-sacrifice is treated in the entry Odin.

See also Billing's Girl; *Ljódatal*; *Loddfáfnismál*; Mead of Poetry; Odin
References and further reading: Klaus von See, *Zur Gestalt der Hávamál: Eine Studie zur eddischen Spruchdichtung* (Frankfurt/Main: Athenäum, 1972).

HEID

Name taken by Gullveig, according to *Völuspá*, stanzas 21–22, when she begins practicing seid:

21. She remembers the war of peoples first in the world,
When Gullveig with spears they studded
And in Hár's hall burned her;
Thrice burned, thrice born,
Often, unseldom, though she yet lives.
22. Heid they called her, wherever she came to houses,
A seeress skilled in prophecy, she observed magic staffs;
She performed seid, wherever she could, she performed seid in a trance,
She was ever the joy of an evil woman.

In the sagas Heid is a common name for seeresses, and it is also found in a genealogy in *Hyndluljód*, stanza 33, of Hrímnir's kin, presumably giants. The adjective *heid*, "gleaming," and the noun *heid*, "honor," would suit nicely here as well.

See also Gullveig; Seid

HEIDRÚN

Goat who bites the foliage of Lærad, the tree at Valhöll.

Grímnismál, stanza 25, is the most important source:

> 25. Heidrún is the name of the goat, who stands at the hall of Herjafödr [Odin]
> And bites from the limbs of Lærad.
> She will fill a barrel with the bright mead;
> That drink can never run out.

In *Gylfaginning* Snorri Sturluson paraphrased these lines.

> That goat, who is called Heidrún, stands up on Valhöll and bites foliage off the limbs of that tree, which is famous and which is called Lærad. From her teats runs that mead, with which she fills a barrel each day; it is so much, that all the einherjar get fully drunk on it.

Thus Snorri draws Heidrún into the notion of the endless feasting of the einherjar, making her a parallel to Sæhrímnir, the boar who is cooked each day and is whole again by evening.

Heidrún is found in one other place in eddic poetry, namely, the closing stanzas of *Hyndluljód*. The frame of the poem is a dialogue between Freyja and Hyndla, who appears to be a giantess, and in the end the exchanges are increasingly acerbic. After the "Short *Völuspá*" has ended, Freyja asked for some sort of "memory-beer" to be brought for her boar (who is perhaps Óttar, her protégé). Hyndla responds with two stanzas:

> 46. Turn away from here! I desire to sleep;
> You'll get little of fair opportunities from me;
> You run about, noble friend, out at nights,
> As if with he-goats Heidrún were traveling.
> 47. You ran up to Ód ever howling,
> You jumped quickly into the sheets,
> You run about, noble friend, out at nights,
> As if with he-goats Heidrún were traveling.

Accusations of sexual forwardness are nothing new for Freyja, but adding lasciviousness to the slender dossier of Heidrún changes it considerably and stresses the intoxicating nature of the beer that flows from her. She would thus seem to be less a nurturer and more associated with the Odinic side of the activities at Valhöll. This would seem to me to negate the idea advanced by some of the older scholarship that Heidrún should have a connection with fertility ritual or even, I think, that the first syllable in her name should have referred to the mead consumed at cult events, as some of the handbooks and encyclopedias report. The etymology of the name is unknown, although that first syllable would probably have been understood in Viking and medieval Scandinavia as "bright." Although the second syllable is identical with the noun "rune," no one would have understood it as such, since many common names use it (e.g., Gudrún).

> *See also* Eikthyrnir; Freyja; *Hyndluljód*
>
> *References and further reading:* There is no study limited to Heidrún. The notion that *Heid-* means "sacrificial mead" was, as far as I know, advanced by Jan de Vries in his *Altgermanische Religionsgeschichte* (Berlin: W. de Gruyter, 1956–1957), still the standard handbook of Germanic religion despite its relative age. Readers who thirst for more about Heidrún's mead may wish to consult Stefán Einarsson, "Some Parallels in Norse and Indian Mythology," in *Scandinavian Studies: Studies Presented to Dr. Henry Goddard Leach on the Occasion of His Eighty-Fifth Birthday*, ed. Carl F. Bayerschmidt and Erik J. Friis (Seattle: University of Washington Press for the American-Scandinavian Foundation, 1965), 21–26, but what they find will be abbreviated and speculative.

HEIMDALL

Important but enigmatic god, the "guardian of the gods" and perhaps a boundary figure.

Snorri has this to say of Heimdall in his catalog of the æsir in *Gylfaginning:*

> One is called Heimdall. He is called White-god. He is large and holy. Nine maidens, all sisters, bore him. He is also called Hallinskídi and Gullintanni (Gilded-teeth); his teeth were made of gold. His horse is called Gulltopp (Gold-top). He lives at Himinbjörg near Bilröst. He is the guardian of the gods and sits there at the end of heaven to guard the bridge from mountain giants. He needs less sleep than a bird. Night and day he sees a hundred leagues away; he also hears it when grass grows on the earth or wool on sheep or anything else that can be heard. He has a trumpet called the Gjallarhorn, whose blast can be heard in all the worlds.

In *Skáldskaparmál* Snorri adds more tantalizing information when he tells how kennings can be made for Heimdall:

> By calling him the son of nine mothers or guardian of the gods, as was written above, or White-god, enemy of Loki, seeker of Freyja's necklace. A sword is called the head of Heimdall; it is said that he was struck against a man's head. That is treated in the poem *Heimdalargaldr*, and thereafter the head is called fate of Heimdall; the sword is called fate of man. Heimdall is the owner of Gull-

This figure with its imposing horn, from a stone cross on the Isle of Man, recalls Heimdall and the Gjallarhorn. (Werner Forman/Art Resource)

topp. He is also the visitor to Vágasker (Wave-skerry) and Singastein, when he fought with Loki for the Brísinga men. He is also called Vindhlér (Wind-shelter). Úlf Uggason versified for a long time in *Húsdrápa* about this story, and it is said that they were in the form of seals. He is also the son of Odin.

We have one fragment from the poem *Heimdalargaldr,* quoted by Snorri in *Gylfaginning* right after the passage just translated. In it the god himself speaks, saying that he is the son of nine mothers and the son of nine sisters. This must have been a poem in which Heimdall told of his life and exploits, and it would have been nice to have more of it preserved, for we understand only very imperfectly why a head should be called Heimdall's sword. Was the blow with the head fatal? Did Heimdall have nine lives, one for each mother? If he died from the head blow, how can he still be around in the mythological present? Several sources say that he will sound the Gjallarhorn at the onset of Ragnarök, and

Snorri adds in *Gylfaginning* that Heimdall and Loki will square off in the final battle and that they will kill each other.

Snorri's statement to the effect that Úlf Uggason versified extensively about the previous battle between Heimdall and Loki points out another sad loss, for only one stanza has survived. Thus the myth of a possible loss or theft of the Brísinga men and its recovery by Heimdall is forever lost to us.

We do have some potential information on Heimdall's mothers, but it is conflicting. In *Skáldskaparmál* Snorri speaks of the nine daughters of Ægir and Rán. These fulfill the condition of being sisters, and since many of them bear names meaning or associated with the waves of the sea, Heimdall could somehow be the daughter of nine waves. Alternatively, he may be the one referred to in stanzas 35–38 of *Hyndluljód,* in the "Short *Völuspá*."

> 35. A certain one was born in days of yore,
> With greatly increased power, of the race of gods;
> Nine bore him, a man full of grace [?],
> Giant maidens on the edge of the earth.
>
> . . . .
>
> 37. Gjálp bore him, Greip bore him,
> Eistla bore him and Eyrgjafa,
> Úlfrún bore him and Angeyja,
> Imdr and Atla and Járnsaxa.
> 38. That one was increased by the might of the earth,
> Of the wave-cold sea and the blood of a sacrificial boar.

Many of these names are those of known giantesses. Thor killed Gjálp and Greip and got Magni on Járnsaxa. Given Odin's propensity for dallying with giantesses, this lot would fit the notion of Odin as the father of Heimdall, even if it cannot be demonstrated that they are sisters. It would be nice if the birthplace "on the edge of the earth" and the "wave-cold sea" could be associated with Ægir's daughters, but no one has yet figured out how to do so successfully. Perhaps there were two traditions about Heimdall's mothers.

The son of nine mothers, Heimdall is also, according to the prose header to the eddic poem *Rígsthula,* the progenitor of the social classes of humans. This prose states that Heimdall was traveling and came to a settlement by a coast, where he called himself Ríg. The poem goes on to tell how Ríg is entertained at three households, where he spends time in his hosts' beds. The results are slaves, farmers, and nobles. Possibly related to this is the request of the seeress in *Völuspá* for a hearing, in the first stanza of the poem.

> I ask for a hearing of all the holy races
> Greater and lesser, kinsmen of Heimdall.

The notion of Heimdall as guardian of the gods is not limited to Snorri. *Grímnismál*, stanza 13, which Snorri quoted in *Gylfaginning* in connection with his description of Heimdall cited above, uses the expression, and Loki's somewhat strange insult, in *Lokasenna*, appears to refer to it:

> Shut up, Heimdall! For you in days of yore
> An ugly life was allotted:
> With a dirty wet back you will ever be
> And wake, guardian of the gods.

If the "dirty wet back" has to do with being out in all weathers, then perhaps the name Vindhlér has to do with the same idea.

Heimdall's preternatural hearing may be the subject of an obscure verse in *Völuspá*, stanza 26.

> She knows that Heimdall's hearing is hidden
> Under the holy tree, accustomed to brightness;
> She sees a river washed with a muddy waterfall
> From the pledge of Valfödr [Odin]—would you know yet more?

The "pledge of Valfödr" is his eye, sacrificed for supernatural vision. Apparently Heimdall put some portion of his hearing, or perhaps an ear, in the well at the base of Yggdrasil in order to obtain his special powers of hearing. Although he displays few other similarities with Odin, Heimdall does occasionally dispense wisdom, as when, in *Thrymskvida*, he suggests that Thor should dress up as Freyja in order to get back his hammer. But this passage is troubling, for it says that Heimdall, "whitest of gods, / could see well into the future, / like other vanir." There are no other indications of Heimdall's membership in the vanir. Nor has his whiteness ever been explained.

Heimdall seems to have a certain connection with peripheral locations: born (if we take him to be the subject of the stanzas in *Hyndluljód*, as I do) at "the edge of the earth," encountering humans by a coast, stationed at the end of heaven to guard against giants. These places are all to some extent boundaries: between land and sea, between the world of the gods and that of the giants. Being born "in days of yore" also situates Heimdall at a temporal periphery. Heimdall's other main action in the mythology involves not a spatial but a temporal boundary, namely, his sounding of the Gjallarhorn at the outset of Ragnarök. The main source is *Völuspá*, stanza 46:.

> Mím's sons sport, and the world tree trembles
> At the old Gjallarhorn.

Loudly blows Heimdall, the horn is aloft,
Odin is speaking to Mím's head.

In *Gylfaginning* Snorri paraphrased this verse and added the information that Heimdall blows the Gjallarhorn in order to awaken all the gods for a meeting to deal with the oncoming forces of chaos.

Of all the gods, Heimdall has the closest connection with an animal, namely, the ram. According to *Skáldskaparmál*, a form of his name, Heimdali, is a word for ram, and Heimdali and Hallinskídi turn up in the thulur for ram.

See also Ægir's Daughters; Gjallarhorn; *Hyndluljód; Rígsthula*

References and further reading: My opening definition of Heimdall, above, incorporates the title of an article by Jan de Vries, "Heimdallr, dieu énigmatique," *Études germaniques* 10 (1955): 257–268, which tries to solve the enigma through etymology: *Dall* means something like "spontaneous energy" and was the god's original name, *Heim*, "world," having been added later. As far as I can see, this etymology has gained no adherents and gets us no closer to the solution than does the standard etymology, "World-gleam," which contributed to all sorts of nature-mythological interpretations. Nor does Hugo Pipping's reading of the name as "World-tree" in his *Eddastudier*, vol. 2, Studier i nordisk filologi, 17:3, and Skrifter utgivna av Svenska litteratursällskapet i Finland, 189 (Helsinki: Mercator, 1926), 120–130. Two Lund dissertations scrutinized Heimdall. The first was that of Åke Ohlmarks, *Heimdalls Horn und Odins Auge: Studien zur nordischen und vergleichenden Religionsgeschichte*, vol. 1: *Heimdall und das Horn* (Lund: C. W. K. Gleerup, 1937), which uses suspect methodology to reach suspect conclusions. The second, just four years later, was that of Birger Pering, *Heimdall: Religionsgeschichtliche Untersuchungen zum Verständnis der altnordischen Götterwelt* (Lund: C. W. K. Gleerup, 1941), who argued that "guardian of the gods" originally meant something more like a household spirit or brownie. Georges Dumézil, "Comparative Remarks on the Scandinavian God Heimdallr," in his *Gods of the Ancient Northmen*, ed. Einar Haugen, Publications of the UCLA Center for the Study of Comparative Folklore and Mythology, 3 (Berkeley and Los Angeles, University of California Press, 1973), 126–140, argues by means of a Celtic parallel for Ægir's daughters as Heimdall's mother. Kurt Schier, "*Húsdrápa* 2: Heimdall, Loki und die Meerniere," in *Festgabe für Otto Höfler zum 75. Geburtstag*, ed. Helmut Birkhan, Philologica Germanica, 3 (Vienna: W. Braumuller, 1967), 577–588, makes sense out of the stanza in Úlf's poem about the struggle between Heimdall and Loki. M. Meyer, "Beiträge zur germanischen Mythologie," *Arkiv för nordisk filologi* 23 (1907): 245–256 (esp. 250–256), addressed the idea of Heimdall as a boundary figure. Rudolf Much, "Der nordische Widdergott," in *Deutsche Islandforschung 1930*, vol. 1: *Kultur*, ed. Walther Heinrich Vogt, Veröffentlichungen der Schleswig-Holsteinischen Universitätsgesellschaft, 1928:1 (Breslau: F. Hirt, 1930), 63–67, made the most powerful case yet for Heimdall as ram. The most recent article devoted wholly to Heimdall is now rather long in the tooth: Franz Rolf Schröder,

"Heimdall," *Beiträge zur Geschichte der deutschen Sprache und Literatur* (Tübingen) 89 (1967): 1–41. It provides Indo-European and Mediterranean context but leaves us no closer to a satisfactory understanding of this enigmatic figure.

HEL

Ruler of the world of the dead; daughter of Loki and Angrboda, one of the three monsters that resulted from that union.

Grímnismál, stanza 31, tells of the three roots of the world tree Yggdrasil. Hel lives under one, frost giants live under another, and humans live under the third. Hel's abode is frequently described as having one or more halls, all surrounded by a wall with an imposing gate called variously Helgrind (Hel-gate), Nágrind (Corpse-gate), and Valgrind (Carrion-gate). The way there is call Helveg (Hel-road), and many texts speak of dying as going to or being held by Hel.

Snorri Sturluson's *Gylfaginning* tells how Odin foresaw the trouble that Loki's three monstrous children—the Midgard serpent, Hel, and Fenrir the wolf—would make. He had them brought to him and each was put somewhere relatively safe (although the binding of the wolf Fenrir was not accomplished without the loss of Týr's hand).

Hel he threw into Niflheim [Fog-world] and gave her power over nine worlds, that she should host all those who were sent to her, and they are those who die of illness or old age. She has a large residence there, and the walls are extremely high and the gate huge. Éljudnir [Rain-damp] is the name of her hall, Hunger her plate, Starving her knife, Ganglati her serving boy, Ganglöt her serving woman, Stumbling Block the threshold that leads in, Kör [Sickbed] her bed, Blíkjanda-böl [Pale-misfortune] her bedhangings. She is half dark blue and half flesh color. For this reason she is easily recognized and rather stooping but fierce.

Most of these details are not found outside of Snorri, but the notion of nine netherworlds is not uncommon.

When older poetry says that people are "in" rather than "with" Hel, we are clearly dealing with a place rather than a person, and this is assumed to be the older conception. The place Hel (or the noun *hel*) originally probably just meant "grave." The personification probably came later.

See also Angrboda; Loki

References and further reading: H. R. Ellis Davidson, *The Road to Hel: A Study of the Conception of the Dead in Old Norse Literature* (Cambridge: Cambridge University Press, 1943).

HERMÓD

Son (or servant) of Odin, journeyed to Hel to try to have Baldr restored to the living. The question of Hermód's status (son or servant) is posed by the use of the ambiguous expression *sveinn Óðins,* "Odin's lad," in the main manuscript of Snorri's *Edda* (the other manuscripts say "son" explicitly). There is also a considerable body of evidence suggesting that Hermód may once have been a human hero rather than a god. For example, he is linked with the hero Sigmund in *Hyndluljóð,* stanza 2; both are recipients of gifts from Odin. *Hákonarmál,* stanza 14, puts him at Valhöll awaiting the arrival of the recently defeated Hákon the Good. He is mentioned together with Bragi, who may be the human poet Bragi and not a god. Indeed, Snorri never mentions Hermód in his lists of æsir, although he often seems to be present. Finally, there is the cognate hero Heremod in Old English tradition, both of whose feet are firmly on earth.

If Hermód is Odin's servant, he fulfills a role rather like that of Skírnir, Frey's servant, who was dispatched to the world of the giants to get Gerd as a wife for Frey and to the world of the dwarfs to get the fetter Gleipnir to bind Fenrir. If he is Odin's son, he keeps the Baldr drama within a set of brothers: Baldr the victim, Höd the killer, Hermód the rectifier.

In either case, Hermód's journey to Hel is one of the more picturesque tales in Scandinavian mythology, with many analogues in medieval Christian vision literature and in the heroic legends of the world. He rides off on Odin's horse Sleipnir; passes over the river Gjöll on the Gjallarbrú after being challenged by Módgud; leaps over Helgrind, the gate to Hel's compound; and sits beside his dead brother in Hel's hall. The next day he gets Hel to agree to release Baldr if all creation will weep (it will not), and from the world of the dead he takes back to the gods Odin's ring Draupnir, which was burned on Baldr's pyre, and gifts from Nanna to Frigg.

Hermód is an interesting figure, but the myth is not about him. It is about Baldr and Höd, and they are the ones who return after Ragnarök.

> **See also** Baldr; Gjallarbrú; Hel; Módgud
> **References and further reading:** John Lindow, *Murder and Vengeance among the Gods: Baldr in Scandinavian Mythology,* FF Communications, 262 (Helsinki: Suomalainen Tiedeakatemia, 1997), chapter 4.

HILDISVÍNI (BATTLE-PIG)

Freyja's boar (or her lover or protégé).

Hildisvíni is known only from stanza 7 of *Hyndluljóð.* Freyja is conversing with the giantess Hyndla, and the giantess accuses Freyja of having her husband with her on a trip to Valhöll. Freyja answers:

You are mistaken, Hyndla, I think you are dreaming,
When you say my husband is with me on a trip to Valhöll,
Where a gilded boar glistens, golden-bristled,
Hildisvíni, whom they made for me, skillful,
Two dwarfs, Dáin and Nabbi.

The "husband" in question is not Freyja's husband at all but Óttar, a human whom she has brought along to learn his genealogy. Some translators use "lover" for the noun in question, which literally means "man." The relationship of Freyja and Óttar is mysterious, although the poem makes it clear that Freyja favors him because he has worshipped her. If he appears in this stanza in the shape of a boar, perhaps it is because Freyja has transformed him. Hildisvíni is mentioned nowhere else.

See also Freyja; Gullinborsti; *Hyndluljód*

HIMINBJÖRG (HEAVEN-MOUNTAIN)

Heimdall's home.

Grímnismál, stanza 13, which is part of the list of divine dwellings seen by Odin as he hangs in Geirröd's fire, is the main source:

Himinbjörg is the eighth, there yet they say Heimdall
Rules the cult places;
There the guardian of the gods drinks in the peaceful hall,
Happy, the good mead.

Snorri cites this verse when describing Heimdall in *Gylfaginning*. Paraphrasing it, Snorri writes that Heimdall "lives at Himinbjörg near Bilröst. He is the guardian of the gods and sits there at the end of heaven to guard the bridge from mountain giants." Although the bridge of the æsir leads to the well, which is presumably at the center of the abode of the gods, Snorri's notion of Bilröst as the rainbow may have led him to put Himinbjörg at the end of heaven. Such a conception is, however, consistent with the notion of Heimdall as a boundary figure.

See also Bilröst; Heimdall

HJADNINGAVÍG (BATTLE-OF-THE-FOLLOWERS-OF-HEDIN)

Eternal combat of warriors, incited by Freyja and ended only through the holiness of Olaf Tryggvason.

The fullest version of the story is in *Sörla tháttr*. Freyja has obtained a beautiful necklace (the Brísinga men?) by sleeping with four neighboring dwarfs, but at

Odin's command, Loki has stolen it. When Freyja awakens and misses the neck-lace, she confronts Odin, who tells her she can only have it back by fulfilling one rather strange condition: She must make two kings, each of whom is served by 20 kings, fall out and engage in a battle that through charms and magic will go on without end, unless it is interrupted by a Christian who serves a great king.

Although we never see Freyja or Odin again in the text, this condition is ful-filled when two great kings, Hedin and Högni, have a falling out when Hedin abducts Högni's daughter Hild. This he does through the machinations of Gön-dul, a woman who sits on a throne in a clearing in a dark forest and gives him a magic potion to drink, which clouds his reason. Elsewhere Göndul is a valkyrie name, and a medieval audience might well have recognized an association between it and the word *gandr*, "magic." The two armies meet on an island, and each night and day for 143 years they fight. If someone's head is cloven down to the shoulders, immediately he is made whole, and the battle goes on. Only the arrival and intervention of Ívarr ljómi (Gleam), a retainer of Olaf Tryggvason, brings the battle to an end, an end that is welcomed by the weary warriors, who know that they have been the victims of magic spells.

Although it is of interest in its own right, to my mind the Hjadningavíg is most valuable in the context of Scandinavian mythology for casting a shadow over the life of the einherjar at Valhöll. That life is presented as wholly positive, but the endless battle of the Hjadningar is wholly negative. This has to do in part with the view in *Sörla tháttr* of the pagan gods: Odin is an imperious ruler who covets the possessions of his subjects, Loki is a toady and a thief, and Freyja sells her body for a piece of jewelry. This is most easily explained as a post-pagan view, but the situation is more complicated than that. In the first place, the story was also told by Bragi Boddason the Old, reckoned the first skald, in his *Rag-narsdrápa* (stanzas 7–12), and in his version a woman keeps the battle going by curing men's wounds. This woman is decidedly evil. When Snorri describes the Hjadningavíg in *Skáldskaparmál*, he says that Hild awakens the dead warriors each night so that they can fight the next day, and this is a direct parallel to his presentation of life at Valhöll. Snorri says that the Hjadningavíg will go on until Ragnarök. I believe that the similarity between the Hjadningavíg and life at Val-höll points up the emptiness of a life given over to battles and feasting, an empti-ness, I would add, that is borne out when the einherjar prove to be of use at Ragnarök when the entire world is destroyed.

> ***See also*** Brísinga men; Einherjar; Freyja; Loki; Valhöll
> ***References and further reading:*** In the distressingly familiar pattern of finding for-eign sources, Niels Lukman proposed an Irish annal for *Sörla tháttr* and other texts dealing with the Hjadningavíg in "An Irish Source and Some Icelandic *fornaldarsögur*," *Mediaeval Scandinavia* 10 (1977): 41–57. At least Magnus

Olsen saw a native source, Hallfred vandrædaskáld's memorial poem to Olaf Tryggvason: "Hjadningekampen og Hallfreds arvedraapa over Olaf Tryggvason," in *Heidersskrift til Marius Hægstad fra venner og æresveinar 15de juli 1925* (Oslo: O. Norli, 1925), 23–33. Otto Höfler, *Germanisches Sakralkönigtum*, vol. 1: *Der Runenstein von Rök und die germanische Individualweihe* (Tübingen: M. Niemeyer, 1952), associated the Hjadningavíg and einherjar traditions with an ecstatic Odin warrior cult and the Wild Hunt.

HLIDSKJÁLF

Odin's high seat, with a view over all the worlds.

Although a few skalds called Odin "Lord of Hlidskjálf," Hlidskjálf does not otherwise appear in poetry. It is, however, crucial to two eddic poem, *Grímnismál* and *Skírnismál*, each of which mentions Hlidskjálf in a prose header. In the prose header to *Grímnismál* Odin and Frigg are sitting in Hlidskjálf and see their foster sons Agnar and Geirröd, the one living in a cave, the other a king. Frigg and Odin make a bet over whether Geirröd is stingy with food, and Odin sets off to test the premise. In *Skírnismál* it is Frey who sits in Hlidskjálf and sees something that sets in motion a narrative, namely, the beautiful arms of Gerd, which make him lovesick. Frey sends Skírnir to woo the giantess on his behalf.

In *Gylfaginning* Snorri Sturluson says there is a place or estate called Hlidskjálf, and when Alfödr sat in the high seat there, "he saw over all the worlds and the behavior of each person and comprehended all the things he saw." Although this statement might make it seem that Hlidskjálf is Valhöll rather than a seat, later in *Gylfaginning* Snorri refers explicitly to Hlidskjálf as the high seat. Frey's fateful use of the seat is mentioned in connection with the wooing of Gerd, but the only time Odin actually uses it is to locate Loki after he has run off from the scene of Baldr's murder.

The name Hlidskjálf appears to mean something like "doorway-bench," or perhaps "watchtower."

> ***See also*** Baldr; *Grímnismál*; Loki
> ***References and further reading:*** In an interesting argument, Vilhelm Kiil, "Hliðskjálf og seiðhjallr," *Arkiv för nordisk filologi* 75 (1960): 84–112, juxtaposed Hlidskjálf with the raised dais on which seid performances—attempts to see in other worlds—were apparently carried out.

HLÍN

Minor goddess; possible name for Frigg.

Snorri lists Hlín twelfth in his catalog in *Gylfaginning* of goddesses among the æsir and says, "She is put to watch over those people whom Frigg wishes to protect from some danger. For that reason there is a proverb that the one who gets away *hleinir* ('protects'?)." The name is common as the base word in woman kennings in skaldic poetry. *Völuspá*, stanza 53, says that the second sorrow of Hlín will occur when Odin goes to fight the wolf at Ragnarök, and the bright killer of Beli (i.e., Frey) goes against Surt; "then Frigg's joy will perish." If Hlín is Frigg, her first sorrow would have been the death of Baldr.

HLÓRA

Thor's foster mother, according to Snorri Sturluson in *Skáldskaparmál*.

No other source mentions the name, although it appears to be similar to the Thor name Hlór(r)idi.

HLÓRRIDI

Alternate name for Thor, found in eddic poetry.

Hlórridi is the most common alternate name that Thor takes. It is found in *Hymiskvida*, *Lokasenna*, and *Thrymskvida*, and in the verse of one older skald. The name looks as though it should mean "noisy-rider," but the meaning and etymology are disputed.

HNOSS (TREASURE)

Daughter of Freyja and Ód, according to Snorri Sturluson's *Edda* and according to one of the thulur.

In *Gylfaginning* Snorri says that Hnoss is so beautiful that from her name things that are beautiful and precious are known as *hnossir* (pl.). *Hnoss* is indeed a common noun, but the relationship between it and Freyja's daughter is the opposite of what Snorri said: Hnoss appears in no myth, but Snorri repeats in *Skáldskaparmál* that "mother of Hnoss" is a valid kenning for Freyja.

See also Freyja

HÖD

Baldr's killer, the blind son of Odin.

Höd's role in Baldr's death is found in stanza 32 in the *Codex Regius* version of *Völuspá* in three words: "Höd did shoot." In *Baldrs draumar*, stanza 11, Odin asks the seeress who will kill Baldr. She replies,

> Höd will bear the high praise-tree [Baldr] thither.
> He will be the death of Baldr
> And Odin's son he will deprive of life.

Neither of these stanzas says anything about Höd being blind, or of Loki playing any role in Baldr's death. That, however, is the way Snorri Sturluson has it in *Gylfaginning,* in the best-known version of the story. In response to his bad dreams, Baldr has been made invincible, and all the gods are honoring him by flinging weapons at him. Loki learns that mistletoe did not take the oath not to harm Baldr, and he makes a spear from it.

> And Höd stood on the outside of the circle, because he was blind. Then Loki said to him: "Why are you not shooting at Baldr?" He answers: "Because I cannot see where Baldr is, and also because I have no weapon." Then Loki said to him: "Do as others do and honor Baldr as others do. I will show you where he is standing; shoot this stick at him." Höd took the mistletoe and shot it at Baldr at Loki's direction. The shot flew through Baldr, and he fell dead to the earth.

In the *Gesta Danorum* of Saxo Grammaticus the cognate figure Høtherus is a human king who, like the demigod Balderus, has fallen in love with Nanna. Høtherus and an ally confront Balderus and the gods in a sea battle and gain victory when Høtherus slices the handle off Thor's hammer, the gods' major weapon, with his magic sword. Høtherus then marries Nanna. In a subsequent battle, Balderus defeats him. Balderus is plagued by dreams of his desired Nanna. Høtherus is now chosen king of the Danes, but in his absence the Danes vote again, and this time they choose Balderus. In a following battle, Høtherus is put to flight. In their final battle he deals Balderus a fatal wound. Here again, there is no blindness and no accidental killing.

The name Höd seems quite clearly to mean "battle," which would fit Saxo's version of the story better than Snorri's. In any case, accidental or not, Baldr's death must be avenged, and *Völuspá* and *Baldrs draumar* also agree that vengeance was visited on Höd. Just after saying that Höd did shoot, the seeress who speaks *Völuspá* adds these lines:

> Baldr's brother was   quickly born;
> That son of Odin   killed when he was one night old.
> 33. He did not wash his hands   or comb his head,
> Until he had carried to the pyre   Baldr's adversary.
> Frigg still weeps in Fensalir   the woe of Valhöll.

Similarly, in *Baldrs draumar* Odin asks the seeress who will avenge Baldr, and she replies with another version of the lines just quoted. And Saxo has an elaborate story of how Odin sires the avenger Bous on Rinda (Rind). In *Gylfaginning* Snorri tells how the gods take vengeance on Loki but are silent toward Höd.

However, in *Skáldskaparmál* he lists these kennings for Váli: "son of Odin and Rind," "avenging god of Baldr," "enemy of Höd and his killer." Clearly Snorri's reticence in *Gylfaginning* has to do with his presenting Höd as blind and victim of Loki's trickery.

Höd, however, like the avenger Váli, is one of the æsir who will survive Ragnarök and reinhabit the purged cosmos. Of the æsir, three pairs of brothers survive Ragnarök: Thor's sons Magni and Módi, Odin's avenger sons Vídar and Váli, and Baldr and Höd.

> *See also* Baldr; Magni; Módi; Ragnarök; Váli, Son of Odin; Vídar
> *References and further reading:* John Lindow, *Murder and Vengeance among the Gods: Baldr in Scandinavian Mythology*, FF Communications, 262 (Helsinki: Suomalainen Tiedeakatemia, 1997), chapter 2, discusses the scholarship on Höd. See also the readings suggested in the Baldr entry.

HODDMÍMIR'S FOREST

According to *Vafthrúdnismál,* stanza 45, the place where Líf and Lífthrasir will hide themselves during Fimbulvetr (Mighty-winter, which is to occur at the onset of Ragnarök).

In Hoddmímir's forest Líf and Lífthrasir will have morning dew as nourishment, and from them the race of humans will descend.

Hodd means "treasure" or "gold," and Mímir, of course, is an important if enigmatic mythological figure. If Hoddmímir is identical with Mímir, his forest would presumably be near the well with which Mímir is associated. A tree called Mímameid is found twice in the poem editors call *Fjölsvinnsmál.* Mímameid could be a name for Yggdrasil; if so, Hoddmímir's forest might also have to do with the tree.

HŒNIR

Enigmatic god, involved with such major moments of the mythology as the Æsir-Vanir War, the creation of human beings, and Ragnarök.

Stanzas 17–18 of *Völuspá* tell of the creation of the first humans, Ask and Embla, who were found capable of little and fateless. Odin, Hœnir, and Lódur endow them with the various qualities they need to live. Hœnir's gift is *óð,* which ordinarily means "poetry" and is in fact identical with the first syllable of Odin's name and with that of the shadowy god Ód. In his version of the creation of humans in *Gylfaginning,* however, Snorri refers to wit and movement or possibly emotion at this point, and therefore some observers think *óð* has that meaning when Hœnir gives it to the proto-humans. However, Snorri says that the creators were the sons of Bor, and there is no reason to think that that group included Hœnir. What he gave to the first man and woman must remain a mystery, but if it is poetry, we must imagine a very close connection between Odin and Hœnir.

There is also a close connection with Loki. Thjódólf of Hvin's *Haustlöng*, one of the oldest skaldic poems, refers to Loki twice as "Hœnir's friend" and once as "the tester of Hœnir's courage." The myth that Thjódólf is telling is that of the encounter of Odin, Loki, and Hœnir with Thjazi, and the three also travel together in the episode in heroic legend regarding the wergild (compensation) for the killing of Otr. There, as in the Thjazi myth, Loki is the principal actor, but the presence of Hœnir as one of a triad of traveling gods seems fairly constant.

According to Snorri's story of the settlement following the Æsir-Vanir War in *Ynglinga saga*, chapter 4, Hœnir was sent by the æsir to the vanir along with Mímir as part of the exchange of hostages (men exchanged as a pledge of good faith). Hœnir appeared to have the qualities of a chieftain, and the vanir immediately employed him in that capacity. But Hœnir relied exclusively on the counsels of Mímir, and when Mímir was not present, Hœnir responded to queries by saying, "Let others decide." The vanir therefore deduced that they had been cheated, and they beheaded Mímir and sent the head to Odin, who preserved it and listened to the hidden things it had to say to him. Thus, Hœnir was, indirectly at least, a contributor to Odin's arsenal of techniques for acquiring and mastering wisdom.

For the most part, the survivors of Ragnarök are pairs of second-generation gods: Baldr and Höd, Magni and Módi, Vídar and Váli. But *Völuspá*, stanza 63, adds Hœnir to the list. The line in question says that after unsown fields grow and Baldr and Höd return, Hœnir was able to choose *hlautvið*, which looks as though it should mean something like "wooden lots" ("lot" as in "to cast lots"). If so, the line must mean that Hœnir survived Ragnarök and carried out some sort of divining; some observers understand the line as referring to priestly functions of some sort. Snorri omits Hœnir from his account of Ragnarök and from his catalog of the æsir in *Gylfaginning*, but he does say there that Njörd was exchanged for Hœnir in the settlement of "the gods and the vanir." Snorri does put Hœnir at Ægir's banquet at the beginning of *Skáldskaparmál*, however, so he cannot have thought that Hœnir remained among the vanir. Later in *Skáldskaparmál* Snorri mentions possible kennings for Hœnir, and these are strange indeed: "swift god," "long leg," "mud king." From these kennings has arisen some speculation associating Hœnir with such birds as the crane or stork, but such a surmise can hardly be aligned with his actual role in the mythology. There his salient feature appears to be a close connection with Odin.

See also Æsir-Vanir War; Ragnarök

References and further reading: Bror Schnittger, "Storken som livsbringare i våra fäders tro," *Fornvännen* 11 (1916): 104–118, saw Hœnir as a stork; Eric Elgqvist, "Guden Höner," *Arkiv för nordisk filologi* 72 (1957): 155–172, as a crane; and Folke Ström, "Guden Hœnir och odensvalan" *Arv* 12 (1956): 41–68 (summary in English), as a black stork. The connection with Odin is argued most ably by Franz Rolf Schröder, "Hœnir, eine mythologische Unter-suchung," *Beiträge zur Geschichte der deutschen Sprache und Literatur* (1918): 219–252.

HÖRN

Name for Freyja.

Snorri says in *Gylfaginning* that Freyja has many names because she took on dif-ferent names among the various peoples she encountered when she went to search for her missing husband, Ód. Hörn turns up frequently as a base word for woman kennings in skaldic poetry, and one kenning does equate the name with Freyja: "Praised child of Hörn" for a valuable ax, a precious object, that is, a *hnoss*, which is the name of Freyja's daughter. The meaning of the name is usu-ally taken to be related to the word for linen.

What makes the name Hörn most interesting is its appearance in place-names such as the Swedish Härnevi, which would represent a cult site for Hörn.

> ***See also*** Freyja
> ***References and further reading:*** On the place-names, see Magnus Olsen, "Hærnevi: En gammel svensk og norsk gudinde," *Norske videnskaps-akademi i Oslo, forhandlinger i videnskabs-selskabet i Christiania*, 1908, no. 6: 1–18, and Oskar Lundberg and Hans Sperber, *Härnevi*, Uppsala universitets årsskrift, 1911:1, and Meddelanden från nordiska seminariet, 4 (Uppsala: Akademiska boktryckeriet, 1912). Gunnar Knudsen coined the phrase "pseudotheophoric place-names" to refer to ones wrongly associated with cult and included Härnevi as his main example: "Pseudotheofore stednavne," *Namn och bygd* 27 (1939): 105–115.

HRÆSVELG

Giant, originator of the wind.

Hræsvelg is the subject of a question Odin puts to the wise giant Vafthrúdnir in their contest of wisdom: "Whence comes the wind, / so that it travels over the wave; / even men see it seldom" (*Vafthrúdnismál*, stanza 36). The giant answers in the following stanza:

> He is called Hræsvelg,
> who sits at heaven's end,
> a giant, in the shape of an eagle;

from his wings
they say the wind comes
over all people.

Snorri knew this stanza. He paraphrased and then quoted it in *Gylfaginning* when having Hár answer Gangleri's question "Whence comes the wind?" Snorri added the detail that the giant sat at the north end of heaven and that winds originate from under the eagle giant's wings when he spread them for flight.

Hræsvelg is usually understood as "Corpse-swallower," which would be an appropriate name both for an eagle and a giant, even if it has nothing to do with wind. Jón Hnefill Aðalsteinsson reads the name as "Shipwreck-current," which would agree more readily with the wind moving over the sea.

> ***References and further reading:*** Jón Hnefill Aðalsteinsson, "Gods and Giants in Old Norse Mythology," *Temenos* 26 (1990), reprinted as "Hræsvelgr, the Wind-Giant, Reinterpreted," in Jón Hnefill Aðalsteinsson, *A Piece of Horse Liver: Myth, Ritual, and Folklore in Old Icelandic Sources* (Reykjavík: Háskólaútgáfan, 1998), 13–32.

HRAUDUNG

Human king, father of Agnar and Geirröd according to the prose header to *Grímnismál*.

The name, if not the person, turns up in several other contexts associated with heroic legend rather than with myth. Interestingly, it is also attested as a giant name, probably because it means something like "destroyer."

HRÍMFAXI

Horse that pulls Nótt (Night), according to *Vafthrúdnismál*, stanza 14, and Snorri Sturluson, who paraphrases the stanza in *Gylfaginning*.

Stanza 14 answers a question put by Odin to Vafthrúdnir in stanza 13: "What horse pulls Nótt [across the sky]?"

Hrímfaxi he is named, who pulls each
Night for the useful powers;
Bit-drops [of foam] he lets fall each morning,
Thence comes dew into the valleys.

See also Nótt; Skínfaxi; *Vafthrúdnismál*

HRÍMGRÍMNIR (FROST-MASKED)

Giant invoked in the threat Skírnir makes to Gerd in order to convince her to marry
Frey. The entire passage is thrilling, so I quote it in full:

> 33. Odin is enraged at you, the prince of the æsir [Thor] is enraged at you,
> Frey will hate you,
> You outrageously wicked girl, you have still got
> The powerful rage of the gods.
> 34. Let the giants hear, let the frost-giants hear,
> The sons of Suttung, members of the æsir,
> How I forbid, how I ban,
> Joy of men to the maid,
> Use of men to the maid.
> 35. Hrímgrímnir is the name of the giant who shall possess you,
> Down below Nágrind [the gate to Hel's realm].
> There let wretches on the roots of the tree
> Give you goat piss.
> A better drink you will never get,
> Maiden, from your mouth,
> Maiden, to your mouth.
> 36. Thurs [Giant] I carve for you and three staves
> *Ergi* [sexual perversion] and madness and impatience;
> So I can erase it, as I carved it,
> If need be.

At this point, Gerd capitulates, and the marriage is arranged.

It is clear that Hrímgrímnir (whose name is included in the thulur for giants
but is not found elsewhere) is part of something bigger. If she will not marry
Frey, Gerd is to be denied all ordinary sexual congress, and that is clear (stanza
34). But the consequences of such denial are social. Despite being married (or
perhaps I should say mated), she will live in social exile, her wine turned not to
water but to worse (stanza 35). And all of this has a mental component as well
(stanza 36). No wonder she changed her mind.

> ***See also*** Frey; Gerd
> ***References and further reading:*** On Skírnir's curse in general, see Joseph Harris,
> "Cursing with the Thistle: *Skírnismál* 31, 6–8, and OE Metrical Charm 9,
> 16–17," *Neuphilologische Mitteilungen* 76 (1975): 26–33.

HRINGHORNI (RING-HORN)

Baldr's funeral ship, according to Snorri Sturluson in *Gylfaginning.*
The gods were unable to launch the ship and called for the help of the giantess
Hyrrokkin. She flung the ship down the rollers so fiercely that flames emerged

and the earth shook. Presumably with the launching of the ship Snorri intended a floating cremation, as is described in some heroic literature.

The name of the ship could refer to a ring or circle at the prow, as was found on the Oseberg ship, a funeral ship buried near the Oslo fjord during the ninth century.

See also Baldr; Hyrrokkin
References and further reading: In my *Murder and Vengeance among the Gods: Baldr in Scandinavian Mythology*, FF Communications, 262 (Helsinki: Suomalainen Tiedeakatemia, 1997), chapter 3, I discuss the related evidence for floating funerals.

Dragon-headed post from the Oseberg ship burial. (Werner Forman/Art Resource)

HRÓDVITNIR

Wolf, father of Hati, probably Fenrir. Paraphrasing *Grímnismál*, Snorri Sturluson writes in the *Gylfaginning* of his *Edda* that Hati Hródvitnisson (son of Hródvitnir) will swallow the moon. The identification with Fenrir comes from *Lokasenna*, stanza 39. Loki has just reminded Týr that Fenrir ripped his hand off. Týr responds:

> I lack my hand, and you lack Hródvitnir;
> A baleful loss for each.
> Nor does the wolf have it well, who in bonds shall
> Await the judgment of the gods.

The name Hródvitnir (or Hródrsvitnir, another form of the name) means something like "famous wolf."

See also Fenrir; Hati Hródvitnisson; Máni; Sól; Týr

HROPT

Alternate name for Odin, perhaps the one most commonly found in skaldic and eddic poetry.

The meaning of this name is disputed, but some observers think there is a connection with Odin's erotic activity, especially his seduction of Rind so as to beget an avenger for Baldr. The best evidence for this surmise is the fact that in Book 3 of Saxo's *Gesta Danorum*, which describes this seduction, Odin takes the name Rofterus (in Book 9 he takes the similar name Roftarus when he cures Siwardus [Sigurd] in such as way as to give him the nickname "snake-in-the-eye").

> *See also* Odin; Rind
>
> *References and further reading:* Magnus Olsen, "En iagttagelse vedkommende Balder-diktningen," in *Studier tillägnade Axel Kock, tidskriftens redaktör, 1888–1925*, Arkiv för nordisk filologi, 40, supplement (Lund: C. W. K. Gleerup), 169–177, argued the connection with the seduction of Rind.

HRUNGNIR

Strongest of the giants, defeated by Thor in a formal duel.

The myth is retained in the skald Thjódólf of Hvin's *Haustlöng*, stanzas 14–20, and in the *Skáldskaparmál* of Snorri's *Edda*. As Snorri tells it, there are four scenes: Odin's initial encounter with Hrungnir, Thor's journey to the duel, the duel itself, and the aftermath. Thjódólf tells only the middle two, although he hints at the last. Stanzas 14–16 of *Haustlöng* describe Thor's journey to the duel, as the entire cosmos reacts—mountains shake and the earth is in flames. Stanzas 17–19 tell of the giant's standing on his shield and of weapons flying at each other, Thor's hammer and the giant's whetstone. In stanza 20 Thjódólf hints at the removal of the piece of whetstone from Thor's head, but we learn no more.

According to Snorri, the onset of the story takes place when Odin is riding Sleipnir and encounters the giant Hrungnir mounted on Gullfaxi (Gold-mane). They exchange words, and soon Hrungir is pursuing Odin in a giant rage. He rides all the way into Ásgard, where the gods are required to give hospitality. Drunk, the giant boasts he will move Valhöll to Giantland and kill all the giants except Freyja and Sif, whom he will keep for himself. The gods call on Thor, but because Hrungnir is a guest no blows may be exchanged. The two therefore agree to a duel, to be held at Grjótúnargard (Stony-farm-enclosure). The giants, especially, realize that the duel is important, for Hrungnir is the strongest of them.

The travel scene is highly attenuated in *Skáldskaparmál*. Thor arrives at the dueling place with Thjálfi, who is not in Thjódólf's version. Nor is the clay monster Mökkurkálfi (Mist-calf), whom the giants have built to be Hrungnir's second and who is equipped with the heart of a mare. Mökkurkálfi is not much use, however; he wets himself at the sight of Thor and is easily killed by Thjálfi.

Thjálfi's big contribution is to tell Hrungnir that Thor will attack from below. The giant stands on his shield and thus cannot use it to protect himself against the hammer Mjöllnir. Thor flings his hammer, and the giant flings his whetstone in return. The weapons meet in midair. The hammer shatters the whetstone and finds its mark, killing Hrungnir, but a piece of the whetstone lodges in Thor's head. He lies under Hrungnir's body until his three-year-old son Magni (three nights old, according to some manuscripts of Snorri's *Edda*!) lifts it off, saying that he could have killed the giant easily.

Thor is visited by the seeress Gróa, who is to sing the whetstone out of his head. When Thor thinks the cure is imminent, he wishes to reward her, and he tells her that he carried her husband Aurvandil back from Giantland in a basket. A toe was sticking out and it froze, so Thor broke it off and threw it up into the sky to make the star Aurvandilstá (Aurvandil's toe). He tells her Aurvandil will soon be home. At this news Gróa loses her concentration, and the piece of whetstone never does get out of Thor's head.

The most important aspect of this myth is of course that Thor is able to defeat the strongest of giants in a formal duel. Duels had a certain legal status, and the gods therefore once again ratified their hierarchical superiority over the giants. However, in my view it is also important that Thor is able in the end to clean up a mess first made by Odin, and in so doing we even learn that he put a star in place, thereby taking on a bit of the cosmogonic role usually held by Odin. The myth shows not only how close the rivalry between the gods and giants is, but also how close the rivalry between Odin and Thor is.

> *See also* Magni; Módi; Thjálfi; Thor
>
> *References and further reading:* Kemp Malone, "Hrungnir," *Arkiv för nordisk filologi* 61 (1946): 284–285, proposes an etymology for Hrungnir meaning "big person, strong man." In his *Gods of the Ancient Northmen*, ed. Einar Haugen, Publications of the UCLA Center for the Study of Comparative Folklore and Mythology, 3 (Berkeley and Los Angeles: University of California Press, 1973), 68–71, Georges Dumézil makes the argument that the story involves the initiation of Thjálfi by Thor, in the killing of the made monster, and several eminent scholars have accepted this hypothesis. My analysis of the story is to be found in "Thor's Duel with Hrungnir," *Alvíssmál: Forschungen zur mittelalterlichen Kultur Scandinaviens* 6 (1996): 3–18.

HUGIN (THOUGHT) AND MUNIN (MIND)

Odin's two ravens.

In eddic poetry, Hugin and Munin are mentioned in *Grímnismál*, stanza 20:

> Hugin and Munin fly each day
> Over the earth.

Helmet plate from Vendel, showing what might be Odin accompanied by Hugin and Munin and confronted by a serpent. (Statens Historiska Museum, Stockholm)

> I am worried about Hugin, that he not come back,
> And yet more worried about Munin.

Why they fly is indicated by Snorri Sturluson, who says in *Gylfaginning*, just before quoting the above stanza,

> Two ravens sit on his [Odin's] shoulders and say into his ear everything they see

or hear. Their names are Hugin and Munin. He dispatches them at daybreak to fly over all the world and they return at breakfast time. From this he becomes wise about many events, and thus he is called the Raven-god.

In chapter 8 of his *Ynglinga saga* Snorri gives a euhemerized version: Odin has two ravens to whom he had taught speech. They fly all around and report back to him.

The ravens' connection with Odin may be age-old, for Migration Period bracteates frequently portray a figure with birds near his head, and many observers believe this motif is Odin and his ravens. Hugin and Munin are attested as raven names in early skaldic poetry. The ability to send one's "thought" and "mind" may be related to the trance-state journey of shamans. The worry about their return, expressed in the stanza from *Grímnismál*, would be consistent with the danger the shaman faces on the trance-state journey.

> ***See also*** Bracteates; Odin
> ***References and further reading:*** Hugin and Munin are treated among Albert Morey Sturtevant's "Comments on Mythological Name Giving in Old Norse," *Germanic Review* 29 (1954): 68–71.

HVEDRUNG

Alternate name for Loki.

Völuspá, stanza 55, describing the vengeance that Vídar takes on Fenrir, calls the beast "the son of Hvedrung," and the skaldic poem *Ynglinga tal*, by Thjódólf of Hvin, uses the kenning "Hvedrung's maiden" for Hel. As Fenrir and Hel make up two of Loki's three monstrous offspring, Hvedrung must be Loki.

The thulur list Hvedrung as an Odin name, but it is found nowhere.

> ***See also*** Fenrir; Hel; Loki

HVERGELMIR (HOT-SPRING-BOILER)

Spring located near the center of the cosmos.

The major source is *Grímnismál*, stanza 26:

> Eikthyrnir is the name of a hart, who stands at the hall of Herjafödr [Odin]
> And bites from the limbs of Lærad.
> Yet from his horns it drips into Hvergelmir,
> Thence all waters have their ways.

In *Gylfaginning* Snorri Sturluson assigns Hvergelmir to the mythic past:

> It was many ages before the earth was created, that Niflheim was made, and in the middle of it is the spring Hvergelmir, and from it flow those rivers that are

so named: Svöl (Cool), Gunnthrá (Battle-pain), Fjörm (Rushing), Fimbulthul (Mighty-wind or Mighty-speaker), Slíd (Dangerous) and Hríd (Storm), Sylg (Slurp) and Ylg (She-wolf), Víd (Wide), Leipt (Flash).

Although he does not state it explicitly, these rivers appear to be the Élivágar, which Snorri begins describing in the next paragraph. But they are not all the rivers that flow from Hvergelmir according to Snorri. Later in *Gylfaginning* Snorri says that drops from the horn Eikthyrnir flow down into Hvergelmir, and from it flow these rivers:

Síd, Víd, Sœkin, Eikin, Svöl, Gunnthrá, Fjörm, Fimbulthul, Gípul, Göpul, Gömul, Geivimul—these flow into the settlements of the æsir. These are named too: Thyn, Vín, Thöll, Höll, Grá, Gunnthráin, Nyt, Nöt, Nönn, Hrönn, Vína, Vegsvínn, Thjódnuma.

Elsewhere in *Gylfaginning* Snorri says that there are countless serpents in Hvergelmir with the dragon Nídhögg.

See also Eikthyrnir; Nídhögg

HYMIR

Hardheaded giant; host and fishing buddy of Thor when Thor hooks the Midgard serpent; owner of the kettle Thor gets to brew the beer of the gods; father of Týr.

Thor's interactions with Hymir are found in the (probably late) eddic poem *Hymiskvida* and in Snorri's *Gylfaginning*. According to *Hymiskvida*, Hymir has the kettle that the gods need to brew beer, but he gives it to Thor after Thor is able to pass the test of breaking a cup. This he does, following the advice of Týr's mother, by throwing it at the head of the giant, which is harder than any cup. The giant says the gods can have the kettle if they can lift it, but only Thor can pass this second test. On the way home Hymir leads a force of giants against Thor, and Thor kills them all.

Snorri makes of Hymir a less-imposing figure. He hosts Thor when the latter appears in the form of a young man, but he clearly has doubts about the lad's abilities. Thor is able to dispel these doubts, and when the two go fishing it is Thor who pushes the envelope. They venture into uncharted waters, and when Thor hooks the Midgard serpent, the giant—apparently out of fear, not any solidarity with his jötun kin—cuts the line, so that the serpent probably survived the encounter, according to Snorri. Hymir apparently does not, as Thor smacks him overboard.

According to *Hymiskvida*, Hymir is the father of Týr, one of the æsir, and this makes Hymir unique (Loki has a giant father, Fárbauti, but Loki is only

Sandstone carving discovered at Gosforth Church in Cumberland depicting Thor and Hymir fishing for the Midgard serpent. (Society of Antiquaries)

numbered among the æsir, not a real member of the group). If Hymir really succeeded in making a marriage with one of the female æsir, as the poem suggests, he is the only such success story of the jötnar. Besides Týr, his son, he apparently had daughters who remained giants: In *Lokasenna*, stanza 34, when Njörd challenges Loki, Loki responds with this unflattering stanza:

Shut up, Njörd. You were sent
    from here to the east
A hostage for the gods;
Hymir's maidens used you as
    a urinal
And pissed in your mouth.

It is not impossible that "Hymir's maidens" is simply a kenning for giantesses, since Hymir is often the modifier in kennings for giants. However, there is a parallel with Geirröd, whom Thor also visits and whose two threatening daughters he kills. Perhaps here we see a comparison between helpless old Njörd and Thor, the god of might.

The etymology of Hymir's name has not been satisfactorily explained.

See also Geirröd; *Hymiskvida;* Thor

References and further reading:
Preben Meulengracht Sørensen's article on Thor's fishing expedition is "Thor's Fishing Expedi-

tion," in *Words and Objects: Towards a Dialogue between Archaeology and the History of Religion*, ed. Gro Steinsland (Oslo: Norwegian University Press, 1986), 257–278. Franz Rolf Schröder's attempt to recover older stages of the myth of the acquisition of the kettle is "Das Hymirlied: Zur Frage verblasster Mythen in den Götterliedern der *Edda*," *Arkiv för nordisk filologi* 70 (1955): 1–40. A basic treatment is Konstantin Reichardt, "*Hymiskvida*: Interpretation. Wortschatz. Alter," *Beiträge zur Geschichte der deutschen Sprache und Literatur* 57 (1933): 130–156, which provoked the response of Jan de Vries, "Das Wort Godmálugr in der *Hymiskvida*," *Germanisch-Romanisch Monatsschrift* 35 (1954): 336–337. C. W. von Sydow, "Jätten Hymies bägare," *Folkminnen och folktankar* 1 (1914): 113–150, is a folkloristically oriented study of the motif of breaking a cup on Hymir's skull. A detailed and useful comparison of Snorri's and the *Hymiskvida* poet's presentation of Thor's fishing expedition may be found in Alois Wolf's "Sehweisen und Darstellungsfragen in der *Gylfaginning*: Thors Fischfang," *Skandinavistik* 7 (1977): 1–27.

HYMISKVIDA

Eddic poem, detailing Thor's visit to a giant, his fishing up of the Midgard serpent, and his acquisition of a huge kettle in which to brew beer.

The poem is found in both of the main manuscripts of eddic poetry, the title only in the lesser of the two, AM 748 4to. In *Codex Regius* it is situated between *Hárbardsljód* and *Lokasenna* and was probably regarded by the compiler as a Thor poem in the manuscript.

As the poem begins, a feast is in the offing (stanzas 1–2), and a giant, presumably Ægir, thinking of vengeance, bids Thor get a kettle in which to brew beer (stanza 3). The gods are at a loss, until Týr tells Thor (stanza 4) that to the east dwells a giant, the very wise Hymir, Týr's father, who has a huge kettle, a league deep (stanza 5), which might be obtained through cunning (stanza 6). Týr and Thor set out and travel until they come to Egil, who is herding Hymir's goats (stanza 7). Stanza 8 is puzzling:

> The son met the mother, much loathsome to him,
> She had nine hundred heads.
> Another still went forth, all in gold,
> White about the brows, to bear beer to her son.

This second woman bids the two gods hide under a kettle (stanza 9). Hymir returns home (stanza 10), and Týr's mother tells Hymir that his son and Thor are there. Pillars burst and fall when he gazes upon them, so fierce is his anger (stanza 12–13), but he must fulfill his duties as a host. At dinner, Thor alone eats two of Hymir's oxen (stanza 15). They agree to go fishing the next morning (stanza 16). Thor says he will row if the giant will fetch the bait, but the giant sends Thor on that expedition (stanzas 17–18). Thor tears the head off one of Hymir's oxen (stanza 19). The scene shifts abruptly to the fishing expedition. Thor asks Hymir to row further out, but the giant demurs (stanza 20). Hymir fishes up two whales, but then Thor casts his line (stanza 21). With the ox head as bait, he fishes up the Midgard serpent (stanza 22), draws it aboard, and smashes it with his hammer (stanza 23). As the whole cosmos reacts, the serpent sinks into the sea (stanza 24). Hymir is downcast as they row back to shore (stanza 25), and he asks Thor to help him moor the boat (stanza 26). Thor hauls it all the way up to the giant's house (stanza 27). Hymir bids Thor break a cup (stanza 28), but he cannot (stanza 29). The woman counsels him to throw it at the head of the giant (stanza 30). Thor does so and breaks the cup (stanza 31). The giant now offers Thor and Týr the kettle, if they can lift it (stanza 32). Týr is unable to do so (stanza 33), but Thor picks it up and they leave (stanza 34). A pack of giants led by Hymir pursues them (stanza 35), and Thor kills them all with his hammer (stanza 36). They are further delayed because one of Thor's goats is lame, which Loki caused (stanza 37). The giants were paid with blows (stanza 38), and Thor got the kettle for brewing beer (stanza 39).

In *Gylfaginning* Snorri relates the story of the fishing expedition, and although *Hymiskvida* must have been his principle source, there is a huge difference: Snorri says that in his fear the giant cut the line, allowing the serpent to sink into the water and making it unclear whether the hammer thrown after it struck the target with any effect. The poem, on the other hand, seems to suggest that Thor killed the serpent or at least dealt it a mighty blow. Preben Meulengracht Sørensen has explained the differences between the versions as involving not only a time difference but also differing conceptions of the relationship between the gods and their adversaries as Christianity approached and was adopted. Snorri also has a few other interesting details, of which perhaps the most interesting is that Thor strikes the giant with his fist and throws him overboard.

Scholars are agreed that the poem itself is fairly late, dating from the eleventh or even, according to the most radical (and in my view quite unlikely) view, from around the time Snorri was writing. But the central myth, the fishing up of the Midgard serpent, was widely known and popular during the Viking Age, as both skaldic poetry and rock carvings attest. The earliest skald, Bragi Boddason the Old, has a section of Thor's encounter with the Midgard serpent in his *Ragnarsdrápa,* and Úlf Uggason, working in Iceland circa 985, also has it. Bragi is describing a shield, and Úlf is describing the carvings in a hall, so we know that the story was popular in image form. But there are also Viking Age rock carvings that without doubt portray the scene: at Altuna, Sweden, and Hørdum Ty, Denmark, and on the fragment from the church at Gosforth, England.

The myth of the acquisition of the kettle, on the other hand, is not widespread. There appears to be an allusion to it in the *First Grammatical Treatise,* an Icelandic work of the twelfth century, but otherwise it is unknown outside the *Poetic Edda,* even if Ægir's banqueting seems to presuppose it. Nevertheless, the gods' acquisition of precious objects from the world of the giants is a constant of the mythology. And there is a good deal of logic in the notion that Odin obtained the mead of poetry—that is, the mental part of inspiration—and Thor obtained the physical object in which beer, the reflex of the mead in the human world, is made. Furthermore, Franz Rolf Schröder has argued for comparisons in Indic myth that would make possible the reconstruction of an Indo-European original. This section of the poem is also interesting in that it assigns to the god Týr a giant father and a mother who sides with the æsir against her husband. Týr would be the only one of the æsir (other than Loki), whose status as a member of the æsir the mythology spectacularly unravels, to have such a father.

Loki's laming of Thor's goat in stanza 37 is not known from other sources. In Snorri's account of the journey of Thor to Útgarda-Loki, the human boy Thjálfi inadvertently lames one of Thor's goats, and it is as compensation for this injury that Thjálfi and his sister Röskva become Thor's human servants. A connection between Loki's and Thjálfi's laming of the goats may be vitiated by the possibly malign motive of Loki in *Hymiskvida,* but Loki and Thjálfi (and Týr!) share the role of Thor's companion on journeys to the world of the giants. Thus, *Hymiskvida* tantalizes in many details, even if the central myth, the fishing up of the Midgard serpent, was central to the mythology.

See also Egil; Hymir; Loki; Mead of Poetry; Midgard Serpent; Röskva; Thjálfi; Útgarda-Loki

References and further reading: Preben Meulengracht Sørensen's article on Thor's fishing expedition is "Thor's Fishing Expedition," in *Words and Objects: Towards a Dialogue between Archaeology and the History of Religion,* ed. Gro Steinsland (Oslo: Norwegian University Press, 1986), 257–278. Franz Rolf Schröder's attempt to recover older stages of the myth of the acquisition of the kettle is "Das Hymirlied: Zur Frage verblasster Mythen in den Götterliedern der *Edda,*" *Arkiv för nordisk filologi* 70 (1955): 1–40. A basic treatment is Konstantin Reichardt, "*Hymiskvida:* Interpretation. Wortschatz. Alter," *Beiträge zur Geschichte der deutschen Sprache und Literatur* 57 (1933): 130–156, which provoked the response of Jan de Vries, "Das Wort Godmálugr in der *Hymiskvida,*" *Germanisch-Romanisch Monatsschrift* 35 (1954): 336–337. C. W. von Sydow, "Jätten Hymies bägare," *Folkminnen och folktankar* 1 (1914): 113–150, is a folkloristically oriented study of the motif of breaking a cup on Hymir's skull. A detailed and useful comparison of Snorri's and the *Hymiskvida* poet's presentation of Thor's fishing expedition may be found in Alois Wolf's "Sehweisen und Darstellungsfragen in der *Gylfaginning:* Thors Fischfang," *Skandinavistik* 7 (1977): 1–27.

HYNDLULJÓD

Eddic poem, consisting of a visit by Freyja to the giantess Hyndla to retrieve genealogical information and including within it the "Short *Völuspá*."

The poem is found only in *Flateyjarbók*, an Icelandic manuscript from the end of the fourteenth century with a focus on materials concerning the kings of Norway. A prose header to the poem states that it was recited about Óttar heimski (The Foolish), and indeed the poem itself traces this Óttar's genealogy, although his identity remains unknown. The genealogical material is inserted into a frame story of Freyja's visit to Hyndla, whom she calls her friend and sister but who lives in a cave and apparently rides a wolf. At the end of the poem, Hyndla tells Freyja that she wishes to sleep, which is reminiscent of the seeresses called up by Odin to perform in *Völuspá* and *Baldrs draumar*. In the last stanza Freyja explicitly calls Hyndla a giant's bride.

The early stanzas give information about the principal æsir. In stanzas 2 and 3 Freyja says that Herjafödr (Odin) gives gold to men. He gave Hermód a helmet and byrnie and Sigmund a sword. "To his sons he gives victory and to his sons riches" ("to his sons" is often changed by editors to "to some"). "He gives speech and brains to men, sailing wind to men and poetry to poets, courage to many a warrior." In stanza 4 Freyja turns to Thor, to whom she will sacrifice, she says, to make him ever well disposed to her companion, "although he does not care for the brides of giants." The two then apparently travel. Hyndla accuses Freyja of having her husband or lover (apparently Óttar) along on the way to Hel, but Freyja denies the accusation. Stanza 9 refers to a wager between Óttar and the hero Angantýr, which some have taken to be the motivation for the poem. Stanza 10 shows why Freyja is partial to Óttar.

> He made an altar for me, loaded up with stones,
> Now that gravel has turned into [burned to?] glass;
> He reddened with the blood of nine cattle;
> Óttar ever believed in the goddesses.

In stanza 11 the speaker, evidently still Freyja, requests a tallying up of genealogical information, and this information fills stanzas 12–28. Then the speaker, now presumably Hyndla, addresses Óttar directly, and her stanzas frequently end with the refrain "That is all your family, foolish Óttar." This family of foolish Óttar involved dynastic lines, such as the Skjöldungar, Skilfingar, Ödlingar, and Ynglingar; some famous heroes, such as Sigurd, Gunnar, and Högni; and a few names that arouse interest from the point of view of the mythology. There is a Fródi, apparently Óttar's maternal grandfather, and a Nanna, the daughter of Nökkvi; neither of these, however, seems to be imagined as anything other than a human ancestor of Óttar.

Toward the end of the poem, in stanza 45, Freyja asks that "memory-beer" be brought to or by means of her boar, so that he (the boar? Óttar? Are they one and the same?) may remember everything when he and Angantýr recount their genealogies. Here the relationship between the two female figures turns increasingly antagonistic, and as the poem draws to a close, Hyndla has apparently brought the beer, mixed with poison. Freyja has the last word:

> Your spoken wish will have no effect,
> Even if, giant's bride, you promise evil;
> He will drink the precious beverage,
> I ask all the gods to help Óttar.

Thus described, the poem puts Freyja in the role ordinarily played by Odin, the member of the æsir who calls upon a member of the giant race to gain information in spoken form, as in *Völuspá* and *Baldrs draumar*, and triumphs verbally over the giant at the end of the encounter, as in *Baldrs draumar* and *Vafthrúdnismál*. Although an overt connection with a protected human is not part of that Odinic form, Odin certainly does have a close connection with human heroes, probably the closest of any deity.

The formal connection with *Völuspá* accords with the common scholarly understanding that some portion of *Hyndluljód* is the "Short *Völuspá*." We have the title from Snorri, who quotes stanza 33 in *Gylfaginning*. This stanza says that all seeresses descend from Vidólf, all witches from Vilmeid, all bearers of seid from Svarthöfdi, and all giants from Ymir. Since the last use of the refrain "That is all your family, foolish Óttar," occurs in stanza 29, where the speaker turns to the æsir, specifically Baldr, it would seem that the "Short *Völuspá*" begins there, and it would seem to run through stanza 44, which echoes the ending stanzas of *Völuspá*:

> Then will come another, yet more powerful,
> Although I dare not name that one;
> Few now seem farther into the future,
> And yet Odin will meet the wolf.

Like *Völuspá*, the "Short *Völuspá*" is punctuated by a refrain, not "Would you know more?" but rather "Do you wish to go yet further?" or "Do you wish yet more?" But despite the reference to Ragnarök in the last stanza, the "Short *Völuspá*" offers not a sweep of mythic history but rather a disjointed set of mythic allusions and mythological information. Stanza 29 indeed gives a brief précis of the Baldr story (he died and was avenged by Váli); most of the rest of the poem tells who was descended from or married to whom; stanza 35 (and possibly stanzas 36–38) tell of the birth of one with nine mothers, presumably Heimdall; and stanzas 40–41 are about Loki. Stanza 41 has information found nowhere else: Loki got pregnant by a woman (seemingly by eating a woman's heart, but the lines are obscure) and every female monster on earth was the result.

Another way to view the poem is to focus on Óttar's visit to the otherworld, and such a view will lead one to medieval and Christian analogs. Certainly most scholars have dated the poem to the post-Conversion period, most often the twelfth century.

> **See also** Freyja, *Völuspá*
>
> **References and further reading:** Jere Fleck, "Konr–Óttar–Geirrøðr: A Knowledge Criterion for Succession to the Germanic Sacred Kingship," *Scandinavian Studies* 42 (1970): 39–49, thought *Hyndluljóð* was part of a pattern in which a prince obtained sacral information with the help of a divine patron. Aron Gurevich argued something similar in his "*Edda* and Law: Commentary upon *Hyndluljóð*," *Arkiv för nordisk filologi* 88 (1973): 72–84, but he thought that the poem had more to do with means of inheriting property in Norway than with some distant Germanic sacral kingship. Like Gurevich, Gro Steinsland, *Det hellige bryllup og norrøn kongeideologi: En analyse av hierogami-myten i Skírnismál, Ynglingatal, Háleygjatal, og Hyndluljóð* (N.p.: Solum, 1991), operates with the idea of the received poem as a single entity rather than an interpolated mess. She sets the poem in "a milieu in which knowledge of the origin of the royal family in a holy marriage between a god and a giant woman will have been among the important elements of royal ideology" (p. 259).

HYRROKKIN (FIRE-SMOKED)

Giantess, according to Snorri Sturluson the one who launched Baldr's funeral ship. Hyrrokkin is not mentioned by name in extant poetry, with one notable exception: Thorbjörn dísarskáld includes her in the catalog of giants he credits Thor with killing in one of the two little late-tenth-century fragments addressed directly to Thor. However, the *Húsdrápa* of Úlf Uggason, which was composed in Iceland around 985, refers to a figure who must be Hyrrokkin, to judge from Snorri's account of Baldr's funeral in *Gylfaginning*. Here is the relevant part of what Snorri said about Baldr's funeral:

> And the æsir took Baldr's body and transported it to the sea. Hringhorni was the name of Baldr's ship. It was the greatest of ships. The gods wanted to launch it and make on it Baldr's funeral pyre, but the ship would not budge. Then Hyrrokkin, an ogress, was sent for from Jötunheimar. She arrived riding a wolf with poisonous snakes for reins, and when she dismounted, Odin called to four berserks to look after the horse, and they could not hold it unless they killed it.

Then Hyrrokkin went to the prow of the ship and shot it forward at the first try so that sparks leapt out of the runners and all the lands shook.

Úlf's stanza, number 12 in the conventional numbering, is as follows:

The very powerful Hild of the mountains [giantess] caused the sea-Sleipnir to trudge forward; but the wielders of the helmet flames [warriors] of Hropt [Odin] felled her mount.

Úlf's stanza was certainly known to Snorri (*Húsdrápa* is only retained in Snorri's *Skáldskaparmál*), and it does not appear that he needed to have known any other stanzas in order to have written what he did in *Gylfaginning*. However, it is important to recall that Úlf's *Húsdrápa* was composed to put into words the carvings in a hall in western Iceland, and even if the hall did not survive the two centuries that separated it from Snorri, descriptions of it could easily have done so, including fuller narratives about the carvings in it.

Hyrrokkin was clearly a relatively important figure in the last decades of paganism in Iceland. Her name remains unexplained. Perhaps she was shriveled and dark, giving her a monstrous appearance like some of Thor's other victims, such as Hengankjöpa (Slack-jaw).

See also Baldr

References and further reading: Otto Höfler, "Balders Bestattung und die nordischen Felszeichnungen," *Anzeiger der Österreichischen Akademie der Wissenschaften*, phil.-hist. Kl., 88 (1951): 343–372, argued pictorial continuity between Bronze Age rock carvings and the carvings in the Icelandic hall described in Úlf's *Húsdrápa* and then went on to explain Hyrrokkin and the other details in Baldr's funeral as misinterpretations of an old pictorial cult scene; needless to say, this is a bit speculative. In the third chapter of my *Murder and Vengeance among the Gods: Baldr in Scandinavian Mythology*, FF Communications, 262 (Helsinki: Societas Scientiarum Fennica, 1997), I presented the story about Hyrrokkin as an encounter between Odin and a giantess in which Odin triumphs and his will, in this case a proper funeral for Baldr, is carried out.

IDAVÖLL

Assembly field of the æsir in *Völuspá* and Snorri's *Gylfaginning*; associated with temporal beginnings.

Idavöll is mentioned twice in *Völuspá*. The first instance is in stanza 7, just after they have established time reckoning by naming day and night and the other parts of the temporal cycle in stanza 6.

The æsir assembled at Idavöll
Those who altar and temple high timbered.

They created wealth, smithed riches,
Forged tongs and made tools.

When Idavöll appears again in the poem (in stanza 60), it is a reappearance, after the demise and resurrection of the cosmos, just after the seeress has seen the earth come up for a second time.

The æsir will assemble at Idavöll
And adjudge the powerful Midgard serpent,
And there remember might
And Fimbultýr's [Odin's] ancient runes.

Snorri paraphrases these verses. For the first one, he puts Idavöll in the middle of the stronghold of the gods but says nothing about assembly. He appears to put Gladsheim and Vingólf on Idavöll. He paraphrases the second stanza as follows:

Vídar and Váli will live, because the sea and Surt's fire will not have harmed them, and they will dwell at Idavöll, where Ásgard used to be.

As is so often the case, much of the discussion has centered on the etymology of the word, or in this case, the first syllable. Idavöll means either "eternal field" or perhaps "shimmering field" or even "field of pursuits [of the gods]." The first makes the most sense, given that Idavöll is the terrestrial equivalent of the paired second-generation gods and their gaming pieces and memories that survive the mythological present and Ragnarök.

See also Game of the Gods; Ragnarök; Váli, Son of Odin; Vídar

IDUN

Guardian of the apples of the gods; given over to and retrieved from the giant Thjazi. The story is found in the skaldic poem *Haustlöng*, by Thjódólf of Hvin, and in the *Skáldskaparmál* section of Snorri Sturluson's *Edda*. The story begins with Odin, Hœnir, and Loki traveling and unable to cook an ox. An eagle in the tree above claims responsibility and says the ox will cook if he may have some. However, when he tries to take a vast amount, Loki strikes at him with a staff. The staff sticks to the eagle and to Loki's hand, and the eagle flies off with Loki in tow. As he bangs against things, Loki agrees to the eagle's demand: that he bring him Idun and her apples. This he does by luring Idun into the forest, where the eagle, who is actually the giant Thjazi, arrives and carries her off. Without their apples, the gods grow old and gray, and they force Loki to agree to get Idun back.

In Freyja's falcon coat he flies to Jötunheimar, changes Idun into a nut, and flies off with her. Thjazi pursues in the form of an eagle. The gods kindle a fire just as Loki flies into Ásgard, and Thjazi's feathers are singed and he falls to the earth and is killed by the gods.

This is one of the most dangerous moments for the gods in the mythological present, for giants are not supposed to be able to mate with goddesses. The fact that the gods grow old and gray—that is, display mortality—indicates what would happen if the flow of females, ordinarily from the giants to the gods, were to be reversed. What follows immediately in Snorri is Skadi's quest for vengeance, which ends with her becoming married to Njörd.

Although *Haustlöng* calls Idun the "maiden who understood the eternal life of the æsir" but does not mention the apples, in Snorri's version of the story Idun's apples clearly function as a symbol of the immortality of the gods. Indeed, when he presents Idun in *Gylfaginning,* Snorri says she is the wife of Bragi:

> She keeps in her bag the apples that the gods are to chew when they grow old, and then all become young again, and so shall it be until Ragnarök.

In *Skírnismál* stanzas 19–20, Skírnir offers and Gerd rejects 11 apples of gold. These are the only other prominent apples in the mythology, and some observers associate them with Idun's apples. The bucket that contained apples on the ninth-century Norwegian Oseberg funeral ship also deserves mention. However, the presumed etymological meaning of Idun—"ever young"—would permit her to carry out her mythic function without apples.

In *Lokasenna,* stanza 16, Idun asks Bragi not to quarrel with Loki, but in the following stanza Loki accuses Idun of having slept with the killer of her brother. The identity of her brother and the killer remain unknown.

See also Skadi; Thjazi

References and further reading: In her *Prolonged Echoes: Old Norse Myths in Medieval Icelandic Society,* vol. 1: *The Myths* (Odense: Odense University Press, 1994), Margaret Clunies Ross makes clear the importance of the direction of the passage of marriageable women, and on pages 115–119 she analyzes the Idun-Thjazi myth in some detail. See also her "Why Skadi Laughed: Comic Seriousness in an Old Norse Mythic Narrative," *Maal og minne,* 1989: 1–14. From the older scholarly literature may be cited Sophus Bugge's "Iduns æbler: Et bidrag til de nordiske mythers historie," *Arkiv för nordisk filologi* 5 (1889): 1–45 (characteristically, he thought the apples were borrowings into Old Scandinavian), and Anne Holtsmark, "Myten om *Idun* og *Tjatse* i Tjodolvs *Haustlǫng,*" *Arkiv för nordisk filologi* 64 (1949): 1–73, who argued for a background in ritual drama.

IFING

River separating the worlds of gods and giants.

Ifing is known only in *Vafthrúdnismál*, stanza 16:

> Ifing is the name of the river that divides for the sons of giants
> And for the sons of gods the earth;
> It will run open throughout all ages
> There will never be ice on the river.

A river on which ice will never form is one that runs swiftly and therefore is extremely difficult to ford.

ING

Figure found in the Old English *Rune Poem,* implied in the *Germania* of Tacitus, and associated with the Frey names Yngvi and Ingunar-Frey.

Ing is the name of the rune that stands for the sound *-ng-.* In the Old English *Rune Poem* (eighth or ninth century?), the verse in question runs as follows:

> Ing was first among the East Danes
> Seen by people, until he afterwards eastward
> Went over the wave; a cart ran after him.
> Thus the Heardingas named this hero.

The cart was associated with the vanir from the time of Nerthus and endured even into the jocular account of the worship of Frey in *Ögmundar tháttr dytts.* Scholars have associated the Heardingas, who must be a people or a dynasty, with the Haddingjar, twin or multiple warriors in their turn associated with the Danish King Hadingus in Book 1 of Saxo's *Gesta Danorum;* Hadingus is said to have established an annual sacrifice to Frey which the Swedes call Frøblot.

In chapter 2 of his *Germania,* composed around the end of the first century C.E., Tacitus writes this about the Germanic peoples:

> They celebrate in ancient songs . . . a god Tuisto, born from the earth, and his
> son Mannus as the origin and founders of their people. To Mannus they assign
> three sons, from whose names are called the Ingaevones near the ocean, those
> in the center as Herminones, and the rest Istaevones.

Ing must be the son of Mannus after whom the Ingaevones (more often known as the Ingvaeones) are named. The connection with the sea is interesting, and one might speculate that the Old English *Rune Poem* testifies to a movement of the cult of Ing away from the coast toward the territory that had once been that of the central Herminones. If the Baltic is involved, one might even put Sweden on Ing's itinerary.

> *See also* Frey; Haddingjar; Hadingus, Ingunar-Frey; Yngvi
>
> *References and further reading:* See Wolfgang Krause, "Ing," *Nachrichten der Akademie der Wissenschaften in Göttingen*, phil.-hist.-Kl., 10 (1944): 229–254, for an argument that the name originally meant "man" and was associated with fertility through the sun. Also see Henrik Schück, "Ingunar Frey," *Fornvännen* 10 (1940): 289–296, which argued that Ingun was the earth; Franz Rolf Schröder, *Untersuchungen zur germanischen und vergleichenden Religionsgeschichte*, vol. 1: *Ingunar-Frey* (Tübingen: J. C. B. Mohr [P. Siebeck], 1941), which argued for Ingun as a fertility goddess associated with a holy tree, and Walter Baetke, *Yngvi und die Ynglingar: Eine quellenkritische Untersuchung über das nordische "Sakralkönigtum,"* Sitzungsberichte der sächsischen Akademie der Wissenschaften zu Leipzig, Phil.-hist.-Kl., 109:3 (Berlin: Akademie-Verlag, 1964), which argued that the materials concerning Frey and the Ynglingar cannot be used to advance a notion of sacral kingship.

INGUNAR-FREY

Name for Frey.

This form of Frey's name is found in *Lokasenna*, stanza 43, where Byggvir uses it of his master, and in the so-called *Great Saga of St. Olaf*, where it is said that Thjódólf of Hvin's *Ynglinga tal* traces the ancestors of King Rögnvald of Vestfold "back to Ingunar-Frey, as pagans called their god." Thjódólf's poem is retained in Snorri Sturluson's *Ynglinga saga*, where Snorri refers to Yngvi-Frey. Clearly the two forms of the name are related, and on a purely linguistic basis one would say "Yngvi-Frey" has a Scandinavian form and "Ingunar-Frey" a West Germanic form; *Beowulf* 1319 refers to the king of the Danes as *frea Ingwina* (lord of the friends of Ing), and a figure named Ing is also found in the Old English *Rune Poem*. However, Norse *Ingunar* cannot be directly equated with Old English *Ingwina*, and what the Norse form means remains open to debate. Formally it looks like a genitive singular (Ingun's Frey), and scholars have speculated that Ingun could have been the earth or some other female deity. There may also be an association with the West Germanic people called the Ingvaeones.

> *See also* Frey; Ing
>
> *References and further reading:* Henrik Schück, "Ingunar Frey," *Fornvännen* 10 (1940): 289–296, argued that Ingun was the earth; Franz Rolf Schröder, *Untersuchungen zur germanischen und vergleichenden Religionsgeschichte*, vol. 1: *Ingunar-Frey* (Tübingen: J. C. B. Mohr [P. Siebeck], 1941), argued for Ingun as a fertility goddess associated with a holy tree.

INTERPRETATIO GERMANICA

"Germanic interpretation," that is, the translation of the Roman days of the week by the Germanic peoples at some point during the Migration Period.

Although the Roman weekdays were named after planets, the Germanic peoples who undertook the translation seem to have relied on the Roman gods whose names the planets bore and to have tried to equate those gods with their own. In the cases of the sun and the moon, the translation was obvious: Sunday and Monday. The other cases, however, were more difficult.

Dies Martis, the day following "Moon-day," bore the name of Mars, god of war and battle. The Germanic peoples equated him with *Tiwaz, who was to become Týr in Scandinavia and Tiw in England, whence Tuesday. Thus, although about all Týr does in the extant mythology is lose his hand to the wolf Fenrir (and provide the gods with a laugh when he does so), we can surmise that he derives from a warrior god of considerable importance.

Dies Mercurii bore the name of Mercury, who was associated with travel and commerce (whence our words "mercantile" and "merchandise"). Mercury carried forward a number of the traits of the Greek Hermes, who was known for his cunning, taste for theft, invention of the lyre, and accompanying of the dead to Hades. This set of characteristics fits Odin strikingly: He relies on cunning and treachery; he is the thief of the mead of poetry and is deeply associated with that craft (cf. the lyre of Hermes); he is associated with the dead (the einherjar) and visits the abode of the dead (in *Baldrs draumar*). Mercury was associated with commerce, to be sure, but he was also changeable (whence our word "mercurial" in that meaning), as Odin certainly was. Odin therefore got the day of Mercury, Old English Wodnesdæg, our Wednesday.

Dies Jovis carried in it the name of Jupiter, the head of the Roman pantheon, heir to Zeus in the Greek pantheon. One of his accouterments was a thunderbolt that he heaved across the sky, and this may have contributed to the choice of the translation of his day into that of the thunderer, Thor, giving us Thursday.

Dies Veneris bore the name of Venus, goddess of love. The deity the Germanic peoples chose to render her name was at that time *Frija, and that gives us Friday. *Frija was the predecessor of Frigg, however, not of Freyja.

Dies Saturni bore the name of Saturn, the old Roman harvest god. Curiously, the Germanic peoples do not seem to have equated him with any of their gods. Our name "Saturday" reflects a simple borrowing of his name, as does Dutch *zaterdag*. Scandinavian *lördag/lørdag* means "washday."

These translations offer us some sense of both the stability and innovation of the oral tradition that carried the mythology forward from the Migration Period to the High Middle Ages, from somewhere near the northern border of the Roman Empire to the Scandinavian outpost on Iceland. We see that Týr has lost most of the glory implied by the etymology of his name, which derives from the same Indo-European root as the names of Zeus and Jupiter and of our word "deity" (compare Latin *deus*); his predecessor may once have been a far greater warrior than Týr seems to be in the extant mythology. We surmise that the original Odin is seen in his fickle and cunning aspects, not in his role as lord of hosts and ruler of the pantheon. Similarly, we surmise that the predecessor of Thor might possibly once have been the head of the pantheon, and that the predecessor of Frigg may once have been inspired love the way Freyja does in the texts that have come down to us.

Some of the variations of the names in the various Germanic languages are also of interest. German *Dienstag* and Dutch *dinsdag*, "Tuesday," are based on an adjective *thingsus*, "protector of the thing or assembly," used to describe the war god, and this suggests that the predecessor of Týr had a connection with lawful assembly that is hardly to be seen in the god as we known him. German *Mittwoch*, "Wednesday," may suggest an aversion to Odin, but Dutch *woensdag* and Scandinavian *onsdag* still retain Odin's name. Ironically enough, in Iceland, which bequeathed the mythology to us, the weekday names are not based on the Germanic interpretation but are merely numbered (first day, second day, etc.). If there was a special aversion to the names of the ancient deities at the time of the conversion, it must have been short-lived.

See also Interpretatio Romana

References and further reading: Udo Strutynski, "Germanic Divinities in Weekday Names," *Journal of Indo-European Studies* 3 (1975): 368–384.

INTERPRETATIO ROMANA

"Roman interpretation," that is, translations of the Germanic gods into the Roman equivalents.

Although Caesar has something to say about the Germanic gods, this notion refers especially to Tacitus, *Germania*, chapter 9, in which Tacitus attempts a discussion of gods, cult, and divination. Mercury, he says, receives the greatest worship, even human sacrifice. Animals are sacrificed to Hercules and Mars, and a portion of the Suebi sacrifice to Isis (an Egyptian goddess who was known to the Romans), in what Tacitus regards as a ritual of foreign origin because of the use of a ship.

In the Interpretatio Germanica, we know the Latin weekday names that were being translated, but here we are on less-certain ground. Indeed, we cannot know the extent to which the Interpretatio Romana represents Germanic peoples trying to equate their deities with Roman ones and Romans trying to figure out the Germanic deities. We can make guesses about the reaction of Germanic peoples to the iconography of Roman gods, and we can make guesses about the forms of the myths that might have attended the Germanic gods, but the enterprise is difficult. Still, when we bring into the picture the Interpretatio Germanica, which presumably occurred a few centuries after Tacitus wrote, the presumed correspondences become fairly clear. In the Interpretatio Germanica Odin is the equivalent of Mercury, and Týr is the equivalent of Mars. Hercules is not used in the interpretatio, but we must believe that Thor was one of the principal deities of the Germanic peoples, and, like Thor, Hercules was a renowned slayer of monsters. Thus, Tacitus tells us about just three gods, the same three who were pressed into service when the days of the week were translated. Tacitus also tells us about one goddess, whom he calls Isis, and in the Interpretatio Germanica only one goddess was used, namely Frigg, for Venus. Even if Isis is not a rendering of Frigg's predecessor, the parallel of three males and one female is striking.

> ***See also*** Interpretatio Germanica
>
> ***References and further reading:*** Georg Wissowa, "Interpretatio Romana: Römische Götter im Barbarenlande," *Archiv für Religionswissenschaft* 20 (1916–1919): 1–49.

JÁRNSAXA (ARMED-WITH-AN-IRON-SWORD)

Giantess.

Hyndluljóð, stanzas 35–38, tell of one "with greatly increased power, of the race of gods," born of nine giant maidens and therefore probably Heimdall. The list of giantesses begins with Gjálp and Greip and ends with Járnsaxa. Snorri too has a Járnsaxa, who is identified briefly in *Skáldskaparmál* as the mother of Magni, the three-year-old prodigy who alone of the æsir is able to lift the leg of the lifeless giant Hrungnir off Thor when Thor lies pinned under it after their duel. Odin disparages the relationship when he says at the end of the story that Thor did wrong to offer the splendid horse Gullfaxi to the boy, the son of a giantess, rather than to himself, the father of Thor. *Skáldskaparmál* says that a valid kenning for Sif is "one who shares a man with Járnsaxa."

> ***See also*** Thor

JÁRNVID (IRON-WOODS)

Forest where giantesses live.

Völuspá, stanza 40, mentions one such giantess, almost certainly Angrboda:

> To the east sat the old lady in Járnvid
> And raised there the kinfolk of Fenrir.

In the *Gylfaginning* section of his *Edda*, Snorri Sturluson paraphrases this stanza:

An ogress lives east of Midgard in the forest called Járnvid. In that forest dwell those troll women, who are called Járnvidjur (Ironwoodites). The old ogress raises as her sons many giants and all in the form of a wolf, and from them come wolves.

Stanza 3 of *Háleygjatal*, composed by the skald Eyvind Finnsson toward the end of the tenth century, refers to a Járnvidja (Ironwoodite) who is apparently Skadi.

See also Angrboda; Mánagarm

JÖRD (EARTH)

The earth, personified; consort of Odin and mother of Thor.

The Thor kenning "son of Jörd" is attested twice (with different words for "son") in skaldic poetry from the pagan period and is also found in the eddic poems *Lokasenna* and *Thrymskvida* and in the thulur. In *Skáldskaparmál*, discussing poetic diction, Snorri says that Thor may be called "son of Jörd" and that Jörd may be called "one who shares a man with Frigg." In *Gylfaginning*, after enumerating the *ásynjur* and describing the valkyries, Snorri says that "Jörd, the mother of Thor, and Rind, the mother of Váli, are numbered among the *ásynjur*." Rind is certainly a giantess, and to be "numbered among the æsir" is to be from some other group originally. Jörd must have been a giantess in the beginning. If so, Odin's marriage (or, more likely, sexual relationship outside marriage, perhaps not even a willing one on her part) to Jörd should be regarded as parallel to his other strategically minded relationships with giantesses. Rind is a good example; he seduced her by means of magic (seid) in order to sire Váli, the avenger of Baldr. It is instructive to think of Thor in this context. Is he the ultimate avenger?

Earlier in *Gylfaginning* Snorri has a confused discussion of Jörd, in connection with Alfödr (Odin):

The earth was his daughter and his wife. With her he made [*sic*] the first son, and that is Ása-Thor.

Snorri's use of the definite article in this passage suggests a desire to keep separate the earth and the goddess Jörd (Earth). A few lines later Snorri gives a genealogy of Jörd: She is the daughter of Annarr (Second) and Nótt (Night), daughter of the giant Nörfi or Narfi. Yet Jörd, without the definite article, is ordinarily regarded as Thor's mother. *Völuspá*, stanza 50, calls Thor the "son of Hlódyn," an etymologically unclear name that must be the same as Jörd.

JÖTUNHEIMAR (GIANT-WORLDS)

That part of the cosmos inhabited by giants.

The fact that this term is plural may indicate that there were multiple areas inhabited by giants, as opposed to the single enclosure of the gods (Ásgard). In the world of humans there were multiple places where the trolls might live: mountains, forests, and so forth—any of the unsettled areas surrounding the farmstead.

KVASIR

God whose blood is used to make the mead of poetry.

Toward the end of the tenth century, the skald Einar Helgason skálaglamm, in his *Vellekla*, referred to poetry as "Kvasir's blood." This accords with the story of the origin of the mead of poetry, as told by Snorri Sturluson in the *Skáldskaparmál* section of his *Edda*. The peace between the æsir and vanir was sealed when both groups spat into a kettle. The gods wished to make the token of their peace more permanent, so they fashioned a man out of this spittle. He was Kvasir, and "he is so wise, that no one can ask him a question he cannot answer." He went about the world spouting wisdom and was murdered by the dwarfs Fjalar and Galar, who mixed his blood with honey and made the mead of poetry from it. They told the æsir, in one of the few really funny lines in this mythology, that he had choked on his wisdom. Apparently this outrageous lie did not trouble the æsir.

In the *Gylfaginning* section of his *Edda*, Snorri described Loki's attempts to evade the vengeance of the æsir after the killing of Baldr. He changed himself into a salmon and jumped in the river, but when the æsir arrived at his distant hideout, the first of the æsir to approach was Kvasir, "the wisest of all the æsir." He recognized in the ashes of a fire the form of a net—a technology yet to be invented, according to the myth—and the æsir made a net to help capture Loki. Here we have one of those discrepancies in chronology that characterize myth in general and this mythology in particular: Kvasir had to die in what I call, in chapter 2, the "near past," that is, early on in the mythology, since the incorporation of vanir and æsir and Odin's use of poetry are part of the mythic present. At the same time, Loki's punishment is fairly late in the mythic present, so Kvasir ought to be long dead. Yet here he is. This Kvasir is consistent with the one Snorri presents in chapter 4 of his *Ynglinga saga*, in which the Æsir-Vanir War is presented historically. There Kvasir, the wisest of the vanir, is sent to the æsir as a pledge of peace at the end of the hostilities.

See also Æsir-Vanir War; Mead of Poetry

LÆRAD
Tree, almost certainly the world tree.
The major source is *Grímnismál*, stanzas 25–26:

> 25. Heidrún is the name of the goat, who stands at the hall of Herjafödr [Odin]
> And bites from the limbs of Lærad.
> She will fill a barrel with the bright mead;
> That drink can never run out.
> 26. Eikthyrnir is the name of a hart, who stands at the hall of Herjafödr [Odin]
> And bites from the limbs of Lærad.
> Yet from his horns it drips into Hvergelmir,
> Thence all waters have their ways.

In *Gylfaginning* Snorri Sturluson paraphrased these lines. He says that the goat Heidrún "bites foliage off the limbs of that tree, which is famous and which is called Lærad." She provides endless mead, and the hart Eikthyrnir is the source of numerous rivers, according to Snorri.

The reasons for equating Lærad with Yggdrasil begin with Lærad's location at Odin's hall, which would be at the center of the cosmos. Yggdrasil too has animals about it, although they are perhaps more directly threatening than Heidrún and Eikthyrnir. Hvergelmir too is associated with both.

The form of the name varies, and many etymologies have been proposed. If, however, the first component is *Læ-*, "betrayal," the Norse would have understood the name as "arranger of betrayal," and such a name might just fit for Yggdrasil, Odin's steed, that is, the "horse" on which he was hung and was given in a self-sacrifice.

See also Eikthyrnir; Heidrún; Yggdrasil
References and further reading: Albert Morey Sturtevant, "Etymological Comments upon Certain Old Norse Proper Names in the *Eddas*," *Publications of the Modern Language Association* 67 (1952): 1145–1162.

LAUFEY
Loki's mother, used in the matronymic formula "Loki, son of Laufey."
The name is not found in skaldic poetry. In eddic poetry "son of Laufey" is a frequent kenning for Loki (*Lokasenna*, stanza 52—in which Loki uses it of him-

self—and *Thrymskvida,* stanzas 18, 20). In *Gylfaginning* Snorri tells us when he introduces Loki that he was "the son of Fárbauti the giant and of Laufey or Nál," and in *Skáldskaparmál* he says that "son of Laufey" is a valid kenning for Loki (along with "son of Fárbauti" and "son of Nál"). Snorri refers to Loki darkly as "son of Laufey" on a couple of occasions, as when he calls Loki "the one who makes most evil," or when he says that Thökk, the hag who would not weep Baldr out of Hel, was thought to have been Loki, the son of Laufey.

Laufey herself is found in no myths. Her name looks as though it should mean "Leaf-island," but that would be a strange name. *Sörla tháttr* says she was slender and feeble, and for that reason was called Nál (Needle), but the late date of the text makes this piece of information suspect. What is most striking about Laufey is that we always read of Loki Laufeyjarson and never of Loki Fárbauta-son (to use the grammatically correct forms). There were no last names in old Scandinavia (indeed, there are in principle no last names in Iceland today). One had a given name and a patronymic, except in those rare cases when the father was unknown or unsavory, in which case one had a matronymic. The fact that his father Fárbauti was a giant was presumably something that Loki—and Odin—would rather not be reminded of, especially since in this mythology kinship is ideally reckoned exclusively through male lines. (Consider the fact that Odin has a giant mother and that sex with giantesses is one of his weapons.) Was Laufey, then, a goddess? She is listed with goddesses in one of the thulur, and having a goddess as a mother might have been what enabled Loki to be "enumerated among the æsir," as Snorri put it in *Gylfaginning.* If Laufey was a goddess, then Loki's genealogy as offspring of a giant father and a goddess mother would be the same as that of his children with Angrboda, namely the Midgard serpent, Fenrir the wolf, and Hel, all great enemies of the gods, and this might help explain his ultimate allegiance.

See also Loki

LÉTTFETI (LIGHT-FOOT)

Horse name found in *Grímnismál,* stanza 30, which lists the horses the æsir ride each day when they go to make judgments at Yggdrasil.

Snorri Sturluson includes Léttfeti in his list of the horses of the æsir in *Gylfaginning* but does not assign the horse to any specific god. Léttfeti is also listed in the thulur for horses.

LÍF AND LÍFTHRASIR

The humans who will survive Ragnarök and repopulate the world.

In *Vafthrúdnismál*, stanza 44, Odin asks what humans will live after Fimbulvetr has passed. Vafthrúdnir replies in stanza 45.

> Líf and Lífthrasir, still they will conceal themselves
> In Hoddmímir's forest;
> The morning dews they will have as food for themselves,
> From them people will be nourished.

In the *Gylfaginning* section of his *Edda*, Snorri Sturluson paraphrases and quotes this stanza, adding the information that the lineage of Líf and Lífthrasir will be so great that the entire world will be populated.

See also Hoddmímir's Forest; Ragnarök

LIT (COLOR, COUNTENANCE)

Dwarf killed by Thor at Baldr's funeral, according to Snorri.

The killing of Lit, which appears only in *Gylfaginning*, appears almost to be an incidental. The gods have had to send for Hyrrokkin in order to launch Baldr's immobile funeral ship, and Baldr's body is aboard, as is that of his wife Nanna, who according to Snorri died of grief:

> Then Thor stood by and consecrated the pyre with Mjöllnir, and before his feet
> ran a certain dwarf; he is called Lit. And Thor kicked with his foot and knocked
> him into the fire, and he was burned up.

Lit is indeed listed among the dwarfs in the catalog of dwarfs (in stanza 12) and among the dwarfs in the thulur. His name appears to be the common noun for "color, countenance" which is one of the features endowed (in the plural) to Ask and Embla by the gods in *Völuspá*, stanza 18, but has no particularly logical association with dwarfs. There is, however, apparently a second Lit, one who is mentioned by Bragi Boddason the Old, who is taken to be the first skald: "grasp-offerer of the men of ancient Lit," that is, one who offers opportunities to grapple. This is a Thor kenning, and the race with whom Thor would wrestle would be giants, not dwarfs, and if the men of Lit are giants, so was Lit himself. Furthermore, in one of the manuscripts of Thorbjörn dísarskáld's stanza directed to Thor, the god is praised for killing Lit; in the other manuscripts, it is Lút. So was Lit a giant who became a dwarf, or were there two beings with this name?

The evidence hardly permits us to draw a conclusion, but it would not have been inappropriate for Thor to have killed a giant in some earlier version of the funeral of Baldr.

> *See also* Baldr; Dwarfs; Thor
>
> *References and further reading:* Otto Höfler, "Balders Bestattung und die nordischen Felszeichnungen," *Anzeiger der Österreichischen Akademie der Wissenschaften*, phil.-hist. Kl., 88 (1951): 343–372, argued pictorial continuity between Bronze Age rock carvings and the carvings in the Icelandic hall described in Úlf's *Húsdrápa* and then went on to explain Lit as a cult dancer cavorting in some old pictorial cult scene and subsequently misinterpreted; needless to say, this is a bit speculative.

LJÓDATAL

Section of the poem *Hávamál,* usually thought of as comprising stanzas 146–164, although it would be possible to construe 138–164 as a single section.

The *Ljódatal* (Enumeration of Chants), spoken in the first person by Odin, lists the effects of 18 songs or chants that work magic, although the charms themselves are not given. Odin is supposed to have obtained nine powerful songs from his giant maternal uncle in the course of his self-sacrifice, and there does seem to be a kind of qualitative difference between the first of nine chants and those that follow. The first two charms appear to have to do with cures, the next several with battle (e.g., charms for dulling enemies' blades, diverting arrows, redirecting enmities to those from whom they originated, quelling fire in a hall, which would have to do with battle if one thinks of the burnings in the sagas and Icelandic historical record of the Sturlung Age). The eighth is rather strange, ironic even, in the mouth of Odin: "Wherever hate grows, among the sons of a prince, that I can quickly repair." In the ninth Odin announces that he can still storms and high seas. With the tenth there is something of a break, since he says that he can cause witches not to be able to find their way back to their shapes and minds. The tenth and twelfth are battle charms, but the tenth at least differs from the earlier charms in that it does not work on objects (swords, fetters, flames) but, rather, offers blanket protection for his followers. The twelfth announces an Odinic connection with hanged men. From the fourteenth onward there seems to be a sort of progression, from mythological knowledge, the acquisition of important qualities (wealth for the æsir, success for the elves, cognition for Odin), to sexual matters and powers of seduction. The last he will never teach to maid or man's wife, "only to the one who casts an arm about him or is his sister." The conjunction "or" in this language can sometimes mean "and," which would mean that only an unthinkable act of incest would cause this charm to be revealed. Powers of seduction have been a persistent subject in the poem, as evidenced by the so-called Odin's examples, of which the one with a positive outcome resulted in the acquisition of the mead of poetry. In *Hárbardsljód* Odin boasts of having his way with giant girls. Perhaps the most important use of powers of seduction (or rape) comes in the Baldr story, in which his solution to the murder of his son and heir by another son is to sire an avenger, Váli, on a giantess.

LODDFÁFNISMÁL

Section of the poem *Hávamál,* usually thought of as comprising stanzas 111–137.

This section gets its name from a refrain repeated 20 times: "I advise you now, Loddfáfnir, / that you learn counsels, / you will have use of them, if you learn them, / they will be good for you, if you obtain them." Loddfáfnir is otherwise unknown, and the name is not helpful. The first component, *Lodd-,* may mean something like "shaggy," and the second is identical with the name of the giant Fáfnir in heroic tradition, who changed himself into a dragon to hoard the gold he had obtained by killing his brother and who in turn was killed by Sigurd. What a "Shaggy-Fáfnir" might be (or a shaggy dragon or shaggy shape-changer) remains unknown.

The section begins with a verse using language that could relate to the exchange of wisdom in sacral contexts and that is clearly anchored in the mythology.

This worn cross in Lancashire, like many northern-English Viking Age sculptures, contains scenes from Norse legend. (Axel Poignant Archive)

It is time to recite
at the seat of the sage by the well of Urd:
I saw and was silent,
I saw and I considered,
I listened to the speeches of men;
I heard runes being judged,
nor were they silent about counsels, at the hall of Hár,
in the hall of Hár;
I heard them say this.

I have rendered the verb *þylja* as "recite," although "chant" might be another acceptable translation. The noun I rendered with "sage," *thulr*, is related; its cognate in Old English, *þyle*, means "orator." The identity of the speaker is not clear. If, however, we accept that the title *Hávamál* really does mean "Words of Hár [the High One]," then Odin may be speaking. Alternatively, we may be hearing either a narrator's voice or, perhaps, that of Loddfáfnir. In any case, the remainder of the section consists of counsels *(ráð)* introduced by the refrain. Many of these counsels are similar to those of the gnomic section of the poem (which includes such aphorisms as "Keep and make friends"; "Be cautious when drinking beer"; "Limit conversation with foolish people"), but certain of them, especially toward the end of the list, relate easily to myths about Odin. Thus, for example, Loddfáfnir is advised to treat guests generously and to heed the words of grizzle-haired men, counsel that would have been useful to Geirröd when Odin visited that human king and was maltreated *(Grímnismál)*.

LÓDUR

Enigmatic god who helps endow Ask and Embla with life.

Lódur is found only in the version of cosmogony preserved in *Völuspá*. Three æsir have found Ask and Embla on the land, fateless and capable of little. In stanza 19, Odin, Hœnir, and Lódur endow them with three characteristics. Lódur's gift is blood, ruddiness, or vital warmth, and also good coloring. In the *Gylfaginning* section of his *Edda*, Snorri Sturluson adds some details and changes others. The creator gods in his version are the sons of Bor (i.e., Odin, Vili, and Vé). The third, who is structurally equivalent to Lódur, gives appearance, speech, hearing, and vision.

Except in the Odin kenning "Lódur's friend," Lódur is unknown, and the etymology is unclear. Many attempts have been made to understand Lódur as an alternate name for some other god, most often Loki. The main argument in favor of Loki is that he is known to travel with Odin and Hœnir, as when they encounter Thjazi or Andvari. Odin is also known as "Lopt's friend," and Lopt is definitely a Loki name. There have also been attempts to associate Loki with Lódur through the runic name Logathore, but this is problematic.

Besides Loki, Frey has been proposed as the underlying identity of Lódur. According to this scenario, Lódur would have been a fertility figure.

> ***See also*** Ask and Embla; Hœnir
>
> ***References and further reading:*** Edgar C. Polomé has contributed a study focusing exclusively on Lódur: "Quelques notes à propos du dieu énigmatique scandinave Lóðurr," *Revue Belge* 33 (1955), and his "Some Comments on *Völuspá*, Stanzas 17–18," in *Old Norse Literature and Mythology: A Symposium*, ed. Edgar C. Polomé (Austin: University of Texas Press, 1969), 265–290, is also relevant; it associates Lódur with the vanir.

LOFN

Minor goddess.

Snorri lists her eighth in his catalog in *Gylfaginning* of goddesses among the æsir and says, "She is so gracious and good to call on that she gets permission from Alfödr [Odin] or Frigg for the intercourse of people, men and women, although otherwise it would be banned or forbidden; because of that *lof* [praise] is derived from her name, and that which is much *lofat* [praised] by people." Scholars follow Snorri in accepting a connection between the name Lofn and the root *lof-*, "praise." Although Lofn herself is unattested elsewhere, her name turns up frequently as the base word in woman kennings in skaldic poetry. As with many of the other minor goddesses, some scholars believe that she may just be Frigg under another name.

> ***See also*** Alfödr; Frigg

LOGI (FIRE)

Opponent of the æsir in the myth of Thor's visit to Útgarda-Loki.

When the æsir reach the hall of Útgarda-Loki, the giant informs them that no one can stay who does not excel at some kind of skill or knowledge. Loki responds first: "I have that talent, which I am wholly ready to test, that there is no one here inside who can eat his food faster than I can." Útgarda-Loki agrees that that would indeed be a talent, and he calls forth Logi for an eating contest with Loki.

Then a wooden platter is taken and carried into the center of the hall, laden with meat. Loki sits himself at one end and Logi at the other, and each eats as fast as he can, and they meet in the middle of the platter. Loki has eaten all the meat off the bones, but Logi has eaten all the meat off the bones and also the platter, and it seems to everyone that Loki has lost the contest.

Only later does Útgarda-Loki reveal to the æsir: "The one named Logi was wildfire, and he burned the tray no more slowly than the meat." The æsir lose the other contests as well, failing to recognize not only the word for "fire" but also words for "mind" and "old age."

Logi is named as one of the three elemental sons of Fornjót in *Fundinn Noregr* (Norway Found), as the beginning of *Orkneyinga saga* (The Saga of the Orkney Islanders) is sometimes called, and in a section of *Flateyjarbók* called *Hversu Noregr byggdisk* (How Norway Was Settled). There appears to be no connection between this tradition and the story of the gods' visit to Útgarda-Loki.

See also Loki; Útgarda-Loki

LOKASENNA

Eddic poem.

Lokasenna (Loki's Verbal Duel) is found only in *Codex Regius* of the *Poetic Edda*, between *Hymiskvida* and *Thrymskvida*. The compiler of the manuscript therefore understood it as a Thor poem. *Lokasenna* consists of 65 stanzas mostly in *ljóðaháttr*; a few stanzas are in *galdralag* and have quite a heightened effect. The poem is preceded by a prose header, interrupted in a few places by prose sentences tying the stanzas together, and followed by a prose colophon.

The prose header follows the rubric "About Ægir and the Gods." It states that Ægir, having obtained the kettle "as was just told" (i.e., in *Hymiskvida*) to brew beer, had invited the gods to a feast. All but Thor were there, many æsir and elves, and the room was lit by gold instead of a fire. The beer served itself, and the place was one of great sanctuary. Ægir's servants won much praise, and Loki could not stand to hear that and killed one of them, Fimafeng. The gods chased him away, but he returned.

The poem itself consists of a series of dialogues between Loki and various characters, verbal exchanges in which Loki for the most part tells the god to whom he is speaking to shut up and then reveals some unflattering fact about that god. The first exchange, however, is not with a god but with Eldir, a surviving servant of Ægir. Loki learns that the gods are discussing their prowess, states his intention to enter the hall, and dismisses Eldir as a verbal opponent. In the remainder of the poem Loki jousts verbally with 14 of the gods and goddesses. Here is a catalog of the deities and the major insults directed toward them: Bragi, cowardice; Odin, swore blood-brotherhood with Loki, often gave victory to the weaker; Idun, slept with the killer of her brother; Gefjon, sold herself for a bauble; Frigg, slept with Vili and Vé (and Loki takes responsibility for Baldr's death); Freyja, slept with her brother; Njörd, abused by Hymir's daughters, sired Frey on his sister; Týr, lost his hand to Fenrir, cuckolded by Loki; Frey, abandoned his sword to obtain Gerd; Byggvir, cowardice; Heimdall, dirty wet back; Skadi, Loki participated in killing her father and has slept with her; Sif, cuckolded Thor with Loki; Beyla, filthy dairymaid; Thor, cowered in some giant's glove, probably Skrýmir's, and could not open the bag of provisions strapped shut by Skrýmir. There are also accusations directed at Loki, most accusing him of *ergi* (sexual perversion), some reminding him of the binding of his son the wolf. The poem is finally resolved when Loki retires from the hall under the threat of a blow from Thor's hammer: "I spoke before the æsir, / I spoke before the elves, / what my mind incited me to; / but for you alone / I will go out, / for I know that you will strike" (stanza 65). In the final stanza Loki tells Ægir that this is his final party and that he will lose his possessions to fire.

The prose colophon follows a rubric "About Loki" and tells an abbreviated version of the story that Snorri presents as the vengeance taken by the æsir on Loki for Baldr's death. Loki flees and hides in the form of a salmon but is captured and bound under a poisonous snake. Sigyn, Loki's wife, catches the poison in a bowl, but when she goes to empty it, Loki struggles, and that causes earthquakes.

Many of Loki's accusations are known from other sources, such as the incest of the vanir, the possession of Frigg by Vili and Vé, Týr's loss of his hand, and Thor's journey to Útgarda-Loki. Many others are to be found only here, including many of the accusations of sexual misbehavior directed at the female members of the æsir. Byggvir and Beyla are known only from this poem. Although some observers have found it difficult to imagine that believers would tell and listen to such scurrilous material about their gods, there are analogues from other religions. Furthermore, an argument for a late origin for the poem would be more easily built on its language and possible analogues from classical literature, which would not have been known in Iceland before the twelfth century. On the other hand, the primacy of Thor over Loki would accord with Thor's prominence in the waning decades of paganism, and if the real point of the poem is not just that Thor alone can make Loki stop but rather that Thor *can* do so— that is, if the poem ultimately pits Loki's mouth against Thor's hammer—it would be consistent with many of the other mythological poems of the *Poetic Edda*, which involve conflict and ultimately tell us about hierarchy: Odin is better than giants, men, and even Thor with words *(Vafthrúdnismál, Grímnismál,* and *Hárbardsljód),* and Thor is better than Alvíss with words *(Alvíssmál).* On this one occasion, at least, Loki is better than all the gods with words, but Thor can silence him. It is instructive to compare this myth with that of Thor's duel with Hrungnir, for in both Odin is unable to prevent the extension of hospitality to someone who ought not to receive it, both recipients say things that should not be said (in Hrungnir's case that he will possess Ásgard and Freyja), and in both cases Thor's hammer gets Odin out of this tight spot.

This face carved on a furnace stone and found on the beach in Jutland may be that of Loki. The lines cut across the closed mouth bring to mind Loki's punishment of having his lips sewn together for having lost a wager. (Werner Forman Archive/Art Resource)

See also Loki

References and further reading: Philip N. Anderson, "Form and Content in the *Lokasenna:* A Re-evaluation," *Edda,* 1981: 215–225. A. G. van Hamel, "The Prose-Frame of *Lokasenna,*" *Neophilologus* 14 (1929): 204–214. Joseph Harris, "The *Senna:* From Description to Literary Theory," *Michigan Germanic Studies* 5 (1979): 65–74. John McKinnell, "Motivation in *Lokasenna,*" *Saga-Book of the Viking Society* 22 (1987–1988): 234–262.

LOKI

Trickster figure, lives among the gods but will fight with the giants at Ragnarök.

In my view the single most significant line about Loki in the sources comes at the end of the catalog of æsir in the *Gylfaginning* section of the *Edda* of Snorri Sturluson: Loki is "also numbered among the æsir," that is, he is counted as one of them even though he may actually not be one. Indeed, given the principle of reckoning kinship along paternal lines only, Loki is no god but a giant, since he has a giant father, Fárbauti. His mother, Laufey or Nál, may well have been one of the æsir, but that should not count. And Loki is himself the father of three monsters, the Midgard serpent, the wolf Fenrir, and Hel, by the ogress Angrboda. With his wife Sigyn he has the son(s) Nari and/or Narfi.

It seems that Loki's allegiance is for the most part with the æsir during the mythic present, but that in the mythic past, when he mated with Angrboda, and in the mythic future, at Ragnarök, he is unabashedly against them. In the mythic present he travels with Odin and Hœnir in both the Thjazi and Andvari stories, and he travels with Thor in the Útgarda-Loki story and in one version of the story of Thor's visit to Geirröd. Often it is Loki whose actions set the complications of a story in motion: For example, he is stuck to Thjazi and agrees to deliver Idun and her apples; he is starved by Geirröd and agrees to deliver Thor without his weapons. Sometimes when things go wrong the æsir assume it is Loki's fault even when no blame has entered the story, as in the story of the master builder of the wall around Ásgard. But in that story and others, he is willing to fix things; for example, he causes the

This stone found in Cumbria depicts a bound figure, perhaps Loki. (Axel Poignant Archive)

six precious objects of the gods to be made in connection with replacing Sif's hair, which he had mysteriously cut off. (These six objects, made by dwarfs, are Sif's golden headpiece, Odin's spear Gungnir and his ring Draupnir, Thor's hammer, and Frey's boar Gullinborsti and his ship Skídbladnir.)

Not infrequently Loki sacrifices his honor (or worse) to help the æsir, as when he changes himself into a mare to seduce the master builder's horse and bears a foal from it, not something that would enhance a man's reputation in the hyper-masculine society that was medieval Iceland. Similarly, dressing as the handmaiden of Freyja (that is, of Thor very reluctantly in drag) would leave him

Panel from the Thorwald Cross from Andreas on the Isle of Man, showing Odin being devoured by his ancient foe, the wolf. (Werner Forman/Art Resource)

open to charges of effeminacy. Then there is the method he used to make Skadi laugh when the gods were compensating her for the loss of her father, Thjazi: He tied a rope around his testicles and the beard of a she-goat and both bleated as Loki fell into Skadi's lap. Loki shares this sexual ambiguity with Odin, who practiced the effeminate magic called seid, and in fact the two were blood brothers. It seems likely to me that Odin entered into blood-brotherhood with Loki in an attempt to head off future mortal conflict with him. If so, Odin failed.

Loki's unequivocally negative actions should probably begin with his mysterious struggle with Heimdall, apparently over the Brísinga men, which Loki may have stolen. This incident is obscure, but his vicious insulting of the gods and goddesses in *Lokasenna* is crystal clear. Worse yet is his arranging the death of Baldr, the first death among the æsir and almost certainly the event that leads inevitably to Ragnarök. I would assign both *Lokasenna* and Baldr's death to the last stages of the mythological present, when Loki is beginning to reveal his true colors. *Lokasenna* and Snorri's *Edda* agree that Loki was bound in revenge, either for the reviling of the gods or for his role in Baldr's death. But in the early stages of the mythic future he will break free. And according to *Völuspá*, stanza 51, he will pilot a ship from the east full of Muspell's peoples, the enemies and ultimate destroyers of the gods and the cosmos.

In that sense we may say that Loki has a chronological component: He is the enemy of the gods in the far mythic past, and he reverts to this status as the mythic future approaches and arrives. In the mythic present he is ambiguous, "numbered among the æsir."

> *See also* Andvari; Baldr; Bound Monster; Brísinga men; Heimdall; Idun; *Lokasenna*; Muspell; Ragnarök, Skadi; Thjazi; Útgarda-Loki
>
> *References and further reading:* The literature on Loki is vast, and most of it is in German and the Scandinavian languages. Everyone agrees that there was never any cult of Loki, and everyone agrees that he was important, but beyond that it is difficult to generalize. Older (and even some modern) critics thought he could be associated with natural phenomena, such as fire (Wagner made of him Loge in the Ring Cycle) or air, the latter based on his name Lopt. The most consistently useful stand of the scholarship reads Loki against the trickster figures of Native American and African traditions: Trickster thinks only of the present and never of the future, is creative but destructive at the same time, and often has a connection with sexuality. Such a view characterizes the book of Jan de Vries, *The Problem of Loki*, FF Communications, 110 (Helsinki: Suomalainen tiedeakatemia, 1933), who brings out the dual aspects of culture hero and trickster. A later book in English is that of Anna Birgitta Rooth, *Loki in Scandinavian Mythology*, Skrifter utgivna av Kungliga humanistiska vetenskapssamfundet i Lund, 61 (Lund: C. W. K. Gleerup, 1969). Using an extremely strict historical-geographical method and regarding anything found elsewhere as having been borrowed into Scandinavia, Rooth is left with

a spider as the hypothetical Loki. Ulf Drobin, "Myth and Epical Motifs in the Loki-Research," *Temenos* 3 (1968): 19–39, goes beyond a research survey to read Loki as the player of an essentially epic (i.e., narrative) role. Still the most useful recent piece is that of Jens Peter Schjødt, "Om Loke endnu engang," *Arkiv för nordisk filologi* 96 (1981): 49–86, which sees Loki as a mediator. Schjødt contributed a brief but concise history of Loki research in the encyclopedia article "Loki" in *Medieval Scandinavia: An Encyclopedia*, ed. Philip Pulsiano et al., Garland Encyclopedias of the Middle Ages, 1; Garland Reference Library of the Humanities, 934 (New York and London: Garland Publishing, 1993), 394–395.

LOPT

Alternate name for Loki.

The name is common in eddic poetry and is also used by the early skalds. When Snorri Sturluson describes Loki in his catalog in the *Gylfaginning* section of his *Edda,* he begins by calling him "Loki or Lopt."

This alternate Loki name appears to be a masculine form of a feminine noun meaning "sky," and it seems certain to me that medieval Scandinavians would have understood it as related to the sky. Perhaps we should think of Loki flying about in Freyja's falcon coat.

See also Loki

MAGNI (THE STRONG)

Son of Thor.

The tenth-century skaldic *Thórsdrápa,* by Eilíf Godrúnarson, uses "father of Magni" as a kenning for Thor (stanza 21), as does the eddic poem *Hárbardsljód* (stanzas 9 and 53). Magni is mentioned on only one other occasion in poetry, in *Vafthrúdnismál,* stanza 51, but it is an important occasion. Odin has just asked the giant Vafthrúdnir who will control the possessions of the gods:

> Vídar and Váli will inhabit the holy places of the gods,
> When Surt's fire dies down;
> Módi and Magni will have Mjöllnir
> And will bring about a cessation of killing.

Snorri knew this myth and employed it in his account of Ragnarök and its aftermath. Magni and his bother Módi are, then, second-generation gods—like Vídar and Váli and Höd and Baldr—who will survive Ragnarök and participate in the new world order. They will possess Mjöllnir, Thor's hammer, with which

Thor killed countless giants. If my translation of the last line above is correct, Mjöllnir will help them end the ceaseless cycle of slayings that had characterized the mythological present. The text is difficult at this point, however, and many editors and translators choose to alter it to read "at the cessation of the battle of Vingnir (Thor)." In either case, their possession of Mjöllnir is part of the larger pattern here of continuity from the old mythological order to the new one.

Vídar and Váli are both gods of vengeance, and Magni too undertakes an act in the mythological present that, even if it is not vengeance, is at least aimed at his father's opponent in the aftermath of a battle. At the end of Thor's duel with Hrungnir, which we have from *Skáldskaparmál* in Snorri's *Edda*, Thor lies pinned under the lower leg of the dead giant:

> All the æsir came up, when they heard that Thor had fallen, and were going to get the leg off him, but they couldn't move it at all. Then Magni arrived, the son of Thor and Járnsaxa. He was three nights old [three years old, according to some manuscripts of Snorri's *Edda*]. He threw the leg off Thor and said: "What a pity, father, that I came so late; I think I could have smacked the giant down into Hel with my fist, if I had encountered him." Thor stood up and greeted his son well and said that he would become a great man. "I wish," he said, "to give you the horse Gullfaxi, which Hrungnir possessed." But Odin spoke up and said that Thor did wrong when he gave the horse to the son of a giantess and not to his father.

Járnsaxa (Armed-with-an-iron-sword) as the giantess mother of Magni is known only from Snorri, who elsewhere in *Skáldskaparmál* says that a kenning for Sif, Thor's legitimate wife, is "one who shares a man with Járnsaxa." Otherwise Járnsaxa is known as one of the nine giant mothers of Heimdall (*Hyndluljód*, stanza 37). Having a giantess mother increases Magni's similarities with Vídar and Váli, the sons of Odin and the giantesses Gríd and Rind respectively. Furthermore, Magni's precocious acts as an infant find a parallel in the vengeance taken by Baldr's brother, presumably Váli, when one night old (*Völuspá*, stanza 32).

See also Hrungnir; Módi; Thor; Váli, Son of Odin; Vídar

MÁNAGARM (MOON-DOG)

Monstrous hound, destroyer of the moon or sun according to Snorri Sturluson.

Garm turns up often as the base word in kennings, where it means "destroyer," and Mánagarm thus has the form of a kenning, for the first part of the name is just the genitive case of the word "moon." Only Snorri knows about Mánagarm, but his description of the beast, early in *Gylfaginning*, is memorable. He has just mentioned an old giantess, one of the Járnvidjur (Ironwoodites) who gives birth to many sons, all in the form of wolves.

> And it is said, that the most powerful of that family will be the one who is called Mánagarm. He is filled with the life of all people who die, and he will swallow the heavenly bodies, and bespatter with blood the heaven and all the sky. Thence the sun will lose its shine, and winds will not be gentle and will roar hither and yon.

Snorri is obviously following *Völuspá*, stanzas 40 and 41, and he quotes them directly after this passage. Stanza 40 agrees that a Járnvidja gives birth to the families of Fenrir, and that one of them will swallow the *tungl*, "in the form of a troll." How Snorri got from this stanza to Mánagarm is unknown.

I have left *tungl* untranslated because it truly is ambiguous in this context. It means something like "heavenly body," and from the end of Snorri's prose passage we would think that here it means "sun." Mánagarm as "Destroyer-of-the-moon," on the other hand, suggests the opposite.

See also Garm

MÁNI (MOON)

The moon, personified.

In *Vafthrúdnismál*, stanza 22, Odin asks the wise giant Vafthrúdnir whence the moon and sun came to travel over people. The giant responds in stanza 23:

> Mundilfœri he is called, the father of Máni
> And also of Sól the same;
> Into heaven shall they turn each day,
> So that people can reckon years.

Reginsmál, stanza 23, uses "sister of Máni" as a kenning for the sun. There also, however, seem to be kennings in the skaldic corpus for giantesses suggesting a marriage or sexual union between Máni and a giantess, for example, "desired woman of Máni" used by Guthorm sindri. If Máni had such a relationship with a giantess, it has left no other trace in the extant mythology.

Snorri concocts a somewhat different story: Mundilfœri is a man who had two children who were so beautiful that he named them Máni and Sól (i.e., Moon and Sun), and the gods punished this act of pride by placing the children in heaven to serve the actual heavenly bodies, which the gods had created. Máni controls the motion of the moon and its waxings and wanings. He took two human children up from earth, Bil and Hjúki, and they accompany him and can be seen from earth.

As part of the creation of the æsir, that is, the cosmos, Máni must be destroyed at Ragnarök, but this is not explicitly stated, except perhaps by Snorri, who tells about Mánagarm, who will swallow a heavenly body that may be the moon.

> *See also* Bil and Hjúki; Mánagarm; Mundilfœri; Sól.
>
> *References and further reading:* Although Máni obviously figured prominently in nineteenth-century solar mythological readings of the mythology, such readings have faded away. An exception was Leonhard Franz, "Die Geschichte vom Monde in der Snorra-Edda" *Mitteilungen der Islandfreunde* 10 (1922–1923): 45–48, which argued for a kind of lunar mythology. Ernst Alfred Philippson, *Germanisches Heidentum bei den Angelsachsen*, Kölner anglistische Arbeiten, 4 (Leipzig: B. Tauchnitz, 1929), nicely surveyed the evidence for the worship of the moon and sun among the Germanic tribes who migrated to England. Rudolf Much, however, had the last word. His "Mondmythologie und Wissenschaft," *Archiv für Religionswissenschaft* 37 (1941–1942): 231–261, shows pretty convincingly that moon mythology cannot have been of much importance.

MANNUS (MAN)

Figure involved in the origin of the Germanic peoples according to the *Germania* of Tacitus, probably the first human being.

In chapter 2 of his *Germania*, Tacitus writes the following statement:

> They celebrate in ancient songs . . . a god Tuisto, born from the earth, and his son Mannus as the origin and founders of their people. To Mannus they assign three sons, from whose names are called the Ingaevones near the ocean, those in the center as Herminones, and the rest Istaevones.

The name Tuisto appears to have in it the root of the word "two," and this has reminded many observers of Ymir, whose name meant something like "doubled." Ymir sired the races of frost-giants through monstrous hermaphroditic conception, and Tuisto may well have done something similar. Mannus (Man) would be the first human being, whose procreation would be done in the usual human way. From the first human come the Germanic tribes.

> *See also* Ymir
>
> *References and further reading:* A fine general treatment of Tuisto and the sociogonic creation story in *Germania* is that of Marco Scovazzi, "Tuisto e Mannus nel II capitolo della *Germania* di Tacitus," *Istituto Lombardo: Accademia di scienze e lettere, rendiconti, classe di letteri* 104 (1970): 323–336.

MARDÖLL

Name for Freyja.

Snorri says in *Gylfaginning* that Freyja has many names because she took on different names among the various peoples she encountered when she went to search for her missing husband, Ód. There is no other direct evidence that Mardöll is a name for Freyja except the kenning "tear of Mardöll" for gold, which relies on the story of Freyja weeping golden tears for her missing husband Ód. The meaning of the name Mardöll is disputed.

> *See also* Freyja

MATRES AND MATRONES

Groups of females worshipped in the Germanic area that came into contact with Rome during the first five centuries or so C.E.

Matres is Latin for "mothers," and *matrones* is Latin for "matrons." These were celebrated in statues and inscriptions, of which more than 1,000 are known. Many of the names are Germanic, but others are not, and most scholars accept that the cult was both Germanic and Celtic. As groups of women, the *matres* and *matrones* bear a resemblance to the norns, valkyries, and dísir of the mythology that was recorded much later.

One of the many Germanic stone carvings depicting one of the Matres/ Matrones. (Rijksmuseum van Oudheden)

> *See also* Dísir; Norns
> ***References and further reading:***
> Everything on this subject is written in German. To my mind the most useful is Heinrich Hempel, "Matronenkult und germanische Mütterglaube," in his *Kleine Schriften zur Vollendung seines 80. Lebensjahres am 27. August 1965*, ed. Heinrich Mattias Heinrichs (Heidelberg: C. Winter, 1966), 13–37.

MEAD OF POETRY

Intoxicating beverage that makes anyone who drinks it a poet or scholar.

The mead of poetry was, like many precious things, originally fashioned by dwarfs, and like many other precious things, the æsir obtained it from the giants. The story is told most fully in the *Skáldskaparmál* section of Snorri Sturluson's *Edda*.

As a token of the end of hostilities between them, the æsir and vanir mix their spittle in a bowl, and out of that they make Kvasir, the wisest being. He goes around the world dispensing wisdom but is killed by two dwarfs, Fjalar and Galar, who mix his blood with honey and, in the kettle Ódrerir, ferment this mixture into the mead of poetry. Then the dwarfs invite the giant Gilling and his wife to visit. They kill Gilling by overturning their boat, and the wife by dropping a millstone on her head. Gilling's son Suttung comes looking for compensation for his parents' deaths, and when he abandons the dwarfs on a rock on a seat that will be covered at high tide, the dwarfs give him the mead of poetry. Suttung puts it into the mountain Hnitbjörg, storing it in Ódrerir and two other vessels, Bodn and Són, under the care of his daughter Gunnlöd.

Odin sets off to Giantland calling himself Bölverk (Evil-deed). He comes upon the nine slaves of the giant Baugi, Suttung's brother, and tosses a whetstone in the air. As the slaves rush to catch the whetstone, the scythes they are carrying swing about, and they are all killed. Odin then takes service with Baugi and agrees to do the work of the nine slaves for one drink of the mead of poetry. When the wages are due they apply to Suttung, but he refuses to pay. Odin produces a drill called Rati ("Traveler" or "Madman") and has Baugi drill a hole into Hnitbjörg. I now let Snorri take up the story:

> Then Baugi said that he had bored into the mountain, but Bölverk blew into the borehole, and shavings flew back at him. And so he found out that Baugi wished to deceive him, and he had him bore into the mountain. Baugi drilled some more, and when Bölverk blew into the hole a second time, the shavings flew in. Then Bölverk changed himself into a snake and crawled into the borehole, and Baugi struck at him with the drill but missed. Bölverk went to where Gunnlöd was and slept with her for three nights, and she granted him three drinks of the mead. In the first he drank everything in Ódrerir, in the second everything in Bodn, in the third everything in Són, and so he had all the mead. Then he changed himself into an eagle and flew off as quickly as he could, but when Suttung saw the eagle flying, he changed himself into an eagle and flew after him. But when the æsir saw where Odin was flying, they put their barrel out front, and when Odin came over Ásgard, he spat up the mead into the barrel. But Suttung was so close to catching him that he sent some mead out the back, and this was not saved. Everyone who wished had some of that, and it is called the bad poets' share. But Odin gave the mead to the æsir and to those humans who could compose verse.

Hávamál, stanzas 13–14, may refer to this myth:

13. The heron of obliviousness it is called, which hovers over beers,
It steals the mind of people;
In this bird's feathers I was fettered
At Gunnlöd's place.
14. I was drunk, I was overdrunk
Visiting wise Fjalar;
That beer is best which restores
For each man his mind.

Although these stanzas are among others that warn about excessive drinking, they appear to allude to some version of the story in which Odin visited Fjalar. If there was such a version, it has left no other trace.

Hávamál refers explicitly to Odin's acquisition of the mead of poetry in stanzas 104–110. Odin says that he visited Suttung (104) and got a drink of the mead from Gunnlöd (105).

106. The mouth of the drill I had make room for me
And bore through the rock;
Over and under me stood the paths of the giants;
Thus I risked my head.

Ódrerir has "come up" to the world of men (107), but Odin would not have been successful if he had not used Gunnlöd (108). The next stanza has an incident lacking in Snorri's version of the myth:

109. The next day the frost giants went,
To ask counsel of Hár, in the hall of Hár,
About Bölverk they asked, if he had come among the gods,
Or if Suttung had killed him.

Stanza 110 ends the section by reporting that "Odin left Suttung deceived and made Gunnlöd weep."

Besides the giants' search for Bölverk in Odin's hall, this version also differs from Snorri's in that Ódrerir appears to be the mead itself, rather than a vessel in which it was kept. It also has no mention of Baugi, who is found only in Snorri's account. It is possible that both these differences have to do with Snorri's (mis)interpretations of the *Hávamál* stanzas. The *Hávamál* stanzas do not make the shape-changing explicit, and they leave out Suttung's pursuit of Odin and the portion of the mead urinated out for bad poets.

The mead of poetry is one of the most valuable assets of the gods, for wisdom tended to be encoded in verse; indeed, Snorri says in *Ynglinga saga* that

Odin spoke only in verse. The magic songs that he obtains in *Hávamál* are also clearly relevant to the mead that makes one a master of poetry.

> ***See also*** Baugi; Gunnlöd; Suttung
>
> ***References and further reading:*** Georges Dumézil was interested in the mead of poetry in its Indo-European context from the time of one of his very first publications in the 1920s. In chapter 1 of his *Gods of the Ancient Northmen*, ed. Einar Haugen, Publications of the UCLA Center for the Study of Comparative Folklore and Mythology, 3 (Berkeley and Los Angeles: University of California Press, 1973), Dumézil integrates the story into the larger issue of the incorporation of the æsir and vanir into a single group. Snorri's version of the story is explored by Roberta Frank, "Snorri and the Mead of Poetry," *Speculum Norroenum: Norse Studies in Memory of Gabriel Turville-Petre*, ed. Ursula Dronke, Guðrún P. Helgadóttir, Gerd Wolfgang Weber, and Hans-Bekker Nielsen ([Odense:] Odense University Press, 1981), 155–170. Two other interesting if speculative articles are A. G. van Hamel, "The Mastering of the Mead," in the volume *Studia Germanica tillägnade Ernst Albin Kock den 6 december 1934* (Lund: C. Blom, 1934), 76–85, and John Stephens, "The Mead of Poetry: Myth and Metaphor," *Neophilologus* 56 (1972): 259–268. A book on the mythic role of intoxicating beverages in general is Renate Doht, *Der Rauschtrank im germanischen Mythos*, Wiener Arbeiten zur germanischen Altertumskunde und Philologie, 3 (Vienna: K. M. Halosar, 1974).

MEILI

Brother of Thor and therefore presumably son of Odin.

The name is found in the twice-attested Thor kenning, "Meili's brother." Since Thor is Odin's son, Meili must also be Odin's son.

MERSEBURG CHARMS

Two Old High German charms with analogs in Scandinavian mythology.

The First Merseburg Charm is for getting out of bonds, and it refers to women called Idisi who freed warriors from fetters. These women would seem to be cognate with the dísir of Scandinavian mythology.

The Second Merseburg Charm is for an injury:

> Phol and Wodan went to the forest.
> Then Balder's horse sprained its foot.
> Then Sinthgunt sang charms, and Sunna her sister;
> Then Friia sang charms, and Volla her sister;
> Then Wodan sang charms, as he well could:
> be it bone-sprain, be it blood-sprain, be it limb-sprain:
> bone to bone, blood to blood,
> limb to limb, so be they glued together.

Phol may be identical with Fulla in Scandinavian, and Wodan is certainly Odin. Most observers accept that Balder is identical with Baldr, although some think that Balder here may be a noun meaning "lord." Clearly there is no narrative connection with the Scandinavian materials, where Baldr, horses, and sprains have no particular association. However, Karl Hauck has argued in a series of works that some bracteates show a related scene containing Baldr, Odin (understood as a healing god), and a horse.

> *See also* Baldr; Bracteates; Dísir
> *References and further reading:* A mainline general treatment of the gods of the Merseburg Charms is Felix Genzmer, "Die Götter des zweiten Merseburger Zauberspruches," *Arkiv för nordisk filologi* 63 (1948): 55–72, who sees Phol as a male counterpart to Fulla. Another interesting study is that of Axel Olrik, "Odins ridt," *Danske studier* 22 (1925): 1–18. The most important of the many articles discussing the relationship of Baldr and the Second Merseburg Charm is Franz Rolf Schröder, "Balder und der zweite Merseburger Spruch," *Germanisch-Romanische Monatsschrift* 34 (1953): 161–183. But Karl Helm answered with a vigorous "no" his own question, "Balder in Deutschland?" (Baldr in Germany? [by which he meant on the continent in general]), *Beiträge zur Geschichte der deutschen Sprache und Literatur* 67 (1944): 216–222, and included the Balder of the Second Merseburg Charm as one of his "Erfundene Götter" ("invented gods"), in *Studien zur deutschen Philologie des Mittelalters: Festschrift zum 80. Geburtstag von Friedrich Panzer*, ed. Richard Kienast (Heidelberg: C. Winter, 1950), 1–11.

MIDGARD (CENTRAL-ENCLOSURE)

The home of humans.

Völuspá, stanza 4, refers to the sons of Bur as "the ones who fashioned Midgard." *Grímnismál*, stanza 41, is more explicit, since it ties the creation of Midgard to the parturition of Ymir's body and makes clear the benefit to humans:

> 41. And from his brows the blithe gods made
> Midgard for the sons of men;
> And from his brain the tough-minded clouds
> Were all formed.

In *Hárbardsljód*, stanza 23, Thor makes explicit his role in keeping Midgard safe for humans:

> I was to the east and I killed giants,
> Evil maidens who were going to the mountain;
> Great would be the race of giants, if they all lived;
> Few humans would live under Midgard.

"Under Midgard," an expression that is found elsewhere in eddic poetry, suggests that Midgard was something protective, or rather, that it was not so much the space enclosed for humans as the enclosure or wall itself. This agrees with Snorri Sturluson's description, in the *Gylfaginning* section of his *Edda*, of the way the æsir made the earth:

> It [the earth] is disk shaped, and around the outside is the deep sea, and along the edge of the sea they gave lands to the giants to settle, and inside on the earth they made a stronghold around the earth on account of the enmity of the giants, and for this wall they used Ymir's eyebrows, and they called the stronghold Midgard.

Although Midgard was made "for the sons of men," most of the manuscripts of Snorri's *Edda* agree that when Thor set off to visit Hymir, he left from Midgard, not Ásgard. Perhaps this shows the special connection between Thor and humans.

Unlike nearly all the mythological places, Midgard has cognates in other Germanic languages and must have been a common conception.

See also Ásgard; Ymir

References and further reading: In the second chapter of *Den dubbla scenen: Muntlig diktning från Eddan till Abba* (Stockholm: Prisma, 1978), Lars Lönnroth has an interesting reading of the hypothetical performance situation of the opening stanzas of *Völuspá*, in which the building of Midgard might be paralleled by the building of the home of a chieftain in Iceland.

MIDGARD SERPENT

Mighty beast sunk in the sea encircling the earth, a son of Loki, and Thor's greatest opponent.

The Midgard serpent, also known as Jörmungand (Mighty-snake), was one of the three in the monstrous brood sired by Loki on Angrboda. When Odin saw the danger the three posed, he had them fetched, and he dispatched the serpent into the sea, Hel into the underground realm of the dead, and the wolf Fenrir to a cave after he had been bound (not without

Brooch found in Öland, Sweden, depicting a beast reminiscent of the Midgard serpent. (Werner Forman/Art Resource)

some inconvenience, especially for Týr). We have this story from the *Gylfaginning* section of Snorri Sturluson's *Edda*, where he says this about the serpent:

Thor stands in a boat with a raised hammer near the bottom of an eleventh-century rune stone from Altuna. From his left hand dangles the ox-head bait while the serpent coils below. (National Museum of Denmark)

And when they came to him, he threw the serpent into the deep sea that lies around all lands, and that serpent grew so much, that he lies in the middle of the ocean around all lands and bites his tail.

Here a word on medieval cosmology may be in order. The world was a flat disk, with the earth in the center and the sea all around. Thus the serpent is about as far away from the center, where men and gods lived, as Hel might be under the earth in the world of the dead, inaccessible to the living. The fact that he bites his tail means that he forms a complete circle around men and gods.

The Midgard serpent was especially the enemy of Thor (just as Fenrir was of Odin, and Hel, we might say, was of Baldr). *Völuspá* and Snorri agree that they were to meet at Ragnarök. But they also had a famous meeting during the mythic present, when Thor fished up the Midgard serpent out of the sea and threw his hammer at the beast.

The myth turns up in the poetry of the some of the earliest skalds. In addition, it was popular as a subject on carvings in the late Viking Age.

See also Thor

MÍMIR (MÍM, MÍMI)

Enigmatic god associated with wisdom, Odin, and the well at the center of the cosmos.

In eddic poetry Mímir turns up only in the expressions "Mímir's head" and "Mímir's well." There is a myth behind the first expression, told in the early chapters of Snorri Sturluson's *Ynglinga saga* and therefore meant to be understood as history. At the end of the Æsir-Vanir War, according to chapter 4, the æsir sent Mímir, along with Hœnir, to the vanir as part of the exchange of hostages (men exchanged as a pledge of good faith). Hœnir appeared to have the qualities of a chieftain, and the vanir immediately employed him in that capacity. But Hœnir relied exclusively on the counsels of Mímir, and when Mímir was not present, Hœnir responded to queries by saying:

"Let others decide." The vanir therefore deduced that they had been cheated. They beheaded Mímir and sent the head to Odin, who preserved it and listened to the hidden things it had to say to him. Thus in *Völuspá*, stanza 46, as the seeress describes the onset of Ragnarök, she has these things to say:

> Mím's sons sport, and the world tree trembles
> At the old Gjallarhorn.
> Loudly blows Heimdall, the horn is aloft,
> Odin is speaking to Mím's head.

Note first that the form of the name here is Mím, not Mímir. This suggests that more than one figure may have been conflated to make the Mímir we have in the mythology. Mím's sons would presumably be the æsir (from whom Mím was sent in the mythic near past to the vanir, as I have just said).

Mím's head, to use the form that the eddic poets did, is also found in *Sigrdrífumál*, stanza 14.

> Then Mím's head spoke
> Wisely the first word,
> And told true staves.

This is followed by a list of runes that may be carved, and such a list also precedes the stanza. Odin is of course connected with the origin of runes, as he is more generally with the wisdom that may be derived from Mím's head.

The form Mímir is associated with the well. Here is what Snorri Sturluson says in the *Gylfaginning* section of his *Edda*. He is talking about the world tree, Yggdrasil.

> Under that root, which turns toward the frost giants, is Mímisbrunn [the well of Mímir], in which wisdom and human knowledge are hidden, and that one is called Mímir, who owns the well. He is full of wisdom, because he drinks from the well using the horn Gjallarhorn.

The seeress of *Völuspá* mentioned this well in connection with Odin's wisdom:

> I know fully, Odin, where you hid your eye:
> In the famous well of Mímir.
> Mímir drinks mead each day
> From the pledge of Valfödr [Odin].

The passage is usually understood to mean that Odin gave away one of his eyes to gain mystic vision, and that he did so by putting the eye in Mímir's well. The *Völuspá* poet apparently imagined that the eye could be used as a kind of drinking vessel, unless what the stanza means is that the whole well could be called "pledge of Odin." That mead can be drunk from it is not surprising, since mead confers wisdom.

The location of Mímir's well beneath the root that runs toward the frost giants suggests a connection, perhaps primal, between Mímir and the giants, even though we know that Mímir was a member of the æsir in the mythic near past. Here again we may be dealing with a conflation of figures and conceptions. But the location near Yggdrasil also may help illuminate the tree called Mímameid (Mími's-tree), which is found twice in the poem editors call *Fjölsvinnsmál.* Mímameid could be a name for Yggdrasil; if so, Hoddmímir's forest might also have to do with the tree.

Etymologically, Mímir is associated with our word "memory," and this provides attractive possibilities for interpretation. Memory is something valued and especially understood by Odin, but misunderstood and undervalued by the vanir. It stands at the very center of the Odinic universe.

> ***See also*** Gjallarhorn; Hoddmímir's Forest
> ***References and further reading:*** A. LeRoy Andrews, "Old Norse Notes 7: Some Observations on Mímir," *Modern Language Notes* 43 (1928): 166–171, offered a satisfyingly romantic interpretation, making Mímir's head a drinking skull (there is, sad to report, no evidence of drinking from skulls). On Mímir and memory, see Margaret Clunies Ross, *Prolonged Echoes: Old Norse Myths in Medieval Icelandic Society,* vol. 1: *The Myths* (Odense: Odense University Press, 1994), 213–215.

MÓDGUD (BATTLE-WEARY)

Maiden who guards the Gjallarbrú; encountered by Hermód on his journey to Hel attempting to retrieve Baldr.

Módgud is found only in Snorri, who states explicitly that she guards the bridge. In the narrative, she asks Hermód his name and family and informs him that five troops of dead men rode over the bridge yesterday.

> And yet my bridge resounds no less under you alone, and you do not have the countenance of dead men. Why do you ride the road to Hel?

Hermód asks whether Baldr has come that way. Módgud replies that he has and adds that the way to Hel lies down and north.

Módgud fills to some extent the epic role of one who challenges the hero upon arrival, often near a body of water, but she also functions as a donor figure here by giving Hermód the information he needs. She thus seems to have more a narrative than a mythic or religious function.

> ***See also*** Baldr; Gjallarbrú; Hermód

MÓDI (ANGRY-ONE)

Son of Thor.

Hymiskvida, stanza 34, uses the kennings "father of Módi" and "husband of Sif" for Thor, and in *Skáldskaparmál* Snorri agrees that "father of Módi" is a Thor kenning.

Unlike Magni, Thor's other son, Módi has no particular role in the mythological present. With Magni, however, and with Odin's sons Vídar and Váli and the victim Baldr and his killer Höd, Módi will survive Ragnarök. In the aftermath he will inherit Mjöllnir along with his brother, as *Vafthrúdnismál,* stanza 55, states, and as Snorri reports in *Gylfaginning* when he quotes the stanza.

Of the six second-generation gods who are to survive Ragnarök, Módi has the thinnest dossier. But his name turns up frequently enough as the base word in man kennings that he must have been fairly well-known.

See also Magni; Ragnarök; Váli, Son of Odin; Vídar

MUNDILFŒRI

Father of the sun and moon.

The main evidence for this figure is *Vafthrúdnismál,* stanza 23. In stanza 22, Odin asks the wise giant Vafthrúdnir whence the moon and sun came to travel over people. The giant responds in stanza 23:

Mundilfœri he is called, the father of Máni
And also of Sól the same;
Into heaven shall they turn each day,
So that people can reckon years.

Snorri concocts a somewhat different story: Mundilfœri is a man who had two children who were so beautiful that he named them Máni and Sól (i.e., Moon and Sun), and the gods punished this act of pride by placing the children in heaven to serve the actual heavenly bodies, which the gods had created. Sól drives the horses that pull the sun, and Máni controls the motion of the moon and its waxings and wanings.

Various explanations have been offered for the name (which varies in significant ways in the sources). If the first component, *mundil-,* is associated with *mund,* "period of time," then the name might be a kind of kenning for moon, something like "he who causes periods of time to move."

See also Máni; Sól

MUSPELL

Probably a giant; being associated with Ragnarök and the origin of the cosmos.

In eddic poetry Muspell is associated with groups, Muspell's peoples (*Völuspá*, stanza 51), and Muspell's sons (*Lokasenna*, stanza 42). Both refer to the hordes of evil beings that will invade the world at Ragnarök to fight with the gods. Snorri Sturluson, in the *Gylfaginning* section of his *Edda*, made copious reference to the sons of Muspell at Ragnarök, but he also referred to Muspell in connection with the origin of the cosmos.

> That part of Ginnunga gap, which faced the north, was filled with a load and heaviness of ice, and in from there drizzle and a gust of wind; and the southern part of Ginnunga gap turned toward those sparks and embers, which flew out of Muspellsheim. . . . Just as cold and all bad things came from Niflheim, all that which came from Muspell was hot and bright, but Ginnunga gap was as calm as a windless sky, and when the warm breeze met the frost, it melted and dripped. And from those drops of poison life emerged, with the power that the heat sent, and it grew into a human form, and that one is called Ymir, but the frost giants call him Aurgelmir, and all the families of frost giants descend from him.

Although it has been argued that this passage suggests that Muspell is a place, the notion seems hardly credible. Rather, it seems that Muspell presides over a fiery region outside the realm of the gods, and from there some chaos beings will come when Ragnarök is at hand; after all, the world is to be consumed by flames.

There are fascinating cognates in other Germanic languages. Old High German has a poem that modern editors call *Muspilli* because that word is to be found in it as a word for the subject of the poem, the Christian Last Judgment. In the Old Saxon *Heliand*, an epic about Christ, the form *mudspell* is to be found, with the same meaning. Taking into account the medieval Icelandic materials as well, scholars are inclined to understand the word as referring to the fiery end of the earth. The figure in Scandinavian mythology would be a personification of that notion.

See also Ginnunga gap

References and further reading: Most of the work on Muspell-Muspilli-Mudspell is in German. The most recent book, that of Heinz Finger, *Untersuchungen zum "Muspilli,"* Göppinger Arbeiten zur Germanistik, 244 (Göttingen: Kummerle, 1977), doubts the close parallel between the German and Scandinavian conceptions.

NAGLFAR

Ship that will transport the forces of chaos at Ragnarök.

Völuspá, stanza 50, has a list of bad things that will happen at Ragnarök, ending with "Naglfar casts off."

In the *Gylfaginning* section of his *Edda*, Snorri Sturluson has more information. At Ragnarök:

> It will also happen that that ship Naglfar will get loose. It is made of the nails of dead men, and for that reason it is worth warning that if men die with uncut nails they greatly increase the materials for Naglfar, which the gods and men would least wish them to do.

Earlier Snorri had said that "Naglfar is the largest ship; Muspell owns it."

The information about uncut nails is not found outside of Snorri. Naglfar looks as though it should mean "Nail-farer," but other etymologies have been proposed. Of these I find most attractive the idea that "nail" is a metonym for a ship, whose planks were fastened with nails.

See also Muspell

References and further reading: Nails to hold planks together are the centerpiece of the interpretation of Hallvard Lie, "Naglfar og Naglfari," *Maal og minne*, 1954: 152–161.

NAGLFARI

First husband of Nótt (Night).

We have this information only from Snorri Sturluson, who describes Nótt's marriages in the *Gylfaginning* section of his *Edda*. In this first, and otherwise unknown, marriage, a child named Aud (Wealth) was produced. No further mention is to be found.

NÁL (NEEDLE)

Mother of Loki, apparently a secondary name of Laufey.

Only the late *Sörla tháttr* states explicitly that Nál and Laufey are the same person:

> There was a man called Fárbauti. He was an old man and was married to that woman who was named Laufey. She was both slender and weak, and for that reason she was called Nál [Needle].

Nál is unknown in skaldic and eddic poetry.

See also Fárbauti; Laufey; Loki; *Sörla tháttr*

NANNA

Wife of Baldr, burned on the funeral pyre with him.

No vernacular source has very much to say of Nanna. Snorri is the most informative. In the *Gylfaginning* section of his *Edda*, he does not mention Nanna when he presents Baldr. When he comes to Forseti, he says that Forseti is the son of Baldr and Nanna Nepsdóttir (Nep is otherwise wholly unknown). In the description of Baldr's funeral Snorri refers to her again as Nanna Nepsdóttir and says that when she, Baldr's wife, saw his body on the pyre, she "burst from grief" and was placed there alongside him. She accompanied him to Hel and sent back with Hermód some linen cloth for Frigg and a finger ring for Fulla, just as Baldr returned the ring Draupnir to Odin.

In the *Gesta Danorum* of Saxo Grammaticus, Nanna is a human woman, the pivot of a love triangle involving the demigod Balderus and the human king Høtherus. Høtherus gets the girl, and Balderus dies, still presumably loving her, killed by Høtherus.

Völuspá, stanza 30, refers to valkyries as "Nannas of Odin." I have used a capital letter, as though it were a name, but it is also possible that there was a common noun, *nanna*, which would have meant something like "woman." There is an account of a Rus (probably Swedish) Viking Age funeral in the writings of an Arab traveler, Ibn Fadlan, in which a slave girl is sacrificed at the funeral of her master, just as Nanna dies at Baldr's funeral and is burned beside him. Was Nanna a *nanna*? It seems unlikely, but considering the possibility will give some idea of the interpretive difficulties offered by Scandinavian mythology.

> ***See also*** Baldr; Forseti; Höd
>
> ***References and further readings:*** I consider in excruciating detail all the relevant Nanna details and spin a very speculative hypothesis about Nanna and *nanna* in chapter 3 of my *Murder and Vengeance among the Gods: Baldr in Scandinavian Mythology*, FF Communications, 262 (Helsinki: Societas Scientiarum Fennica: 1997).

NARI AND/OR NARFI

Son(s) of Loki.

In the *Gylfaginning* section of his *Edda*, Snorri introduces Loki as one "also numbered among the æsir." At the end of this introduction, Snorri tells about the vengeance taken on Loki for his role in the death of Baldr. First the gods capture Loki:

> Then three stone slabs were taken and stood on edge and holes cut in each. Then Loki's sons, Váli and Nari or Narfi, were seized. The æsir turned Váli into the form of a wolf, and he tore apart Narfi, his brother. Then the æsir took his

guts and bound Loki with them across the three sharpened stones; one is under his shoulders, the second under his loins, and the third under the hollows behind his knees, and these bonds turned to iron.

The same vengeance is described in the prose colophon to *Lokasenna*, there of course motivated by Loki's insulting of all the gods. Again Loki tries to hide but is taken. "He was bound with the guts of his son Nari. But Narfi, his son, turned into a wolf." Narfi's metamorphosis is not explained.

There is thus considerable confusion here. Nari may also be Váli (otherwise the name of a son of Odin), and Nari may or may not be the same as Narfi. To make matters worse, there is another Narfi or Nörfi, the father of Nótt (Night), whose name turns up as Nör in the eddic poems.

See also Nótt; Váli, Son of Loki

NERTHUS

Goddess of the Germans, described by the Roman historian Tacitus toward the end of the first century C.E.

Tacitus has mentioned a whole set of tribes:

> There is nothing noteworthy about them individually, except that in common they worship Nerthus, that is, Mother Earth, and they believe her to intervene in the affairs of humans and to ride among people. There is on an island of the ocean a sacred grove, and in it a consecrated cart, covered with cloth. A single priest is allowed to touch it. He perceives the entry of the goddess into the shrine and follows with veneration as she is led away drawn by cows. Then a period of rejoicing, places of festival, as many as are honored to receive and entertain her. They do not enter into war; they do not take up arms. Every weapon is hidden. Peace and quiet are then alone known, and then alone loved, until the same priest returns the goddess, when she has had her fill of human conversation, to her temple. Thereafter the cart, the cloth, and, if you wish to believe it, the deity herself, are washed in a secret lake. Slaves serve her, whom the same lake swallows. Hence there is a secret terror and a holy ignorance about what that may be, which they only see to die.

Both Frey and Freyja are associated with carts, and Njörd is especially associated with water. Indeed, "Nerthus" is the feminine form of what the name "Njörd" would have looked like during the time Tacitus wrote. The identification with Mother Earth probably has much less to do with Jörd in Scandinavian mythology than with fertility goddesses in many cultures. In short, Nerthus looks very much like one of the vanir, although her cult is attested more than a millennium before the Scandinavian sources were recorded, and Tacitus's description of her cult may tell us something about the later cult of the vanir.

See also Frey; Freyja; Vanir

References and further reading: The etymological relationship between Njörd and Nerthus, as well as the similar relationship between Frey and Freyja, is best set forth by Axel Kock, "Die Göttin Nerthus und der Gott Niorpr," *Zeitschrift für deutsche Philologie* 28 (1896): 289–294. In "The Votaries of Nerthus," *Namn och bygd* 22 (1934), 26–51, Kemp Malone surveyed the evidence about the tribes who worshipped Nerthus and located the cult somewhere near the Limfjord, in Jutland, Denmark. Eric Elgquist, *Studier rörande Njordkultens spriding bland de nordiska folken* (Lund: Olin, 1952), used place-name evidence to discuss the dissemination of the Njörd cult among the Nordic peoples, which he thinks originated in southern Jutland. Edgar Polomé, "À propos de la déesse Nerthus," *Latomus* 13 (1954): 167–200, sees the Nerthus cult as associated with the fertility of the soil, and he thinks agriculture was primarily a female activity at the time that Tacitus was writing.

NIDAFJÖLL

Mountains in the underworld.

Stanza 66, the last stanza of *Völuspá*, says the dragon Nídhögg, carrying corpses, will come flying down from the Nidafjöll. This conception of the place is clearly a negative one, but in *Gylfaginning* Snorri says that at Ragnarök the hall Sindri—a good hall, made of gold, in which good and righteous people shall dwell—will stand upon the Nidafjöll. Snorri's source here was *Völuspá*, stanza 37, which locates the hall of the family of Sindri on Nidavellir, that is, on plains, not mountains. Why he would make this change is unclear.

The second component of Nidafjöll, *fjöll*, just means "mountains" (compare the English "fell"). The first part, however, could be one of at least two things: the darkness of the waning moon or a dwarf name (Nidi).

See also Nidavellir; Nídhögg; Sindri

NIDAVELLIR

Plains, perhaps in the underworld, site of a splendid hall.

We find the Nidavellir only in *Völuspá*, stanza 37:

> There stood to the north, on the Nidavellir,
> A hall of gold, of the family of Sindri.

Snorri conflated these plains with the mountains called Nidafjöll and said that it was there the hall Sindri was located. Presumably plains and mountains are related. The first part of each name could be the darkness of the waning moon or a dwarf name (Nidi).

See also Nidafjöll; Sindri

NÍDHÖGG (EVIL-BLOW)

Dragon associated with Yggdrasil, the world tree.

Grímnismál mentions Nídhögg in two stanzas:

> 32. Ratatosk is the name of a squirrel who shall run
> on the ash of Yggdrasil;
> words of an eagle he shall carry down
> and say to Nídhögg below.

and

> 35. The ash of Yggdrasil suffers difficulty,
> more than men may know;
> a hart bites from below, yet on the side it rots;
> Nídhögg harms it from below.

Snorri adds that the words transported down by the squirrel are hostile and that he carries them in both directions, and that Nídhögg is a snake or dragon, one of many who live below one of the roots of Yggdrasil.

Völuspá gives Nídhögg a role at Ragnarök. As the world dissolves into chaos, as the seeress sees murderers, oath breakers, and adulterers wading through heavy currents, "There Nídhögg sucked / the corpses of the departed, / the wolf tore men apart." But more important is Nídhögg's appearance in stanza 66, the very last one in the poem:

> There the dark dragon comes flying,
> The gleaming snake, down from the Nidafjöll;
> In his feathers he carries—he flies over the field—
> Does Nídhögg, corpses—now she must sink down.

This stanza follows the seeress's discussion of the reemergence of the earth and the æsir, and it is not difficult to imagine a performance of *Völuspá* in which this last stanza, with the dragon zooming overhead, would suggest the advent of Ragnarök and thus would be a particularly effective way to end the performance, a real surprise ending. But whether or not one takes an interest in this surmise about oral performance, it is clear that Nídhögg was an important symbol of chaos and the looming end of the world.

See also Ratatosk, Yggdrasil

NIFLHEIM (FOG-WORLD) AND NIFLHEL (FOG-HEL)

World of the dead.

If we are to distinguish between the two, we would say that Niflheim is the ancient underworld, where Hel has her domain, and Niflhel is the ninth underworld of the dead.

Niflheim is unknown in poetry but is mentioned several times by Snorri Sturluson in the *Gylfaginning* section of his *Edda.* It is ancient because it somehow existed before the world was created.

> It was many ages before the earth was created, that Niflheim was made, and in the middle of it is the spring Hvergelmir, and from it flow those rivers that are so named: Svöl (Cool), Gunnthrá (Battle-pain), Fjörm (Rushing), Fimbulthul (Mighty-wind or Mighty-speaker), Slíd (Dangerous) and Hríd (Storm), Sylg (Slurp) and Ylg (She-wolf), Víd (Wide), Leipt (Flash).

In discussing Ginnunga gap, Snorri contrasts all the cold and bad things in Niflheim with the heat of Muspell, but he does not elaborate further. However, he does place Niflheim centrally in his discussion of the world tree:

> The ash is the greatest and best of all trees. Its limbs stretch over the entire world and rise above heaven. Three roots of the tree hold it up and stretch out widely. One is among the æsir, the second among the frost giants, where Ginnunga gap used to be, the third stands over Niflheim. Under that root is Hvergelmir, and Nídhögg gnaws the roots from below.

Thus Snorri gives Niflheim both a cosmogonic and cosmological function. It also has a role in the mythic present as the abode of the dead. This Snorri explains when he discusses the three monstrous children of Loki, each of whom is banished by the æsir: Odin casts the Midgard serpent into the sea, and the æsir bind the wolf Fenrir. As for Hel,

> Hel he [Odin] threw into Niflheim and gave her power over nine worlds, that she should host all those who were sent to her, and they are those who die of illness or old age. She has a large residence there, and the walls are extremely high and the gate huge. Éljudnir [Rain-damp] is the name of her hall, hunger her plate, starving her knife, Ganglati her serving boy, Ganglöt her serving woman, stumbling block the threshold that leads in, Kör [Sickbed] her bed, Blíkjanda-böl [Pale-misfortune] her bedhangings. She is half dark blue and half flesh color. For this reason she is easily recognized and rather stooping but fierce.

Unlike Niflheim, Niflhel is found in eddic poetry. In *Vafthrúdnismál*, stanza 43, Odin tells the giant Vafthrúdnir how he has come to be so wise:

About the runes of the giants and of all the gods
I can tell the truth
Because I have come through each world.
From nine worlds I came below Niflhel;
Thither men die out of Hel.

This stanza seems to say that Niflhel is some lower version of Hel, into which some people go when they die. That complexity appears to be missing in the other reference to Niflhel in eddic poetry, namely, stanza 2 of *Baldrs draumar*, which says that Odin traveled "down into Niflhel" when he went to explore the implications of Baldr's bad dreams.

In the *Gylfaginning* section of his *Edda*, Snorri mentions Niflhel, and he appears to be paraphrasing and expanding the stanza from *Vafthrúdnismál*. Well behaved persons, he says, will be with Alfödr, "but evil men will go to Hel and thence to Niflhel; that is down in the ninth world."

The confusion between Niflheim and Niflhel is neatly summed up by variation in the manuscripts of Snorri's *Edda*. In describing the fate of the giant master builder of the wall around Ásgard, two of the four main manuscripts say that Thor bashed the giant's head and sent him to Niflheim, and the other two say that Thor sent him to Niflhel.

See also Ginnunga gap; Hel

NJÖRD

God, member of the vanir group.
According to Snorri's *Gylfaginning* Njörd lives in heaven at Nóatún (Boathouse); he rules the motion of the wind and stills the sea and fire; he should be called on for seafaring and fishing. He is so wealthy that he can endow land and money and should be called on for that purpose. He came to the æsir in exchange for Hœnir as a settlement established between the æsir and vanir. He is married to Skadi but the marriage failed, since he prefers to live by the sea and she in the mountains. Although Snorri cites two stanzas about this marriage, the poem from which they are taken is lost, and Njörd does very little in mythic narrative. His role in taking Skadi to wife was anything but active, and otherwise he is known, other than as the father of Frey and Freyja, only as a hostage, from the vanir to the æsir and also apparently to the giants (*Lokasenna*, stanza 34).

The story of the arrangement of Njörd's marriage to Skadi is told in *Haustlöng* and *Skáldskaparmál*, and Njörd plays a very passive role. The entire mythic complex involves travel by Odin, Loki, and Hœnir, the disruption of their food supply by Thjazi, the capture of Loki when the staff he uses to strike

Thjazi in eagle form sticks to the giant, and the subsequent removal of Idun and her golden apples to Thjazi. Loki is forced to undertake the rescue of Idun and does so in bird form. According to *Skáldskaparmál*, he changes Idun into a nut and flies off with her in his claws, and Thjazi, again in the form of an eagle, flies in pursuit. After Loki's arrival with Idun, the gods light a fire that singes Thjazi's feathers and causes him to crash inside the gate of Valhöll, where the gods kill him. Here the much shortened account in *Haustlöng* ends.

Skáldskaparmál continues with the aftermath. Thjazi's daughter Skadi puts on armor and sets off to demand compensation. In Ásgard she agrees to accept a husband from among the gods as compensation, and the gods offer her a choice based on the lower legs alone (Old Icelandic *fótr*, the term used, actually denoted the foot or the foot and leg). Seeing a particularly nice pair, she says, "I choose this one; there can be little ugly about Baldr," but she has chosen Njörd. Her final condition is that the gods should make her laugh, and Loki succeeds in doing so by tying a rope about his testicles and the beard of a she-goat and then, while each brays, falling onto Skadi's lap.

Most observers assign the story as a whole to Loki's dossier, for he is the only constant. The play with castration and inverted sex roles is obvious; indeed, it runs throughout the story. Skadi puts on helm and armor and sets off in the role ordinarily taken by a male kinsman to obtain compensation or extract vengeance for the death of her father Thjazi, presumably as sole surviving heir. Compensation in the form of a spouse ordinarily involves the giving of a bride, and it appears, then, that Njörd has somehow been feminized, just as Skadi has put on men's clothing and taken up a task ordinarily in the male realm. An analogue to the choice of spouse by lower legs may be in the scene in *Kormáks saga* in which Kormák first meets Steingerd, who will be the object of his desire throughout the saga. When her ankles peep forth from under her skirts, Kormák utters a verse indicating that he has fallen in love with her even though he does not know her. Reading this scene against the myth of Skadi's choice of Njörd would accord directly with the gender inversions there. It is also worth pointing out that the name "Skadi" is grammatically masculine.

We know nothing about Njörd outside this myth that particularly addresses his sexuality per se; indeed, among the vanir he took to wife his sister, as was the custom in that society, and fathered Frey and Freyja, and he offers his siring of Frey as a counter to Loki's accusation concerning his humiliation by giantesses while he was a hostage. Beyond that, however, the evidence is perhaps equivocal. The name "Njörd" can be derived etymologically from that of Nerthus, the goddess described by Tacitus from around the end of the first century C.E. The etymological equivalence can suggest either that some time during the first millennium the sex of the deity changed, that the deity was hermaphroditic, or, perhaps most likely, that there was once a male-female pair, like Frey and Freyja, with identical or nearly identical names.

As Snorri says, Njörd joined the æsir as a hostage (a man exchanged as a pledge of good faith) at the end of the war between the æsir and the vanir. He also, according to *Lokasenna*, stanza 34, spent time among the giants as a hostage. His status as hostage is then doubled. It is important to recall that hostages in Viking and medieval Scandinavia were persons exchanged as surety for various kinds of agreements and were ordinarily not to be mistreated. However, in *Lokasenna*, stanza 34, Loki insults Njörd by claiming that when he was a hostage among the giants, the daughters of Hymir urinated in Njörd's mouth. No satisfactory explanation of this motif has been provided (few have been attempted), but it would seem most reasonable to regard it as reflecting a complete loss of social status. Since it has also been suggested that bare legs or feet would in a European medieval public context be viewed as signs of humility or shame, it would appear that these two myths share a common feature, one that is perhaps ultimately associated with the hierarchically low status of the vanir within the community of the gods. However, place-names indicate worship of Njörd (Nerthus?) in many parts of Scandinavia, sometimes paired with the god Ull. Here it is difficult to reconcile myth and cult.

> ***References and further reading:*** Carol J. Clover, "Maiden Warriors and Other Sons," *Journal of English and Germanic Philology* 85 (1986): 35–49, and "Regardless of Sex: Men, Women, and Power in Early Northern Europe," *Speculum* 68 (1993): 363–387. Margaret Clunies Ross, "Why Skaði Laughed: Comic Seriousness in an Old Norse Mythic Narrative," *Maal og minne,* 1989: 1–14. John Lindow, "Loki and Skaði," *Snorrastefna: 25.–27. júlí 1990,* ed. Úlfar Bragason, Rit Stofnunar Sigurðar Nordals, 1 (Reykjavík: Stofnun Sigurðar Nordals, 1992), 130–142.

NORNS
Collective female spirits.

Poets, especially in eddic verse, speak repeatedly of the judgment *(dómr)* or verdict *(kviðr)* of the norns, and this means death or a life lived out, so that death is imminent. One of the thulur says, "Norns are called those women who shape what must be," and the noun related to the verb "shape" (medieval Icelandic *skapa*), medieval Icelandic *sköp,* which means something like "fate," is also used with the norns.

Snorri describes the norns explicitly in *Gylfaginning*. He is discussing the center of the universe, where the gods dwell, close by Yggdrasil. "A beautiful hall stands there under the ash tree by the well, and out of that hall come three maidens, those who are thus named: Urd, Verdandi, Skuld. These maidens shape

A scene from an eighth-century whalebone box known as the "Frank's Casket." On the right is a group of three women, identified by some observers as norns. (Werner Forman/Art Resource)

lives for people; we call them norns." Here Snorri is paraphrasing a stanza in *Völuspá*, stanza 18 in the *Codex Regius* version of the poem:

> Thence come maidens,
> much knowing,
> three of them, out of that lake,
> which stands under the tree.
> They call Urd one,
> the second Verdandi
> —they carved on a stick—
> Skuld the third.
> They established laws,
> they chose lives
> for the children of people,
> fates of men.

Snorri's version of the stanza has the maidens emerging from a hall, not a lake, and the seemingly more plausible hall is also found in the other version of *Völuspá*, in *Hauksbók*. These three norns, then, had a cosmic function ("established laws") as well as the function of shaping people's fates. Their names are transparent. Urd is similar to the past tense of the verb *verða*, "to become" and thus means something like "Became" or "Happened." It is cognate with Old English *wyrd*, "fate, destiny" and related words in Old High German and Old Saxon. Verdandi is the present participle of *verða*, "Becoming" or "Happening." Skuld is derived from the modal verb *skulu*, which is cognate with English "shall" and "should," and probably then means "Is-to-be" or "Will-happen." Thus these three norns in their names cover the past, the present, and the future. Of these three, only Urd seems to be known in tradition outside this passage, most importantly in connection with a well, the Urdarbrunn (Well-of-Urd), which is found in poetry. Skuld is also found as a valkyrie name.

Snorri goes on in this passage. "There are additional norns, who come to each child, when it is born, to shape the life, and these are related to the gods, but others are of the family of the elves, and the third ones are of the dwarfs." He quotes *Fáfnismál*, stanza 13, in which the dying Fáfnir tells Sigurd that the norns are very "differently born / they have not a family together; / some are related to the æsir, / some to the dwarfs, / some are the daughters of Dvalin." Fáfnir is answering a question from Sigurd that is no longer easy to understand: "Who are those norns, / who go under duress / and choose mothers from sons?"

Snorri's statement about the three kinds of norns seems to suggest that he thought the norns related to the æsir came to the children of humans; perhaps the elf norns came to elves and the dwarf norns to dwarfs. Certainly a norn came to the dwarf Andvari, or to his ancestors, for he says in *Reginsmál*, stanza 2: "[A] wicked norn / shaped us in days of old, / that I should go in the water" (the reference is to his sporting in rivers in the form of a salmon). Snorri ends his discussion of the norns in *Gylfaginning* by having Hár respond to Gylfi's comment that the norns give very different fates to different people. "Good norns of good family give a good life, but those people whose destiny is not good, bad norns cause that."

The skald Hallfred Óttarson vandrædaskáld coined the expression "long-maintained fates of the norns" to refer to the paganism he abandoned when he converted to Christianity. However, a runic inscription at the entrance to the church at Borgund in Sogn, Norway, says "Thórir carved these runes on St. Olafs day when he came by here. The norns did both good and bad. They shaped a lot of sorrow for me." In much more recent folklore, the porridge put out for the spirits at childbirth is called *nornegraut*, "norn's porridge." If, then, there is a unified concept of the norns, it is that they are responsible for fate, and that they act especially at childbirth.

NÓTT (NIGHT)

Personification of the night.

Nótt is found in *Vafthrúdnismál*, stanza 25, Vafthrúdnir's response to Odin's question in stanza 24, "Whence comes the day / that goes over people / or the night with tides?"

> Delling he is called, he is Dag's [Day's] father,
> And Nótt was born to Nör.
> New moon and tides the useful powers created
> For people to tell time.

In *Gylfaginning* Snorri has an interesting expansion of the idea in this stanza:

> Nörfi or Narfi was a giant who lived in Jötunheimar. He had a daughter named Nótt [Night]; she was swarthy and dark, as she had the lineage for. She was married to Naglfari; their son was Aud. Next she was married to Ánar; their daughter was Jörd [Earth]. Last she married Delling, and he was of the lineage of the æsir. Their son was Dag, according to his paternal heritage.

Why Nótt had so many marriages is unclear, but it does seem obvious that in Snorri's view the third marriage was the best, since it led to day.

Alfödr (Odin) gave horses to Nótt and Dag so that they could be pulled across the sky in wagons. Nótt's horse is Hrímfaxi (Frost-mane), and drippings from his bit, according to Snorri, cause dew.

See also Dag; Hrímfaxi

ÓD

Husband of Freyja.

Ód is little mentioned in poetry. The *Völuspá* poet referred to Freyja as Ód's maid, and in a puzzling reference in the end of *Hyndluljód*, Freyja's giantess interlocutor tells Freyja, "You ran to Ód, / ever longing." In other words, Ód's existence has to do with Freyja.

The same is the case in Snorri Sturluson's *Edda*. In the *Gylfaginning* section Ód appears first when Snorri is discussing Freyja.

> She is married to Ód, and their daughter is Hnoss. . . . Ód went away on long journeys, and Freyja weeps for him, and her tears are red gold. Freyja has many names, and the reason for that is that she called herself by various names when she went about among unknown peoples looking for Ód.

Although "Ód's bed-friend" is a Freyja kenning in skaldic poetry, Ód's journeys are not mentioned in the older poetry, and Freyja's journeys in search of him are completely undocumented.

Clearly the name of Ód (Óðr) is related to that of Odin (Óðinn); indeed, the linguistic relationship is identical to that between Ull and Ullin. In favor of a close relationship between the gods represented by the two names is the fact that Odin frequently travels (although no one seems to miss him); against it is the fact that Snorri so clearly keeps the two apart.

See also Freyja

References and further reading: The argument for associating Ód and Odin is made most forcefully by Jan de Vries, "Über das Verhältnis von Óðr und Óðinn," *Zeitschrift für deutsche Philologie* 73 (1954), 337–353, a response to two works that sought to separate the two: Lee M. Hollander, "The Old Norse God Óðr," *Journal of English and Germanic Philology* 49 (1950): 4–8, and Ernst Philippson, *Die Genealogie der Götter in germanischer Religion, Mythologie, und Theologie,* Illinois Studies in Language and Literature, vol. 37, part 3 (Urbana: University of Illinois Press, 1953).

ODIN (OLD NORSE ÓÎINN)

God of poetry, wisdom, hosts, and the dead; in the received mythology head of the pantheon.

Odin's father was Bur, son of Búri, the form licked from the salt blocks by the proto-cow Audhumla. Odin's mother was Bestla, a giantess, the daughter of Bölthorn. His very genealogy, therefore, replicates a basic operational pattern, namely, that the gods take as wives (or make children with) the females of the giant group.

With his brothers Vili and Vé, Odin created the cosmos out of the body of the proto-giant Ymir, whom they killed. Here too a basic operational pattern of the mythology is to be found: Gods kill giants, but not vice versa. This killing of Ymir, however, was a killing within a family, if one accepts that kinship is reckoned both through the father and mother, as it was in real life in medieval Scandinavia and probably in older Germanic society. For that reason, the mythology seems to privilege kinship reckoned only through the father.

There is much kinship to be reckoned with when it comes to Odin, one of whose alternate names is Alfödr (All-father). Odin is hardly the father of all, but he is the father of many within the mythology. Thor is the most important of Odin's sons, but there is also a set of younger sons who will survive Ragnarök: Váli and Vídar, young gods of vengeance. The most important of his roles as father, however, is as father of Baldr, the first god to die. When Baldr dies, all the gods are struck dumb, but it is Odin who best understands the implications.

Die for stamping the decorative plaques on seventh-century Swedish helmets. (Statens Historika Museum, Stockholm)

As the name Alfödr might also suggest, Odin is head of the pantheon, at least as it is presented in the sources recorded in the thirteenth century. Snorri Sturluson is explicit on this point in the *Gylfaginning* section of his *Edda*, and the compiler of the main manuscript of the *Poetic Edda* must have had the same idea, for he ordered the poems about the gods and put Odin's poems first. We also see him as a leader in the opening chapter of *Ynglinga saga*, the first chapter in Snorri Sturluson's *Heimskringla*, which presents Odin as a king who leads his people from Tyrkland to Scandinavia, where he founds a dynasty.

Odin's most important characteristic is his wisdom. One of the most intriguing myths of Odin tells of his acquisition of wisdom through self-sacrifice, recounted in stanzas 138–145 of *Hávamál*, the so-called *Rúnatal*, which leads to the *Ljódatal*. Stanza 138 is justly famous:

> I know that I hung
> on the wind-swept tree
> nine entire nights,
> wounded with a spear,
> given to Odin,
> myself to myself,
> on that tree,
> of which no man knows
> of what roots it runs.

The "wind-swept tree" must be Yggdrasil, the world tree, and information about its roots belongs to the kind of cosmological knowledge that is Odin's specialty. Nine is of course the most charged number in the mythology, and the spear is Odin's special weapon. The next stanza apparently states that Odin was deprived of food and drink; screaming, "I took up [or learned] the runes." In stanza 140 Odin says he learned nine powerful songs or chants from the famous son of Bölthor, the father of Bestla, and got a drink of the precious mead, poured from Ódrerir.

As mentioned above, Bestla was Odin's mother, and Bölthor her father (elsewhere the form of the name is Bölthorn), so the one who taught him the nine powerful songs is his maternal uncle, who, like his maternal grandfather and mother, is a member of the race of the giants. It is worth recalling that Odin also acquired knowledge from Vafthrúdnir, the wisest of giants, from the seeress who speaks in *Völuspá*, and from Hel (in *Baldrs draumar*). Ódrerir is either the mead of poetry itself or, in Snorri's reading, the name of one of the pots into which the mead was delivered. Earlier in *Hávamál* there was an account of Odin's acquisition of the mead of poetry from the giant Suttung through the seduction or rape of his daughter, Gunnlöd. One way to reconcile that version, which was repeated by Snorri and appears to have been ubiquitous, with this one is to assume that Odin entered a shamanic trance or even died on the tree and that his spirit traveled to Giantland and acquired the mead while the body was left behind. Such a reading is enhanced by stanza 145 of *Hávamál*, which appears to end this account of the self-sacrifice: "Thus Thund [Odin] carved / for the judgments of peoples, / where he arose / when he came back." Stanza 141 brings the incident to its logical conclusion: "Then I started to become fertile / and to be

Die for stamping the decorative plaques on seventh-century Swedish helmets. (Statens Historika Museum, Stockholm)

Die for stamping the decorative plaques on seventh-century Swedish helmets. (Statens Historika Museum, Stockholm)

Die for stamping the decorative plaques on seventh-century Swedish helmets. (Statens Historika Museum, Stockholm)

wise / and to grow and to thrive; / a word for me from a word / sought a word, / a deed for me / sought a deed." All this, apparently, from his "taking up" the runes.

Within the mythological present Odin uses his wisdom to order himself atop the hierarchy of all creatures. In the eddic poem *Hárbardsljód* he outwits Thor and even makes it impossible for that god to cross a body of water, which is part of Thor's everyday functioning. In *Vafthrúdnismál* he defeats the wisest of giants in a contest of wisdom. In *Grímnismál* he carries out an ecstatic wisdom performance while hung in the fire of the human king Geirröd, who falls on his sword at the end of the poem and is therefore succeeded by his son Agnar; thus Odin determines the succession of kings among human beings.

Odin continues to seek out wisdom in the mythological present. *Vafthrúdnismál* might be regarded as an Odinic thrust in that direction, for the giant Vafthrúdnir answers all but one of Odin's cosmogonic and mythological poems. But more to the point are *Völuspá*, in which Odin causes a seeress to arise and recount the mythological past, present, and future, and *Baldrs draumar*, in which Odin travels to the world of the dead to investigate Baldr's bad dreams.

Odin lives at Valhöll (Carrion-hall), where the einherjar sport each day and night. He is therefore a god of the dead, and in fact in *Ynglinga saga* Snorri Sturluson says that Odin could awaken the dead to learn secret things from them.

Etymologically, Odin's name meant something like "leader of the possessed." In Viking and medieval Scandinavia, few could have missed the connection with the word *óðr*, which could mean "poetry" and "frenzy." Odin has a great many alternate names—more than 150, all counted. He takes a different name in virtually each of his myths and often travels in disguise, but it is also worth remembering that he is the god of poetry, and that the most important feature of this poetry's style is that it has a vast number of nouns and within semantic categories these nouns are interchangeable.

Part of a tapestry from Skog, Sweden, with three figures who have often been identified as Odin, Thor, and Frey, although recent research has cast doubt on this identification. (Werner Forman/Art Resource)

Odin presides over the banishing of the Midgard serpent and Hel to the outer ocean and the underworld, respectively, as well as the binding of Fenrir. At Ragnarök Fenrir will run free and will destroy Odin, only to have vengeance taken on him by Vídar. The cosmos will reemerge from the fires and chaos of Ragnarök, but Odin will not be there.

> ***See also*** Audhumla; Baldr; *Baldrs draumar*; Bestla; Fenrir; *Grímnismál*; *Hárbardsljód*; Hel; Midgard Serpent; *Vafthrúdnismál*

References and further reading: As the preeminent figure in Norse mythology, Odin figures in nearly every work about it. To understand Odin is to understand the mythology, and vice versa. As throughout this book, I recommend Margaret Clunies Ross's *Prolonged Echoes: Old Norse Myths in Medieval Icelandic Society,* vol. 1: *The Myths* (Odense: Odense University Press, 1994), as the best first step in that direction. There have of course been countless studies that focus on Odin, but many of them have debated whether he is a latecomer to the Germanic pantheon. I do not think he is, but in any case, the date of his arrival does not help in understanding the mythology itself.

ÓDRERIR

Either a pot in which the mead of poetry was preserved or the mead itself. *Hávamál* has two ambiguous references. The first is stanza 107:

> The well-acquired appearance have I used well,
> Little is lacking to the wise;
> Because Ódrerir has now come up
> To the men of the holy place of earth.

The second is stanza 140:

> Nine magic songs I got from the famous son
> Of Bölthor, Bestla's father,
> And I got a drink of the precious mead,
> Poured from [by? to? of? for?] Ódrerir.

In the *Skáldskaparmál* section of his *Edda,* Snorri Sturluson is quite explicit. Ódrerir is the kettle in which the dwarfs Fjalar and Galar fermented the blood of Kvasir into the mead of poetry. There were two other barrels, Bodn and Són. Today most scholars would accept that it was Snorri who explicitly made Ódrerir into a kettle instead of the mead itself.

See also Mead of Poetry

References and further reading: Snorri's role in the reinterpretation of his sources is explored by Roberta Frank, "Snorri and the Mead of Poetry," *Speculum Norroenum: Norse Studies in Memory of Gabriel Turville-Petre,* ed. Ursula Dronke, Guðrún P. Helgadóttir, Gerd Wolfgang Weber, and Hans-Bekker Nielsen ([Odense:] Odense University Press, 1981), 155–170.

ÖGMUNDAR THÁTTR DYTTS OK GUNNARS HELMINGS (THE TALE OF ÖGMUND DINT AND GUNNAR HALF)

Tale containing putative information about the cult of Frey in Uppsala.

The tale is found in manuscripts of the *Saga of Olaf Tryggvason,* none of them earlier than the fourteenth century. When the tale was composed is unknown, but few think the tale can antedate the fourteenth century.

The tale falls into two parts, one about each of the characters named in the title (itself an invention of modern editors). The link between the tales is a cloak, which Ögmund borrows from Gunnar and wears when he carries out a vengeance killing at the court of King Olaf. Mistaken for the killer, Gunnar flees the court for Sweden. There he meets the woman who has been chosen by the pagans to serve as the wife of Frey, actually a statue with a demon in it. In a humorous series of dialogues, she allows Gunnar to stay with her longer and longer, each time warning him of Frey's displeasure, which Gunnar says he will gladly endure if he has her good wishes. Then the time arrives for the pagan ceremonies, and Gunnar must pull Frey's wagon. When he tires of that, he wrestles with Frey. Things are going badly until he calls on Olaf Tryggvason, at which point the demon abandons the statue and runs off.

Gunnar now decides to impersonate Frey. The Swedes are impressed that their god can eat and drink, and they are especially happy that his wife is pregnant, although they do wonder somewhat at his now wishing to be propitiated with gold and silver, fine clothing, or other precious things. Times are good, and the fame of Frey spreads to Norway. Olaf suspects what is going on and has Gunnar returned to Norway. Gunnar and his wife are baptized and keep the faith ever after.

Although the tale certainly is amusing, and despite its obvious medieval Icelandic Christian perspective, it does accord with certain features known elsewhere of the worship of Frey and similar figures such as Fródi and Njörd, namely, the pulling about in a wagon and the ascribing of good times to the deity. But rather than being of direct source value, the presence of these features may simply tell us what learned men surmised about Frey in medieval Iceland.

> ***See also*** Frey; Fródi, Njörd
>
> ***References and further reading:*** Alexander Haggerty Krappe, "La légende de Gunnar Half (Olafs saga Tryggvasonar, Chap. 173)," *Acta Philologica Scandinavica* 3 (1928–1929): 226–233, thought the tale reflected actual ritual practice, in which a man played the deity, but in "Der Göttertrug im Gunnarsþáttr helmings," *Zeitschrift für deutsches Altertum* 71 (1934): 155–166, Helga Reuschel argued exactly the opposite, namely, that the text has no independent value for the history of religion.

RAGNARÖK (JUDGMENT-OF-THE-POWERS)

Demise of the gods and of the cosmos at the end of the mythological present.

Although most Viking Age poets and modern scholars use the form above, Snorri Sturluson was among those who used the form "Ragnarøkkr" (Twilight-of-the-gods), which became famous as the title of the last opera, *Götterdämmerung* (Twilight of the Gods), in Richard Wagner's Ring Cycle. It will do equally well as a designation of the end of the gods' day on earth.

The most powerful presentation of Ragnarök is that of the *Völuspá* poet. Depending on where one believes it begins, this section of the poem takes up as much as the last 30 of the 66 stanzas of the poem in the standard editions. In my view it has certainly begun by stanza 39:

> She saw wading there through heavy currents
> Men who forswore oaths and murderers,
> And the one who seduces another's beloved;
> There Nídhögg sucked
> the corpses of the departed,
> The wolf tore men apart—would you know more?

Stanzas 40 and 41 refer to the loss of the sun and the moon. In stanzas 42–43 mysterious cocks crow the onset of the end, and in 44, which reappears verbatim as 49 and 58, Garm howls and the wolf runs free. In 45 the bonds of kinship break down:

> Brothers will fight and kill each other,
> Cousins will destroy kinship.
> It is hard in the world, much whoredom,
> An ax age, a sword age, shields are split,
> A wind age, a wolf age, before the world falls;
> No man will spare another.

Heimdall sounds the Gjallarhorn, and the world tree Yggdrasil shudders. Giants leave from the east to attack the land of the gods, and the Midgard serpent thrashes in the deep sea. Loki is seen steering a ship from Giantland in the attack.

> 52. Surt travels from the south with the enemy of twigs [fire],
> The sun shines from the swords of the carrion-gods,
> Mountains resound, and ogresses roam,
> Humans tread the road to Hel, and the sky is riven.
> 53. Then the second sorrow of Hlín [Frigg] occurs,

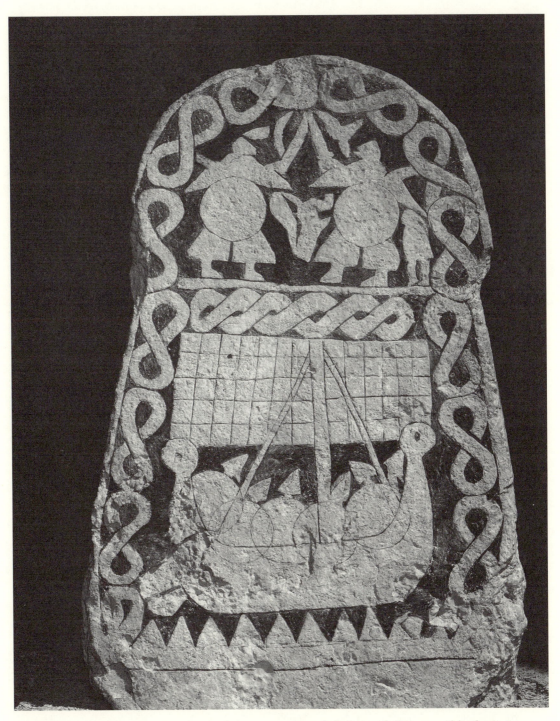

Picture stone from Smiss, Gotland, showing warriors fighting and ship, possibly depicting fallen warriors' voyage to the afterlife. (The Art Archive/Historiska Museet Stockholm/Dagli Orti)

Stone carving from Lindisfarne, England (ninth century C.E.). The procession of warriors is reminiscent of forces gathering for the final battle of Ragnarök. (Axel Poignant Archive)

> When Odin goes to fight with the wolf,
> And the killer of Beli [Frey] the bright one, against Surt;
> Then Frigg's joy will perish.

Vídar avenges Odin, but still Thor, the mightiest of the gods, has not taken the field. This he does in stanza 56:

> Then comes the great son of Hlódyn [Earth],
> Odin's son goes to fight with the wolf;
> Strongly strikes the guardian of Midgard,
> All men will redden the earth;
> Nine paces goes the son of Fjörgyn [Earth]
> Exhausted from the snake, unconquered by enmity.

The demise of the gods is followed by the demise of the cosmos they had created. The sun turns black, the earth sinks into the sea, smoke and flames lick the sky itself.

But Ragnarök has two parts, and the second involves rebirth. The earth arises from the sea, and a new generation of gods inhabits it. They have reminiscences of their forebears and some mysterious gaming pieces that link them to what went before. Höd and Baldr are there, reconciled, and Hœnir too has survived the conflagration, for he "chooses lot-sticks," that is, he performs some sort of ritual activity. According to the *Hauksbók* redaction of the poem, "the powerful one" then comes, and this looks like a reference to the Christian deity.

Snorri paraphrases these verses and adds a few details, of which the most salient is the presence of Odin's sons Vídar and Váli and Thor's sons Magni and Módi, who will possess Thor's hammer Mjöllnir, in the new world that follows Ragnarök. Snorri also, following *Vafthrúdnismál*, says that humans will survive into the new world, through Líf and Lífthrasir.

Besides *Völuspá* and Snorri, Ragnarök figures in numerous other sources.

> ***See also*** Game of the Gods; Líf and
> Lífthrasir; Nídhögg; *Völuspá*
> ***References and further reading:*** The
> study of Ragnarök cited most often
> is that of Axel Olrik, *Ragnarök:*
> *Die Sagen vom Weltuntergang,*
> trans. Wilhelm Ranisch (Berlin and
> Leipzig: W. de Gruyter, 1922), a
> German translation of two earlier
> long works in Danish on the sub-
> ject. It is extremely erudite and fas-
> cinates on every page, but its

*This tenth-century cross at Gosforth in Cum-
bria is the largest surviving piece of sculpture
in England from before the Norman conquest.
It is interlaced with scenes from the crucifix-
ion of Christ as well as scenes from Ragnarök.
(Axel Poignant Archive)*

conclusion, that much of the material entered Scandinavia from the Middle East, no longer seems helpful in understanding the mythology as we have it. A study in English, arguing an ultimate association with ritual, is that of John Stanley Martin, *Ragnarǫk: An Investigation into Old Norse Concepts of the Fate of the Gods*, Melbourne Monographs in Germanic Studies, 3 (Assen: Van Gorcum, 1972).

RÁN

Goddess of the sea.

Rán is not in eddic verses, but in skaldic poetry she is encountered fairly frequently, in kennings having to do with the sea (e.g., "Rán's way" for waves) and in woman kennings where her name is the base word (e.g., "Rán of the down covering"). The thulur list Rán among the *ásynjur*, but she is never seen among them or the gods in general in the materials that were left us. Snorri reports in *Skáldskaparmál* that Rán is the wife of Ægir and that they have nine daughters, whose names have to do with the waves. More interestingly, he also says that she has a net with which she hunts men who go to sea. The prose header to the eddic poem *Reginsmál* and *Völsunga saga* say that Loki went to Rán and borrowed her net in order to capture the dwarf Andvari, who had changed himself into a pike and was sporting in the river.

But the net was surely primarily used to drag the drowning to their deaths. This conception, or something like it, appears to be realized in a line from one of the most famous skaldic poems, Egil Skallagrímsson's *Sonatorrek* (Loss of Sons). According to *Egils saga* (which many critics believe was written by Snorri himself), Egil composed this poem after his son Bödvar was drowned in the nearby fjord. The saga says that Egil's other son had previously died, and that after the loss of Bödvar, Egil wished to die, but that his daughter Thorgerd tricked him into taking some nourishment and then coerced him into composing a memorial poem for Bödvar. In the seventh of the 25 extant stanzas, Egil says something like this:

> Much has Rán harried about me,
> I am wholly bereft of beloved friends;
> The sea tore the bonds of my family,
> A powerful thread right out of me.

As the poem ends, Egil complains of Odin's treatment of him but admits that the gift of poetry is a consolation.

If the text of *Sonatorrek* as we have it is genuine, it would date from around 960 (*Egils saga* is from the first half of the thirteenth century, but the full text of

Sonatorrek is only retained in seventeenth-century copies of a fifteenth-century manuscript). Verses from *Fridthjófs saga*, which is post-classical, play on the idea of drowning as visiting Rán and refer to her as an ill-bred or immoral woman.

> *References and further reading:* Carlo Alberto Mastrelli, "Sul nome della gigantessa Rán, *Studi germanici*, new ser. 4, 3 (1966): 253–264, discusses the etymology of the name, which is quite obscure. Certainly an etymology connecting the name with the noun *rán*, "theft," would agree with some of the sentiments adduced above. Franz Rolf Schröder, "Die Göttin des Urmeeres und ihr männlicher Partner," *Beiträge zur Geschichte der deutschen Sprache und Literatur* (Tübingen) 82 (1960): 221–264, is centered on Nerthus and Njörd but also includes discussion of Rán and Ægir.

RATATOSK (BORE-TOOTH)

Squirrel who lives on Yggdrasil, the world tree.

Grímnismál, stanza 32, says this:

> Ratatosk is the name of a squirrel who shall run
> on the ash of Yggdrasil;
> words of an eagle he shall carry down
> and say to Nídhögg below.

According to Snorri in *Gylfaginning*, the words the squirrel transports are hostile ones, and he carries them in both directions, between the eagle atop the tree and the dragon Nídhögg below. Thus, the world tree is not only threatened by the harts and the dragon that chew on it and by its rotting side; it also bears, in the fauna it supports, verbal hostility. In the sagas, a person who helps stir up or keep feuds alive by ferrying words of malice between the participants is seldom one of high status, which may explain the assignment of this role in the mythology to a relatively insignificant animal.

> *See also* Yggdrasil

REGNATOR OMNIUM DEUS

God who is ruler of all; found in Tacitus, *Germania,* chapter 39.

The expression refers to the god in the sacred grove in which the Semnones conduct their cult, involving, according to Tacitus, a human sacrifice. The grove is so sacred that worshippers bind themselves with a chain when they enter, and if they fall, they must wiggle out without help. The whole superstition, as Tacitus puts it, rests on the idea that "the tribe originated here and the god who is ruler of all is here."

The association with binding suggests such collective words for the gods as *bönd* and *höpt,* but the regnator omnium deus is clearly a single god, a head god of the Germanic pantheon around 100 C.E. (as the pantheon was understood by a Roman historian). The Interpretatio Germanica associated Thor with Jupiter, but the aspect of binding would appear to suggest the "war-fetters" that Odin can put on enemy troops, and more generally the binding that is characteristic of so-called first-function Indo-European gods (gods of sovereignty in the scheme devised by Georges Dumézil).

> **See also** Gods, Words for; Interpretatio Germanica; Interpretatio Romana
> **Reference and further reading:** Gustav Neckel, "Regnator omnium deus," *Neue Jahrbücher für Wissenschaft und Jugendbildung* 2 (1926): 139–150.

RÍGSTHULA

Eddic poem describing the origin of the social classes.

The poem is found only in *Codex Wormianus* (AM 242 folio) of Snorri Sturluson's *Edda,* a manuscript from the first half of the fourteenth century. A prose header states that Heimdall went traveling, and when he came to a coastal settlement he called himself Ríg. The poem itself refers only to Ríg.

Ríg visits three households. In the first and third he is fed, and one assumes that his feeding in the second household has been lost. After dining in each household, he goes off to bed, and there he spends three nights between the man and woman of the household. Nine months later the woman gives birth to a son, who in turn finds a mate and has offspring.

The first household is that of Ái and Edda, which mean something like "Great-Grandfather" and "Great-Grandmother." They eat coarse bread and a broth made from boiled calf. Edda's son is Thrall, who has thick fingers, an ugly face, and a crooked back, and he busies himself with heavy lifting. To his farm comes Thír (Bondswoman), and they have children who manure the fields, look after pigs and goats, and dig turf. From them come slaves.

Ríg comes next to the household of Afi and Amma (Grandfather and Grandmother). There is a chest on the floor. Slaves could not own property, so a chest leads one to think of a manumission ritual, in which a freed slave symbolically climbs onto a chest. The woman is neatly dressed, and it would have been nice to learn what food was served. In any case, after nine months Amma bears a son Karl (Man). He tames oxen to plow with, builds barns, and in short does what a farmer would do. He marries Snør (Daughter-in-law), and they have sons, many of whose names indicate social status; these are difficult to translate, but some, for example, were used of individuals in the medieval king's court. The daughters have similar names. We do not learn what these offspring do, but from them descend the (landowning) farmers.

The third household is that of Fadir and Módir (Father and Mother). Mother is sewing and wearing fashionable garments, and the food served is fine bread and meats, washed down with wine. Módir bears the son Jarl. The noun is cognate with English "earl." "Jarl" was the title of the ruler of the Trondheim area (the Hladir jarls) and in the High Middle Ages came to mean something like "duke." He is trained in warfare, and Ríg takes a special interest in him. Emissaries are sent to the hall of Hersir (Chieftain) to ask for the hand in marriage of Erna (Vigorous?). They marry and have sons, whose names are nouns like "son," "child," "heir," "kinsman," and "related-one." The youngest is Kon, whom Ríg trains, especially in runes. Kon learns the speech of birds and is encouraged by an aviary adviser to wage war, against Dan and Danp, two kings who turn up elsewhere in legendary prehistory. Here the poem breaks off, perhaps prematurely.

Kon the young is twice called "Konr ungr," which many observers believe the poet meant to suggest the noun *konungr*, "king." Given the poet's lack of inhibition elsewhere in his naming strategies, one might think that if he had wished to call this individual King he might have done so directly, especially since "Konr ungr" is grammatically awkward in medieval Icelandic. Still, it does not seem implausible that the poet would have wished to proceed from the class of warriors or nobility to the monarch.

Discussion of the poem is frustrating. One wing has sought Celtic influences, since the name of the progenitor in the poem looks a bit like Old Irish *ri/rig*, "king." Dumézil saw a shifted reflection of his tripartite Indo-European structure, with the functions being displaced downward (see chapter 1). Others have thought that the poem must be of medieval origin, for a society that actually engaged in slaveholding, it is argued, would hardly derive slaves and the rest of the population from a single progenitor, and more important, the division into three groups is typical of medieval social thinking, even if the three groups would ordinarily be laborers, warriors, and priests. Thomas Hill argued for an ultimate connection with the Old Testament story of the sons of Noah.

Although *Rígsthula* offers a social-foundation myth, it had little effect on the mythology as it is understood for the purposes of this book. Snorri never recounts any aspect of it, and there are no kennings based on it or references to it elsewhere, with the possible exception of the reference to all the holy families as the kin of Heimdall in *Völuspá*, stanza 1. Even that accords poorly with the poem, for no holy families descend from Ríg (who is in fact only called Heimdall in the prose header to the poem).

See also Heimdall

References and further reading: The Celtic hypothesis is explored in Jean Young, "Does Rígsþula Betray Irish Influence?" *Arkiv för nordisk filologi* 49 (1933): 97–107, and Nora K. Chadwick, "Pictish and Celtic Marriage in Early Literary

Tradition," *Scottish Gaelic Studies* 8 (1958): 56–115. An English translation of George Dumézil's 1958 French original is "The Rígsthula and Indo-European Social Structure," trans. John Lindow, in Dumézil, *Gods of the Ancient Northmen*, ed. Einar Haugen, Publications of the UCLA Center for the Study of Comparative Folklore and Mythology, 3 (Berkeley and Los Angeles: University of California Press, 1973), 118–125. Analyses associating *Rígsthula* with the later Middle Ages are Klaus von See, "Der Alter der Rígsþula," *Acta Philologica Scandinavica* 24 (1957–1961): 1–12, reprinted in von See, *Edda, Saga, Skaldendichtung: Aufsätze zur skandinavischen Literatur des Mittelalters* (Heidelberg: C. Winter, 1981), 84–95, with an addendum on pages 514–516; and Thomas D. Hill, "Rígsþula: Some Medieval Christian Analogues," *Speculum* 61 (1986): 79–89.

RIND

Mother of Váli, the avenger of Baldr, and therefore sexual partner of Odin.

Rind is listed among the thulur for *ásynjur*, but with no indication of a relationship with Odin or Váli. However, in *Gylfaginning* Snorri says that Rind, "the mother of Váli," is enumerated among the *ásynjur*. *Baldrs draumar*, stanza 11, states that Rind bore Váli and that "that son of Odin" will fight when one night old, and in his catalog of the æsir in *Gylfaginning* Snorri says that Váli is the son of Odin and Rind. The relationship between Odin and Rind was apparently not a normal one: In his *Sigurdurdrápa*, composed around 960 if the stanza is genuine, the Icelandic skald Kormák Ögmundarson says that Odin used magic (seid) on Rind, presumably to beget Váli. Saxo too has the story of Odin begetting an avenger for Baldr, and it too is unsavory. Having learned from a seer that the Rutenian princess Rinda is to bear the avenger of Balderus, Othinus sets out to seduce her. Acting as a soldier, he takes up residence with her father, wins victories, and presses his suit, but she rejects him. A second visit, this time acting as a smith, also fails. On the third visit, Othinus acts as a knight, but when he finally makes some progress toward his goal it is by touching the girl with a rune-carved stick, which drives her mad; here is the potential parallel with Kormák's stanza. Othinus now assumes the guise of a woman to gain entry to the girl's chamber, but he only succeeds in his goal when Rinda falls sick. Dr. Othinus prescribes a potion so foul that the patient must be bound when she takes it. She is duly bound, and Othinus rapes her. The result of the rape is Bous.

The use of seid, especially by men, was considered shameful, and Othinus's rape of Rinda, not least because it involved cross-dressing, was hardly the deed of a man of honor. Saxo reports that the gods were so disgusted by Othinus's cross-dressing that they banished him and replaced him with Ollerus (who would be Ull in medieval Icelandic), who took Othinus's title and name. After ten years, Bous killed Høtherus, and Othinus returned to Byzantium, where Saxo located the euhemerized gods, and ousted Ollerus.

> *See also* Baldr; Bous; Seid; Ull; Váli, Son of Odin

RÖSKVA (RIPE?)

Servant of Thor, sister of Thjálfi.

Snorri tells in *Gylfaginning*, at the beginning of the myth of Thor's visit to Útgarda-Loki, how Röskva and Thjálfi were given to Thor as a settlement after Thjálfi had damaged the bones of one of Thor's goats while eating it, so that the goat could not be properly revived by the god. Röskva plays no role in the mythology, but the gender of the pronouns Snorri used in the continuation of the journey to Útgarda-Loki shows that Röskva was along. In *Skáldskaparmál* Snorri says that "lord of Thjálfi and of Röskva" is a Thor kenning. Besides Snorri, there is tenth-century evidence of the existence of Röskva, since the poet Eilíf Godrúnarson referred to Thjálfi as "brother of Röskva."

> *See also* Egil; Thjálfi; Thor; Útgarda-Loki
> *References and further reading:* My analysis of the encounter with Röskva's family
> is found in "Thor's Visit to Útgarda-Loki," *Oral Tradition* 15 (2000): 170–186.

SÆHRÍMNIR

Pig cooked at Valhöll, the unending food source of the einherjar.
The key passage is stanza 18 of *Grímnismál*.

> Andhrímnir in Eldhrímnir
> Has Sæhrímnir boiled
> Best of pork, yet few knew,
> On what the einherjar are nourished.

In *Gylfaginning* Snorri explains the passage as follows: Gylfi/Gangleri wonders how the einherjar are fed, given that there are so many of them. Hár responds:

> What you say is true, a great many of them are there, but many more shall there yet be, and yet it will seem too few, when the wolf comes calling. But never will there be so great a crowd of men in Valhöll, that the flesh of that pig, who is named Sæhrímnir, will run out on them. He is boiled each day and is whole again by evening.

The names of the cook, the pot, and the eternal pork are joined by the element *hrímnir,* which is derived from the word for soot on a cookpot. The element

And- could refer to (or could have been understood by Snorri as referring to) the front of the cook, who would be facing the cookpot as he worked his culinary magic, and "Fire-sooty" would make sense for the pot, but the pig's name is far from clear. It certainly looks as if it means "sea-sooty," which some modern observers read as "sooty sea beast." The name would, I suppose, do in a pinch for the famous New Orleans preparation blackened redfish, but it does seem somewhat out of place for the best of pork. Those troubled by this fish-beast problem have proposed understanding the first syllable as somehow having to do with boiling, but that makes philological fish into fowl.

See also Eldhrímnir; Sæhrímnir

SÆMING

Son of Odin or Frey and ancestor of the Hladir jarls.

Sæming is mentioned in the prologue to Snorri Sturluson's *Edda,* the prologue to his *Heimskringla,* and in *Ynglinga saga,* the first saga in *Heimskringla.* In all three texts, Snorri is operating on the principle of euhemerism; that is, on the belief that there was a historical Odin who led the æsir from Asia to Scandinavia. In each case he appears to be building on *Háleygjatal,* a poem from the end of the tenth century by the skald Eyvind Finnsson skáldaspillir.

In the prologue to his *Edda* Snorri says that after Odin settled in Sweden he went north to the coast, where he established his son Sæming as the ruler of Norway, "and the kings of Norway, the jarls and other powerful people, traced their lineage to him, as it says in *Háleygjatal.*" In the prologue to *Heimskringla,* however, Snorri says that according to *Háleygjatal,* Sæming was the son of Yngvi-Frey. And in *Ynglinga saga,* he quotes a stanza of *Háleygjatal* (stanza 3 in the editions) saying it is about Sæmund, although he is not mentioned in it by name. The verse is not clear, but it seems to suggest that Odin sired someone on Skadi (which is unknown elsewhere). Snorri explains it as follows:

> Njörd got that wife, who was called Skadi. She did not wish to have intercourse with him and was married afterward to Odin. They had many sons. One of them was called Sæming.

SÁGA

Minor goddess.

Snorri lists her second in his catalog in *Gylfaginning* of goddesses among the æsir, after Frigg, and says only that she lives at the great farm Søkkvabekk

(Sunken-bank?). In *Grímnismál*, stanza 7, Odin includes Søkkvabekk as the fourth of the residences he surveys and says that cool waves resound over it; "there Odin and Sága / drink through all the days, / happy, out of a golden cup." The similarity of Søkkvabekk to Fensalir, Frigg's dwelling; Odin's open drinking with Sága; and the usual etymology of the name, which relates it to the verb *sjá*, "to see" and understands her as a seeress, have led most scholars to understand Sága as another name for Frigg.

SEID

A form of magic and divination, associated in the mythology especially with Odin. Snorri Sturluson offered a description of seid as carried by a euhemerized Odin during Scandinavian prehistory:

> Odin knew that art called seid, which the greatest power accompanied, and he carried it out himself. Through it he could determine the fates of men and things yet to happen, and also to arrange death or bad luck or ill health for people, and further to take the mind or strength of people and give it to others. And this magic art, when it is carried out, is accompanied by so much *ergi* [sexual perversion] that it did not seem shameless for men to indulge in it, and so this art was taught to priestesses.

The connection with females is widespread. Freyja is said to be the one who brought seid to the æsir (*Ynglinga saga*, chapter 4), and in *Völuspá*, Gullveig/Heid (who may also be Freyja) practices it.

The sagas have many accounts of seid set in pre-Christian Iceland, again mostly practiced by women. The most famous of these is in *Eiríks saga rauda* (The Saga of Erik the Red), which is set in Greenland just before the conversion to Christianity. Famine has overrun a certain region, and a seid-woman is asked to prophesy its duration. She ascends a platform, songs are sung, and she makes contact, she says, with spirits. She predicts a quick end to the famine and a prosperous future for the woman, herself a Christian, who helped with the magic songs. Besides this divination, other examples of seid in the sagas are like that described for Odin, in that seid can be used to do bad things for people.

As the master of wisdom and of verse, Odin would naturally be the mythological figure closest to this kind of magic, and in fact one skald says that Odin used seid on Rind, whom he seduced or raped to beget an avenger for Baldr. Freyja, on the other hand, never uses it.

In the scholarly discussion of seid, most of which has to do not with the mythology but with an attempt to unravel the historical background, some scholars point to shamanic practices, especially in northern Eurasia.

See also Gullveig; Heid; Rind

References and further reading: The most recent general discussion of seid may be found in Thomas A. DuBois, *Viking Ages Religions* (Philadelphia: University of Pennsylvania Press, 1999). For those who can read Swedish, Dag Strömbäck, *Sejd: Textstudier i nordisk religionshistoria*, Nordiska texter och under-sökningar, 5 (Stockholm: H. Geber; Copenhagen: Levin & Munksgaard, 1935), offers a thorough and well-balanced study.

SIF (IN-LAW-RELATIONSHIP)

Thor's wife, mother of Magni and Módi.

Although Sif plays only a small role in the mythology, the use of the kenning "husband of Sif" for Thor is found in both skaldic and eddic poetry.

Sif's major myth has to do with her golden headpiece, which was made for her by dwarfs after Loki cut off her hair. Five other precious objects, all of them of extreme mythological importance (e.g., Thor's hammer), were also made at the same time. It is easy to lose sight of the fact that the gods got all these objects because Thor forced Loki to replace Sif's hair.

Twice Sif appears in connection with accusations of cuckoldry made to Thor. In *Hárbardsljód*, stanza 48, Odin accuses Sif of having a lover at home, but he does not elaborate. In *Lokasenna*, stanza 54, Loki does elaborate. When Sif tells Loki that she is blameless, Loki responds:

> You would be alone if that were so,
> Wary and fierce toward a man;
> I know one, I'm pretty sure,
> Who cuckolded Thor,
> And that was the sly Loki.

But Loki makes this accusation about all the goddesses. Sif's faithfulness to Thor is difficult to judge. Nor does the meaning of her name shed any light on that topic.

See also Dwarfs; Loki

References and further reading: Margaret Clunies Ross, "Þórr's Honour," in *Studien zum Altgermanischen: Festschrift für Heinrich Beck*, ed. Heido Uecker (Berlin and New York: W. de Gruyter, 1994), 43–76, puts the making of Sif's gold headpiece into the context of Thor's responsibility to look after his female relations.

SIGYN

Wife of Loki, mother of Nari or Narfi.

We know nothing of Sigyn's background, but she is mentioned as early as the pre-Christian skald Thjódólf of Hvin, who in his *Haustlöng* called Loki the "cargo of the arms of Sigyn." In the mythology Sigyn's only role is to hold a basin over Loki's head to catch the venom dripping from a snake under which he is bound, punished either for his role in the death of Baldr *(Gylfaginning)* or his insulting of all the gods (prose colophon to *Lokasenna*). *Völuspá*, stanza 35 appears to refer to this scene. The seeress is speaking:

> She saw a prisoner lie in a grove of valleys
> A malevolent figure identical to Loki;
> There sits Sigyn, thought not at all
> Glad about her husband—would you know more?

See also Loki; Nari and/or Narfi

SINDRI (SLAG)

A person connected with a golden hall, or the hall itself.

Völuspá, stanza 37, says that Sindri's family owns a splendid hall:

> There stood to the north, on the Nidavellir,
> A hall of gold, of the family of Sindri.

Who the family of Sindri might be is a puzzle. The second half of the stanza refers to a second hall, Brimir, that is, a beer hall of a giant, but it is unclear whether a break or continuation is meant. The connection of the name with forging and the gold of Sindri's hall might suggest the dwarfs. Indeed, Nidavellir might be the fields of the dwarf Nidi. If they are not Nidi's fields, they are probably dark fields, and this concept too would accord with the notion of Sindri as a dwarf. And someone through whose hands the main manuscript of Snorri's *Edda* passed evidently did think Sindri was a dwarf, for he wrote "Brokk and Sindri" in the margin near where the story of Brokk's smithing of the precious objects of the gods is told. This occurred after the Middle Ages, however.

Snorri, on the other hand, wrote in *Gylfaginning* that Sindri was the name of a hall that will stand upon the mountains called Nidafjöll. It will be a good hall, made of gold, in which good and righteous people shall dwell when Ragnarök arrives.

See also Brokk; Nidavellir

SJÖFN

Minor goddess.

Snorri lists Sjöfn seventh in his catalog in *Gylfaginning* of goddesses among the æsir and says this about her: "She does much to turn the minds of people to love, men and women. From her name love is called *sjafni*." The noun *sjafni* is indeed included in the thulur as a love word, but the goddess herself is otherwise unknown. The name is used as the base word in three woman kennings. As with many of the other minor goddesses, some scholars believe that she may just be Frigg under another name.

SKADI

Wife of Njörd, daughter of Thjazi, and a giant by birth but still regarded as a member of the æsir.

Skadi is mentioned as the daughter of the giant Thjazi in several sources, including *Grímnismál*, stanza 11, and *Hyndluljód*, stanza 31 (part of the "Short Völuspá"). In each of these stanzas Thjazi is specifically identified as a giant. *Grímnismál* says Skadi inhabits Thrymheim, the old homestead of her father.

The circumstances of Skadi's marriage to Njörd, one of the foremost of the vanir, are told only by Snorri. In *Skáldskaparmál* he tells how the marriage came about in the first place. Following Thjazi's abduction of Idun, Thjazi is killed by the æsir during her retrieval. Apparently he has no male relative to seek compensation, for Skadi acts in this role.

> And Skadi, the daughter of Thjazi the giant, took helmet and byrnie and all weapons of war and went to Ásgard to avenge her father, but the æsir offered her a settlement and compensation, and the first [part] was that she should choose a husband for herself and choose by the lower legs and not see any more than that. Then she saw some exceedingly attractive lower legs of a man and said, "I choose this one; there can be little ugly about Baldr." But it was Njörd of Nóatún. She also had in her settlement what she thought the æsir would not be able to accomplish, and that was to make her laugh. Then Loki tied a rope around the beard of a she-goat and the other end around his testicles, and they both pulled on it and each screamed loudly, and then Loki fell into Skadi's lap; and then she laughed. And so the conditions of the settlement with her were met by the æsir.

Frey too is married to a giantess, Gerd, and although the other gods sire children by giantesses, these are the only two marriages of gods to giantesses. It would therefore appear, as Margaret Clunies Ross has shown, that because of their lower hierarchical status, the vanir cannot choose wives from among the æsir and must take them from the giants. But the situation is even stranger with Njörd, since he is not the chooser but the chosen. It would appear that the gods tricked Skadi somehow, but our understanding of the lower-leg beauty contest is imperfect. Baldr is a young and handsome god; Njörd is by this point in the mythological present an old man. (A note on "lower-leg": The word used refers both to the foot and to the foot, ankle, and calf running up to the knee; since the word in question, *fótr*, is cognate with our word "foot," that is the translation one often sees.)

Loki's sport with the goat clearly plays on themes of castration, and making a goddess laugh may have associations with ritual. However, Loki and Skadi have a special relationship in any case. Snorri in *Gylfaginning* and the prose coda to *Lokasenna* agree that when Loki was bound, it was Skadi who hung over his face the poisonous snake whose venom Sigyn catches in a pot. When Sigyn is out emptying the pot, the venom drips on him and causes his tectonic writhings. And in *Lokasenna*, stanzas 49–52, Loki and Skadi engage in an angry exchange in which Loki boasts not only that he has seduced her (he says this of all the goddesses) but also that he took the lead when her father was killed.

The marriage between Skadi and Njörd is a failure. In *Gylfaginning* Snorri says that Skadi wishes to live in her father's home in the mountains, while Njörd wishes to be by the sea. They compromise on nine nights in each place, but the arrangement fails. Snorri cites two verses, one spoken by each, on the disadvantages of the other's home, and these presumably are from some otherwise lost eddic poem. He ends this discussion by telling us a bit more about Skadi:

> Then Skadi went up into the mountains and lives in Thrymheim, and she goes about much on skis with a bow and arrow and shoots game. She is called snow-shoe-god or snowshoe-dís.

The concept of Skadi as snowshoe-dís is unknown in the narrative sources, but she bears this cognomen not infrequently in early skaldic poetry. In *Lokasenna*, stanza 51, she refers to her cult places, and there are place-names that verify the worship of Skadi, especially in Sweden. Since Ull is also called snowshoe-god and seems to have been popular in Sweden, some scholars have seen a special connection between the two. But there is a Norwegian connection according to *Ynglinga saga*, which says that after her marriage to Njörd Skadi had multiple sons from Odin, ancestors of the Hladir jarls. Whether she is the mother of Frey and Freyja is unknown. In the prose header to *Skírnismál*, when Frey is ailing, Njörd asks Skadi to talk with him, and according this tradition, then, she speaks the first stanza of the poem, asking Skírnir to intervene. Snorri, too, in the section just following the description of the failed marriage of Njörd and Skadi, says that Njörd sired Frey and Freyja "afterward." But *Ynglinga saga* numbers Frey among the hostages exchanged at the end of the war between the æsir and vanir, and there he implies strongly that Frey and Freyja are the offspring of a marriage between Njörd and his sister.

See also Æsir-Vanir War; Loki; Thjazi, Vanir

References and further reading: The circumstances leading to the marriage of Skadi and Njörd are discussed by Margaret Clunies Ross, "Why Skaði Laughed: Comic Seriousness in an Old Norse Mythic Narrative," *Maal og minne*, 1989: 1–14, and John Lindow, "Loki and Skaði," in *Snorrastefna: 25.–27. júlí 1990*, ed. Úlfar Bragason, Rit Stofnunar Sigurðar Nordals, 1 (Reykjavík: Stofnun Sigurðar Nordals, 1992), 130–142. Hjalmar Lindroth, "En nordisk gudagestalt i ny belysning genom ortnamn," *Antikvarisk tidskrift för Sverige* 20 (1915), and Franz Rolf Schröder, *Untersuchungen zur germanischen und vergleichenden Religionsgeschichte*, vol. 2: *Skadi und die Götter Skandinaviens* (Tübingen: C. B. Mohr, 1941), are the most important treatments of the possible background in cult.

SKÍDBLADNIR

Frey's magic ship (but attributed once to Odin).

Grímnismál mentions Skídbladnir in stanzas 43–44. Stanza 43 is devoted to the ship:

> The sons of Ívaldi went in days of yore
> To create Skídbladnir,
> The best of ships, for bright Frey,
> The useful son of Njörd.

The story referred to is that of the creation of six wondrous objects for the gods by the dwarfs: Sif's golden hair, Skídbladnir, Draupnir; Gullinborsti, Gungnir, and Mjöllnir, told by Snorri in *Skáldskaparmál*. Stanza 44 of *Grímnismál* lists the best of various things, and begins "The ash Yggdrasil, it is the best of trees, / and Skídbladnir of ships." Snorri quoted this stanza in *Gylfaginning*, and it prompted Gangleri to ask in what way Skídbladnir was the best of ships. Hár answered:

> Skídbladnir is the best of ships and made with the greatest skill, but Naglfar is the largest ship; Muspell owns it. Some dwarfs, the sons of Ívaldi, made Skídbladnir and gave the ship to Frey. It is so large that all the æsir may be aboard with weapons and armor, and it has a fair wind, as soon as the sail is hoisted. But when it is not to be sailed on at sea, then it is made of so many pieces and with such great skill that it may be folded up like a handkerchief and kept in one's wallet.

Rock carving found at Tegneby, Sweden, showing ships, men with giant axes and bird heads, and worshippers around a possible sun disk. (Statens Historiska Museum, Stockholm)

Partly based on this explanation (which is repeated in *Skáldskaparmál* in the story of the making of the ship by the dwarfs), scholars sometimes suggest that the name Skídbladnir means something like "put together using thin pieces of wood." Of course, that description fits to some extent any ship with planks.

In chapter 7 of *Ynglinga saga,* Snorri assigns the ship to Odin and associates it with his magic skills:

> He could also, by words alone, extinguish fire and calm the sea and turn the wind in any direction he wished, and he had that ship which was called Skídbladnir, on which he traveled over great seas, and it could be folded up like a cloth.

Snorri seems to have imagined Skídbladnir here as part of Odin's shamanic attributes, for he had just told how Odin could change shape and travel in animal form to distant lands on his or other people's business. And in *Ynglinga saga* Snorri also downplays the connection of Njörd and Frey with the sea, and that may also have contributed to the unique assignment to Odin.

The ship was an important part of life in Viking and medieval Scandinavia, and it clearly had important symbolic as well as practical value. The Bronze Age

"Sun-Chariot" from Trundholm, Denmark. Found in fragments and reconstructed, it may offer a Bronze Age predecessor of Skínfaxi. (Werner Forman/Art Resource)

rock carvings have ships on them, and many of the Gotland picture stones from the eighth century depict ships crowded with armed warriors. Wealthy people were sometimes buried in ships, and Baldr's was only one of many funerals in the older literature in which the corpse was burned on a ship. We might conclude that when Frey has it, Skídbladnir is a symbol of wealth and plenty to be regarded as parallel to the cart associated with the cult of the vanir; when Odin has it, Skídbladnir is a means of traveling to the other world.

> ***See also*** Dwarfs; Frey; Odin
> ***References and further reading:*** A thorough discussion of Skídbladnir is found in Rudolf Simek, "Skíðbladnir," *Northern Studies* 9 (1977).

SKÍNFAXI (SHINING-MANE)

Horse that pulls Dag (Day), according to *Vafthrúdnismál,* stanza 12, and Snorri Sturluson, who paraphrases the stanza in *Gylfaginning.*

Stanza 12 answers a question put by Odin to Vafthrúdnir in stanza 11: "What horse pulls [across the sky] Dag (Day)?"

> Skínfaxi he is named, who pulls the shining
> Dag for people;

Best of horses it seems among the Hreidgoths [i.e., people],
Ever the mane shines from the horse.

See also Dag; Hrímfaxi; *Vafthrúdnismál*

SKÖLL

Wolf; follows the sun in the sky and will swallow it.
Grimnismál, stanza 39, tells of the wolves who threaten the sun:

Sköll is the name of a wolf who accompanies the shining god
As a defense of the forest;
And the other Hati, he is the son of Hródvitnir,
That one shall be before the bright bride of heaven.

These lines are enigmatic. Snorri paraphrased them as follows in *Gylfaginning*:

Gangleri said: "The sun moves fast, and almost as if she were frightened; she would not hasten her journey more, if she feared her death." Then Hár answers: "It is not surprising that she goes quickly. The one who seeks her is right nearby, and she has no other way out than to run away." Then Gangleri said: "Who is it who makes this trouble?" Hár says: "It is two wolves, and the one who chases her is Sköll; she is afraid of him, and he will take her, and the one who runs in front of her is called Hati Hródvitnisson, and he will take the moon."

I rendered the last word of this passage "moon," although it can mean either sun or moon. Clearly Snorri has adapted these wolves to his notion of Ragnarök, when Garm will bay and Fenrir will get loose to slay Odin. Sköll (or Skoll; the form varies) is not known from other sources. Sköll is identical with a poetic noun meaning "loud noise"; Skoll would be associated with a root meaning "deceiver."

See also Hati Hródvitnisson; Máni; Sól

SKRÝMIR (BIG-LOOKING)

The name taken by the giant Útgarda-Loki when he travels with and deceives Thor.
The story is told in *Gylfaginning*, and Snorri is wholly consistent: The giant with whom Thor and his companions travel is Skrýmir, and the one whose hall they visit is Útgarda-Loki. Only at the end of the entire story does Útgarda-Loki reveal that he was Skrýmir.

Loki refers to Skrýmir and Thor's inability to open the food pack sealed by him in *Lokasenna*, stanza 62; in stanza 60 he had referred to Thor cowering in the giant's glove but did not name Skrýmir. Odin refers to the same incident but calls the giant Fjalar, not Skrýmir, in *Hárbardsljód*, stanza 26. Skrýmir is listed as a giant among the thulur, but the name seems also to have been taken by a few humans, according to some early skaldic stanzas.

> ***See also*** Útgarda-Loki
>
> ***References and further reading:*** A standard work cited with relation to Skrýmir is C. W. von Sydow's study of giants in the mythology, "Jättarna i mytologi och folktro," *Folkminnen och folktankar* 6 (1919): 52–96, which uses Skrýmir as a kind of paradigm of the qualities of great size and control of powers of deception von Sydow thought to be typical of giants. See also Friedrich von der Leyen, "Utgarðaloke in Irland," *Beiträge zur Geschichte der deutschen Sprache und Literatur* 33 (1908): 382–391; C. W. von Sydow, "Tors färd till Utgård," *Danske studier*, 1910: 65–105, 145–82; Alexander Haggerty Krappe, "Die Blendwerke der Æsir," *Zeitschrift für deutsche Philologie* 62 (1937): 113–124; and Michael Chesnutt, "The Beguiling of Þórr," in *Úr Dölum til Dala: Guðbrandur Vigfússon Centenary Essays*, ed. R. W. McTurk and A. Wawn, Leeds Texts and Monographs, 11 (Leeds: Leeds Studies in English, 1989), 35–63. Nora K. Chadwick looked to Russian tradition in "The Russian Giant Svyatogor and the Norse Útgartha-Loki," *Folklore* 75 (1964): 243–259. Anatoly Liberman focuses ultimately on etymology but has much to say about myths of Loki in his "Snorri and Saxo on Útgardaloki, with Notes on Loki Laufeyjarson's Character, Career, and Name," in *Saxo Grammaticus: Tra storiografia e letteratura. Bevagna, 27–29 settembre 1990* (Rome: Editrice "Il Calamo," 1992), 91–158. My analysis is in "Thor's Visit to Útgarða-Loki," *Oral Tradition* 15 (2000): 1–17.

SLEIPNIR

Odin's horse.

Grímnismál, stanza 44, has a list of things that are the foremost in various categories (Yggdrasil of trees, Odin of the æsir, and so forth), and Sleipnir is included as the best of horses. Snorri agreed; in *Gylfaginning* Snorri has a little list of the horses of the æsir, which he begins with Sleipnir. "Sleipnir is best; Odin owns him; he has eight legs." Later Snorri quotes *Grímnismál*, stanza 44, and this prompts Gangleri to ask about Sleipnir. Hár responds with the story of the building of Ásgard. The giant master builder has agreed to do the work only with the help of his horse, Svadilfari. If he succeeds in meeting the deadline, the gods must pay him Freyja, the sun, and the moon. Three days before the deadline the work is nearly complete, and Loki, who the gods say advised them to make the deal, must act. He changes himself into a mare and distracts Svadilfari, and without the horse the work cannot be finished. The master builder goes into a giant rage, thus revealing himself as a giant, and the gods call on Thor to kill him. Not much later Loki bears a gray eight-legged foal, the best of horses among the gods. This

Lärbro Tängelgårda stone from Gotland with rider on an eight-legged horse, probably Odin on Sleipnir. (The Art Archive/Historiska Museet Stockholm/Dagli Orti)

story is alluded to in *Hyndluljód*, stanza 40, which is part of the "Short *Völuspá*," although in this stanza it is not absolutely clear that Loki played the female role:

> Loki sired the wolf on Angrboda,
> And got Sleipnir on Svadilfari. . . .

The so-called *Thórgrímsthula*, an anonymous poetic fragment cited in Snorri's *Skáldskaparmál*, numbers Sleipnir among the excellent horses it knows of. The excellence or indeed superiority of Sleipnir is actually what triggers the duel between Thor and Hrungnir, since according to *Skáldskaparmál*, Hrungnir first gets into a dispute with the æsir when he and Odin each claim to possess the best horse.

As would befit the horse of Odin, Sleipnir is used for trips to the world of the dead. The second stanza of *Baldrs draumar* tells what happens after Baldr has had disquieting dreams:

Picture stone from Alskog Tjängvide, Gotland, showing a rider on an eight-legged horse, perhaps Sleipnir, being greeted by a female, perhaps a valkyrie at Valhöll. Note the other figure overhead. (The Art Archive/Historiska Museet Stockholm/Dagli Orti)

> Up rose Odin, god of the ages,
> And on Sleipnir he placed a saddle.
> He rode down from there to Niflhel
> Met a dog, which came out of Hel.

In the Baldr story in Snorri's *Gylfaginning*, when Hermód rides to the world of the dead to try to bring Baldr back, it is on Sleipnir's back. After riding nine dark nights he crosses the Gjallarbrú and finally comes the gates of Hel.

> Then he dismounted from the horse and girded it fast, mounted and drove with
> his spurs, and the horse leap so powerfully over the gate that he came nowhere
> near it.

Book 1 of Saxo Grammaticus's *Gesta Danorum* contains an episode that many scholars think is related to Odin, Sleipnir, and journeys to the otherworld.

The hero king Hadingus is brought into contact by a one-eyed old man with a wanderer called Liserus. Together they challenge Lokerus, lord of Kurland, but they are defeated. They ride away from the battle on a horse to the old man's home, and Hadingus is given a potion that invigorates him. On the return ride Hadingus looks down to see that the horse is speeding through the air.

The connection with the world of the dead grants a special poignancy to one of the kennings in which Sleipnir turns up as a horse word. This is "sea-Sleipnir," which Úlf Uggason used in the section of his *Húsdrápa* describing Baldr's funeral. The kenning stands for Baldr's funeral ship. Baldr's funeral was one of the scenes carved as decoration in the hall of Óláf pái (Peacock) in western Iceland, circa 985, which Úlf was describing in *Húsdrápa*. His use of Sleipnir in the kenning may show that Sleipnir's role in the failed recovery of Baldr was known at that time and place in Iceland; it certainly indicates that Sleipnir was an active participant in the mythology of the last decades of paganism.

Some of the eighth-century picture stones from the island of Gotland, including those of Alskog Tjängvide and Ardre VIII, show eight-legged horses, and most scholars accept that these represent Sleipnir. A rider sits on each, and some scholars think this is Odin; indeed, above horse and rider on the Alskog Tjängvide stone is a horizontal figure with a spear, perhaps a valkyrie. A woman greets the rider holding a cup, and the entire scene has been interpreted as the arrival of the rider in the world of the dead.

Sleipnir's eight legs have been interpreted as an indication of great speed or as being connected in some unclear way with cult activity.

> **See also** Gjallarbrú; Hadingus; Loki; Odin
> **References and further reading:** Although there are no studies that limit themselves exclusively to Sleipnir, Gutorm Gjessing devotes a chapter to him in his study of the horse in art and cult, "Hesten i førhistorisk kunst og kultus," *Viking* 7 (1943): 5–143. The Ardre VIII picture stone is the subject of a stimulating book by Ludwig Buisson, *Der Bildstein Ardre VIII auf Gotland: Göttermythen, Heldensagen und Jenseitsglaube im 8. Jahrhundert n. Chr.*, Abhandlungen der Akademie der Wissenschaften in Göttingen, phil.-hist. Kl., 3. Folge, 102 (Göttingen: Vandenhoeck & Ruprecht, 1976).

SLÍDRUGTANNI (DANGEROUS-TOOTH)

Alternative name for Gullinborsti, Frey's boar.

Snorri states in both *Gylfaginning* and in *Skáldskaparmál* that Slídrugtanni is an alternative name for Gullinborsti, but the name is found nowhere else. Since Gullinborsti is used once as an adjective ("gold-bristled") to describe Freyja's boar, Hildisvíni, and since the poet Úlf Uggason refers to Frey's boar in his *Húsdrápa* not by name but as "the one with golden bristles," it would seem possible that the adjective *gullinborsti* might in time have replaced an original name, such as Slídrugtanni.

See also Frey; Gullinborsti; Hildisvíni

SNOTRA

Minor goddess.

Snorri lists her thirteenth in his catalog in *Gylfaginning* of goddesses among the æsir and says this about her: "She is wise and of gentle bearing. From her designation the one who is *hóflátr* is called a wise woman or man." The name is clearly connected to the adjective *snotr*, "wise," and a wise person would then be *hóflátr*, "moderate," a sentiment that the gnomic stanzas of *Hávamál* would support.

SÓL (SUN)

The sun, personified.

Although the sun is mentioned frequently in older poetry, it is seldom personified. Even a kenning like "hall of the sun" for sky may not suggest personification, given the rules of kenning formation. In poetry, only *Vafthrúdnismál* is certain in its personification of the sun. In stanza 22 Odin asks the wise giant Vafthrúdnir whence the moon and sun came to travel over people. The giant responds in stanza 23:

> Mundilfœri he is called, the father of Máni
> And also of Sól the same;
> Into heaven shall they turn each day,
> So that people can reckon years.

Snorri concocts a somewhat different story in *Gylfaginning:* Mundilfœri is a man who had two children who were so beautiful that he named them Máni and Sól (i.e., Moon and Sun), and he married Sól to a man called Glen. The gods punished this act of pride by placing the children in heaven to serve the actual heavenly bodies, their creation.

> Sól drives those horses that pull the carriage of that sun that the gods had created to light the worlds, out of that spark that flew from Muspellsheim. Those horses are called Árvak and Alsvin; and under the span of the horses the gods put two wind bellows to cool them, and in some learning that is called Ísarnkól.

Sól's brother Máni controls the motion of the moon and its waxings and wanings. That Sól is female and Máni male probably has to do with the grammatical gender of the nouns: Sól is feminine and Máni masculine. Máni may have had some connection with the race of giants, but no such connection is suggested for Sól. Sól's husband Glen is unknown outside this passage.

When *Völuspá*, stanza 57, says of Ragnarök that "[t]he sun turns black, the earth sinks into the sea," there is no indication that either is personified. In *Gylfaginning*, however, Snorri continues his account of the personified sun. Gangleri begins the exchange:

> "The sun moves fast, and almost as if she were frightened; she would not hasten her journey more, if she feared her death." Then Hár answers: "It is not surprising that she goes quickly. The one who seeks her is right nearby, and she has no other way out than to run away." Then Gangleri said: "Who is it who makes this trouble?" Hár says: "It is two wolves, and the one who chases her is Sköll; she is afraid of him, and he will take her, and the one who runs in front of her is called Hati Hródvitnisson, and he will take the moon."

I rendered the last word of this passage "moon," although it can mean either sun or moon. (Try reading the passage to see what sense you make of it if Hati too takes the sun.) I have also rendered the animate pronoun "she" and "her," even though Snorri's use of the definite article at the beginning of the passage may suggest that he has dropped the personification or is speaking of the sun the gods created; I used the animate pronoun because I have trouble imagining a spark experiencing fear. Snorri is following *Grimnismál*, stanza 39 here, but that passage is silent on whether Hati will attack either heavenly body.

Snorri ends the catalog of the *ásynjur* that comes later in *Gylfaginning* with a note to the effect that Sól and Bil, "whose natures were explained above," are numbered among them.

The sun was of course a focus of older nature mythological and solar mythological interpretations of Scandinavian and other mythologies, but as the relatively short length of this article shows, it would not be easy to make a case for a central role of the sun in Scandinavian mythology as we have it.

> ***See also*** Bil and Hjúki; Glen; Hati Hródvitnisson; Máni; Sköll
>
> ***References and further reading:*** For an attempt to argue for sun worship in Scandinavia (other than in today's winter charter trips from dark Scandinavia to the sunny Mediterranean), see Vilhelm Kiil, "Er de nordiske Solberg minner om soldyrkelse?" *Maal og minne*, 1936: 126–175, who asked whether the place-name Solberg, which transparently means "Sun-mountain," might not be involved, even if only for the Bronze Age. The most recent work I know to foreground the importance of the sun (even if through symbols) in the extant mythology is Régis Boyer, *Yggdrasil: La Religion des anciens Scandinaves*, Bibliothèque historique (Paris: Payott, 1981). Boyer wrote that three aspects of nature run throughout Scandinavian religion from the Bronze Age to the

extant mythology: the sun, liquid, and the earth. Baldr, Týr, and Thor, Boyer writes, were aligned with the sun, as were, during the Viking Age, law and war. This book is rarely cited, but to those who can read French it offers an idiosyncratic interpretation.

SÖRLA THÁTTR

Text famous for its presentation of the Hjadningavíg, the unending battle, but also of interest for its presentation of the world of the gods in its opening pages.

Generically *Sörla tháttr* is a short *fornaldarsaga* (on saga genres, see chapter 1). It is found only in *Flateyjarbók*, an important Icelandic manuscript from the end of the fourteenth century, where it is one of the many *thættir*, "short narratives," interwoven into the *Great Saga of Olaf Tryggvason*.

The opening lines present a version of the Learned Prehistory familiar from the beginning of Snorri's *Ynglinga saga:* To the east of Vanakvísl in Asia lived the Æsir (here openly understood as "Asians") in their capital city Ásgard. Odin was the king, and it was a place of great pagan activity. He established Njörd and Frey as chieftains presiding over the sacrifices. Freyja was the daughter of Njörd. Up to this point there is nothing new. But then follows the statement that Freyja was a follower of Odin and was his concubine. Seeing a beautiful necklace (the Brísinga men?) being made by four neighboring dwarfs, she desires it, but they will only part with it if each of them gets to spend a night with her. She agrees, and four nights later she owns the necklace. Now Loki is introduced, as another of Odin's retainers. Loki finds out about the necklace and tells Odin of it, and Odin commands Loki to get the necklace. This Loki accomplishes by turning himself into a fly and getting into Freyja's impenetrable bedchamber (an otherwise unknown motif). To make Freyja turn over so that he can get at the necklace, Loki turns himself into a flea and bites her; he then flees with the necklace. When Freyja awakens and misses the necklace, she confronts Odin, who tells her she can only have it back by fulfilling one rather strange condition: She must make two kings, each of whom is served by 20 kings, fall out and engage in a battle that through charms and magic will go on without end, unless it is interrupted by a Christian who serves a great king.

Although we never see Freyja or Odin again in the text (although a mysterious woman calling herself by the valkyrie name Göndul does appear), this condition is fulfilled when two great kings, Hedin and Högni, have a falling out when Hedin abducts Högni's daughter Hild. Their armies fight each day for 143 years, until the arrival and intervention of Ívarr ljómi (Gleam), a retainer of Olaf Tryggvason.

The courtly setting, with Freyja and Loki presented as retainers of Odin, is interesting, as is the open presentation of Freyja's sexual willingness. The introduction of Loki begins with his parents Fárbauti and Laufey (who is called Nál [Needle], we are told, because of her slender physique), and the text goes on to explain, without as far as I can see the slightest trace of irony, that he was known for his cunning. For these reasons the text would appear to be post-classical.

See also Hjadningavíg

References and further reading: Jan de Vries, *The Problem of Loki*, FF Communications, 110 (Helsinki: Suomalainen tiedeakatemia, 1933), 125–141, treats the text. Niels Lukman, "An Irish Source and Some Fornaldarsögur," *Mediaeval Scandinavia* 10 (1977): 41–57, locates a potential source among Irish annals. Helen Damico, "*Sörlaþáttr* and the Hama Episode in *Beowulf*," *Scandinavian Studies* 55 (1983): 222–235, argues that the Hama episode in *Beowulf* should be read against mythological rather than legendary-historical models.

STARKAD

The most famous divine hero.

Starkad was a favorite of Odin and was hated by Thor. A scene found in *Gautreks saga* has Starkad brought before 12 æsir. Odin and Thor bestow alternate aspects of his life to come: Odin gives three lifetimes, and Thor counters with a dastardly deed to be committed in each; Odin gives great weapons, and Thor says he will never own land; Odin gives him wealth, and Thor says he will never enjoy it; Odin gives victory in battles, and Thor promises many wounds in each; Odin gives the gift of poetry, and Thor says he will never remember his compositions; Odin gives standing among the highest in society, and Thor says the common man will despise him. This exchange had begun with Thor's statement that Starkad would be childless because his paternal grandmother, Álfhild, had preferred a giant to Thor. This seems to allude to an incident told in one redaction of *Hervarar saga ok Heidreks konungs*. A figure called Starkad Áludreng (Ála-boy) carried off a woman called Álfhild. Her father called on Thor, who killed Starkad Áludreng.

This Starkad Áludreng had eight arms. Saxo Grammaticus has a character called Starcatherus (Starkad) with six arms, and he says Thor tore away four of them to make him normal. In addition, a stanza composed in the waning days of paganism and addressed directly to Thor praises him for killing Starkad. Saxo's Starcatherus dies voluntarily at the hand of the son of a king he had killed.

There must indeed have been conflicting traditions about the figure or figures known as Starkad. In Saxo's Starcatherus, however, there is a single figure, however complex his character. He is a major figure in Books 6–8 of *Gesta Danorum*. He certainly lives out the gifts and counter-gifts bestowed on him (in Saxo only by Odin): He lives to an enormous age; he is a great warrior, invincible in battle, and an accomplished poet, but he commits dastardly deeds. The first is the murder of King Víkar, at Odin's request, during a supposedly mock sacrifice (in Icelandic tradition, this killing is portrayed as unintended). The second is probably Starkad's flight from a battlefield in Jutland, and the third is clearly the murder of King Olo, whom he had served at the great battle of Brávellir. Starkad killed Olo for a bribe while the king was bathing.

> *See also* Dísablót
>
> *References and further reading:* Georges Dumézil wrote extensively about Starkad. See first his *The Destiny of the Warrior,* trans. Alf Hiltebeitel (Chicago and London: University of Chicago Press, 1971), and *The Stakes of the Warrior,* trans. David Weeks, ed. Jaan Puhvel (Berkeley and Los Angeles: University of California Press, 1983). Another classic treatment arguing a mythic background is Jan de Vries, "Die Starkadsage," *Germanisch-Romanisch Monatsschrift* 36 (1955): 281–297, reprinted in his *Kleine Schriften,* ed. Klaas Heeroma and Andries Kylstra (Berlin: W. de Gruyter, 1965), 20–36. James Milroy, "Starkaðr: An Essay in Interpretation," *Saga-Book of the Viking Society* 19 (1974–1977), 118–138, attempts to read Starkad as a "literary myth." For useful analysis of Starkad in Saxo, consult Inge Skovgaard-Petersen, *Starkad in Saxo's Gesta Danorum: History and Heroic Tale* (Odense: Odense Universitetsforlag, 1985).

SURT

Giant particularly associated with Ragnarök.

Völuspá, stanza 52, sets Surt's departure to do battle with the gods as part of the general chaos that will reign when the world ends at Ragnarök and makes it clear that he has to do with the conflagration that will ensue:

> Surt travels from the south with the enemy of twigs [fire],
> The sun shines from the swords of the carrion-gods,
> Mountains resound, and ogresses roam,
> Humans tread the road to Hel, and the sky is riven.

Previously, in stanza 47, the poet had called the wolf who swallows the sun "the companion of Surt."

Asking where the last battle will take place, the giant Vafthrúdnir puts it this way in stanza 17 of *Vafthrúdnismál:* Tell me, he says,

> What that field is called where will meet in battle
> Surt and the beloved gods.

In *Fáfnismál,* Sigurd asks the dying dragon Fáfnir a very similar question. Tell me, he says,

14. What that island is called, where they will mix in a sword game,
Surt and the æsir together.

Fáfnir responds:

15. Óskópnir it is called, and there shall all
The gods make play with spears.

These passages suggest strongly that Surt and his fire could stand for all of Ragnarök. Another exchange in *Vafthrúdnismál* strengthens this supposition. Odin asks about the aftermath of Ragnarök, and Vafthrúdnir responds:

50. Which æsir will rule the possessions of the gods,
When Surt's fire dies down?
51. Vídar and Váli will inhabit the holy places of the gods,
When Surt's fire dies down.

Surt plays an active role at Ragnarök, for according to *Völuspá*, stanza 53, he goes up against Frey and kills him.

As is usual, Snorri Sturluson has more to say. In the *Gylfaginning* section of his *Edda*, he assigns Surt to the fiery world of Muspell:

That one is called Surt, who sits there at the end of the world as a guardian.
He has a burning sword, and at the end of the world he will travel and harry
and defeat all the gods and burn the entire world with fire.

When Snorri gets to Ragnarök at the end of *Gylfaginning*, he writes that Surt rides first of the sons of Muspell, with fire before and after him, with a sword that shines more brightly than if the sun were reflected from it. After the individual gods have fallen, Surt casts fire over the earth and burns the entire world. The name Surt is used in poetry as a general name for a giant. It meant something like "black," as if he were charred.

See also Muspell; Ragnarök
References and further reading: Bertha S. Phillpotts, "Surt," *Arkiv för nordisk filologi* 21 (1905): 14–30, argued that Surt was a "volcano-giant," which would give him a special association with Iceland, where volcanic activity remains common. Indeed, when a volcanic island erupted fresh from the waters off Iceland in 1963, it was named Surtsey (Surt's-island).

SUTTUNG

Giant from whom Odin obtains the mead of poetry.

Suttung is mentioned in both major versions of the story of Odin's acquisition of the mead of poetry, in *Hávamál*, stanzas 104–110, and the *Skáldskaparmál* of Snorri Sturluson's *Edda*. In one sense we might say that the story of the mead of poetry, especially as Snorri spells it out, is a story about Suttung's family. Suttung obtains the mead, in compensation for their murder of his parents, from the dwarfs Fjalar and Galar, who made it from the blood of Kvasir. He entrusts the mead to his daughter Gunnlöd, to whom Odin gains access after Suttung's brother Baugi drills a hole into the mountain where Gunnlöd is staying. Only after Odin leaves in the form of an eagle does Suttung play an active role: Also in the form of an eagle, he pursues Odin. The pursuit is so close that Odin cannot get all the mead back into the possession of the æsir, and he urinates a bit out; this portion makes bad poets. Thus we have Suttung to blame for the lyrics of most pop songs.

See also Baugi, Fjalar; Gunnlöd; Mead of Poetry

SYN

Minor goddess.

Snorri lists Syn eleventh in his catalog in *Gylfaginning* of goddesses among the æsir and says this about her: "She manages the doors of the hall and closes the doors before those who are not to go in, and she is established at assemblies as a defense against those cases which she wishes to disprove. Thus there is a proverb that *syn* [denial] is seen when someone says no." The goddess is otherwise unknown, but her name does appear in the thulur and a few times in woman kennings in skaldic poetry.

SÝR (SOW)

Name for Freyja.

Snorri says in *Gylfaginning* that Freyja has many names because she took on different names among the various peoples she encountered when she went to search for her missing husband, Ód. Freyja bears this name in no extant narrative, but the skaldic kenning "tear of Sýr" supports it, and it is listed in the thulur. Freyja as "sow" would accord with the notion of her as a fertility deity.

See also Freyja

THJÁLFI

Thor's human servant and companion.

The story of how Thjálfi and his sister Röskva came to be Thor's human servants is told as part of the first section of the long myth of Thor's visit to Útgarda-Loki in Snorri's *Gylfaginning*. Traveling with Loki, Thor comes to the home of a certain farmer and arranges lodgings for the night. Thor slaughters his goats and boils them and then invites the farmer and the rest of the household to eat the meat; they are to cast the bones onto the skins, which he has spread out nearby. While they are eating, Thjálfi, the farmer's son, cuts one of the bones with his knife to get at the marrow. The next morning Thor waves his hammer over the piles of skin and bones, and the goats arise whole, but one is lame. Thor goes into a rage, and in their terror the humans beg for mercy. Seeing their fear, Thor relents, and in compensation he takes Thjálfi and Röskva, and they have been his servants ever since.

Although most of the attention paid to this story has focused on the revival of the goats, I believe that a far more important aspect is the relationship between humans and gods. Because of a failure to carry out a ritual properly, the god is angry, and the humans rightly fear his wrath. But when they beg for mercy he grants it, and the result is a closer relationship between the humans and the gods.

Thjálfi accompanies Thor on the next leg of the journey, which is to the land of the giants, and he carries Thor's pack. When Útgarda-Loki calls for demonstrations of skill or ability, Thjálfi, "the swiftest of all humans," proposes a footrace. He loses three heats to Útgarda-Loki's retainer Hugi, and although he comes a bit closer in each heat, even in the third he is only halfway around the course when Hugi has finished. Later we learn that Hugi is the same as the noun *hugi*, "thought"; that is, he is Útgarda-Loki's thought, so the defeat is hardly humiliating, as is indeed the case with the other contests undertaken at Útgarda-Loki's court by Loki and Thor.

In the *Skáldskaparmál* of his *Edda*, Snorri tells the story of Thor's duel with Hrungnir, and there too Thjálfi plays a role, both as Thor's second and as the killer of a secondary monster. Thjálfi contributes materially to Thor's victory over Hrungnir, the strongest of giants, by falsely warning Hrungnir that Thor will attack from below. The giant stands on his shield and therefore cannot use it when Thor hurls the hammer at him. Thjálfi, meanwhile, faces Mökkurkálfi, a figure nine leagues tall and three leagues wide, made of clay but with the heart of a mare, which is unsteady when Thor approaches. Indeed, the clay giant was so consumed with fear when Thor approached that he wet himself. After giving the details of the closely matched encounter between Thor and Hrungnir, Snorri adds laconically "and Thjálfi attacked Mökkurkálfi, who fell with little glory."

Hrungnir is defeated, and Thjálfi attempts to lift Hrungnir's lifeless leg off Thor but cannot; that job is left to Thor's infant son Magni. Magni's success after Thjálfi's failure may give some indication of the god-human hierarchy in the mythology.

Following Georges Dumézil, many observers, especially those who, like Dumézil, approach the material from the Indo-European side, see here a reflection of warrior initiation: Under the tutelage of an elder warrior, the initiant "slays" a made monster. I find the theory attractive even though there is nothing in Snorri's text to indicate that Thjálfi's status changes after the encounter with Mökkurkálfi, which we would expect in an initiatory context. Made monsters turn up in all sorts of cultures, not always in initiatory contexts (e.g., golems).

According to the *Thórsdrápa* of the tenth-century skald Eilíf Godrúnarson, Thjálfi accompanied Thor on his journey to the giant Geirröd. The ninth and tenth stanzas seem to show Thjálfi clinging to Thor as the river Vimur rises, but neither of them is fearful. Apparently Eilíf thought Thjálfi participated in the struggles with Geirröd and his daughters alongside Thor. A half-stanza that editors put at the end of the poem seems to give the two equal weight:

Angry stood Röskva's brother,
The father of Magni struck for gain.
Neither Thor's nor Thjálfi's
Stone of strength [heart] trembled with fear.

Snorri has Loki accompany Thor on this journey, and indeed it sometimes seems that there was a structural slot, "companion of Thor," that was filled sometimes by Loki and sometimes by Thjálfi. The etymology of the name is unclear, but it was used in the human community too, as several Swedish runic inscriptions show.

See also Egil; Geirröd; Loki; Röskva; Thor; Útgarda-Loki

References and further reading: My analysis of the encounter with Thjálfi's family is found in "Thor's Visit to Útgarda-Loki," *Oral Tradition* 15 (2000): 170–186. Georges Dumézil presents the evidence for Thjálfi and Mökkurkálfi as an initiation story in chapter 4, "From Storm to Pleasure," in his *Gods of the Ancient Northmen*, ed. Einar Haugen, Publications of the UCLA Center for the Study of Comparative Folklore and Mythology, 3 (Berkeley and Los Angeles: University of California Press 1973), 66–79. The notion of Thjálfi and Loki as reflexes of the same character, the companion of the thunder god, was argued by Axel Olrik, "Tordenguden og hans dreng," *Danske studier* 2 (1905): 129–146.

THJAZI

Giant, father of Skadi, abductor of Idun and her apples.

The story is found in the skaldic poem *Haustlöng*, by Thjódólf of Hvin, and in the *Skáldskaparmál* section of Snorri Sturluson's *Edda*. Odin, Hœnir, and Loki are traveling and find themselves unable to cook an ox. An eagle in the tree above claims responsibility and says the ox will cook if he may have some. However, when he tries to take a vast amount, Loki strikes at him with a staff. The staff sticks to the eagle and to Loki's hand, and the eagle flies off with Loki in tow. As he bangs against things, Loki agrees to the eagle's demand: that he bring him Idun and her apples. This he does, and without their apples, the gods grow old and gray. They force Loki to agree to get Idun back. In Freyja's falcon coat he flies to Jötunheimar, changes Idun into a nut, and flies off with her. Thjazi pursues in the form of an eagle. The gods kindle a fire just as Loki flies into Ásgard, and Thjazi's feathers are singed and he falls to the earth and is killed by the gods.

This is one of the most dangerous moments for the gods in the mythological present, for giants are not supposed to be able to mate with goddesses. The fact that the gods grow old and gray—that is, display mortality—indicates what would happen if the flow of females, ordinarily from the giants to the gods, were to be reversed.

> *See also* Idun; Skadi
>
> **References and further reading:** In her *Prolonged Echoes: Old Norse Myths in Medieval Icelandic Society*, vol. 1: *The Myths* (Odense: Odense University Press, 1994), Margaret Clunies Ross makes clear the importance of the direction of the passage of marriageable women, and on pages 115–119 she analyzes the Idun-Thjazi myth in some detail. Another interesting approach is that of Anne Holtsmark, "Myten om *Idun* og *Tjatse* i Tjodolvs *Haustlǫng*," *Arkiv för nordisk filologi* 64 (1949): 1–73, who argued for a background in ritual drama.

THOR

God who specializes in killing giants.

Thor is the son of Odin and Jörd (Earth), the wife of Sif, and the father of sons Módi and Magni and a daughter Thrúd. Virtually all of Thor's myths have to do with giantslaying. He slays the strongest giant, Hrungnir, in a duel. He kills Geirröd, and more famously Geirröd's daughters, on a visit to that giant. He kills Thrym, and all the giants in his family, when he goes off to Thrym in the guise of Freyja, supposedly to be given to Thrym in exchange for Thor's stolen hammer. He kills Hymir and a host of giants when he goes off to Hymir's home in Giantland to acquire from him a huge kettle in which the gods will brew beer. He kills the giant who built the wall around Ásgard. His greatest struggle was with the Midgard serpent, the most powerful giant of all, whom he fished up out of the

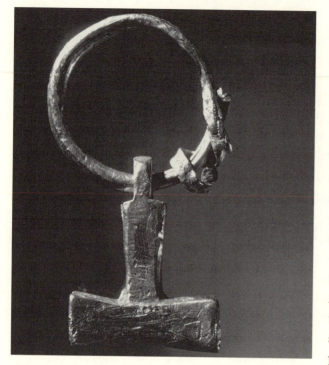

A hanging amulet of Thor's hammer. (Ted Spiegel/ Corbis)

deep sea. Earlier skaldic sources suggest that Thor killed the monster, but Snorri Sturluson contradicts this in the *Gylfaginning* section of his *Edda*. Snorri and *Völuspá* have him meet the serpent again at Ragnarök. They kill each other, but Thor staggers back nine steps before succumbing to the serpent's poison, and this suggests a kind of small victory snatched from the greater defeats the gods are suffering.

Thor also kills dwarfs, although less deliberately. In *Alvíssmál* he keeps the dwarf who is trying to woo his daughter up until sunrise answering questions about poetic vocabulary (not otherwise a known interest of Thor's), and the sun's first ray kills the dwarf. At Baldr's funeral he redirects his anger at the giantess Hyrrokkin to the dwarf Lit, whom he kicks into the fire.

Thor could be outdone through the use of magic, an area into which he never ventures. Thus, when traveling with the giant Skrýmir, Thor is unable to kill him because, as he learns later, the giant magically redirected the blows of Thor's hammer. After Skrýmir and Thor part ways, Thor and his traveling companions are defeated in various contests at the hall of Útgarda-Loki partly through magic, as when Thor thinks he is lifting a cat but is in fact lifting the Midgard serpent, and partly through linguistic dullness, as when Thor fails to realize that the old lady he wrestles named "Old Age" is in fact old age. A similar lack of linguistic awareness, or perhaps a lack of awareness of poetic forms, makes Thor come out the loser when he engages in a contest of words with a ferryman, Odin in disguise, in *Hárbardsljód*. But Thor is the only god capable of shutting Loki up when he is reviling all the gods in *Lokasenna*, and Thor is also the one who contributes most to the capture of Loki that leads to his binding.

Thor very frequently travels in the company of an assistant, most often Thjálfi but also on occasion Loki or Týr. Thjálfi is a human, and his accompanying Thor indicates the close relationship between Thor and humans, a relationship also attested by the metal artifacts known as Thor's hammers. These objects, miniature hammers that were worn about the neck, are the only indica-

Two of the most elaborate of Thor's hammers, made of silver. The figure on the chain was found in Erikstorp, Sweden, along with a hoard of treasure. The hammer on the left is from Kabbara, Sweden, also found with a hoard of treasure. (Statens Historiska Museum, Stockholm)

tion from the archaeological record of talismans associated with specific accouterments of the gods. Thor was probably the most important god of late paganism, as is suggested by the presentation in medieval Scandinavian sources of the conversion as a struggle between Thor and Christ.

During the last years of paganism in Iceland, poets left us with two fragments of poems addressed directly to Thor, in the second person. These are mostly lists of giants he killed. Some of the giants are known, but some are not, and it is clear that we no longer have all the relevant mythology about Thor. It would be nice to know, for example, about his killing of Thrívaldi (Thrice-powerful), who may be associated with a nine-headed giant mentioned by the skald Bragi. One of the interesting aspects of these lists of Thor's victims is the relative frequency of female names. Thor was not just a giantslayer but also a giantess-slayer. The forces of chaos had a strong female side.

A small bronze, 6–7 cm high, from Eyrarland, Iceland, identified by some observers as Thor. (Werner Forman/Art Resource)

Thor is persistently presented as crossing rivers. The most spectacular of these rivers is Vimur, but there is another set he crosses, according to *Grímnismál*, stanza 29:

> Körmt and Örmt and two Kerlaugar,
> Those Thor shall cross,
> Each day, when he goes to judge
> At the ash of Yggdrasil.

Thor's crossing of rivers may have to do with the fact that he does his business mostly in the realm of the giants, who live on the other sides of boundaries, but it is also worth recalling the symbolic association between giants and water, as can be seen in the abode of the Midgard serpent out in the deep sea.

See also Ásgard; Baldr; *Bergbúa tháttr;* Geirröd; *Hárbardsljód;* Hrungnir; *Hymiskvida;* Midgard Serpent; *Thrymskvida;* Útgarda-Loki

References and further reading: The most recent book on Thor was published quite some time ago, and in Swedish: Helge Ljungberg, *Tor: Undersökningar i indoeuropeisk och nordisk religionshistoria,* vol. 1: *Den nordiska åskguden och besläktade indoeuropeiska gudar: Den nordiska åskguden i bild och myt,* Uppsala universitets årsskrift, 1947:9 (Uppsala: Lundequistska Bokhandeln, 1947; summary in French). But there are many recent articles in English. These include Margaret Clunies Ross, "An Interpretation of the Myth of Þórr's Encounter with Geirrøðr and His Daughters," in *Speculum Norroenum: Norse Studies in Memory of Gabriel Turville-Petre,* ed. Ursula Dronke, Guðrún P. Helgadóttir, Gerd Wolfgang Weber, and Hans-Bekker Nielsen ([Odense:] Odense University Press, 1981), 370–391, "Two of Þórr's Great Fights according to Hymiskviða," in *Studies in Honour of H. L. Rogers,* ed. Geraldine Barnes and D. A. Lawton, Leeds Studies in English, 20 (Leeds: University of Leeds, 1989), 7–27, and "Þórr's Honour," in *Studien zum Altgermanischen: Festschrift für Heinrich Beck,* ed. Heiko Uecker (Berlin and New York: W. de Gruyter, 1994), 48–76; Margaret Clunies Ross and B. K. Martin, "Narrative Structures and Intertextuality in *Snorra Edda:* The Example of Þor's Encounter with Geirrøðr," in *Structure and Meaning in Old Norse Literature,* ed. John Lindow, Lars Lönnroth, and Gerd Wolfgang Weber, Viking Collection, 3 (Odense: Odense University Press, 1986), 56–72; John Lindow, "Thor's *hamarr," Journal of English and Germanic Philology,* 93 (1994): 485–503, "Thor's Duel with Hrungnir," *Alvíssmál: Forschungen zur mittelalterlichen Kultur Scandinaviens* 6 (1996): 3–18, "Þrymskviða, Myth, and Mythology" in *Germanic Studies in Honor of Anatoly Liberman,* ed. Martha Berryman, Kurt Gustav Goblirsch, and Marvin Taylor, NOWELE, 31/32 (Odense: Odense University Press, 1997), 203–212, "Thor's Visit to Útgardaloki," *Oral Tradition* 15 (2000): 170–186.

THRÚD (STRENGTH)

Daughter of Thor.

We know about Thrúd only from kennings. Snorri says in *Skáldskaparmál* that "father of Thrúd" is a valid Thor kenning, and there is evidence that skalds indeed used the kenning. Thrúd also turns up as the base word in woman kennings. What is most interesting, however, is a kenning for the giant Hrungnir in Bragi Boddason the Old's *Ragnarsdrápa,* stanza 1: "thief of Thrúd." The kenning suggests a now lost myth of the abduction of Thrúd by the giant, portrayed on the shield that Bragi is describing a century or so before the conversion to Christianity. Such a myth could certainly have added an extra dimension to the duel between Hrungnir and Thor.

See also Hrungnir; Thor

References and further reading: In "Þórr's Honour," *Studien zum Altgermani-schen: Festschrift für Heinrich Beck,* ed. Heiko Uecker (Berlin and New York: W. de Gruyter, 1994), 48–76, Margaret Clunies Ross discusses Thor's need to look after his females, a need that the myth of the abduction of Thrúd, if it existed, would have involved.

THRÚDGELMIR (STRENGTH-YELLER)

Primeval giant.

Thrúdgelmir is mentioned only in stanza 29 of *Vafthrúdnismál.* Odin has asked Vafthrúdnir who was the oldest of the æsir or kin of Ymir. The answer is three generations of giants: Aurgelmir, Thrúdgelmir, and Bergelmir. Aurgelmir, according to this poem, was the proto-giant whose hermaphroditic monstrous acts of procreation produced the race of giants (he was Ymir by another name, according to Snorri). And some event involving Bergelmir, probably his funeral, was the oldest event that Vafthrúdnir himself actually remembered. Thrúdgel-mir has no story. He is not mentioned in Snorri or anywhere else. Perhaps the poet felt compelled to give the proto-giants a three-generation genealogy and invented Thrúdgelmir. His name is the most obvious of the three, and that could suggest that it did not come down in oral tradition.

See also Aurgelmir; Bergelmir; Ymir

THRÚDHEIM (STRENGTH-WORLD)

Home of Thor.

In *Grímnismál,* when the disguised Odin, hung between the fires, is given a drink by the young Agnar (stanza 3), he begins to pronounce his visions. Thrúd-heim, the first thing he reports seeing, is the subject of the whole of stanza 4:

> A land is holy, which I see situated
> Near the æsir and elves;
> Still in Thrúdheim shall Thor be,
> Until the powers are riven.

In *Gylfaginning* and *Ynglinga saga* Snorri says consistently that Thor lives in Thrúdvangar, not Thrúdheim, although one manuscript of the *Edda* does refer to Thrúdheim where the others have Thrymheim, the residence of the giant Thjazi and his daughter Skadi. However, in the euhemerized discussion of the æsir in Tyrkland, Snorri says that Trór, "whom we call Thor," conquered for himself the kingdom of Thrace, "which we call Thrúdheim." At its first men-tion in *Gylfaginning,* Thrúdvangar is also called a kingdom.

See also Thrúdvangar; Thrymheim

THRÚDVANGAR (STRENGTH-FIELDS)

Home of Thor.

This name is not attested in poetry, but it is Snorri's preferred form. When he introduces Thor in *Gylfaginning*, Snorri calls him the strongest god and says that he has a kingdom "where it is called Thrúdvangar, and his hall is called Bilskírnir." In *Ynglinga saga*, chapter 5, Thrúdvangar is the place assigned to Thor when Odin gives residences to his principal followers after arriving in Sweden.

See also Bilskírnir; Thrúdheim

THRYMHEIM (DIN-WORLD)

Home of the giants Thjazi and Skadi.

Grímnismál, stanza 11, includes this place in the list of residences of gods:

> The sixth is called Thrymheim, where Thjazi lived,
> That powerful giant;
> Now Skadi there still inhabits, shining bride of the gods,
> The ancient dwelling of her father.

Thus the marriage of Skadi to Njörd, after the death of her father, qualifies her residence for inclusion in the list of gods' residences despite her giant ethnicity. In *Gylfaginning* Snorri names Thrymheim ("that dwelling, which her father had owned; it is on some mountains, where it is called Thrymheim") as the place where Njörd and Skadi spent nine nights alternating with their nine nights at Nóatún, Njörd's residence, before the marriage broke up; in the mythological present, Thrymheim is Skadi's residence. In one manuscript of Snorri's *Edda* the scribe wrote "Thrúdheim" where the other manuscripts have "Thrymheim." Thrúdheim is supposed to be Thor's residence. We might also perhaps expect the giant Thrym to dwell at a place named after him, but Thrymheim is the only mythological name beginning with *Thrym-*, and there is no connection with the giant Thrym.

See also Njörd; Skadi; Thrúdheim; *Thrymskvida*

THRYMSKVIDA (THE POEM OF THRYM)

Eddic poem telling of Thor's recovery of his hammer from the giant Thrym.

The poem is found only in *Codex Regius* of the *Poetic Edda*. It begins with Thor awakening in anger to find his hammer missing (stanza 1). He calls on Loki (2), and the two visit Freyja and ask to borrow her feather coat (3). She agrees (4), and Loki flies off to Giantland (5). There Thrym sits, the lord of the domain (6), and a dialogue ensues in which Thrym admits having the hammer and demands in exchange Freyja as his bride (7–8). Loki flies back to Ásgard (9), where Thor greets him (10). Loki delivers the news (11). Once more the two go to visit Freyja to ask her to go off to Giantland (12), which she adamantly refuses to do (13). The æsir assemble (14), and wise old Heimdall suggests dressing up Thor as Freyja (15–16). Thor demurs, citing the potential stain on his manhood (17), but Loki reminds him of the stakes: "The giants will immediately / inhabit Ásgard, / unless you get your hammer / back for yourself" (18). The gods dress Thor as a bride (19), and Loki states a willingness to go along as a serving woman (20). Mountains break and the earth burns as they travel (21). In Giantland Thrym has the giants prepare for Freyja's arrival (22–23). But when the feast begins, the bride eats an entire ox, eight salmon, and all the delicacies intended for the ladies, and "she" drinks three barrels of mead (24). The giant wonders at this appetite (25), but Loki responds that Freyja has not eaten for eight nights, so eager was she to come to Jötunheimar (26). Thrym lifts the bride's veil and is horrified by the burning eyes it conceals (27). Loki counters that Freyja has not slept for eight nights, so eager was she to come to Jötunheimar (28). Thrym's sister asks for a gift of love (29), but Thor asks that the hammer be brought in to hallow the marriage (30). The final two stanzas show Thor in a familiar role:

> 31. Hlórridi [Thor]'s heart laughed in his breast
> when the tough-minded one received the hammer.
> First he killed Thrym, the lord of the giants,
> And he smashed the entire family of the jötun.
> 32. He killed the aged sister of the jötnar,
> the one who had asked for a bridal gift.
> She got a bash instead of a multitude of rings.
> Thus Odin's son got his hammer back.

This myth is utterly unknown in other sources, and scholars have therefore speculated that it must have been of very late date, that is, from the late twelfth or even the thirteenth century. However, many arguments have been advanced about possible Indo-European cognates, myths about the theft and recovery of a thunder weapon. Furthermore, it is possible that a very old myth might only have been rendered into eddic poetry at a late date, although there is still the problem that only the late skalds make any reference to the myth. But whatever the date of myth and poem, *Thrymskvida* is absolutely consistent with the rest of the mythology. As in *Hymiskvida*, Thor travels with an assistant in order to retrieve a valuable object from the giants. As in the myth of his visit to Geirröd, Thor travels to Giantland with a companion but without his weapons, and he kills male and female giants there. His disguise as a woman appears strange, but

Odin too was open to accusations of perversion (as cross-dressing was understood in medieval Scandinavian culture), and that the god of might should have
to undergo this apparent humiliation shows how close the ongoing battle is
between gods and giants. The poem as we have it also shows how stupid the
giants are, for Thrym allows Loki to talk him out of the evidence that is right
before him.

    See also Loki; Thor

    References and further reading: An Indo-European background was suggested by
    Georges Dumézil in his very first publication, *Le festin d'immortalité, étude
    de mythologie comparée indo-européenne,* Annales du museé Guimet, biblio-
    thèque des études, 34 (Paris: Geuthne, 1924), but *Thrymskvida* never figured
    large in the Dumézilian ouevre. The most detailed discussion of a possible
    Indo-European background is that of Franz Rolf Schröder, "Thors Hammerhol-
    ung," *Beiträge zur Geschichte der deutschen Sprache und Literatur* (Tübin-
    gen) 87 (1965): 1–42. Samuel Singer, "Die Grundlagen der Thrymskvidha,"
    Neophilologus 17 (1931): 47–48, proposed Arabic as well as Indo-European par-
    allels, and Martin Puhvel, "The Deicidal Otherworld Weapon in Celtic and
    Germanic Mythic Tradition," *Folklore* 83 (1972): 210–219, saw a myth of a
    cosmic struggle between celestial gods, probably of Indo-European origin.
    Alfred Vestlund, "Åskgudens hammare förlorad: Ett bidrag till nordisk rit-
    forskning," *Edda* 11 (1919): 95–119, and Wolfgang Schultz, "Die Felsritzung
    von Hvitlycke und das *Edda*-Lied von Thrym," *Mannus* 21 (1929): 52, argued
    for a possible ritual background, Vestlund mostly on the basis of the text itself
    and Schultz through a hypothetical connection with Bronze Age rock carvings.
    In his huge monograph on Thor, *Tor: Undersökningar i indoeuropeisk och
    nordisk religionshistoria,* vol. 1: *Den nordiska åskguden och besläktade
    indoeuropeiska gudar: Den nordiska åskguden i bild och myt,* Uppsala uni-
    versitets årsskrift, 1947:9 (Uppsala: Lundequistska Bokhandeln, 1947; sum-
    mary in French), Helge Ljungberg worked with the assumption that Thor was
    a thunder god and explained the apparently jocular view of Thor expressed in
    Thrymskvida as the result of the relative scarcity of summer thunder in Ice-
    land. Others have sought the origin of *Thrymskvida* in loans from various
    places. Edith Smith Krappe, "The *Casina* of Plautus and the *Þrymskviða*,"
    Scandinavian Studies 6 (1920): 198–201, argued for Ireland; Otto Loorits, "Das
    Märchen vom gestohlenen Donnerinstrument bei den Esten," *Sitzungs-
    berichte der Gelehrten Estnischen Gesellschaft,* 1930: 47–121, argued for Rus-
    sia; and Uku Masing, "Die Entstehung des Märchens vom gestohlenen
    Donnerinstrument (Aarne-Thompson 1148B)," *Zeitschrift für deutsches Alter-
    tum* 81 (1944): 23–31, argued for the Middle East. The classic argument for a
    late date was advanced by Jan de Vries in "Over de dateering der Þrymskviða,"
    Tijdschrift voor nederlandse taal- en letterkunde 47 (1928): 251–372, which
    followed by only a few years the valiant attempt of Jöran Sahlgren in his
    Eddica et scaldica. Fornvästnordiska studier, Nordisk filologi, undersökningar
    och handlingar, 1 (Lund: C. W. K. Gleerup, 1927–1928) to prove that *Thryms-
    kvida* had to antedate the late-tenth-century *Eiríksmál. Thrymskvida* as par-

ody is the subject of Heinrich Matthias Heinrichs, "Satirisch-parodistische Züge in der Þrymskviða," in *Festschrift für Hans Eggers zum 65. Geburtstag*, ed. Herbert Backes (Tübingen: M. Niemeyer, 1972; also issued as a supplement to *Beiträge zur Geschichte der deutschen Sprache und Literatur* [Tübingen], 94, Supplement). Otto Höfler, "Götterkomik: Zur Selbstrelativierung des Mythos," *Zeitschrift für deutsches Altertum* 100 (1971): 371–389, wonders how believers could laugh at a deity; A. Ya Gurevich, "On the Nature of the Comic in the Elder Edda: A Comment on an Article by Professor Höfler," *Mediaeval Scandinavia* 9 (1976): 127–137, tries to provide an answer. Peter Hallberg, "Om Þrymskviða," *Arkiv för nordisk filologi* 69 (1954): 51–77, proposed Snorri Sturluson as the author of *Thrymskvida*, and various arguments for and against were advanced until Gustav Lindblad, "Snorre Sturlasson och eddadiktningen," *Saga och sed*, 1978: 17–34, showed convincingly that Snorri had little association with eddic poetry in any way. My own analysis of the poem is in "Þrymskviða, Myth, and Mythology," in *Germanic Studies in Honor of Anatoly Liberman*, ed. Martha Berryman, Kurt Gustav Goblirsch, and Marvin Taylor, NOWELE, 31/32 (Odense: Odense University Press, 1997), 203–212.

TUISTO

Proto-being of the Germanic peoples, according to the *Germania* of Tacitus.

In chapter 2 of his *Germania* Tacitus writes the following statement:

> They celebrate in ancient songs . . . a god Tuisto, born from the earth, and his son Mannus as the origin and founders of their people. To Mannus they assign three sons, from whose names are called the Ingaevones near the ocean, those in the center as Herminones, and the rest Istaevones.

The name Tuisto appears to have in it the root of the word "two," and this has reminded many observers of Ymir, whose name meant something like "doubled." Ymir sired the races of frost giants through monstrous hermaphroditic conception and is presented in the mythology as essentially a negative figure; indeed, his killing makes possible the creation of the cosmos. Tuisto, on the other hand, is "celebrated," and there is nothing negative about him in what Tacitus says. He is the father of Mannus (Human), who in turn produces the tribes of human beings.

> **References and further reading:** A fine general treatment of Tuisto and the creation story in *Germania* is that of Marco Scovazzi, "Tuisto e Mannus nel II capitolo della *Germania* di Tacitus," *Istituto Lombardo: Accademia di scienze e lettere, rendiconti, classe di letteri* 104 (1970): 323–336. The "doubled" nature of Ymir and identity with Tuisto were argued by Richard M. Meyer, "Beiträge zur altgermanischen Mythologie," *Arkiv för nordisk filologi* 23 (1907): 245–256, and "Ymi-Tuisto," *Arkiv för nordisk filologi* 25 (1909): 333.

TÝR

One of the æsir, lost his hand in the binding of the wolf Fenrir.

This event is alluded to directly in *Lokasenna*, stanza 38. Loki is upbraiding Týr:

> Shut up, Týr. You never knew how
> To mediate something good between two people
> Your right hand, that one will I mention
> Which Fenrir tore from you.

"To mediate something good between two people" is the standard translation, but an attractive alternative, given what happens next, would be "to carry something well with two [hands]."

Snorri tells the myth twice in *Gylfaginning*. On the first occasion, he is describing Týr and as a token of Týr's bravery:

> when the æsir enticed the wolf of Fenrir to permit the fetter to be put on him,
> then he did not believe that they would release him, until they placed the hand
> of Týr as a pledge in his mouth. And when the æsir were unwilling to release
> him, then he bit the hand off, where it is now called the "wolf's joint" [wrist],
> and Týr is one-handed and not called a peacemaker.

A few pages later Snorri tells the full story. When the gods learned that Loki's evil offspring with Angrboda were being raised in Jötunheimar, they discovered through prophecy that this brood would be trouble for them, and Odin had them brought to him. He cast the Midgard serpent into the sea and Hel into the world of the dead. For reasons that are unclear (because Odin had a connection with wolves? Because Loki was Odin's blood brother?), the gods raised the wolf with them, and only Týr was brave enough to feed it. But when they saw how quickly it was growing and reconsidered the prophecies, they decided to bind the wolf. First they tried with two ordinary fetters, but the wolf easily broke them. The gods now turned to magic. Alfödr (Odin) sent Skírnir to the dwarfs to obtain a fetter, Gleipnir (perhaps "Entangler"), made from cat noise and woman beard and mountain roots and bear sinews and fish breath and bird spittle. On the island Lyngvi (Heathery) in the lake Ámsvartnir (Red-black), they invited the wolf to let himself be bound again. Needless to say, the wolf was suspicious. What renown could there be in bursting this fetter, which looked like a silken band? Fenrir stipulated that someone had to place his hand in his mouth.

> And each of the æsir looked at another and thought that now their troubles had
> doubled, but none would put forth his hand, until Týr stretched forth his right

hand and put it into the mouth of the wolf. And when the wolf moved, then the fetter hardened, and the more he struggled, the sharper it became. Then all the gods laughed except Týr; he lost his hand.

Lokasenna, stanzas 37–40, comprise an exchange between Týr and Loki. Loki boasts that Fenrir tore off Týr's hand; Týr responds that although he may be missing his hand, Loki is missing Hródrsvitnir, that is, the famous wolf Fenrir. *Málsháttakvædi*, a poem of the twelfth or thirteenth century and usually thought to have been composed in the Orkneys, is the only poem to refer to the binding of Fenrir. It has been argued that Týr and Fenrir appear on the eighth-century Alskog Tjängvide picture stone from Gotland.

In *Hymiskvida* Týr accompanies Thor to the giant Hymir to get a huge kettle in which to brew beer. Týr is the one who knows of the existence of this cauldron, and he tells Thor about it in what the poet calls a "great loving counsel," which is stanza 5 of the poem:

> There dwells east of the Élivágar
> Exceedingly wise Hymir, at the edge of heaven.
> My father, the powerful one, owns a kettle,
> A huge pot, a league deep.

Hymir is indeed a giant, and how Týr got a giant for a father is one of the true mysteries of this mythology. The identity of his mother also poses a problem. She is mentioned in stanza 8:

> The son met the mother, much loathsome to him,
> She had nine hundred heads.
> Another still went forth, all in gold,
> White about the brows, to bear beer to her son.

Is Týr's mother the loathsome multiheaded creature or the golden one bearing beer? Neither possibility is attractive. If the monster is Týr's mother, he would appear to be wholly of giant stock. If the golden one is his mother, she may be one of the æsir, and a union between giant and goddess violates every principle of the mythology. However, we can console ourselves with the notice in the *Skáldskaparmál* section of Snorri Sturluson's *Edda* that a kenning for Týr is "son of Odin." In any case, one of these women, probably the second one, since she is referred to as "the beautiful concubine" (stanza 30), gives Thor useful advice when he is required to break a cup: He must throw it at the giant's head. With the cup broken, the gods can now take the kettle, but Týr cannot lift it. Thor lifts it, and they depart with yet another valuable object obtained from the giants.

According to Snorri Sturluson in the *Gylfaginning* section of his *Edda*, Týr will fight with another bound monster at Ragnarök (Fenrir will be busy with Odin). This is Garm, who was bound at Gnipahellir but who will run free as the end of the world approaches. He and Týr will kill each other.

Týr's name is found in the weekday name Tuesday, which is a translation of Latin *Dies Martis* (Day of Mars); as Mars was a god of war, so must the Germanic predecessor of Týr have been. Etymologically Týr's name is related to an Indo-European root meaning "deity" (e.g., compare Latin *deus*), and in fact the formal plural of Týr would be *tívar*, and this is attested as a collective for all the gods. This would also explain such Odin names as Sigtýr (Victory-Týr) or Hangatýr (Týr-of-the-hanged).

> ***See also*** Fenrir; Garm
>
> ***References and further reading:*** The alternative translation of *Lokasenna*, stanza 38, is discussed by Alfred Jakobsen, "*Bera tilt með tveim:* Til tolkning av Lokasenna 38," *Maal og minne,* 1979: 34–39, reprinted in his *Studier i norrøn filologi* ([Trondheim:] Tapir, 1979), 43–48. On the Alskog Tjängvide picture stone from Gotland, see Karl Helm, "Zu den gotländischen Bildsteinen," *Beiträge zur Geschichte der deutschen Sprache und Literatur* 62 (1938): 357–361.

ULL

Enigmatic god.

Although *Grímnismál*, stanza 5, assigns Ull a home at Ýdalir (Yew-dales), Ull is only a shadowy figure in the preserved mythology. Snorri Sturluson included him in the catalog of æsir in the *Gylfaginning* section of his *Edda* toward the end of the list (only Forseti follows), where he had this to say about him:

> There is one called Ull, the son of Sif and stepson of Thor. He is such a good archer, and so good on skis that none can compete with him. He is also fair of face and has the ability of a warrior. It is good to call on him in a duel.

In the *Skáldskaparmál* section of his *Edda*, Snorri says that Ull may be called Sif's son and Thor's stepson as well as god of skis, of bows, of hunting, and of shields, and these kennings are attested in skaldic poetry. Regarding shields, it should be noted that a shield might be called "Ull's ship," which suggests perhaps that he transported himself on it, rather as a snow boarder today might. In Book 3 of his *Gesta Danorum*, Saxo Grammaticus has a character called Ollerus, who is clearly Ull in Latin form. This figure replaced Odin when that god was exiled because of disgust over his rape of Rinda to get an avenger for Balderus. When Odin returns, Ollerus is in turn exiled and finally killed. He was, Saxo

Detail of Sparlösa rune stone from Vastergötland, Sweden, around 800 C.E., interpreted by Niels Åge Nielson as depicting a sacrifice to Ull. (The Art Archive/Dagli Orti)

says, such a cunning magician that he could travel over the sea on a bone; Viking Age bone skates are known from the archaeological record.

Two curious passages in eddic poetry refer to Ull, one to his grace (*Grímnismál*, stanza 42), the other to an oath sworn on his ring (*Atlakvida*, stanza 30). These tantalizing details might be connected with the story in Saxo to suggest that Ull was some kind of sovereign figure. The etymology of his name, which means something like "glory," might suggest that he was once a sky god of some sort, but, except for relatively infrequent displays of the Northern Lights, there isn't much glorious sky in the deep Scandinavian winters, when skis and skates are useful. Ull turns up frequently in place-names in Norway and Sweden, and he must once have been an important god.

> **See also** Rind
> **References and further reading:** The small scholarly literature devoted to Ull
> depends largely on the place-name evidence and is concerned with recon-
> structing a cult that is far older than the mythological records that are the
> subject of this book. Niels Åge Nielsen argues bravely but, I fear, on rather
> sparse evidence, that the Sparlösa runic inscription (ca. 800 c.e.?) is all about
> Ull (whom he regards as identical to Frey), in "Frey, Ull, and the Sparlösa
> Stone," *Mediaeval Scandinavia* 2 (1969): 102–128.

URDARBRUNN (WELL-OF-URD)

Well at the center of Ásgard.

Völuspá, stanza 19, associates the well with Yggdrasil, the world tree:

> I know an ash tree that stands, called Yggdrasil,
> A tall tree, sprinkled with white mud;
> Thence come the dews that run into valleys,
> Forever it stands green over the Urdarbrunn.

In the *Gylfaginning* section of his *Edda*, Snorri Sturluson mentions the roots of Yggdrasil.

> The third root of the ash stands in heaven and under that root is that well which
> is very holy and is called the Urdarbrunn; there the gods have their place of
> judgment. Each day the æsir ride up there on Bilröst.

Urd was one of the norns, and if we take literally the name of this well, it must have a special association with fate. Under another root of Yggdrasil is Mímisbrunn, the well of Mímir, and here Odin has pledged his eye, presumably for supernatural vision or foresight. These wells are thus powerful symbols in the mythology.

> **See also** Mímir; Norns; Yggdrasil

ÚTGARD (OUTER-ENCLOSURE)

Where the giants live.

This term is actually only attested in Snorri Sturluson's account of Thor's visit to Útgarda-Loki, in the *Gylfaginning* of Snorri's *Edda*, but it fits conceptually with the widely known terms Ásgard (Enclosure-of-the-æsir) and Midgard (Central-enclosure), the worlds of gods and men, respectively. The name Útgarda-Loki means "Loki-of-the-Útgards (pl.)," and I find attractive the idea that gods and men live in single spaces, whereas the giants are spread about on the periphery of the world. The medieval worldview of our sources conceived of the world as a round disk, with the ocean all the way around it, and Snorri in fact says in *Gylfaginning* that the gods gave land along the beaches of this circular cosmos for the giants to settle in.

> *See also* Ásgard; Midgard

ÚTGARDA-LOKI (LOKI-OF-THE-ÚTGARDS)

Giant; host, opponent, and deceiver of Thor and companions.

The myth of Thor and his companions' visit to Útgarda-Loki is told at considerable length in Snorri's *Gylfaginning*, of which it makes up nearly one-sixth. It may conveniently be divided into three parts: Thor's visit to the family of Thjálfi and Röskva, the journey of Thor and his companions in the company of Skrýmir, and the events at the hall of Útgarda-Loki. I treat the first part at greater length in the entry on Thjálfi and here will only repeat that, accompanied by Loki, Thor visits a human family, and because of a violation concerning Thor's goats, Thor acquires his human servants Thjálfi and Röskva.

Thor, Loki, and Thjálfi then set out for Jötunheimar and cross a large body of water. At night they shelter in an empty hall. After an earthquake they move into a smaller inner room, and throughout the night, as Thor stands watch, they hear loud noises. In the morning they learn that the noises were the snoring of a huge fellow who calls himself Skrýmir, and that the hall they cowered in was his glove. They agree to travel together, sharing their provisions. However, Skrýmir puts the food in his sack, and Thor is later unable to undo the knot while the big man sleeps. In a rage Thor strikes Skrýmir with his hammer, Mjöllnir, but Skrýmir merely wakes up and mildly asks whether a leaf has fallen on him. Twice more in the night Thor bashes Skrýmir with Mjöllnir. The first time Skrýmir asks whether an acorn fell on him, the second time whether it was bird droppings that had awakened him. In the morning they part ways.

Thor and his companions now come to the hall of Útgarda-Loki, another huge man, and Útgarda-Loki tells the æsir that no one can stay in the hall who is not the master of some skill or ability. When Loki claims to be an enormous eater, an eating contest is set up between Loki and Logi, a retainer of Útgarda-Loki. Loki eats all the food, but Logi eats all the food and the wooden platter it was served on. Next Thjálfi, the "swiftest of men," runs a footrace with Útgarda-Loki's retainer Hugi. Although Thjálfi loses by less in each of the three heats, he still loses. Finally, contests are set for Thor. He is to drain a drinking horn but cannot despite three huge quaffs. He is to lift a cat but can only get one paw off the ground. Finally, he wrestles with an old woman called Elli and is thrown.

The next morning Útgarda-Loki leads his guests out of the hall and explains the whole thing. He was Skrýmir, and he had used magic deceptions on them. The food bag was bound in iron, and he deflected the three hammer blows onto the landscape, and the result was three valleys. Then, in the hall, Loki's opponent Logi was actually fire (the meaning of the noun *logi*) and Thjálfi's opponent Hugi was actually thought (the meaning of the noun *hugi*). Thor's drinking horn was connected to the sea, and his quaffs created low tide; the cat was actually the Midgard serpent; and Elli was old age (the meaning of the noun *elli*). Thor raises the hammer again, but Útgarda-Loki and the hall vanish.

Útgarda-Loki is clearly a giant by ethnicity as well as in stature. Thor and his companions have set off for Jötunheimar, and Útgardar (Outer-enclosures, found only here) corresponds nicely to Ásgard, the enclosure of the æsir, and Midgard, the central enclosure where humans live. But even without these place-names, Útgarda-Loki and his companions could only be giants, because only giants contest with the gods. And although they appear to win their contests, they did so only by using magic, and their victories were hollow in that, despite them, Thor performed cosmogonic acts, creating the tides and three mountain valleys. Where Thor and his company went wrong was in failing to understand names as nouns, and linguistic abilities belong primarily to Odin. Indeed, in his control of magic and in outwitting Thor through language, Útgarda-Loki is a highly Odininc figure. Why he should bear the name Loki is unclear, but it may have to do with a demonization of Loki in the later Middle Ages.

Loki taunts Thor with cowering in a glove in *Lokasenna*, stanza 60, and says that Thor did not even think himself to be Thor. Furthermore, he taunts Thor with being unable to open the food pack (stanza 62). Thor does not deny the charges; he simply threatens to bash Loki with the hammer, and this threat finally causes Loki to desist. In *Hárbardsljód*, stanza 26, Odin repeats the accusation that Thor forgot who he was while he cowered in a glove, and adds that he was afraid to sneeze or fart, lest Fjalar should hear; Fjalar is presumably Skrýmir.

In Book 8 of *Gesta Danorum* Saxo tells of the voyage of Thorkillus to Utgarthilocus, a prophet. On the way there is a problem with food, but it is caused by a lack of fire. Finally Thorkillus and his companions reach Utgarthilocus, a smelly bound monster in a dark, snake-infested cave. This Loki appears to have more to do with the bound Loki of the Norse-Icelandic tradition than with Útgarda-Loki.

Much of the discussion of the Útgarda-Loki story has sought for origins to the east or to the west. Those who have commented on the story itself have mostly thought that it lacks mythic import. I disagree, since I think the story shows not only Thor's creative side and the constant threat he poses to the giants but also the hierarchical superiority of Odin to Thor in the verbal arena. At the same time, in the story of the acquisition of Thjálfi and Röskva, Thor shows a special relationship with humans.

> **See also** Fjalar; Röskva; Skrýmir; Thjálfi; Thor
> **References and further reading:** Those who have sought Irish origins include Friedrich von der Leyen, "Utgarðaloke in Irland," *Beiträge zur Geschichte der deutschen Sprache und Literatur* 33 (1908): 382–391; Carl Wilhelm von Sydow, "Tors färd till Utgård," *Danske studier*, 1910: 65–105, 145–82; Alexander Haggerty Krappe, "Die Blendwerke der Æsir," *Zeitschrift für deutsche Philologie* 62 (1937): 113–124; and Michael Chesnutt, "The Beguiling of Þórr," in *Úr Dölum til Dala: Guðbrandur Vigfússon Centenary Essays,* ed. R. W. McTurk and A. Wawn, Leeds Texts and Monographs, 11 (Leeds: Leeds Studies in English, 1989), 35–63. Nora K. Chadwick looked to Russian tradition in "The Russian Giant Svyatogor and the Norse Útgartha-Loki," *Folklore* 75 (1964): 243–259. Anatoly Liberman focuses ultimately on etymology but has much to say about myths of Loki, including this one, in his "Snorri and Saxo on Útgardaloki, with Notes on Loki Laufeyjarson's Character, Career, and Name," in *Saxo Grammaticus: Tra storiografia e letteratura. Bevagna, 27–29 settembre 1990* (Rome: Editrice "Il Calamo," 1992), 91–158. My analysis of the story is in "Thor's Visit to Útgarda-Loki," *Oral Tradition* 15 (2000): 170–186.

VAFTHRÚDNISMÁL

Eddic poem, "Words of Vafthrúdnir."

The poem is the third in *Codex Regius* of the *Poetic Edda*, after *Hávamál* and before *Grímnismál*, and was therefore regarded by the compiler, quite rightly, as an Odin poem. It is also found from stanza 20 onward in the other main manuscript of eddic poetry, AM 748, and Snorri Sturluson quotes many of its stanzas in *Gylfaginning* in his *Edda*. The meter is *ljóðaháttr* throughout, with a few stanzas expanded to *galdralag*, and the structure appears to be very carefully thought out.

The first four stanzas comprise a dialogue between Odin and Frigg in which Odin announces his intention to visit Vafthrúdnir. Frigg tries to dissuade him, because Vafthrúdnir is wisest of all giants, but when Odin persists, she sends him off with wishes for a safe return. Stanza 5 describes his journey and is the only stanza not spoken by one of the actors in the poem. Stanzas 6–9 comprise an introductory dialogue between Odin and the giant, and in stanza 10 Odin (or the narrator?) speaks a gnomic stanza reminiscent of the gnomic stanzas of *Hávamál*. In stanzas 11–18, Vafthrúdnir puts four questions, and Odin answers them: What horse pulls Day (Skínfaxi), what horse pulls Night (Hrímfaxi), what river separates gods and giants (Ifing), and what plain is marked off for the battle between Surt and the gods (Vígríd; it is 100 leagues square). Odin's answers satisfy the giant, and he invites Odin into the hall for a contest on which their lives will depend (stanza 19). The remainder of the poem, stanzas 20–55, consists of 18 questions put by Odin, 17 of which Vafthrúdnir answers.

The first 12 questions are numbered ("Say first, Vafthrúdnir"), and the first nine are further joined by Odin repeating some version of "since people say you are wise and you know" before actually putting the question. Odin's first nine questions concern cosmogony:

1. Whence came the earth? From the body of Ymir.
2. Whence came the moon and sun? They are the children of Mundilfœri, who traverse the heavens for human time reckoning.
3. Whence come day and night with its waning moons? Their parents are Delling and Nör; the gods created them so that people could reckon time.
4. Whence come summer and winter? Their parents are Vindsval and Svásud.
5. Who is the oldest of the æsir or of the giants? Bergelmir, whose father was Thrúdgelmir and grandfather Aurgelmir.
6. Whence came Aurgelmir? From drops of poison out of the Élivágar.
7. How did Aurgelmir beget children? A boy and girl came from under his arm, and one leg begat a six-headed son on the other.
8. What is the first thing you remember? When Bergelmir was placed on a *lúðr* (according to Snorri, something that floated and saved him from the flood created from Ymir's blood).
9. Whence comes the wind? From the giant Hræsvelg, who sits in the form of an eagle at the end of heaven and flaps his wings.

These items are known from other accounts of the creation and structure of the universe. It is, however, worth noting that Vafthrúdnir had also asked about the sun and moon; Odin's questions elicit a response that concedes the role of the gods in ordering time. Odin also elicits the monstrous reproductive acts of the proto-giant, and he ends this sequence by pointing out the location—would exile be the right word?—of a giant to the end of the universe. Gods and men occupy the center.

Questions 10–12 are still numbered, but now instead of saying "since people say you are wise and you know," Odin says "since you know about the fates of the gods," that is, about Ragnarök, and the focus shifts from cosmogony and cosmology to the end of the world and its aftermath:

10. Whence came Njörd? From the vanir, to whom he will return when the end comes.
11. Where do people engage in daily battle? All the einherjar do battle on Odin's landholdings.
12. How do you know about the runes (here perhaps secrets) of the giants and of all the gods? I have been to nine worlds below Hel.

This last question is put in the *galdralag* meter, and the giant rises to the challenge and responds in the same meter.

Now Odin stops numbering and prefaces each of the remaining questions with the refrain "Much have I traveled, much tried, much tested the powers":

13. Who will survive Fimbulvetr? Líf and Lífthrasir.
14. Whence will come the sun again, after Fenrir has overtaken it? Her daughter will ride the paths of her mother.
15. Who are those wise maidens who travel over the sea? Vafthrúdnir's answer to this unclear question is unclear.
16. Which æsir will control the possessions of the gods after Ragnarök? Vídar and Váli, Magni and Módi.
17. What will happen to Odin? He will be killed by the wolf but avenged by Vídar.
18. What did Odin himself say, before Baldr was placed on the funeral pyre, into the ear of his son?

Only Odin knows the answer to this last question, and the giant must yield. "With a doomed mouth," he says, "I spoke my old lore and of Ragnarök. With Odin I was now exchanging my verbal wisdom; you are always the wisest of beings."

Just as Thor defeats Hrungnir, the strongest of giants, in a formal duel, so Odin defeats Vafthrúdnir, the wisest of giants, in a formal verbal duel. Vafthrúdnir's four questions to Odin involved cosmogony, cosmology (Ifing), and Ragnarök. Odin's questions to the giant treat the same issues, at greater length and more adroitly. The changing introductions to the questions are especially effective, and the revelation of Odin's identity in the last question only confirms what is hinted at by the ominous refrain "Much have I traveled," which Odin begins to use just after Vafthrúdnir has reported his own travels to the worlds below Hel. With the last question Odin disrupts the linear sequence, for Baldr died before Ragnarök, and the actual subject of the question is withheld until the final words: "into the ear of his son." In leading to an epiphany and the subsequent death of Odin's interlocutor, *Vafthrúdnismál* parallels the poem that follows it, *Grímnismál*.

What Odin said into the ear of the dead Baldr is the ultimate unknowable. Accounts of Baldr's funeral do not include the motif of a last message from Odin, but the motif is also used to end the riddling sequence in *Hervarar saga*.

> ***See also*** Aurgelmir; Bergelmir; Delling; Élivágar; Gestumblindi; Odin; Ragnarök
> ***References and further reading:*** Surprisingly few studies have been devoted to this beautiful, powerful poem. In *The Origins of Drama in Scandinavia* (Cambridge, England: D. S. Brewer, 1995), 275–280, Terry Gunnell considers it alongside other eddic poems that he thinks could have received dramatic performance.

VÁLASKJÁLF

A hall or abode of the gods.
Grímnismál, stanza 6, tells us of it:

> There is a third residence, where the blissful powers
> Thatched the hall with silver.
> It is called Válaskjálf, where built skillfully for himself
> The god in days of yore.

Who "the god" is we do not know. Snorri Sturluson, however, thought that it was Odin. In the *Gylfaginning* section of his *Edda*, Snorri wrote this, just after he had mentioned Himinbjörg at the end of Bilröst:

> There is yet a great place, called Válaskjálf. Odin owns it. The gods made it and thatched it with shining silver, and there [in it] is Hlidskjálf.

Hlidskjálf is the high seat on which Odin sits himself when he sees into all the worlds.

Válaskjálf could mean "Váli's-bench," or, if the form should be "Valaskjálf" (we cannot know), it could mean something like "Bench-of-the-slaughtered-ones."

> ***See also*** Hlidskjálf

VALHÖLL (CARRION-HALL)

Odin's hall.

Grímnismál, which lists the various abodes of the gods, takes up Valhöll in stanza 8:

> Gladsheim is the fifth, where the gold bright
> Valhöll lies widely situated;
> And there Hropt chooses each day
> Weapon-dead men.

From this it would appear that Valhöll is a hall, perhaps one of many, at Gladsheim (Snorri knew *Grímnismál*, so it is interesting to note that he says Gladsheim was a temple erected at Idavöll by Alfödr [Odin], with 12 high seats). Later in *Grímnismál*, Odin (speaker of the poem) describes Valhöll in more detail:

> Five hundred doors and forty,
> Think I there are at Valhöll;
> Eight hundred einherjar go out of one door,
> When they go to fight with the wolf.

That is stanza 23. The following stanza confuses the issue somewhat by ascribing the same number of rooms to Bilskírnir (the hall of Thor), but stanzas 25 and 26 go back to the hall of Valfödr:

> 25. Heidrún is the name of the goat, who stands at the hall of Herjafödr [Odin]
> And bites from the limbs of Lærad.
> She will fill a barrel with the bright mead;
> That drink can never run out.
> 26. Eikthyrnir is the name of a hart, who stands at the hall of Herjafödr [Odin]
> And bites from the limbs of Lærad.
> Yet from his horns it drips into Hvergelmir,
> Thence all waters have their ways.

Thus there appears to be endless mead at Valhöll, and it is at the source of all waters.

In the *Gylfaginning* section of his *Edda*, Snorri Sturluson used these and other sources to create a vivid picture of Valhöll. At the very onset of the piece, he reads a skaldic stanza in such a way as to suggest that Valhöll was thatched with shields of gold. Later he says that the valkyries are to serve there, that the einherjar feast each day on the flesh of the boar Sæhrímnir and drink the mead provided endlessly by the goat Heidrún each night after doing battle during the day.

The tenth-century poems *Eiríksmál* and *Hákonarmál* have scenes set in Valhöll, where Odin and the others await the arrival of the human kings Eirík Bloodax and Hákon the Good. Valhöll was therefore an important mythological conception as far back as our written records go.

> **See also** Andhrímnir; *Eiríksmál*; Eldhrímnir; *Hákonarmál*; Heidrún, Sæhrímnir
>
> **References and further reading:** For the older scholarship, all of it in German and Scandinavian, see Gustav Neckel's book *Walhall: Studien über germanischen Jenseitsglauben* (Dortmund: F. W. Ruhfus, 1913). As the title says, this book is about Germanic conceptions of the hereafter. Accordingly, Neckel tries to sketch a development from the carrion on the battlefield to the mythological conception of a hall of the dead presided over by Odin. A charming article by Magnus Olsen, "Valhall med de mange dører," *Acta Philologica Scandinavica* 6 (1931–1932): 157–170, imagines that the multiple doors of Valhöll were influenced by Roman amphitheaters, especially the Coliseum. Edith Marold, "Das Walhallbild in den *Eiríksmál* und *Hákonarmál*," *Mediaeval Scandinavia* 5 (1972): 19–33, acknowledges that the portrait of Valhöll in *Hákonarmál* is darker and conceivably more archaic than that of *Eiríksmál* and analyzes especially the duality of the conceptions in *Hákonarmál*.

VÁLI, SON OF LOKI

Used by the gods in their vengeance on Loki for his role in the death of Baldr.

Snorri tells the story in *Gylfaginning*: After the gods have captured Loki, they turn his son Váli into a wolf, and the wolf tears apart his brother Nari or Narfi. The gods bind Loki with the guts of his dead son (and what happens thereafter to Váli is left unstated). The prose colophon to *Lokasenna* in *Codex Regius* of the *Poetic Edda* has the same story, but there the brothers are called Narfi (who changes into a wolf) and Nari (the source of the guts). Snorri may have been influenced by something like *Völuspá*, stanza 34, a half-stanza that is found only in the *Hauksbók* redaction of the poem:

> Then for [or of] Váli one could turn the killing-bonds;
> Quite hard were the fetters, out of guts.

Because the *Hauksbók Völuspá* lacks the Baldr story, however, this stanza appears to connect whatever happened to or for Váli to the aftermath of the battle between the æsir and vanir.

The story as Snorri presents it offers an act of vengeance fitting to the original crime. Loki makes Höd kill his half brother, Baldr; the gods make Váli kill his brother (half brother or not, we cannot tell). Both are under a kind of compulsion, Höd because he is tricked, Váli because he is transformed into a ravening beast. In keeping with this contrast, Höd kills Baldr at a place of sanctuary, whereas Váli kills Narfi in a wretched cave far from anywhere. And the fathers too are in contrast: Odin is free awaiting Ragnarök, whereas Loki is bound.

    See also Baldr; Loki; Nari and/or Narfi; Váli, Son of Odin

VÁLI, SON OF ODIN

Avenger of Baldr; with his brother Vídar, a survivor of Ragnarök.

Only one eddic poem states explicitly that it was Váli who avenged the death of Baldr, namely *Hyndluljód*, stanza 29, the first stanza of the "Short *Völuspá*."

> Eleven æsir were enumerated,
> Baldr who fell by the slayer's mound [the half-line is obscure];
> This Váli declared himself worthy to avenge;
> His brother's killer he slew.

The word for "killer" in the last line is *handbani*, that is, the one whose hand actually strikes the blow, as opposed to the *ráðbani*, "conspirator to murder." Thus we know that Váli's vengeance was taken on Höd, not on Loki. *Baldrs draumar*, stanza 11, and *Völuspá*, stanza 33, say,

> Rind will bear Váli in the western halls,
> That son of Odin will kill at the age of one night;
> He will not wash his hands or comb his head,
> Until he puts on the funeral pyre Baldr's adversary.

(It should be noted that, following virtually every editor, I have inserted the name "Váli" in the first line; there is no word at that point, but the line is defective and requires a name or noun beginning with *v-* because of the demand for alliteration.) Here we learn that Rind is Váli's mother, a motif that is corroborated by Snorri in his catalog of the æsir in *Gylfaginning:* "Áli or Váli is the name of one, the son of Odin and Rind; he is bold in battle and an extremely fortunate shot." This occurs in the catalog just after Vídar, with whom Váli is often paired, has been mentioned and before Ull is listed. In his *Sigurdurdrápa*, composed around 960 if the stanza is genuine, the Icelandic skald Kormák Ögmundarson says that Odin used magic (seid) on Rind, presumably to beget Váli.

    Váli's extreme youth and absence of grooming are described in virtually identical language in *Völuspá*, stanzas 32–33, although the avenger is there just called "Baldr's brother." Váli's precocious age at the moment he takes vengeance finds its closest parallel in the story of Thor's duel with Hrungnir, in which Thor's three-year-old (according to one manuscript, three-night-old) son comes along after the duel and lifts the dead giant's vast leg off Thor, who is pinned helpless beneath it. But the abstention from grooming until vengeance is taken may be more significant. Váli is regularly paired with Vídar, the "silent god," who will avenge his father Odin at Ragnarök; Vídar's silence looks rather like a parallel act of abstention. Tacitus, *Germania*, chapter 31, says of the Chatti, a Germanic tribe, that novice warriors may not shave or groom themselves until they have first slain an enemy.

With Vídar, and with the other pairs Magni and Módi, sons of Thor, and Baldr and Höd, victim and killer, Váli will survive Ragnarök. *Vafthrúdnismál*, stanza 51, is the best source:

> Vídar and Váli will inhabit the holy places of the gods,
> When Surt's fire dies down;
> Módi and Magni will have Mjöllnir
> And will bring about a cessation of killing.

Snorri is, as usual, more explicit. Vídar and Váli survive because neither fire nor the sea can harm them, and with the other surviving gods they inhabit Idavöll, where Ásgard once was, and retain artifacts and memories of their forebears.

The name Váli is understood as deriving from a form meaning "Little-member-of-the-vanir," but Váli has nothing to do with the vanir, and the alternative "Little-warrior" makes more sense. Snorri's alternate name, Áli, is unexplained, except as a supposed derivation from Váli. In Saxo's version of the Baldr story, the avenger of Balderus is Bous, son of Othinus and Rinda. The names Váli and Bous are not related.

See also Baldr; Bous; Idavöll; Rind; Váli, Son of Loki; Vídar

References and further reading: Heinrich Wagner, "Eine-irisch-altnordische hieros gamos-Episode," *Beiträge zur Geschichte der deutschen Sprache und Literatur* 77 (1955), 348–357, argues that the siring of Váli/Bous is a divine marriage, with a parallel in Irish tradition.

VANIR

Subgroup of the gods.

The vanir are distinguished from the æsir, the dominant group to which Odin and Thor and their consorts belong, but they are also subsumed within it, so that the word *æsir* generally refers to both groups. The word *vanir* is related etymologically to the word for "friend" in the Scandinavian languages and to words in other languages meaning "pleasure" or "desire." The vanir joined the æsir as a result of a war between the two groups. The deities explicitly referred to as vanir are Njörd, Frey, Freyja, and possibly Heimdall. Njörd is the father of Frey and Freyja, with his sister, according to Snorri in *Ynglinga saga*, because that was the custom among the vanir. But among the æsir such incestuous liaisons were not permitted, and they therefore ended with the incorporation of the two groups of gods. Scholars generally think of the vanir as gods of fertility, perhaps especially because Frey's major moment in the mythology involves a marriage to the giantess Gerd. But a poetic formula refers to the "wise vanir," and *Thrymskvida*, stanza 15, says that Heimdall can see the future, "like other vanir."

See also Æsir-Vanir War; Frey; Freyja; Heimdall; Njörd

VÁR

Minor goddess.

Snorri lists Vár ninth in his catalog in *Gylfaginning* of goddesses among the æsir and says this about her: "She gives a hearing to the oaths of people and the personal agreements that men and women grant one another; thus those agreements are called *várar* [pl.]. She takes vengeance on those who violate them." The noun *várar* does turn up a few times in references to pledges, especially of a marital nature, but Vár is unknown outside of Snorri's list of goddesses.

VEDRFÖLNIR (STORM-PALE)

Hawk associated with Yggdrasil, the world tree.

This figure is found only in Snorri Sturluson's *Gylfaginning*. Describing Yggdrasil, the world tree, he says,

A certain eagle sits in the limbs of the ash, and it knows a great deal, and between its eyes sits that hawk who is called Vedrfölnir.

Why a hawk should sit between the eyes of an eagle, or what its role might be, Snorri leaves unaddressed. Presumably the hawk is associated with the wisdom of the eagle. Perhaps, like Odin's ravens, it flies off acquiring and bringing back knowledge.

See also Yggdrasil

VÍDAR

God; sometimes called the "silent god;" associated especially with vengeance.

Snorri includes Vídar in his catalog of the æsir in *Gylfaginning*, after Höd and before Áli/Váli. Here Snorri says that Vídar is the silent god, that he has a thick shoe, that he is second in might only to Thor, and that the gods have great support or consolation from him in all struggles. In *Skáldskaparmál* Snorri places

Vídar among the other æsir at the banquet of Ægir and tells us that we may use these kennings for Vídar: "the silent god," "the owner of the iron shoe," "enemy and killer of the Fenris wolf [Fenrir]," "the vengeance god [áss] of the gods [goð]," "the dwelling god [áss] of paternal properties," "the son of Odin" and "brother of the æsir." In his account of Thor's journey to Geirröd in *Skáldskap-armál*, Snorri says that the giantess Gríd, who equips Thor with various pieces of equipment, is the mother of Vídar the silent.

In his vision of the dwellings of the gods in *Grímnismál*, Odin describes Vídar's "land" last, in stanza 17, and says it is grown with brushwood and tall grass:

> There the son gets off the back of a mare,
> The brave one, to avenge his father.

Vídar's silence is unexplained in the texts that have come down to us. Some scholars believe it may derive from ritual silences or other abstentions accompanying acts of vengeance; Baldr's brother, presumably Váli, does not wash his hands or comb his hair until he has laid Baldr's adversary on the funeral pyre (*Völuspá*, stanza 33, and *Baldrs draumar*, stanza 11). As for the shoe, it is definitely associated with vengeance, for Vídar uses his shoe, according to Snorri, to take vengeance on the wolf Fenrir for killing Odin (who is his father, according to *Völuspá*, stanza 56). Just after Snorri has the wolf swallow Odin, he writes this:

> Immediately thereafter Vídar will come forth and put one foot on the lower jaw
> of the wolf. On that foot he will have that shoe, which has been put together for
> all time; it is the leather scraps that people cut out of their shoes by the toes and
> heel, and therefore a person who wishes to take care to help the æsir shall throw
> away the leather scraps. With one hand he takes hold of the upper jaw of the
> wolf and tears apart his gullet, and that will be the death of the wolf.

This shoe is otherwise unknown; tentative identifications of Vídar on the stone crosses at Gosforth, Northumbria, and Kirk Andreas, Isle of Man, do not, as far as I can see, show any special footwear. The issue is further complicated by the existence of an alternative version of Vídar's killing of Fenrir with a sword, in *Völuspá*, stanza 56:

> Then comes the great son of Sigfather [Odin];
> Vídar, to fight with the beast of battle;
> For the son of Hvedrung, he makes stand with his hand
> A sword in the heart; thus the father is avenged.

Hvedrung is surely Loki, since *Ynglinga tal*, stanza 32, refers to Hel as Hvedrung's daughter. The name is also to be found among the thulur as a word for giant, and, confusingly, as an Odin name.

The account in *Vafthrúdnismál*, stanza 53, is perhaps equivocal on the method the vengeance took. Odin has just asked Vafthrúdnir about Odin's fate:

> The wolf will swallow Aldafödr [Odin]
> Vídar will avenge this;
> The malevolent jaws he will cleave
> At the death of the wolf.

The verb "cleave" looks as though it should refer to something done with a sword, but it is just possible that one could imagine tearing a beast apart by its jaws to be an act of cleaving. It is of course not impossible that Snorri introduced this interpretation.

Vídar's major act in the mythology, then, is one of vengeance. In this he is like Váli, the avenger of Baldr, and we may speculate that there may once have been a story about Odin's seduction or rape of Gríd, just as there exists one about his getting Váli on Rind (Bous on Rinda in Saxo). Vídar and Váli are linked not only by acts of vengeance, and by alliteration, but also by virtue of surviving Ragnarök and inhabiting the new world that is to exist. *Vafthrudnismál*, stanza 51, is the best source:

> Vídar and Váli will inhabit the holy places of the gods,
> When Surt's fire dies down;
> Módi and Magni will have Mjöllnir
> And will bring about a cessation of killing.

Snorri is, as usual, more explicit. Vídar and Váli survive because neither fire nor the sea can harm them, and with the other surviving gods they inhabit Idavöll, where Ásgard once was, and retain artifacts and memories of their forebears.

According to Georges Dumézil, Vídar was a cosmic figure derived from an Indo-European archetype. He was aligned with both vertical space (from his foot on the wolf's lower jaw to his hand on the upper jaw) and horizontal space (by means of his step and strong shoe) and therefore served to define the boundaries of space, just as Heimdall defined the boundaries of time. By killing the wolf, Vídar keeps it from destroying the cosmos, which can then be restored in the aftermath of Ragnarök.

See also Fenrir; Idavöll; Ragnarök, Váli, Son of Odin

References and further reading: Georges Dumézil, "Le dieu scandinave Víðarr," *Revue de l'histoire des religions* 168 (1965): 1–13. Thorkild Ramskou, "Ragnarok," *Kuml*, 1953: 182–192. Albert Morey Sturtevant, "Etymological Comments upon Certain Old Norse Proper Names in the *Eddas*," *Proceedings of the Modern Language Association* 67 (1952): 1145–1162.

VÍDBLÁIN (WIDE-BLUED)

Third heaven, according to Snorri's *Gylfaginning.*

There are no other mentions of this place in the mythology. When Snorri mentions it, he adds that the light-elves live there now.

> *See also* Andlang

VÍDBLINDI (WIDE-BLIND)

Giant used in kennings.

The kenning "boar of Vídblindi" in a verse by the poet Hallar-Steinn is explained by Snorri in *Skáldskaparmál* as follows:

> Here whales are called the "boars of Vídblindi." He was a giant and fished up whales at sea like fishes.

An anonymous verse from the thirteenth century appears to call whales "pigs of Vídblindi," and Vídblindi is numbered among the giants in the thulur. He appears to be one of those figures preserved in the verse tradition but not in the mythology.

VIDFINN (WOOD-FINN)

Father of the children who accompany the moon, according to Snorri Sturluson.

These children are Bil and Hjúki, who according to *Gylfaginning* were taken up from earth as they were walking. Although Anne Holtsmark has explained him as the Man in the Moon, what I find most interesting about him is that he is assigned Finnish (in this context almost certainly Sámi) ethnicity. I assume that this assignment has to do with the distance of the moon from the earth and perhaps also with a notion of the moon as a treeless, inhospitable landscape rather like the mountains of Norway.

Some have read the name as "Contrary-Finn" or "Finder," but "Wood-Finn" is, as far as I can tell, the standard reading.

> *See also* Bil and Hjúki
> ***References and further reading:*** Anne Holtsmark, "Bil og Hjuke," *Maal og minne,*
>   1945: 139–154.

VILI AND VÉ

Odin's brothers.

Like Odin, Vili and Vé are the sons of Bur; according to *Völuspá*, stanza 4, they raised the earth and shaped Midgard, and according to the *Gylfaginning* section of Snorri Sturluson's *Edda*, they endowed the first humans with life.

According to Snorri in *Ynglinga saga*, once when Odin had been away on a journey for a particularly long time, Odin's brothers, Vili and Vé, divided his inheritance and both possessed Frigg, but Odin later returned and took her back. Saxo Grammaticus tells a somewhat similar story in Book 1 of the *Gesta Danorum*: In order to adorn herself with gold, Frigga despoils a statue of Othinus and then gives herself to a servant in order to enlist his aid in taking down the statue. In shame Othinus goes into self-imposed exile, and during his exile a sorcerer called Mithothyn takes his place and institutes a change in cult procedures. Upon Othinus's return, Mithothyn flees to Fyn and is killed by the inhabitants there.

Loki knew a version of this story and was not above reminding Frigg about it. In *Lokasenna*, stanza 26, when Frigg tries to silence Loki, he rebukes her:

> Shut up, Frigg! You are Fjörgyn's daughter
> and have ever been most eager for men,
> when Vé and Vili you allowed, wife of Vidrir,
> to embrace you.

See also Bur, Bor; Frigg

VINGÓLF (FRIEND-HALL)

Hall at Ásgard.

Vingólf is known only from Snorri Sturluson, who mentions it twice in the *Gylfaginning* section of his *Edda*. First he says it is a temple near Gladsheim, a truly beautiful building tended by priestesses. Later he says that for all who fall in battle—the einherjar—Odin arranges a place at Valhöll or Vingólf. It is not impossible to reconcile these notions, especially if we see the valkyries serving beer at Valhöll as analogous to the priestesses at Vingólf.

See also Einherjar; Valhöll

VÖLUND

Hero, main subject of the eddic poem *Völundarkvida*.

Although he is once called "countryman of elves" in the poem, and twice "prince of elves," no direct connection with elves is to be seen. Völund appears to be the Scandinavian reflex of Wayland the Smith, who is well known in

A scene from the whalebone box known as the "Frank's Casket." On the right is a Christian image of the adoration of the Magi, while the left side depicts scenes from the legend of Völund. (Werner Forman/Art Resource)

English tradition. In *Thidriks saga,* which either reflects German tradition or is a direct translation of a German book, the character Velent, the son of a giant and a mermaid, is apprenticed to dwarfs, and subsequently, like Völund, he is captured and maimed and exacts a terrible vengeance.

> ***See also*** Elves
> ***References and further reading:*** Ellis H. R. Davidson, "Weland the Smith," *Folklore* 69 (1958): 145–159.

VÖLUSPÁ
Eddic poem, "Prophecy *[spá]* of the Seeress *[völva]*."
Völuspá is the first poem in *Codex Regius* of the *Poetic Edda,* either because its synopsis of the mythology, from the creation to the destruction of the cosmos to its rebirth, invited the compiler to place it there, or because the compiler thought of it as one of the Odin poems, which he had elected to place at the beginning of the collection (or for both reasons). A separate version of the poem exists in *Hauksbók,* a manuscript comprising what is in effect the private library—a collection of historical, religious, and scientific texts—of Hauk Erlendsson, an Icelandic lawman who spent the last years of his life in Norway. The version of *Völuspá* in this manuscript is written in an Icelandic hand from the middle of the fourteenth century and thus may have been added to it after Hauk's death in 1334. Besides these

two full versions of the poem, Snorri Sturluson quotes numerous stanzas in the *Gylfaginning* of his *Edda*, some of them differing slightly in wording from the *Codex Regius* or *Hauksbók* versions. Some scholars therefore operate with the concept of a third version, perhaps oral, that Snorri used, and certainly Snorri cannot have had either of the other versions before him when he wrote.

Völuspá is spoken by a seeress under the compulsion of Valföðr (stanza 1) or Odin. She refers to herself sometimes in the first and sometimes in the third person. She remembers those giants who raised her (stanza 2), before the world had been created (3). The sons of Bur raised up the earth (4), and the gods created time reckoning (5–6), had tools (7), and enjoyed gold until three giant maidens disrupted their joy (8). Upon the counsel of the gods (9), Mótsognir was made the mightiest of dwarfs, and the dwarfs made human images out of earth (10). A catalog of dwarfs occupies the next several stanzas, with somewhat differing versions in the various redactions of the poem. The æsir endowed Ask and Embla with life forces (stanzas 17–18). At this point the poem turns from cosmogony to cosmology and describes the world tree and the norns (19–20, 27–28). The Æsir-Vanir War occupies stanzas 21–24, and 25–26 may allude to the building of the wall at Ásgard. In the *Codex Regius*, but not in *Hauksbók*, there follows the story of Baldr's death and the aftermath of that climactic event (30–35). There follows a description of the moral and cosmic disintegration that characterized Ragnarök, and then the deaths of the gods and the demise of the cosmos itself (57). The last stanzas, however, strike a hopeful note. The seeress sees the earth arise for a second time (59). The æsir—presumably a new generation of them—will assemble, and they will find physical and narrative links to their past (60–61). Unsown fields will grow, and Baldr and Höd will dwell together, presumably reconciled. Ritual activity will be resumed. A stanza to be found only in *Hauksbók* reports that "the powerful one will come from on high, he who rules all." But a dragon will also come flying, with corpses in its grip. Now, the seeress says, "she must sink," and the poem ends.

The lack of Baldr's death in the *Hauksbók* redaction is the major difference between it and the *Codex Regius* version, and it is a significant difference. In *Codex Regius* the onset of Ragnarök follows immediately after and appears to be a direct result of Baldr's death. In the *Hauksbók* text, on the other hand, Ragnarök seems somewhat unmotivated. But the *Hauksbók* text sends to earth "the powerful one, he who rules all," which looks much like an intrusion of the Christian god. Indeed, even without this stanza, there is much in the poem that is reminiscent of Christianity, and in part because it seems to indulge in millennial thinking, scholars have been inclined to date it to the last decades of the tenth century. This dating is uncertain, and attempts to assign the poem's origin to a specific location are even more uncertain.

Völuspá is one of the most powerful and eloquent monuments of Scandinavian mythology, with a beauty of expression that is seldom matched and an overarching view of the mythology that is also peerless. Snorri's otherwise eloquent summary of the mythology in *Gylfaginning* owes much to *Völuspá* but seems clumsy when set alongside it.

> ***References and further reading:*** Régis Boyer, "On the Composition of *Völuspá*," in *Edda: A Collection of Essays,* ed. Robert J. Glendinning and Haraldur Bessason (Winnipeg: University of Manitoba Press, 1983), 117–133. Sigurður Nordal, "Three Essays on *Völuspá*," trans. B. S. Benedikz and J. S. McKinnell, *Saga-Book of the Viking Society* 18 (1970–1971): 79–135, and "The Author of *Völuspá*," trans. B. S. Benedikz, *Saga-Book of the Viking Society* 20 (1978–1979): 114–130. Paul Schach, "Some Thoughts on Völuspa," in *Edda: A Collection of Essays,* ed. Robert J. Glendinning and Haraldur Bessason (Winnipeg: University of Manitoba Press, 1983), 86–116.

VÖR
Minor goddess.

Snorri lists Vör tenth in his catalog in *Gylfaginning* of goddesses among the æsir and says this about her: "She too is wise and so questioning that no item may be concealed from her. It is a proverb that a woman becomes *vör* [aware] of that when she becomes wise." The name Vör is nothing more than the feminine form of the common adjective *varr*, "aware." This goddess is completely unknown outside of Snorri's catalog, but her name occurs twice as the base word in woman kennings in skaldic poetry.

YGGDRASIL (YGG'S-STEED)
The world tree, located at the center of the universe and uniting it.

The seeress who is the speaker in *Völuspá* devotes a stanza to the tree, stanza 19 in the usual editions:

> I know an ash tree that stands, called Yggdrasil,
> A tall tree, sprinkled with white mud;
> Thence come the dews that run into valleys,
> Forever it stands green over the Urdarbrunn.

Grímnismál has a good deal of information about Yggdrasil, all of it, according to the conceit of the poem, spoken by Odin as a kind of vision of holy cosmography. Stanza 44 calls it the "best of trees." Stanzas 29–30 say that the æsir go to the ash of Yggdrasil each day "to judge." Thor goes on foot and the other æsir on horses that are listed in stanza 30; of the ten horse names listed, only one is elsewhere associated with a specific god (Gulltopp, which Snorri says is Heimdall's horse). Stanza 29 implies that the Ás-Brú, the bridge of the æsir usually called Bilröst or Bifröst, leads to the tree.

The next five stanzas are about the tree itself:

> 31. Three roots stand on three roads
> From under the ash of Yggdrasil;
> Hel lives under one, under another the frost giants,
> Human beings under a third.
> 32. Ratatosk is the name of a squirrel who shall run
> on the ash of Yggdrasil;
> words of an eagle he shall carry down
> and say to Nídhögg below.
> 33. There are four harts who with necks bent back
> gnaw on the buds:
> Dáin and Dvalin,
> Duneyr and Durathrór.
> 34. Many snakes lie under the ash of Yggdrasil,
> and may every witless person consider that;
> Góinn and Móinn,—they are the sons of Grafvitnir—,
> Grábak and Grafvöllud;
> Ofnir and Sváfnir, I think will ever
> Eat the branches of the tree.
> 35. The ash of Yggdrasil suffers difficulty,
> more than men may know;
> a hart bites from below, yet on the side it rots;
> Nídhögg harms it from below.

Beset as the tree is according to this account, it will shake and tremble at Ragnarök, according to *Völuspá*, stanza 47, which refers to it as "the aged tree."

Snorri uses and adapts these stanzas (Yggdrasil is not mentioned in other sources) to create a unified description of the tree in *Gylfaginning*, a description that includes information and conceptions not in the eddic poetry. The capital or holy place of the gods is at the ash of Yggdrasil, where the gods pass judgments each day:

> The ash is the greatest and best of all trees. Its limbs stretch over the entire world and rise above heaven. Three roots of the tree hold it up and stretch out widely. One is among the æsir, the second among the frost giants, where Ginnunga gap used to be, the third stands over Niflheim. Under that root is Hvergelmir, and Nídhögg gnaws the roots from below. Under that root which turns toward the frost giants is the Mímisbrunn. . . . The third root [i.e., the first

one] of the ash stands in heaven and under that root is that well which is very holy and is called the Urdarbrunn; there the gods have their place of judgment. Each day the æsir ride up there on Bilröst.

Later Gylfi/Gangleri asks whether there is more to say about the tree. Hár responds:

There is much to tell about it. A certain eagle sits in the limbs of the ash, and it knows a great deal, and between its eyes sits that hawk who is called Vedrfölnir. That squirrel which is called Ratatosk runs up and down the ash and carries malicious words between the eagle and Nídhögg, and four harts run in the limbs of the ash and bite the needles.... And there are so many snakes in Hvergelmir with Nídhögg that no one can count them.

Finally, Snorri quotes a variant of the verse from *Völuspá* with which I began this entry:

I know a besprinkled ash called Yggdrasil
A tall tree, holy with white mud.
Thence come the dews, which run into the valley;
It stands ever green over the Urdarbrunn.

Snorri thus somewhat extends the unifying principle of the tree by allowing it to tower over earth and sky, and he moves it from the world of humans suggested by the location of the roots in *Grímnismál* (humans, giants, and the dead) to the mythological plane (æsir, giants, the underworld). He clarifies the role of the squirrel and eagle, turning the drama that is played out on the tree by these creatures into a duel of words like the ones at which Odin so excels, and he explicitly identifies Nídhögg as a snake or dragon. Unfortunately, he fails to explain the white mud, and that has remained an unsolved mystery.

According to *Hávamál*, stanza 138, Odin hung himself on a wide windy tree with mysterious roots, in a self-sacrifice that led to an acquisition of wisdom. Nearly everyone thinks this tree must be the world tree, and if so, the name Yggdrasil would refer to this myth: Ygg is an Odin name, and the hanged "ride" the gallows. Certainly Odin has a close connection with the tree, and it has even been suggested that he was born from the tree, that is, that the tree is identical with Bestla, Odin's mother.

The tree functions on both the vertical axis (trunk) and the horizontal axis (roots), and structural readings of the mythology, such as those of Eleazar Meletinskij, have suggested that these have varying functions: wisdom on the vertical axis and history on the horizontal axis. And the tree brings not just spatial unity to the mythology; Gro Steinsland showed elegantly through an analysis of *Völuspá* how it also brought chronological unity. Stanza 2 implies its presence in seed; it moves to a symbol of completed creation (stanza 19), gathering place of the gods (27), ancillary to Baldr's death (31), shaking symbol of the imminent demise of the cosmos (46–47), and finally, in the wooden lots chosen by Hœnir (stanza 63) after Ragnarök, it is the symbol of the new world.

In his description of the pagan temple at Old Uppsala written around 1070, Adam of Bremen says that a large yew tree stands in front of the temple and that it is from the branches of this tree that sacrificial victims are hung. The connection with Yggdrasil is obvious: a large tree at the center of the religious landscape. The concept of a "world tree" is widespread in Eurasia, and where shamanism is used the tree is often the path taken by the shaman into the worlds of the spirits.

> ***See also*** Bestla; Níðhögg, Ratatosk
>
> ***References and further reading:*** A good general discussion of the tree in English is that of Hilda Ellis Davidson, "Scandinavian Cosmology," in *Ancient Cosmologies,* ed. Carmen Blacker and Michael Loewe (London: Allen and Unwin, 1975), 172–197. Meletinskij's structural analysis of the mythology is to be found in "Scandinavian Mythology as a System," *Journal of Symbolic Anthropology* 1 (1973): 43–58 and 2 (1974): 57–78; see also Margaret Clunies Ross, *Prolonged Echoes: Old Norse Myths in Medieval Icelandic Society,* vol. 1: *The Myths* (Odense: Odense University Press, 1994), 50–55. Gro Steinsland's study is "Treet i *Völuspá*," *Arkiv för nordisk filologi* 94 (1976): 120–150. The classic study of the world tree is that of Uno Holmberg (Harva), *Der Baum des Lebens,* Annales Acadmiæ Scientiarum Fennicæ, B 16:3 (Helsinki: Suomalainen tiedeakatemia, 1922–1923).

YMIR

The proto-giant killed and dismembered by the gods to create the cosmos.

In *Vafthrúdnismál,* after the wise giant Vafthrúdnir has asked Odin a series of questions, Odin begins to query the giant. His first question is "Whence first came the earth / or heaven above?" Vafthrúdnir responds in stanza 21:

> Out of Ymir's flesh the earth was formed,
> And out of his bones the mountains,
> Heaven from the skull of the frost cold giant,
> And from his "sweat" [blood] the sea.

This stanza is repeated with variations and expansions in *Grímnismál,* stanzas 40–41:

> 40. Out of Ymir's flesh the earth was formed,
> And from his "sweat" [blood] the sea.

Mountains from bones, the tree from hair,
And from his skull, heaven.
41. And from his brows the blithe gods made
Midgard for the sons of men;
And from his brain the tough-minded clouds
Were all formed.

In stanza 28 of *Vafthrúdnismál,* Odin asks Vafthrúdnir who the "oldest of
the æsir / or of the kinsmen of Ymir / might have been in days of yore," and
although the response cites Bergelmir, Thrúdgelmir, and Aurgelmir, the question implies that Ymir was very ancient. That implication is supported by
Völuspá, stanza 3:

That was long ago, when Ymir lived,
There was no sand nor sea nor cool waves;
The earth did not exist nor heaven above,
A gap was gaping, nor was there grass.

The following stanza says that the sons of Bur raised lands; they were "the
ones who created famous Midgard."

Pagan skalds used kennings such as "Ymir's skull" for heaven or "Ymir's
blood" for the sea, so the notion of Ymir as the raw material of the cosmos is
assuredly old. The role of the gods in it, although perhaps implied by *Völuspá,* is
made explicit only by Snorri Sturluson in *Gylfaginning.* But Snorri actually has
several important things to say about Ymir, and the first of these is his role as
proto-giant and progenitor of the race of giants (as *Hyndluljód,* stanza 33 puts it,
all the giants come from Ymir).

In Snorri's version of cosmogony, fundamental oppositions of hot and cold
met in Ginnunga gap, and drops of moisture were the result.

And from those drops of poison life emerged, with the power that the heat sent,
and it grew into a human form, and that one is called Ymir, but the frost giants
call him Aurgelmir, and all the families of frost giants descend from him.

Gangleri asks whether this Ymir is some kind of god, and Hár responds:

In no way do we acknowledge him to be a god; he was evil and all his descendants. We call them frost giants. And it is said that when he slept, he broke into
a sweat, and then there grew under his left arm a man and a woman, and one
leg got a son on the other, and from them come the descendants, that is, the
frost giants. And the old frost giant, we call him Ymir.

Snorri appears to be making an effort here to harmonize the notion of Ymir as the proto-giant with stanzas 30–33 of *Vafthrúdnismál*, in which Aurgelmir is said to have engaged in the monstrous hermaphroditic procreation that Snorri assigns to Ymir. This form of conceiving and bearing offspring is distant from anything that observation of humans or animals could suggest, and although it is not at all uncommon in cosmogonies for hermaphroditic conception and birth to occur, in the context of this mythology it demonstrates once and for all the alien nature of the giants, Ymir's descendants.

Ymir's relationship with the æsir is Snorri's next topic. Also formed out of drops in Ginnunga gap was Audhumla, the proto-cow. Her milk fed Ymir, and she licked Búri, the first of the æsir, out of the salt blocks. Búri sired a son Bor (presumably in the normal way), and Bor married Bestla, the daughter of the giant Bölthorn and therefore a descendant of Ymir. The number of generations is so small that it is tempting to imagine that Bölthorn was one of those who emerged directly from Ymir, but no source makes that explicit.

The sons of Bor, according to Snorri, were Odin, Vili, and Vé, and they created the world. Here is Snorri's account:

> The sons of Bor killed Ymir the giant. And when he fell, so much blood gushed from his wounds, that with it all of the frost giants were killed, except one got away with his family. The giants called that one Bergelmir. He got up on his *lúðr* along with his wife and saved himself there, and from them come the families of the frost giants.

Here again Snorri is striving for consistency with *Vafthrúdnismál*. In *Vafthrúdnismál*, stanza 35, Vafthrúdnir says simply that the oldest thing he remembers was when Bergelmir was placed on a *lúðr*. Snorri clearly understood the *lúðr* as something that would float, and the word might in fact have meant "coffin" or "chest" or some wooden part of a mill; the expected meaning, of a cumbersome musical instrument something like an alphorn, makes no sense either in Snorri or his poetic source. In *Vafthrúdnismál*, Bergelmir could have been placed in his coffin or on some plank of wood, which would suggest his funeral, or perhaps into a cradle at birth. In neither case is there any reason to think of a flood, but that is what Snorri did, presumably as an analogue to the Judeo-Christian flood story.

Snorri's final section about Ymir presents the creation of the cosmos:

> They took Ymir and transported him into the middle of Ginnunga gap and made the earth from him: from his blood the sea and lakes; the earth was made from the flesh, and mountains from the bones, rocks and gravel from the teeth and molars and bones that were broken.... From that blood that ran out of the

wounds and was flowing aimlessly, they made that ocean, when they made the earth and anchored it down, and they put it around the earth, and most people would find it impossible to cross it. . . . They also took his skull [and] made from it the heaven and put it up over the earth with four sides, and under each corner they put a dwarf; they are called East, West, North, and South.

Snorri has the sons of Bor make a medieval cosmos, with the earth in the center and the sea surrounding it, and he adds the details of the cardinal directions represented by dwarfs holding up the sky. He also adds Ymir's teeth to the micro-macro equation.

The slaying of a monster is seen not infrequently in connection with the creation of the universe in mythologies from all around the world, and the creation of the cosmos through a set of micro-macro analogies is not uncommon in Indo-European tradition. Ymir's name originally meant something like "doubled," and scholars associate this etymology with the hermaphroditic procreation in which he indulges and with Tuisto, the primeval being in Tacitus, *Germania,* chapter 2. But perhaps most important for the mythology as a whole, in my view, is that Ymir is a maternal relative of Bor's sons, perhaps as close as their grandfather. To create the cosmos, the gods killed a maternal relative. This may be seen as the first of three killings within the family in the mythology. The second is the death of Baldr at the hands of his half brother Höd, and the third would be the set of killings at Ragnarök, when giants and gods, inextricably linked through Ymir and Audhumla, kill each other off and destroy the cosmos that was created through the first killing.

See also Audhumla; Aurgelmir; Baldr; Bergelmir; Bestla; Bur, Bor; Búri; Tuisto
References and further reading: A comparative reading of the entire set of creation myths was offered by Franz Rolf Schröder, "Germanische Schöpfungsmythen I–II: Eine vergleichende religionsgeschichtliche Studie," *Germanisch-Romanisch Monatsschrift* 19 (1931): 1–26, 81–99 (Ymir is treated in part I). The mysterious *lúðr* is the subject of Anne Holtsmark, "Det norrøne ord *lúðr*," *Maal og minne,* 1946: 49–65. The "doubled" nature of Ymir and identity with Tuisto were argued by Richard M. Meyer, "Beiträge zur altgermanischen Mythologie," *Arkiv för nordisk filologi* 23 (1907): 245–256, and "Ymi-Tuisto," *Arkiv för nordisk filologi* 25 (1909): 333. A splendid analysis of the micro-macro equation is presented by Bruce Lincoln in his *Myth, Cosmos, and Society: Indo-European Themes of Creation and Destruction* (Cambridge, MA: Harvard University Press, 1986).

YNGVI

Name for Frey, sometimes compounded as Yngvi-Frey.

Poets referred to both the Swedes and Norwegians as "Yngvi's people," presumably because of the association of King Rögnvald of Vestfold, Norway, with the Swedish dynasty of the Ynglingar. *Yngvi* also is used in skaldic poetry, following the normal rules of diction, as a noun meaning "king." In the prologue to his *Edda*, Snorri said that Odin (this is the euhemerized Odin, the king who emigrated from Tyrkland to Scandinavia) had a son named Yngvi who succeeded him as king of Sweden. From him descend the lineages called Ynglingar. But in his *Ynglinga saga* Snorri says explicitly that Yngvi was a second name for Frey (chapter 10), and twice he uses the compound Yngvifrey. Snorri also says that the name Yngvi was long used in Frey's lineage as a term of respect. Later, in chapter 17, he puts it this way:

> Dyggvi was the first of his family to be called king; before that they were called *dróttinn* [chieftain], their wives *dróttning* [chieftain's wife; later queen], and the court *drótt* [warrior band]. But each of their lineage was called Yngvi or Ynguni his whole life through, and all the Ynglingar together.

The last sentence must use "the Ynglingar" in the sense of a dynasty rather than a people, and it accords with the poetic usage mentioned above. The form Ynguni (in some manuscripts Yngunni or Yngvin) is not found elsewhere, but it looks very like the West Germanic form in Ingunar-Frey.

See also Frey; Ing; Ingunar-Frey

References and further reading: See Walter Baetke, *Yngvi und die Ynglingar: Eine quellenkritische Untersuchung über das nordische "Sakralkönigtum,"* Sitzungsberichte der sächsischen Akademie der Wissenschaften zu Leipzig, Phil.-hist.-Kl,. 109:3 (Berlin: Akademie-Verlag, 1964), which argues that the materials concerning Frey and the Ynglingar cannot be used to advance a notion of sacral kingship. Also see Wolfgang Krause, "Ing," *Nachrichten der Akademie der Wissenschaften in Göttingen*, phil.-hist.-Kl., 10 (1944): 229–254, for an argument that the name originally meant "man" and was associated with fertility through the sun; Henrik Schück, "Ingunar Frey," *Fornvännen* 10 (1940): 289–296, which argued that Ingun was the earth; Franz Rolf Schröder, *Untersuchungen zur germanischen und vergleichenden Religionsgeschichte*, vol. 1: *Ingunar-Frey* (Tübingen: J. C. B. Mohr [P. Siebeck], 1941), which argued for Ingun as a fertility goddess associated with a holy tree.

PRINT AND NONPRINT RESOURCES

This chapter is intended to give the reader a general picture of important background materials, as well as print resources pertaining more generally to the mythology itself. It is arranged according to the following outline:

Background—Viking and Medieval Scandinavia
    Archaeology
    Etymology
The Conversion of Iceland
Medieval Iceland
Women and Gender
Encyclopedias
Primary Sources—Translations
Primary Sources—Commentary and Analysis
    Eddic and Skaldic Poetry
    Snorri Sturluson
Literary Histories
Mythology—General Treatments
Mythology—Important Studies
Nonprint Resources

The focus is on works in English, but materials in German, and in one case, the Scandinavian languages, have occasionally been included when they seemed particularly important or useful. Guidance for more directed readings on individual aspects of the mythology are found in the sections entitled "References and Further Reading" following the entries in chapter 3.

BACKGROUND—VIKING AND MEDIEVAL SCANDINAVIA

For the Viking Age a number of excellent works exist offering varying treatments: Else Roesdahl, *The Vikings*, trans. Susan M. Margeson and Kirsten Williams

(New York and London: Penguin Books, 1992; Danish original 1987), presents a general survey. Roesdahl is an archaeologist, but she is well informed on the written sources as well, and she offers the most accessible and complete treatment currently available. Peter Sawyer, ed., *The Oxford Illustrated History of the Vikings* (Oxford and New York: Oxford University Press, 1997), contains a collection of chapters by various experts on a number of subjects, based on the latest research. Numerous illustrations enhance the work. R. I. Page, *Chronicles of the Vikings: Records, Memorials, and Myths* (Toronto and Buffalo: University of Toronto Press, 1995) offers a collection of primary source materials with introductions and commentaries. John Haywood, *The Penguin Historical Atlas of the Vikings* (New York and London: Penguin Books, 1995), is a wonderful collection of maps and includes illustrations in color and apt commentary.

Of the many older works on the Viking Age, none is encountered more frequently than Gwyn Jones, *A History of the Vikings*, rev. ed. (New York and London: Oxford University Press, 1984). It is engaging if a bit wordy. Peter Foote and David M. Wilson, *The Achievement of the Vikings: The Society and Culture of Early Medieval Scandinavia* (London: Sidgwick and Jackson, 1970), is unsurpassed in the detail of its expert coverage. A groundbreaking work was that of Peter Sawyer, *The Age of the Vikings*, 2nd ed. (London: E. Arnold, 1971). David Wilson, *The Vikings and Their Origins: Scandinavia in the First Millennium* (New York: McGraw Hill, 1970), is for the general reader. Johannes Brøndsted, *The Vikings* (New York: Penguin, 1965; Danish original 1960), now seems outmoded.

Larger-format illustrated books include James Graham-Campbell and Dafydd Kidd, *The Vikings* (New York: W. Morrow and Co., 1980), the catalog of an exhibition held at the British Museum and the Metropolitan Museum of Art. Published the same year were two similar books: James Graham-Campbell et al., *The Viking World* (New Haven and New York: Ticknor and Fields, 1980), and David M. Wilson, ed., *The Northern World: The History and Heritage of Northern Europe AD 400–1100* (New York: H. N. Abrams, 1980), both perhaps inspired by the exhibition. They all follow in the path of Bertil Almgren et al., eds., *The Viking* (Gothenburg, Sweden: Tre Tryckare, 1967), in including chapters by various experts and rich illustrations, many in color, on large pages. And an explicit exhibition catalog is William Fitzhugh and Elisabeth I. Ward, *Vikings: The Norse Atlantic Saga* (Washington, DC, and London: Smithsonian Institution Press, 2000). It focuses on the Viking expansion west across the Atlantic and is particularly authoritative on the subjects that are best informed by archaeology. A separate chapter is devoted to religion, art, and runes.

Treatments of individual areas abound. For Britain, see H. R. Loyn, *The Vikings in Britain* (London: B. T. Batsford, 1977), P. H. Sawyer, *From Roman Britain to Norman England* (Methuen, London, 1978), Alfred P. Smyth, *Scandinavian Kings in the British Isles, 850–880*, Oxford Historical Monographs (Oxford: Oxford University Press, 1977), and Sir Frank Stenton's standard work, *Anglo-Saxon England*, 3rd ed. (Oxford: Oxford University Press, 1971). For mainland Scandinavia: Klavs Randsborg, *The Viking Age in Denmark: The Foundation of a State* (London: Duckworth, 1980). For Russia and expansion to the east: E. A. Melnikova, *The Eastern World of the Vikings: Eight Essays about Scandinavia and Eastern Europe in the Early Middle Ages*, Gothenburg Old Norse Studies, 1 (Gothenburg, Sweden: Litteraturvetenskapliga Institutionen, Göteborgs Universitet, 1996). For Iceland: Jón Jóhannesson, *A History of the Old Icelandic Commonwealth: Íslendinga saga*, trans. Haraldur Bessason ([Manitoba:] University of Manitoba Press, 1974). For Greenland: Knud J. Krogh, *Viking Greenland: With a Supplement of Saga Texts* ([Copenhagen:] National Museum, 1967).

The Migration Period is well covered in Lucien Musset, *The Germanic Invasions: The Making of Europe, AD 400–600*, trans. Edward and Columba James (University Park: Pennsylvania State University Press, 1975), and Malcolm Todd, *The Early Germans*, The Peoples of Europe (Oxford and Cambridge, MA: Blackwell, 1992).

Medieval Scandinavia has attracted far less general attention than the Viking Age. An exception is Peter Sawyer and Bibi Sawyer, *Medieval Scandinavia: From Conversion to Reformation, circa 800–1500*, Nordic Series, 17 (Minneapolis: University of Minnesota Press, 1993). Otherwise one should consult the national histories. For Denmark: Stewart P. Oakley, *A Short History of Denmark* (New York: Praeger, 1972). For Iceland: Jón R. Hjalmarsson, *History of Iceland: From the Settlement to the Present Day* (Reykjavík: Iceland Review, 1993). For Norway: T. K. Derry, *A History of Norway* (London: Allen and Unwen, 1957). For Sweden: Franklin Scott, *Sweden: The Nation's History* (Minneapolis: University of Minnesota Press, 1977).

Archaeology

This is a field in which things are moving rapidly. As a result, Haakon Shetelig and Hjalmar Falk, *Scandinavian Archaeology*, trans. E. V. Gordon (Oxford: Clarendon, 1937), should be read only for background. Else Roesdahl, *The Vikings*, cited above, will remain the standard for some time to come. The catalogs for the recent Viking exhibitions, especially that of Fitzhugh and Ward, *Vikings: The Norse Atlantic Saga*, also cited above, will give more detail on most topics.

Etymology

The standard etymological dictionary is Jan de Vries, *Altnordisches etymologisches Wörterbuch* (Leiden: E. J. Brill, 1962). Alexander Jóhannesson's *Isländisches etymologisches Wörterbuch* (Bern: Francke, [1951–1956]) is also valuable, but access to entries is through Indo-European roots, so it is not for the uninitiated. Those who cannot read German are referred to Gabriel Turville-Petre's *Myth and Religion of the North: The Religion of Ancient Scandinavia* (New York: Holt, Rinehart, and Winston, 1964; reprint, Westport, CT: Greenwood Press, 1975)—though it is long out of print—which usually includes information of an etymological nature, as do Rudolf Simek, *Lexikon der altgermanischen Mythologie*, translated as *Dictionary of Northern Mythology*, trans. Angela Hall (Cambridge, England, and Rochester, NY: D. S. Brewer, 1993), and Andy Orchard, *Dictionary of Norse Myth and Legend* (London: Cassell, 1997). Another resource is the *American Heritage Dictionary of the English Language*, which contains a glossary of Indo-European roots that is interesting to consult in connection with an etymological discussion involving such roots.

Although there are good introductory works on the study of place-names in the Scandinavian languages, they and nearly all the specialist literature are unavailable in English. Those interested in the use of the gods' names in place-names can, however, easily study the maps in de Vries's *Altgermanische Religionsgeschichte*, Grundriss der germanischen Philologie, 12:1–2 (Berlin: W. de Gruyter, 1956–1957), if they have a German-English dictionary at hand.

Students wishing to learn more about the history of the Germanic languages in general should turn to Orrin W. Robinson, *Old English and Its Closest Relatives: A Survey of the Earliest Germanic Languages* (Stanford: Stanford University Press, 1992), and Hans Frede Nielsen, *The Germanic Languages: Origins and Early Dialectal Interrelations* (Tuscaloosa and London: University of Alabama Press, 1989). For Scandinavian, turn to Einar Haugen, *The Scandinavian Languages: An Introduction to Their History* (Cambridge, MA: Harvard University Press, 1976).

THE CONVERSION OF ICELAND

Dag Strömbäck, *The Conversion of Iceland*, trans. and annotated by Peter Foote, Viking Society for Northern Research, Text Series, 6 (London: Viking Society for Northern Research, 1975), is a model of scholarship, and one need look no further, although more complete treatment, and especially an analysis of the central events at the althingi in 1000 C.E., may be found in Jón Hnefill

Aðalsteinsson, *Under the Cloak: The Acceptance of Christianity in Iceland with Particular Reference to the Religious Attitudes Prevailing at the Time*, Studia Ethnologica Upsaliensia, 4 (Uppsala: Almqvist and Wiksell, 1978). Those deeply pressed for time, those who prefer their history in a popularized form, or those who like pictures could turn to the very short work of Michael Scott Rohan and Allan J. Scott, *The Hammer and the Cross* (Oxford: Alder Publishing, 1980), which presupposes no prior knowledge.

MEDIEVAL ICELAND

Since virtually all the texts of Scandinavian mythology were recorded in medieval Iceland, a knowledge of that society will be helpful. I recommend Jón Jóhannesson, *A History of the Old Icelandic Commonwealth: Íslendinga saga* (cited above), for the historical background up through the thirteenth century. For an excellent anthropological analysis of the Icelandic commonwealth, see first Kirsten Hastrup, *Culture and History in Medieval Iceland: An Anthropological Assessment of Structure and Change* (Oxford: Clarendon, 1985); this work also includes direct commentary on the mythology, especially as regards cosmology. Hastrup's *Island of Anthropology: Studies in Past and Present Iceland*, Viking Collection, 5 (Odense: Odense University Press, 1990), contains other relevant essays by Hastrup, and a collection of essays is to be found in Gísli Pálsson, ed., *From Sagas to Society: Contemporary Approaches to Early Iceland* (Enfield Lock, England: Hisarlik Press, 1992). Books that focus on the interface between history and literature are Preben Meulengracht Sørensen, *Saga and Society: An Introduction to Old Norse Literature*, trans. John Tucker, Studia Borealis/Nordic Studies, 1 (Odense: Odense University Press, 1993; Danish original 1977), and, in the two essays of its introduction, Theodore M. Andersson and William Ian Miller, *Law and Literature in Medieval Iceland: Ljósvetninga saga and Valla-Ljóts saga* (Stanford: Stanford University Press, 1989). Miller's *Bloodtaking and Peacemaking: Feud, Law, and Society in Saga Iceland* (Chicago and London: University of Chicago Press, 1990), is a detailed and thorough analysis of the processes of dispute resolution as they are manifested in the sagas; these processes are in my view directly relevant to the mythology. Students may also find useful Jesse Byock, *Feud in the Icelandic Saga* (Berkeley and Los Angeles: University of California Press, 1982), and Byock, *Medieval Iceland* (Berkeley and Los Angeles: University of California Press, 1988).

WOMEN AND GENDER

The role of women in society and literature has been the subject of several recent investigations. See Judith Jesch, *Women in the Viking Age* (Woodridge, England: Boydell, 1991); Jenny Jochens, *Women in Old Norse Society* (Ithaca, NY: Cornell University Press, 1995), and Jochens, *Old Norse Images of Women* (Philadelphia: University of Pennsylvania Press, 1996). Carol J. Clover argues that gender is less important than power in "Regardless of Sex: Men, Women, and Power in Early Northern Europe," *Speculum* 68 (1993): 363–387.

ENCYCLOPEDIAS

Several encyclopedias offer easy access to relevant information on Norse mythology. Philip Pulsiano, Kirsten Wolf, Paul Acker, and Donald K. Fry, *Medieval Scandinavia: An Encyclopedia*, Garland Encyclopedias of the Middle Ages, 1; Garland Reference Library of the Humanities, 934 (New York and London: Garland Publishing, 1993), offers articles on literary, historical, and archaeological subjects. It supplements the 22-volume Nordic compilation, published in all five Nordic countries, entitled in Swedish *Kulturhistoriskt lexikon för nordisk medeltid från vikingatid till reformationstid* (Malmö, Sweden: Allhems förlag, 1956–1978); the articles are in the Scandinavian languages, but the references may be helpful even to those who cannot read those languages. The *Dictionary of the Middle Ages*, Joseph R. Strayer, general editor, 13 vols. (New York: Scribners, 1982–1989), has extensive coverage of Scandinavia, including articles on Norse mythology. Similarly, *The Encyclopedia of Religion*, Mircea Eliade, editor-in-chief, 16 vols. (New York and London: Macmillan, 1987), contains articles on Indo-European, Germanic, and Scandinavian myth and religion. Those who can read German will find profit in consulting the articles in the new edition of the *Reallexikon der germanischen Altertumskunde*, ed. Heinrich Beck et al. (Berlin and New York: W. de Gruyter, 1973–), many of which are detailed studies of myths and religious topics in their own right. The *Lexikon des Mittelalters*, 9 vols. (Munich and Zurich: Artemis Verlag, 1980–1998), has good articles on medieval history and literature. Scandinavian medieval literature and mythology are also treated in Carl Lindahl, John McNamara, and John Lindow, eds., *Medieval Folklore: An Encyclopedia of Myths, Legends, Tales, Beliefs, and Customs*, 2 vols. (Santa Barbara, CA: ABC-CLIO, 2000).

PRIMARY SOURCES—TRANSLATIONS

Although several attempts have been made to translate the *Poetic Edda*, none has been fully successfully, primarily because of the difficulty of the texts themselves in several places. Henry Adams Bellows, *The Poetic Edda: Translated from the Icelandic with an Introduction and Notes* (New York: American-Scandinavian Foundation, 1923), is still serviceable, although it employs some idiosyncratic spellings (e.g., *Hovamol* for *Hávamál*), and the copious footnotes are to be avoided. Lee M. Hollander, *The Poetic Edda: Translated with an Introduction and Explanatory Notes*, 2nd ed., rev. (Austin: University of Texas Press, 1962), uses an archaic English that is not without interest but usually baffles the ordinary reader. Paul B. Taylor and W. H. Auden, *The Elder Edda: A Selection* (New York: Random House, 1967–1969), is the result of a collaboration between a scholar and a distinguished poet, but its arrangement of the poems is arbitrary, and other translations are more literally accurate. Patricia Terry, *Poems of the Vikings: The Elder Edda* (Indianapolis, IN: Bobbs-Merrill [1969]), also suffers from lapses in accuracy. The most recent translation into English, useful and accessible, is that of Carolyne Larrington, *The Poetic Edda: Translated with an Introduction and Notes* (Oxford and New York: Oxford University Press, 1996). Ursula Dronke is producing an edition of eddic poems; in addition to introductions and notes, it contains English translations facing the Icelandic text. Dronke's translations are splendid, but the work as a whole is intended for an academic rather than a general audience. As of this writing, two volumes have appeared: *The Poetic Edda*, vol. 1, *Heroic Poems: Edited with Translation, Introduction, and Commentary* (Oxford: Clarendon, 1969), and *The Poetic Edda*, vol. 2, *Mythological Poems: Edited with Translation, Introduction, and Commentary* (Oxford: Clarendon, 1997; contains *Völuspá*, *Hávamál*). Finally, Sigurður Nordal's famous and influential edition of *Völuspá*, with commentary, is available in English translation by B. S. Benedikz and John McKinnell, Durham and St. Andrews Medieval Texts, 1 (Durham, England: Durham and St. Andrews Medieval Texts, 1978).

The most recent English translation of Snorri Sturluson's *Edda* is also the best: Anthony Faulkes, *Edda / Snorri Sturluson: Translated from the Icelandic and Introduced*, Everyman Classics, Everyman's Library, 499 (London: Dent, 1987). A translation of most of the mythological passages is offered by Jean I. Young, *The Prose Edda of Snorri Sturluson: Tales from Norse Mythology, Selected and Translated* (Berkeley and Los Angeles: University of California Press, c. 1954). It is accurate, and the introduction by Sigurður Nordal is pleasant, but because it omits most of *Skáldskaparmál* and all of *Háttatal*, it gives a false impression of the work as a whole, and it is not free from occasional bowdlerization. Arthur Gilchrist Brodeur's *The Prose Edda, by Snorri Sturluson: Translated from the Icelandic with an Introduction*, Scandinavian Classics, 5 (New York: American-Scandinavian Foundation, 1916), is long out of print but still quite usable.

Some mythological skaldic verses are gathered in Lee M. Hollander, *The Skalds: A Selection of Their Poems, with Introductions and Notes* (Princeton: Princeton University Press, for the American-Scandinavian Foundation, New York, c. 1945); some may also be found translated and explicated in Gabriel Turville-Petre's *Scaldic Poetry* (Oxford: Clarendon, 1976). Other significant verse may be found in Hollander, *Old Norse Poems: The Most Important Non-Skaldic Verse Not Included in the Poetic Edda* (New York: Columbia University Press, 1936; reprint, Millwood, NY: Kraus Reprint Co., 1973).

The *Gesta Danorum* of Saxo Grammaticus has been rendered into English twice. From the Victorian era is *The First Nine Books of the Danish History of Saxo Grammaticus*, trans. Oliver Elton, with "Some Considerations on Saxo's Sources, Historical Methods, and Folk-Lore," by Frederick York Powell, Publications of the Folk-lore Society, 33 (London: D. Nutt, 1894). Our era found its Saxo in *The History of the Danes / Saxo Grammaticus*, trans. Peter Fisher, ed. Hilda Ellis Davidson (Cambridge, England: D. S. Brewer; Totowa, NJ: Rowman and Littlefield, 1979–1980), which has a very handy commentary by Hilda Ellis Davidson.

Finally, Hermann Pálsson and Magnus Magnus Magnusson, *The Vinland Sagas: The Norse Discovery of America* (Baltimore: Penguin Books, 1965), offers readers the chance to consider for themselves the literary evidence for the Scandinavian excursions to North America half a millennium before Columbus; in the context of this work, it is relevant because of the elaborate description of a seid ceremony in chapter 3 of *Eiríks saga rauda* (The Saga of Erik the Red).

PRIMARY SOURCES—COMMENTARY AND ANALYSIS

Eddic and Skaldic Poetry

Unfortunately, this is perhaps the area in which one is most handicapped by an inability to read German and the Scandinavian languages. A number of commentaries to eddic poetry have appeared over the years, but all are in German, even the one announced by a team of scholars at Frankfurt and manifest in sample texts. The only commentaries, therefore, are those attached to the translations mentioned above. Dronke's is the most satisfying, but she has placed fairly severe limits on going beyond actual textual issues. Larrington's notes are also sound, but I cannot recommend with any enthusiasm anything else on the eddic corpus.

And the case is all but hopeless for skaldic poetry. There are, to be sure, the commentaries accompanying Turville-Petre's and Hollander's translations, but the texts presented are very limited. There are also, of course, monographic treatments of various important skaldic poems, but these texts are so difficult that such treatments tend generally to limit themselves to comment on language and grammar rather than on content. Those who can read the Scandinavian languages can make use of the corpora and commentaries created by Finnur Jónsson and Ernst Albin Kock; on the problems inherent to these, see Roberta Frank, "Skaldic Poetry," in Carol J. Clover and John Lindow, eds., *Old Norse-Icelandic Literature: A Critical Guide*, Islandica, 45 (Ithaca, NY, and London: Cornell University Press, 1985).

An idiosyncratic study of eddic poetry is Eleazar Meletinskij, *The Elder Edda and Early Forms of the Epic*, trans. Kenneth H. Ober, Hesperides, 6, (Trieste: Parnaso, 1998).

Snorri Sturluson

A biography of Snorri Sturluson and consideration of his writing is Marlene Ciklamini, *Snorri Sturluson*, Twayne's World Authors Series, TWAS 493: Iceland (Boston: Twayne Publishers, 1978). It lacks the authority of Sigurður Nordal's magisterial *Snorri Sturluson* ([Reykjavík]: Þór. B. Þorláksson, 1920), but that work has never been translated from the original Icelandic. A fine study of Snorri's *Heimskringla* is Sverre Bagge, *Society and Politics in Snorri Sturluson's Heimskringla* (Berkeley and Los Angeles: University of California Press, 1991). Recent collections of essays about Snorri and his work include *Snorri: Átta alda minning* (Reykjavík : Sögufelag, 1979), a volume in which Icelandic scholars contemplate eight centuries of the memory of Snorri; Úlfar Bragason, ed., *Snorrastefna: 25.–27. Júlí 1990* (Reykjavík: Stofnun Sigurðar Nordals, 1992)—despite the Icelandic title, more than half the essays are in English; Alois Wolf, ed., *Snorri Sturluson: Kolloquium anlässlich der 750. Wiederkehr seines Todestages*, Script Oralia, 51 (Tübingen: G. Narr, c. 1993); and Hans Fix, ed., *Snorri Sturluson: Beitrage zu Werk und Rezeption*, Ergänzungsbände zum Reallexikon der germanischen Altertumskunde, 18 (Berlin: W. de Gruyter, 1998). Margaret Clunies Ross, *Skáldskaparmál: Snorri Sturluson's Ars Poetica and Medieval Theories of Language*, Viking Collection, 4 (Odense: Odense University Press, 1987), sets *Skáldskaparmál* against the learned medieval encyclopedic background. Alexandra Pesch, *Brunaöld, haugsöld, kirkjuöld: Untersuchungen zu den archaologisch überprüfbaren Aussagen in der Heimskringla des Snorri Sturluson*, Texte und Untersuchungen zur Germanistik und Skandinavistik, 35 (Frankfurt am Main and New York: P. Lang, 1996), reads the archaeological record against *Heimskringla*. A German commentary (accompanying a translation) to Snorri's *Gylfaginning* that I have found very useful is that of Gottfried Lorenz, *Snorri Sturluson, Gylfaginning: Texte, Übersetzung, Kommentar*, Texte zur Forschung, 48 (Darmstadt: Wissenschaftliche Buchgesellschaft, 1984). On *Heimskringla*, see Diana Whaley, *Heimskringla: An Introduction*, Viking Society for Northern Research Text Series, 3 (London: University College, 1991).

LITERARY HISTORIES

The most recent general survey in English is that of Jónas Kristjánsson, *Eddas and Sagas: Iceland's Medieval Literature*, trans. Peter Foote (Reykjavík: Hið íslenska bókmenntafélag, 1988). A collection of essays summarizing the state of scholarship and including extensive bibliographies for myth and mythography, eddic poetry, skaldic poetry, kings' sagas, sagas of Icelanders, and romances is Carol J. Clover and John Lindow, eds., *Old Norse-Icelandic Literature: A Critical Guide* (cited above). The *fornaldarsögur* are the most important omission from that collection, but it was somewhat remedied by the publication of Stephen A. Mitchell, *Heroic Sagas and Ballads* (Ithaca, NY, and London: Cornell University Press, 1991).

The relationship between the social conditions and the literature is presented in Preben Meulengracht Sørensen's excellent *Saga and Society: An Introduction to Old Norse Literature* (cited above). Meulengracht Sørensen is particularly good on mythic patterns in the literature in general. Sigurður Nordal, *Icelandic Culture*, trans. and with notes by Vilhjalmur T. Bjarnar (Ithaca, NY: Cornell University Library, 1990) is not, strictly speaking, a literary history, but it offers much that is of interest. Those who read German may turn to Jan de Vries, *Altnordische Literaturgeschichte*, 2 vols., Grundriss der germanischen Philologie, 15–16 (Berlin: W. de Gruyter, 1964), but all the other standard literary surveys are in the Scandinavian languages.

MYTHOLOGY: GENERAL TREATMENTS

Scandinavian myth and religion is a field in which much older work is still read and cited, with the inevitable result that a great percentage of the material is in German and the Scandinavian languages (there is also much of interest in Italian, French, and Russian, among others). It is possible to get a sense of the scholarship up to the early 1980s by consulting my *Scandinavian Mythology: An Annotated Bibliography*, Garland Folklore Bibliographies, 13 (New York: Garland, 1988). If there is a standard reference work, it is Jan de Vries, *Altgermanische*

Religionsgeschichte, 2 vols., 2nd ed., Grundriss der germanischen Philologie, 12–13 (Berlin: W. de Gruyter, 1956–1967). However, there are many introductory works in English that can be recommended. The best in my view remains that of Gabriel Turville-Petre, *Myth and Religion of the North: The Religion of Ancient Scandinavia* (cited above), but it is long out of print. H. R. Ellis Davidson, *Gods and Myths of Northern Europe* (Baltimore: Penguin, 1964), pays less attention to textual detail than I would like but remains in print and is sound. Davidson also contributed a large-format book originally entitled *Scandinavian Mythology* (London and New York: Hamlyn, 1969) and recently reissued as *Viking and Norse Mythology* (New York: Barnes and Noble, 1996); this work has especially attractive plates of many of the more significant artifacts. A very brief treatment, but quite nice, is that of R. I. Page, *Norse Myths* (London: British Museum; and Austin: University of Texas Press, 1990). A very long treatment is the volume in the older series Mythology of All Races by John Arnott MacCulloch (the editor of the series) entitled simply *Eddic* (New York: M. Jones; reprint, New York: Cooper Square Publishers, 1964).

I am not fond of works that in their systematization take readers away from the texts; unlike, say, Greek mythology, Norse mythology is actually found in such a limited textual corpus that it seems to me indefensible to part from it. Thus I cannot recommend the work of the Norwegian historian Peter Andreas Munch, revised by the great philologist Magnus Olsen and available in English as *Norse Mythology: Legends of Gods and Heroes*, trans. Sigure Bernhard Hustvedt (New York: American-Scandinavian Foundation, 1927), although the Norwegian version, with comments added by Anne Holtsmark, is definitely worth a look. Nor do I recommend Brian Branston, *Gods of the North* (New York: Vanguard, n.d. [1955?]), or Kevin Crossley-Holland, *The Norse Myths: Introduced and Retold* (New York: Pantheon Books, 1980).

MYTHOLOGY: IMPORTANT STUDIES

The best modern treatment of the mythology, and one to which every serious reader can turn with profit, is Margaret Clunies Ross, *Prolonged Echoes: Old Norse Myths in Medieval Northern Society*, vol. 1, *The Myths*, Viking Collection, 7 (Odense: Odense University Press, 1994), and vol. 2, *The Reception of Norse Myths in Medieval Iceland*, Viking Collection, 10 (Odense: Odense University Press, 1998). The first volume succeeds admirably in reading the entire mythology as a system in which the ongoing opposition between the gods and giants is read as a struggle involving social hierarchies within a complex symbolic system. Clunies Ross knows the scholarship intimately and has masterful analytic skills; if you read only one book on the mythology (other than the one in your hands now), make it this one. Volume 2 is of more interest in connection with rest of Old Norse–Icelandic literature, but it is equally enthralling.

Two other recent A-to-Z treatments of the mythology have preceded this one. The earlier was that of Rudolf Simek, *Dictionary of Northern Mythology*, cited above; the German original appeared in 1984 in a series of small-format encyclopedias and therefore was presumably formed at least in part to fit the parameters of that series. It is trustworthy and particularly helpful if one is interested in postmedieval manifestations of the mythology in art, literature, and music, for articles ordinarily end with information about such manifestations. Since the work was originally intended for German readers, secondary literature in English is cited only when the author deems it particularly relevant, and full references are not cited. The second such encyclopedia was that of Andy Orchard, *Dictionary of Norse Myth and Legend*, cited above. As is the case with Simek, the scholarship is wholly sound. Orchard's book has greater coverage in that it also takes in heroic legend, and the result is that the mythological entries tend to be somewhat shorter than those in Simek's volume. The book also contains not quite 40 illustrations. A particularly nice touch is the set of appendices listing and offering translations for the numerous names of Odin, dwarfs, giants, and "troll-wives, giantesses and valkyries." Bibliographic citations in the body of the texts are to about 850 items gathered in four lists in the back of the book.

The thinking of Georges Dumézil on Norse mythology and its relationship with Indo-European myth and religion may be found in Dumézil, *Gods of the Ancient Northmen*, ed. Einar Haugen, trans. John Lindow, Alan Toth, Francis Charat, and George Gopen, Publications of the UCLA Center for Comparative Folklore and Mythology, 3 (Berkeley and Los Angeles: University of California Press, 1973). This book comprises a translation of Dumézil's *Les dieux des germains: Essai sur la formation de la religion scandinave* (Paris: Presses Universitaires de France, 1959), and translations of four articles specifically on Scandinavian mythology. Dumézil's later arguments about the displacement of myth into epic are available in Dumézil, *From Myth to Fiction: The Saga of Hadingus*, trans. Derek Coltman (Chicago and London: University of Chicago Press, 1973), which followed by only three years the French original, *Du mythe au roman: La Saga de Hadingus et autre essais* (Paris: Presses Universitaires de France, 1970). His huge study *Mythe et epopée* (Paris: Gallimard, 1968–1975) was rendered piecemeal into English: *The Destiny of a King*, trans. Alf Hiltebeitel (Chicago and London: University of Chicago Press, 1973); *Camillus: A Study of Indo-European Religion as Roman History*, trans. Annette Aronowicz and Josette Bryson, ed. Udo Strutynski (Berkeley and Los Angeles: University of California Press, 1980); *The Stakes of the Warrior*, trans. David Weeks, ed. Jaan

Puhvel (Berkeley and Los Angeles: University of California Press, 1983); *The Plight of a Sorcerer,* ed. Jaan Puhvel and David Weeks (Berkeley and Los Angeles: University of California Press, 1986). Those who long for more Dumézil but cannot read French could turn next to his *Mitra-Varuna: An Essay on Two Indo-European Representations,* trans. Derek Coltman (New York: Zone Books, 1988), a classic of the Dumézilian dossier, or the curious *Riddle of Nostradamus: A Critical Dialogue,* trans. Betsy Wing (Baltimore: Johns Hopkins University Press, 1999). For a vade mecum through the many ins and outs of Dumézil's work up to 1980 or so, see C. Scott Littleton, *The New Comparative Mythology: An Anthropological Assessment of the Theories of Georges Dumézil,* 3rd ed. (Berkeley and Los Angeles: University of California Press, 1982). An incisive non-Dumézilian reading is offered by Jarich G. Oosten, *The War of the Gods: The Social Code in Indo-European Mythology* (London: Routledge, 1985).

Two recent works by Hilda Ellis Davidson, who has contributed greatly to the study of Norse mythology, are *Myths and Symbols in Pagan Europe: Early Scandinavian and Celtic Religions* (Syracuse, NY: Syracuse University Press, 1988), and *The Lost Beliefs of Northern Europe* (London and New York: Routledge, 1993). Where Davidson explores the Celtic interface, Thomas DuBois reminds us of the existence of the religions of the Sámi and Finns in Viking Age Scandinavia: *Viking Ages Religions* (Philadelphia: University of Pennsylvania Press, 1999).

A connection between the texts of eddic poetry and ritual was first argued by Bertha Philpotts, *The Elder Edda and Ancient Scandinavian Drama* (Cambridge, England: Cambridge University Press, 1920). Terry Gunnell, *The Origins of Drama in Scandinavia* (Cambridge, England: D. S. Brewer, 1995), revisits the issue.

NONPRINT RESOURCES

Keying "Norse mythology" into the Google search engine on the world wide web, I got 8,540 hits. Clearly there is a lot of stuff out there. At *http://www.pantheon.org/mythica/areas/norse/,* one of the first sites I visited, I found an A-to-Z listing of the major and minor figures in Norse mythology similar to what is found in this book. This listing is part of *The Encyclopedia Mythica: An Encyclopedia on Mythology, Folklore, and Legend.* Randomly looking at some entries, I found this on Bragi:

> The god of eloquence and poetry, and the patron of skalds (poets) in Norse mythology. He is regarded as a son of Odin and Frigg. Runes were carved on his tongue and he inspired poetry in humans by letting them drink from the mead of poetry. Bragi is married to Idun, the goddess of eternal youth. Oaths

were sworn over the Bragarfull (Cup of Bragi), and drinks were taken from it in honor of a dead king. Before a king ascended the throne, he drank from such a cup.

There are no fewer than six errors in this paragraph (the lingual runes being the most spectacular), and this sad fact leads me to the major point that must be made about materials to be found on the Internet: *Use them at your own risk.* Content is easy to find, but there is no quality control. The Internet is best used to look at things like maps, images (samples of actual Old Norse–Icelandic manuscripts, for example, may be viewed at *http://www.hum.ku.dk/ami*), or the actual text of some primary source. (There are many Internet sites offering primary sources, but my comments in Chapter 4 about primary sources apply here, too.)

I know of two sites with bibliographies. *The Bibliography of Old Norse-Icelandic Studies,* at the University of Odense Library in Denmark, covers the entire field, not just the mythology. Its English-language URL is *http://www. sdu.dk/oub/fagomraa/nordisk/boniseng.htm.* A very brief bibliography of the *Poetic Edda* compiled at the Fiske Icelandic Collection of the Cornell University Library may be found at *http://rmc.library.cornell.edu/Fiske/edda.html.*

Scott Trimble, a former student in my undergraduate class at the University of California at Berkeley on Scandinavian mythology, has built the website *http://www.stst.net/Scandinavian/.* The genealogy page is a brave attempt to concoct a single genealogy for the entire system. Browsing sites that sell term papers, I found that one can obtain an eight-page paper titled "The Giant Loki in Norse Mythology" for $8.95 per page (a few months later the price had risen to $9.95). I didn't buy it, but skimming the summary gave me the impression that I may in fact have already read it.

Look about on the Internet. You will find descriptions of the mythology; encyclopedic listings long and short; student term papers; collections of texts; collections of pictures; close and imaginative retellings of the myths; fiction; poetry and music; Wiccan sites; neopagan sites of various kinds, some including on-line shrines; games; rants and ravings; course curricula; children's literature; comic books; clubs to join; sites devoted in whatever way to individual gods and goddesses; a "scavenger hunt" (actually a list of questions apparently used in a unit on the mythology in some school); a "guest book" to which you can post any comment you like relating, however tenuously, to Norse mythology; instructions to third-grade teachers doing a unit on Norse mythology; instructions for integrating the study of Norse mythology into home schooling; science fiction; astrology. Just exercise care. If it doesn't look right, it probably isn't. After all, if I, an expert in Old Norse–Icelandic mythology, were to devise and print on the Internet plans for a supersonic jet, would you build and fly it?

INDEX

Absalon, 26
Aðalsteinsson, Jón Hnefill, 182
Adam of Bremen, 7, 34, 35, 125, 322
Adils, 94
Ægir, 18, 19, 41, **47–49,** 109, 119, 120, 132, 135, 140
   Bragi and, 86
   daughters of, 47
   feast of, 83, 193
   Fimafeng and, 115
   Gymir and, 156
   Loki and, 215
   Rán and, 47, 258
   Vídar and, 313
Ægir's daughters, **49**
Ægisdrekka, 47
Æsir, 1–2, 19, 22–25, 47, **49–51,** 63, 111, 122
   álfar and, 50
   belief in, 38
   elves and, 109
   jötnar and, 92, 93
   seid for, 52
   vanir and, 2, 41, 51, 53, 206, 225, 311
Æsir-Vanir War, **51–53,** 54, 121, 180, 230, 318
   Hœnir and, 179
   Kvasir and, 207
Afi, 260
Agamemnon, 22
Age of the Sturlings, 18
Agnar, 150, 151, 176
   Hraudung and, 182

   Odin and, 250
   Thrúdheim and, 292
Ái, 260
Alcuin, 120
Aldafödr, 314
Álf of Álfheimar, 94
Álfablót, **53–54,** 110
Álfar, 50, **109–10**
Álfheim, **54,** 110, 123, 150
Álfhild, 94, 281
Alfödr, **55,** 145, 176, 205, 241, 246, 247, 308
   Dag/Nótt and, 92
   Lofn and, 213
   names for, 116
   Odin and, 248
   Skírnir and, 112, 297
Alfred the Great, 5
Algrœn, 79, 80, 117
Ali, 311, 312
Almáttki áss, **55–56**
Alskog Tjängvide, 113, 277, 298
Alsvin, **59,** 60 (illus.), 99, 278
Althingi, 6, 9, 128
Alvíss, 14, 57, 79, 101, 151, 215
Alvíssmál, 13–14, **56–57,** 79, 99, 101, 110, 151, 215, 288
Amma, Karl and, 260
Ámsvartnir, 112, 297
Ánar, 92, 246
Andad, Ítrek and, 134
Andersen, Hans Christian, 36
Andhrímnir, **58,** 104, 107, 263–64
Andlang, **58**

341